Encyclopedia of Rape

Advisory Board

Julie Campbell-Ruggaard
Psychologist, private practice
Oxford, Ohio

Elizabeth Reis
Department of Women's and Gender Studies
University of Oregon, Eugene

Rickie Solinger
Independent Scholar
Lake Mohonk, New York

Encyclopedia of Rape

Edited by MERRIL D. SMITH

GREENWOOD PRESS
Westport, Connecticut • London

Library of Congress Cataloging-in-Publication Data

Encyclopedia of rape / edited by Merril D. Smith.
    p. cm.
    Includes bibliographical references and index.
    ISBN 0–313–32687–8 (alk. paper)
    1. Rape—encyclopedias. I. Smith, Merril D., 1956–
HV6558.E53   2004
   362.883'03—dc22   2004044213

British Library Cataloguing in Publication Data is available.

Library of Congress Catalog Card Number: 2004044213
ISBN: 0–313–32687–8

First published in 2004

Greenwood Press, 88 Post Road West, Westport, CT 06881
An imprint of Greenwood Publishing Group, Inc.
www.greenwood.com

Printed in the United States of America

The paper used in this book complies with the
Permanent Paper Standard issued by the National
Information Standards Organization (Z39.48–1984).

10 9 8 7 6 5 4 3 2

Contents

Preface

This book takes a new approach to the examination and understanding of an old problem: rape. The subject of rape encompasses much more than the actual physical act. There are the people involved; times and places in which rapes have taken place; laws and customs regarding rape; movements against it; art, literature, and other cultural depictions of rape; and social and political events concerning it. The format of an encyclopedia is especially effective for covering this topic because readers can look at the specific entry or entries that interest them, as well as reading further in related entries.

The volume is aimed at general readers and students who desire to learn about rape and rape-related issues. For those who want additional information, there is suggested reading listed under each entry. Additional information can be obtained from the list of resources at the end of the volume.

For two years, 79 scholars from all over the world and from a wide variety of fields—the humanities, social sciences, and medicine—have gathered information and written articles on a variety of topics concerning rape for this project. There are 186 entries in this encyclopedia. The coverage provides explication and descriptions of key terms, concepts, organizations, incidents, institutions, laws, influential works, theories, movements, cases, and individuals associated with rape. Although it is impossible to include every item of significance to the topic in a one-volume reference book, I have tried to be as comprehensive as possible. Readers will note the emphasis in this encyclopedia is on the contemporary United States, but entries that are historically significant, as well as worldwide events and movements, have been included. The result is a volume that covers rape from antiquity to the present.

Entries are listed in alphabetical order. Readers will generally find the subject listed under the most common or popular name. For example, there is an entry under the headwords "Boston Strangler" rather than under Albert DeSalvo, the man convicted of the crimes. However, readers who turn to "Albert DeSalvo" will be directed to the appropriate entry.

Each narrative entry explains the term, gives an overview, and describes its significance. In our rapidly changing world, new information is constantly being revealed, while concepts and ideas are transformed almost before our eyes. All attempts have been made to keep the entries in the volume up to date, accurate, and consistent. Each entry contains cross-references in **bold** type, related entries at the end, and a list of reading suggested by the author of each article. There is a chronology of key rape events, people, and places following the Introduction. The volume contains a Resource Guide of books, movies, and Websites at the end and is fully indexed.

ACKNOWLEDGMENTS

Thanks go to many people who helped in bringing this project to fruition. The process began when Wendi Schnaufer, one of my editors at Greenwood Press, called me to ask if I would be interested in editing this encyclopedia. She was extremely helpful in guiding me through the early stages of this work. Anne Thompson, my other editor at Greenwood, has been a careful and thoughtful reader. She's answered my barrage of emails with efficiency—and sometimes just that needed bit of humor. My advisory board, Julie Campbell-Ruggaard, Elizabeth Reis, and Rickie Solinger, read and offered suggestions on entries. Julie went beyond this role to act as go-between when a contributor became ill. Thanks, Julie!

I could not have completed this book without the help of the contributors who wrote entries for this volume. Some of them wrote multiple entries, and some picked up last-minute entries and delivered polished work to me in record time. I have enjoyed corresponding with all of you, and I have made some friends along the way.

It is indeed helpful to have a supportive and talented family, one willing to listen to me discuss rape at the dinner table. Special thanks to Megan Smith for organizing my computer files, retyping the entries that my computer ate, and doing some proofreading. Sheryl Smith helped me organize lists and cooked some great dinners. Doug Smith read entries, helped me with printing the manuscript, and kept the household going while I worked.

Introduction

Rape has always been a part of human culture. The myths of antiquity included accounts of rape; ancient societies counted rape among the crimes listed in their law codes; and even the Bible contains stories of rape. Throughout the centuries, rape has had an impact on individual women (as well as men and children of both sexes), but it has also affected the evolution and development of cultures all over the world, as women have been abducted as brides, claimed as prizes of war, and enslaved. Unfortunately, rape remains a concern of modern life. Recent headlines make this all too clear, as stories on date rape drugs, attacks by serial rapists, the molestation of children by Catholic priests, and genocidal crimes in Bosnia, Rwanda, and elsewhere pervade the media.[1]

The physical reality of rape has not changed over time: the penetration of a vagina, or other orifice, by a penis (or other object) without the consent of the woman or man being penetrated. What have changed over time and place are definitions about rape, ideas, perceptions, and laws concerning it. Modern laws on sexual assault in the United States and elsewhere recognize that both women and men can be raped, that wives can be raped by their husbands, and that victims often know their attackers. Although rape survivors are still sometimes blamed for provoking their attacks, they may also find support and counseling available to them. For much of history, however, rape has been considered a crime against the woman's father or husband, rather than a crime against the victim. In some areas of the world, that still holds true. In 2002, the Human Rights Commission of Pakistan reported that over 150 women had been sexually assaulted and about 40 women had been killed in "honor killings" in southern Punjab.[2]

Within the United States, rape is all too common, but it remains an underreported crime, since many victims cannot or do not press charges against their attackers. However, in the last few decades, reforms in rape laws have made the process somewhat easier for victims. For example, before the 1970s, rape shield laws and the category of spousal rape did not exist.[3]

The alteration of rape laws within the United States, as well as many other countries, reflects changing ideas about gender and sexuality, as well as redefinitions of rape itself. The feminist movement of the 1960s and 1970s helped to spur along these changes, as many feminists asserted that rape is a crime of violence that threatens all women. In her influential 1975 book *Against Our Will: Men, Women and Rape*, Susan Brownmiller argued that rape is "nothing more or less than a conscious process of intimidation by which *all* men keep *all* women in a state of fear."[4] *Against Our Will* was the first major history of rape. Since its publication, scholarly interest in rape, the study of rape, and the history of rape has grown tremendously.

Yet stigmas against discussing rape and stigmas against rape victims remain. The topic still elicits smirks and innuendo, or religious or moral pronouncements, while actual cases often get bogged down in accounts of "he said/she said." Legal scholar Leslie Francis notes, "Rape is criminal. Rape is gendered. Rape is sexual. In yet another three-word sentence, rape is controversial."[5] But rape is controversial precisely *because* it is a crime that involves sex acts.

At the same time, today there seems to be more freedom to discuss both rape and its effects on victims and survivors. Several survivors of rape have published stories of their ordeals within the last few years. In 2003, for example, Trisha Meili, who previously had been known only as the Central Park Jogger, published an account detailing her experiences since her 1989 attack.[6]

Within the United States, the history of rape is tangled with and connected to race. Native American women were raped first by European explorers who assaulted them and enslaved them as they conquered the Americas. Later, white settlers pushed indigenous people westward and sometimes considered the women they encountered as fair game or prizes. African women were first brought to what is now the United States as slaves in the early seventeenth century. Masters owned their bodies and could use them sexually whenever they wanted to. Their "otherness" both attracted white men and permitted them to portray black women as sexually voracious. This had an effect on white women, too, who were idealized as asexual and pure but who had to pretend they did not know what their husbands, fathers, brothers, and sons were doing. Black men, too, were affected by racial and sexual myths both during slavery when they could not protect their female loved ones and later in their post–Civil War freedom when they were depicted as lusting after white women. This fear of the "black beast" became particularly strong from about 1890 to 1920 and led to the lynching of many black men.

White men, who have considered them "available" for sex because of their "exoticism," or subservience, have also dominated some Hispanic women and Asian American women. The growing populations of Asian Americans and Hispanics in the United States have led to rape counseling services becoming more aware of problems within those groups. However, the terms *Asian American* and *Hispanic* encompass many different groups of people, and therefore it is not easy or even fair to make generalizations about these groups. Some rape crisis centers now offer counseling and legal services in several languages and employ counselors who are familiar with a variety of cultures. In addition to problems they may face from within their own cultures, increased sometimes by the inability to speak English, and/or inhibited by cultural beliefs or taboos, many subgroups within the United States may suffer sexual abuse and not know or be able to report it—or may be afraid to do so.

Besides those based on language, race, and ethnicity, subgroups of rape victims may include gays and lesbians, prisoners of either sex, and the disabled, among others. Rape crises services, law enforcement agencies, and laws now recognize that it is not just young women who are the victims of sexual assaults. Men, who may or may not be gay, rape other men. Children, too, are victimized. Often their molesters are not caught, but the recent publicity concerning the molestation of children by Catholic priests over several decades has focused public awareness on this crime. Child pornography is a growing problem, too, and it has spread due to the availability of Internet sites. The trafficking and slavery of women, men, and children have made sexual slavery and pornography a global industry.

From legitimate reporting of news events to plays, such as *The Vagina Monologues*, and literature, such as *The Color Purple*, to shock advertisements and the most violent pornography, depictions and coverage of rape permeate U.S. culture. Some people will say that it is too much, and to them, no doubt, the idea of an *Encyclopedia of Rape* is controversial, if not unnecessary. I would argue otherwise. It is all the more necessary. By discussing the particulars of rape—specific events, concepts, or people involved—readers can better understand rape as not just a sex act but a crime with real victims. Furthermore, they will learn that there are many definitions and permutations of sexual assault. Understanding the various aspects of rape and how rape has occurred in many different situations and contexts in real life throughout history is the goal of this book. In other words, the purpose of this volume is to educate people about rape.

Rape appears in many guises. There is the actual physical act of rape, which has been defined in various ways and in various places to include only virgins, only women, and only women who have cried out loudly enough to attract witnesses. Regulation of sexuality and punishment of rape has come about through beliefs, laws, and tribal customs. Rape victims may be young or old, male or female, and of any racial group. But rape also appears in art, literature, movies, and mythology, and rape occurs on dates, in marital beds, in prisons, and during war. I have tried to include all these aspects of rape in this encyclopedia.

NOTES

1. See, for example, Glenna Whitley, "He Drugged and Raped Me—and I Couldn't Prove It," *Glamour* (December 2002): 214–217, 242–245; "Center City Rapist," http://www.nbc10.com/news/1413685/detail.html; The Boston Globe: Spotlight Investigation Abuse in the Catholic Church, http://www.boston.com/globe/spotlight/abuse/; Human Rights Watch, http://www.hrw.org.

2. "Rape 'Common' in Punjab," BBC News, http://news.bbc.uk/1/hi/world/southasia/2144241.stm.

3. Susan Estrich, "Rape Shield Laws Aren't Foolproof," http://www.usatoday.co/news/opinion/editorials/20003-07-27-estrich_x.htm; "Spousal Rape Laws: 20 Years Later," The National Center for Victims of Crime, http://www.ncvc.org/policy/issues/spousalrape.

4. Susan Brownmiller, *Against Our Will: Men, Women and Rape* (New York: Fawcett Columbine, 1975), 15. One Internet site consists of a bibliography of rape. See "History of Rape: Bibliography," compiled by Stefan Blaschke, http://de.geocities.com/history_guide/horb/index.html.

5. Leslie Francis, ed., *Date Rape: Feminism, Philosophy, and the Law* (University Park: Pennsylvania State University Press, 1996), vii.

6. Trisha Meili, *I Am the Central Park Jogger: A Study of Hope and Possibility* (New York: Simon and Schuster, 2003).

Chronology of Selected Rape-Related Events

c. 1780 B.C.E.   Code of Hammurabi is written. This famous Babylonian law code declared that a virgin was innocent if raped, but that her attacker should be executed. Married women who were raped were considered to be guilty of adultery and could be executed along with their attackers.

c. 1650–1500 B.C.E.   Code of the Nesilim is written. This ancient Hittite law code included a law stating that a woman who was raped within her own house could be executed.

c. 1075 B.C.E.   Code of Assura is written. This ancient Assyrian law code permitted a husband to kill or punish his wife if she was raped.

c. 990 B.C.E.   King David's daughter, Tamar, is raped by her brother.

c. 750 B.C.E.   Legendary Rape of the Sabine Women takes place following the founding of Rome.

c. 621 B.C.E.   Book of Deuteronomy in the Bible includes laws regarding rape.

c. 509 B.C.E.   Legendary Rape of Lucretia takes place following the expulsion of the Kings of Rome.

429 B.C.E.   Hippocratic Oath initiates the start of ethical opposition to sexual encounters in the doctor-patient relationship.

426 C.E.   Christian philosopher Augustus states the purpose of marriage is procreation.

629   Muslims recognize authority of the Sharia, a complex system of laws and prohibitions and requirements, similar to the Jewish Talmud.

700s   Lady Yeshe Tsogyel, a Tibetan princess and Tantric Buddhist, greets her rapists and transforms the rape into a means of enlightenment for them.

1275	Statute of Westminster I (Clause 13) is written. This English statute made the rape of any woman, virgin or married, a crime. Those found guilty were to be imprisoned for two years.
1285	Statute of Westminster II (Clause 9) is written. This law strengthened the earlier law and sentenced the rapist to death.
1492	Christopher Columbus crosses the Atlantic, leading Europeans to "discover" people, animals, and plants, formerly unknown to them, as well as leading to the exploitation and enslavement of those people.
1559–1562	Titian paints the *Rape of Europa*.
1618	Peter Paul Rubens paints the *Rape of the Daughters of Leucippus*.
1619	Slave ships first bring African slaves to Jamestown, Virginia.
1736	Sir Matthew Hale writes *History of the Pleas of the Crown*, which influenced rape law until the late twentieth century. Hale stated that rape "is an accusation easily to be made and hard to be proved."
1765–1769	Sir William Blackstone writes *Commentaries on the Laws of England*. This work had a profound effect on how rape was prosecuted and how rape victims were treated.
1838	In *People v. Abbott*, New York State, a woman accuses a married minister of rape. He is acquitted because the state's three conditions were not met: the woman must be of good reputation; the woman must show evidence of physical resistance; and the woman must have tried to call for help.
1854	In *People v. Morrison*, New York State, the court declares that the woman must resist by using all of her natural abilities. In the absence of such resistance, there is no rape.
1856–1939	Sigmund Freud's influential theories associate women with passivity and masochism.
1873	Comstock Act prohibits distribution of materials deemed obscene, including information on contraception to rape victims.
1892	Ida B. Wells's *Southern Horrors* is published. It protests the lynching of black men who are often falsely accused of raping white women.
1916	The movie *Birth of a Nation* (D.W. Griffith, 1916) depicts a bestial black man intent on raping a virginal white woman.
1931	In the Scottsboro Boys case, two white women claim to be raped by nine African American men on a freight train. One woman later recants. Several trials result.
	Thalia Massie is raped in Honolulu, Hawaii. Her husband is tried for murdering one of the alleged rapists, and renowned attorney Clarence Darrow represents him in a widely publicized trial.
1932–1946	The Japanese capture and imprison thousands of women in "comfort stations," where they are forced to have sex with Japanese soldiers and sailors.
1937	Rape of Nanking, China, by Japanese takes place.

1938	In November, *Kristallnacht* riots are organized by Nazis against German Jews. Instances of rape of Jewish women occur.
1942	The first rape in the European Theater of Operations (ETO) (World War II) that leads to a military trial, conviction, and prison sentence takes place in Melling, Lancashire, England. The assailant was black, the woman white.
1944	The first execution for rape in the ETO takes place. Two black men are executed on August 11, 1944, in the over-300-year-old prison that the United States had taken over in Shepton Mallet, England (near Bath).
1944–1945	Helene Deutsch's *Psychology of Women* is published. This work is notable for its view that female psychology is characterized by masochism and rape fantasies.
1962–1964	Rape-murders are attributed to the Boston Strangler.
1963	Betty Friedan's *The Feminine Mystique* is published. This influential work focused on the alienation felt by many suburban housewives during this time.
1964	The rape-murder of Kitty Genovese in New York City is ignored by 38 witnesses.
1966	National Organization for Women (NOW) is founded.
1968	U.S. soldiers rape, murder, and pillage My Lai in Vietnam.
1971	First public speak-out against rape takes place at St. Clement's Episcopal Church in New York City.
1972	First rape crisis center opens in Berkeley, California.
1973	U.S. Supreme Court legalizes abortion in *Roe v. Wade*.
1975	Susan Brownmiller's *Against Our Will*, a landmark book on rape, is published.
	In *Cox Broadcasting Corporation v. Cohn*, the Court rules that new agencies have a constitutional right to publish the names of rape victims.
1977	Nebraska becomes the first state to include marital rape within rape laws.
	In *Coker v. Georgia*, the U.S. Supreme Court rules that capital punishment in rape cases is unconstitutional.
early 1980s	The first cases of sexual abuse by clergy of all faiths begin to surface.
1982	New York legislature eliminates the physical resistance requirement in rape cases.
1983	The Big Dan's Tavern case investigates the gang rape of a woman in New Bedford, Massachusetts.
1984	Four out of the six men prosecuted in the Big Dan's Tavern case are convicted.

Weishaupt v. Commonwealth is the first Virginia case of marital rape to deny spousal exclusion.

1986   American college freshman Jeanne Ann Clery is violently raped and murdered in her Lehigh University (Pennsylvania) dormitory room.

Federal Sexual Abuse Act is passed.

1987   North Dakota passes date rape bill.

Real Rape by Susan Estrich is published. This influential book argued that rape by someone known to the victim is just as real as rape by a stranger.

1989   Central Park Jogger Case. In this highly publicized case, a white female investment banker was raped, beaten, and left for dead in Central Park in New York City.

Glen Ridge (New Jersey) case involves sexual assault of a mentally retarded young woman by popular high school athletes.

1990s   More cases of sexual abuse by clergy come to light; there is civil litigation by survivors.

1990   The Crime Awareness and Campus Security Act of 1990, also known as the Student Right to Know and Campus Security Act (Clery Act), is passed. This act requires federally funded colleges and universities to publicly report all campus crimes, including rape.

1991   In *Michigan v. Lucas*, the U.S. Supreme Court upholds the state's rape shield law.

During the Tailhook Convention, male naval aviators sexually harass and molest female naval officers and nonmilitary personnel during nightly gauntlets.

1991–1995   During the Balkans War, thousands of women are raped and impregnated.

1992   Campus Sexual Assault Victims Bill of Rights is passed to prevent rape survivors at college campuses from being revictimized. It also requires colleges and universities to inform victims of sexual assault of their option to report their assault to law enforcement outside of the campus.

Boxer Mike Tyson is convicted of raping Desiree Washington.

1993   North Carolina and Oklahoma are the last states to abolish the spousal exemption clauses in rape laws when spouses are living together.

1994   Megan's Law is passed in New Jersey, followed by similar laws being passed in other states establishing registration of sex offenders and community notifications.

Federal Violence against Women Act (VAWA) is passed.

1995   Violence against Women Office opens as part of the U.S. Department of Justice.

1996   Federal version of Megan's Law is passed.

Drug-Induced Rape Prevention and Punishment Act is passed.

1997   *United States v. Lanier* declares rape by a government official violates the Fourteenth Amendment.

1998   Jeanne Clery Disclosure of Campus Security Policy and Campus Crimes Statistics Act is passed.

             During Rwandan war trials, the United Nations declares that rape is a crime of genocide.

2000   Campus Sex Crimes Prevention Act is passed.

2002   Crisis of priest pedophilia comes to a head in Boston Archdiocese and others; new policy and procedures are developed with some national oversight by the U.S. Conference of Catholic Bishops.

2003   *Lawrence v. Texas* decision overturns criminalization of sodomy between consenting adults.

             Police in Europe and the United States make numerous arrests of people alleged to be involved in Internet child pornography networks.

             Cadets at the U.S. Air Force Academy in Colorado allege that sexual asaults have taken place over a period of many years and charge the academy commanders of ignoring them.

2004   Rapes of U.S. servicewomen on Air Force bases in the Pacific Air Command and on other bases are investigated.

             Marc Dutroux is tried for kidnapping, raping, and murdering four girls in Belgium in the 1990s. He says he is part of a large pedophile ring.

Alphabetical List of Entries

Topical List of Entries

Encyclopedia of Rape

A

ABDUCTION (KIDNAPPING). The words *abduct* and *kidnap* derive from borrowed Latin and Scandinavian words stems. The first recorded uses of *kidnap* in the English language appear in the seventeenth century, while *abduct* appears in the nineteenth century. Today, while legal definitions and terms of the words vary worldwide, common usage refers to taking someone away illegally through force or fraud, with intent to prevent liberation. Abductors usually kidnap with the purpose of carrying out one or more other crimes, such as rape, robbery, **murder**, or a combination thereof.

Abduction and kidnapping existed long before the seventeenth century, especially with regard to rape during wartime. Historically, conquered peoples were considered war spoils and were enslaved. Women were abducted, raped, and deemed wives or concubines of their captors.

Ancient Hebrews captured and made foreign women concubines. Ancient Greeks nabbed and raped women during wartime and made them wives and concubines. Thirteenth-century warlord Genghis Khan returned from conquered tribes with the wives of chieftains. Khan defined a man's highest function as ruining enemies through seizure of possessions and women. In fifteenth-century England, soldiers often gained control of a woman's property through sexual seizure. During the American Revolution, British soldiers abducted women and carried out rapes in war encampments.

Anthropological accounts from the early to the middle twentieth century indicate **gang rape**s of women captured by Yanomamö raiding parties in Venezuela and sexual abduction of women in Kenya by Gusii tribesmen who could not afford bride prices. In the late twentieth century, rape was used as a systematic wartime tool of intimidation and **genocide** in Rwanda, Africa, and **Bosnia-Herzegovina**. Serbian forces organized widespread imprisonment of Muslim and Croat women in detention centers and military brothels, where they endured multiple rapes. An estimated 50,000 women and girls were systematically raped.

Today, the majority of worldwide **victims** of abduction are abducted from, taken to, and moved in vehicles. In the United States, over 35,000 children are abducted annually. Of those, 65 percent of nonfamily kidnapping victims are female. **Sexual predators** often use ruses to gain compliance and lure away children.

Kidnapping is a sudden ordeal that victims do not anticipate. Victims are often too shocked and terrorized to cry for help or resist. Some abductors are motivated to kidnap and rape out of a desire for power and control. They frequently use knives, guns, and threats to intimidate and force. Violence may be used even if a victim is passive.

Abductors often fantasize about, or perceive an imaginary relationship with, victims, who endure hours or days of fear. Trauma normally experienced in a rape situation is intensified and prolonged. There may be multiple rapes by one or more captors. The likelihood of **posttraumatic stress disorder (PTSD)** is increased in sexual abduction cases and multiple rape cases.

Facing constant emotional and physical violence, victims survive by using techniques such as praying, finding routine, and creating relationships with abductors. When attempting to create a relationship with a captor, the victim often shares personal anecdotes and family stories. Listening thoughtfully can reassure the captor that the victim is not a threat. Building a relationship is important when victims are forced to wear hoods to cover their heads, as a hood might psychologically transform the victim from a person to an object in the captor's mind, thereby making murder easier. Surviving three or more days increases chances of being released alive. *See also*: **Comfort Women; Rape of the Sabine Women; Wartime Rape.**

Suggested Reading: Susan Brownmiller, *Against Our Will: Men, Women and Rape* (New York: First Ballantine Books, 1993); Caroline Moorehead, *Hostages to Fortune: A Study of Kidnapping in the World Today* (New York: Atheneum, 1980).

ELIZABETH JENNER

ABORTION. Abortion is the "intentional termination of gestation by any means and at any time during **pregnancy** from conception to full term," according to James Mohr (viii). In 1973, the Supreme Court legalized abortion for all women in the United States, but from the middle of the nineteenth century until the late 1960s, when many states began to liberalize their abortion laws, a rape victim in the United States was barred by law from obtaining an abortion. Prior to the mid-nineteenth century, abortion laws in the United States, as in many European countries, held that the fetus did not become a human being until after quickening, sometime during the fourth or fifth month of pregnancy, when a pregnant woman first sensed movement in her womb. This sensation marked the moment, experts believed, when the soul or human form entered the fetus. Abortion prior to quickening was neither sin nor crime and was not differentiated from spontaneous miscarriage.

Rape **victims** sought and obtained abortions prior to quickening, but a bizarre medical and legal misunderstanding of the relationship between rape and pregnancy characterized the colonial period and persisted well into the twentieth century. Importing medical beliefs widespread in England, colonists, and later Americans, assumed that a woman could become pregnant only if she experienced orgasm during intercourse: A raped woman could not, by definition, become pregnant. Although by the end of the eighteenth century scientists challenged the validity of an inexorable link between pleasure and procreation, medical experts often ignored new findings, or simply modified traditional views, to insist some measure of female **consent** and pleasure was essential to pregnancy.

In the colonial era and beyond, women turned to an array of means to end conception and restore menstruation, relying upon such herbs as savin, tansy, ergot, pennyroyal, snakeroot, and black cohosh. They also adopted other methods: internal douching, bloodletting, severe physical exertion, hot baths, cathartics, even jolts of electricity. By the time of the American Revolution, abortifacient drugs became commercialized, and during the early nineteenth century abortion providers performed relatively safe instrumental abortions.

However, by the mid-nineteenth century, the seemingly widespread phenomenon of abortion began to spark concern among public leaders. Increasingly, abortion seekers were married, native-born, middle- and upper-class Protestant women, rather than the unmarried, seduced young women who evoked public sympathy. The confluence of nativist fears about growing numbers of Irish Catholics, who generally had large families, and the plunging family size among native-born white Americans, sexist anxieties about the rise of the women's movement, and the self-interests of the fledgling American Medical Association, formed in 1847, worked to undermine the hitherto approval of abortion. During the 1850s and 1860s, the American Medical Association launched a crusade to outlaw abortion. Between 1860 and 1890, state legislatures criminalized abortion, though a number of state statutes provided a "therapeutic exception" that allowed abortion to save a woman's life and, in some states, a woman's health. In no state was rape accepted as grounds for abortion. However, many women did find friends, relations, skilled physicians, and other practitioners who endorsed or secretly assisted abortion when their circumstances dictated it. Rape was such a circumstance. After World War II, a number of hospitals around the country established hospital abortion committees that reviewed abortion requests and generally allowed "therapeutic abortions" for women who had been raped.

During the illegal era, some unscrupulous physicians and others sexually or financially exploited vulnerable women in exchange for providing abortions. In some hospitals, women, including some rape victims, could obtain abortions only after agreeing to be sterilized at the same time. In part, this was because rape **survivors** were frequently perceived to be sexually promiscuous. Those who could not find doctors or anyone else to help them end unwanted pregnancies sometimes self-aborted, often permanently damaging or even killing themselves in the process.

Unease over abortion laws grew increasingly visible by the late 1950s. Progressive doctors and lawyers attacked the amorphous, capriciously applied therapeutic exception and sympathized with pregnant rape victims. Members of the American Legal Institute proposed a Model Law calling for abortion law reform to enable raped women who became pregnant to have a legal abortion. During the 1960s, a plethora of nationwide initiatives arose to reform or repeal abortion statutes. This broad-based movement climaxed with the 1973 U.S. Supreme Court decisions in *Roe v. Wade* and *Doe v. Bolton*. State criminal abortion laws were judged unconstitutional for violating the rights of women and doctors. These decisions, however, did not address issues of economic inequality among women and access to abortions, nor was the decision to abort placed wholly within women's control. Since 1973, despite abortion's legality, state legislation and court decisions responding to a powerful and, at times, violent antiabortion movement seriously hampered women's freedom to secure an abortion.

Key developments in medical science in recent decades introduced new ways for rape victims to prevent or halt pregnancy. Beginning in the 1970s and 1980s, a rape survivor could turn to emergency contraception, known as the "**morning-after pill**," to be taken within 72 hours of intercourse or rape. Emergency contraception blocks ovulation, or if ovulation has already taken place, the pills thwart fertilization by preventing the fertilized egg from attaching itself to the uterine wall. Access to emergency contraception, however, is limited; many pharmacies and hospitals fear antiabortion protest.

If a rape victim cannot take advantage of emergency contraception, her alternative is a chemical abortifacient, mifepristone (mifeprex), formerly known as RU-486, which the Federal Drug Administration deemed safe and effective in 1996. This pill blocks progesterone, the hormone essential for a fertilized egg to survive in the wall of the uterus. After taking the pill, the woman later inserts vaginally four tablets of misoprostol to trigger uterine contractions, which approximately four hours later expel the uterine lining with its gestational sac or embryo. As the shifting course of abortion history reveals, the future of abortion pills and abortion rights remains unstable, highly dependent on court and legislature decisions. *See also*: **Infanticide; Physicians/Medical Professionals.**

Suggested Reading: Boston Women's Health Book Collective, *Our Bodies, Ourselves for the New Century* (New York: Simon and Schuster, 1998); Angus McLaren, *Reproductive Rituals* (New York: Methuen, 1984); James C. Mohr, *Abortion in America* (Oxford: Oxford University Press, 1978); Leslie J. Reagan, *When Abortion Was a Crime* (Berkeley: University of California Press, 1997); Joan R. Schroedel, *Is the Fetus a Person?* (Ithaca, NY: Cornell University Press, 2000).

JOYCE AVRECH BERKMAN

ACQUAINTANCE RAPE. *See* Date Rape/Acquaintance Rape.

ADVERTISING. In cutthroat competition with each other for consumer attention, merchandisers have increasingly turned to images of sex and violence. While overt acts of rape are considered too crude for magazine and television advertising, the suggestion of sexual violence may make a casual viewer pause long enough to register a brand name. "Rape," comments Naomi Wolf in *The Beauty Myth*, "is the current advertising metaphor" (79). Shocking the reader into momentary engagement through depictions of sexual transgression can harness the tremendous power of negative publicity. If controversy leads to widespread brand recognition, then the campaign was a success.

The elements of an ad that imply rape may be subtle, but taken altogether the message of sexual violation becomes clear. One ad depicts a woman lying across the seat of an abandoned car with her legs dangling out the door in an unnatural pose. Her clothes and stockings are torn, and her face is turned away. This ad is marketing the bag that sits open on the dirt beside her inert, shoeless foot. Another ad shows a black-and-white alley scene with three young men. Between them is a woman who is suspended off the ground by the back of her jeans while a second man grabs her arm and a third holds her leg. The scene is shot as if caught midaction. Although the product is jeans, the various elements of the ad suggest a **gang rape.**

Often rape is only one possible interpretation of an advertisement. In an ad for perfume, a nude woman reposes on an antique love seat. Her stark white skin is contrasted by vivid red lips. With her head turned slightly into the shadows, it is difficult to tell if her closed eyes are covered in dark makeup or if her face is bruised. One arm is twisted behind her back in a position that would be uncomfortable if she were asleep, which raises the question of whether she is even alive. At first glance, the woman appears to be lying peacefully. It is not until the finer details of the ad are taken into consideration that the possibility of sexual violence becomes apparent.

Yet, should an advertiser take responsibility for every petty little element, most especially when the details hint at charges as serious as rape? Can one read too much into an ad? The average commercial costs half a million dollars to produce and air. In the production phase, thousands of photographs are taken and miles of video are shot. These images are judged, rejected, resized, electronically manipulated, and finally rendered as a finished advertisement. The ads are often relayed back and forth between the ad team, agency executives, the sponsor's marketing division, and their upper-level management. Companies spend over $200 billion a year on campaigns designed by advertising professionals in the hope that they will capture a sizable piece of the trillion-dollar global market. When the stakes are that high and the process so expensive and laborious, there is no question that every element is indeed intentional.

An image sponsored by a shoe company shows the back of a woman running on rough, wet pavement at dusk. She wears a midlength dark coat, stockings, and spike-heeled boots. Her face expresses concern, if not alarm, as she glances over her shoulder at whoever is behind her. Since the scene is shot from the reader's point of view, the pursuer is you. In response to questions about who such ads are designed for, advertisers claim that these images play with **fantasies**. Ads, they say, simply participate in the wider culture's idolization of wealth, romance, youth, and beauty. Although scenes depicting impending sexual violence or its aftermath are not considered a normal part of **popular culture**, they are acceptable enough within the industry that threatening images continue to appear with disturbing regularity. Indeed, fantasies of **sexual coercion** shot from the perpetrator's point of view are typical of violent **pornography**.

A direct link between ads that suggest sexual transgression and actual rape has never been established. Nevertheless, social acceptance and tolerance of these images contribute to a culture of permissiveness, where the idea is conveyed that men can rape with impunity. Most advertising rejects depictions of rape, but the remainder issue the threatening message that women are potential prey. *See also:* **Media.**

Suggested Reading: Jean Kilbourne, *Can't Buy My Love: How Advertising Changes the Way We Think and Feel* (New York: Simon and Schuster, 1999); Naomi Wolf, *The Beauty Myth: How Images of Beauty Are Used Against Women* (New York: Doubleday, 1991).

LINDA D. WAYNE

AFRICAN AMERICANS. The enslavement of African Americans is a core component of the economic and social history of the United States. In 1619, Europeans brought the first ship with African slaves as cargo to Jamestown, Virginia. For some female slaves, rape was part of their initial journey from Africa to the American continent. In one of the earliest accounts of these slave ship voyages, Olaudah

Equiano, an African slave, wrote: "[I]t was almost a constant practice with our clerks and other whites to commit violent degradations on the chastity of the female slaves. . . . I have even known them to gratify their brutal passion with females not even ten years old" (Sollors, 77).

In the system of chattel **slavery** developed in the United States and abolished in 1865, African American slave women were frequently raped. They could be legally raped by their white masters, the young sons of their white masters, and employees of their master, such as white overseers on Southern plantations. In another form of rape, women were sometimes forced to be "breeders," which meant being forced to have sexual relations with black male slaves to produce children for their white masters to enslave.

Connected to the problem of rape were damaging sexual stereotypes of African Americans and continued brutality against them, even after slavery was abolished. This sexual stereotyping and brutal treatment became an important aspect of the legacy of slavery. From the post–Reconstruction period through the 1920s, African Americans were repeatedly lynched by whites in the South without any penalty for the whites. The lynching of black men could include publicly castrating them, burning them alive, or hanging them. A frequent justification for these murders was the accusation that the lynched black men had sexually assaulted white women. These charges did not have to be proven. Myths labeling black men as unable to control their sexual passions, particularly for white women, became rampant in society.

Moreover, citing their sexual "liaisons" with white masters, black female slaves were often depicted by early historians of slavery as sexually promiscuous. These historians falsely represented the rape of black females as consensual sexual relations. Such distortions about black women's sexuality hid the crime of rape committed by white slave owners. Stereotypes about the promiscuity of black females that originated in slavery became part of the image of freed black women. As a consequence of this, in the post–Reconstruction era, many black women were subjected to male **sexual harassment** and sometimes **sexual assault** when working as domestics in white homes (a major form of employment for black women during this period).

The emergence of late-twentieth-century feminist scholarship stimulated a new discussion about the link between rape and racist stereotypes of black men, sometimes with sharp disagreements among scholars. For example, black feminist scholar/activist Angela Davis offered a critique of the racism within several white feminist discussions of rape, including the pioneering text *Against Our Will* by **Susan Brownmiller**. Davis presented arguments supporting the criticism of Brownmiller's text "for its part in the resuscitation of the old racist myth of the black rapist" (Davis, 178). In discussing the widespread problem of rape for women (including experiences of African American women), Brownmiller had defended white women's fear of rape by black men.

For African Americans in contemporary U.S. society, rape occurs most often intraracially, between African Americans, rather than interracially (as is the case for all other racial/ethnic groups, including whites). Black females who have been raped may feel anger, fear, humiliation, depression, numbness, a sense of violation, or shame. Certain racial and gender dynamics produced by U.S. society often intensify the anguish of black women and girls victimized by rape. When seeking help, they may encounter a combination of racism and sexism in the responses by criminal justice officials. For instance, men who are convicted of raping black women tend to get shorter sentences than men who are convicted of raping white women. Some black women who have been raped may be reluctant to report black male perpetrators because they do not want to be accused of contributing to the racist labeling of all black men as rapists. When seeking counseling after being raped, some black women may be labeled as more emotionally "strong," and sometimes it is incorrectly assumed that they need less emotional support.

African American men who are socioeconomically poor are disproportionately incarcerated in prisons throughout the United States. Since rape committed by one inmate against another is a common problem for male prisoners, black men might be perpetrators or **victims** of rape. African American men who are raped in prison may experience fear, anger, humiliation, and an overwhelming sense of powerlessness because there is little public concern about addressing this crime against them.

During the first few hundred years of U.S. history the rape of African American women was a legal act, commonly integrated into the institution of slavery. The relationship between **rape and racism** continued to be a problem that impacted African Americans after slavery was abolished. At great cost to their lives and well-being, racist myths developed in American culture that labeled African American women as "rapable" (always sexually available) and African American men as rapists, especially of white women. Finally, when victimized by rape, there may be experiences that intensify its trauma for African Americans that reflect deeply embedded cultural patterns related to race, gender, sexuality, and socioeconomic status. *See also*: **Rape History in the United States: Seventeenth Century; Rape History in the United States: Eighteenth Century; Rape History in the United States: Nineteenth Century; Rape History in the United States: Twentieth Century; Rape-Lynch Scenario; Southern Rape Complex.**

Suggested Reading: Angela Y. Davis, "Rape, Racism and the Myth of the Black Rapist," in her *Women, Race, and Class* (New York: Random House, 1981), 172–201; Patricia Morton, *Disfigured Images: The Historical Assault on Afro-American Women* (Westport, CT: Praeger, 1991); Charlotte Pierce-Baker, *Surviving the Silence: Black Women's Stories of Rape* (New York: W.W. Norton, 1998); Werner Sollors, ed., *The Interesting Narrative of the Life of Olaudah Equiano, or Gustavus Vassa, the African, Written by Himself* (New York: W.W. Norton, 1991); Jennifer Wriggins, "Rape, Racism, and the Law," in *Rape and Society: Readings on the Problem of Sexual Assault*, ed. Patricia Searles and Ronaly J. Berger (Boulder, CO: Westview Press, 1995), 215–222.

TRACI C. WEST

AFRICAN WOMEN AND GIRLS. Since the mid-1990s, the African **media** have carried reports of endemic rape cases. Hardly a day passes by without a report appearing in local newspapers about rape or defilement. The increasing incidence of rape is due to the growing public awareness of rape and hence the willingness to report rape cases. The sudden coverage of rape cases by the media may be traced, respectively, to two internal and external factors: the surging activism of African women and African response to globalization. The latter factor includes access to television, radio, newsmagazines, and the Internet. Both factors have led to popular awareness that rape is aberrant and criminal and has long-term physical and clinical effects on rape **victims** and their families (*see* **Family**).

Most rape victims in Africa fail to disclose their ordeal, and they do so for a number of reasons. Some victims are intimidated by the rapists, who threaten them with death or bodily harm. Others decide not to report because they fear the **stigma** and ostracism that comes with being raped and/or want to protect their relationships and families. In Congo, for example, husbands frequently abandon wives who have been raped and force them to leave their homes. Given the harsh economic realities, victims of rape in the workplace keep quiet in order to safeguard their jobs. Incestuous rape is shelved because of the concern that it would tarnish the family's name. Rich and powerful men get away with rape by settling rape cases out of the public domain. Also rape victims fail to come forward because they know that the system would fail them. Finally, a number of **date rape** incidents go unreported because the victims blame themselves for associating with the rapists in the first place. Overall, there are more unreported rape cases than there are reported ones. For example, the Nigerian police estimate that about 60 percent of rapes are unreported.

There is a paucity of statistical information on rape in Africa, but the few available statistics can provide an indication of the enormity of rape on the continent. Between April 1, 1999, and August 19, 1999, the Women and Juvenile Unit (WAJU) of the Ghana Police Service recorded 92 cases of rape. Out of these, 25 percent (which is 23 out of 100) related to the defilement of young girls between the ages of one and eight years old. In the Lagos State of Nigeria, four to six females are raped daily. South Africa in 1994 recorded 18,801 cases of rape, and by 2001 the number had reached 24,892. In Egypt, about 10,000 rapes are committed each year.

Although all age groups suffer rape, the evidence shows that those between two years and late teens suffer the most. Young female food and fruit peddlers, mostly in their prepubescence, tend to be the victims of rapists who lure them by pretending to buy whatever the girls are selling. Numerous rape cases include older males who send young girls on errands and rape them thereafter. Due to the acute economic deprivation, rapists are able to entice their victims by offering them food and soft drinks, sometimes laced with intoxicative substances. Some rapists waylay their victims and then resort to violence or threat of death to rape their victims. Date and **gang rape** are common among teenagers, as well. Within families, **incest** and **marital rape** are common but are seldom reported.

In the conflict-ridden zones of Africa, four kinds of rape have been identified. First, genocidal rape is aimed at annihilating an ethnic or political group. This occurred in Rwanda during the 1994 ethnic violence and has carried over to the Congo. Second, political rape is used to punish political opponents of regimes; a very good example is the "Green Bombers" of Zimbabwe, a militia group created by the government. Third is opportunistic rape, that is, when combatants or the police and soldiers run amok and resort to rape in areas of intermittent civil dissonance, as in the case of the oil-rich Niger Delta region of Nigeria. The final one is forced concubinage that involves the conscription and kidnapping (*see* **Abduction/Kidnapping**) of young girls to perform sexual and other services for militiamen and soldiers; this has occurred, for example, in Liberia, the Ivory Coast, the Sudan, and Zimbabwe. All four examples can be seen in the eastern part of the Democratic Republic of Congo, where, according to Human Rights Watch, sexual violence against women is a "war within a war."

African societies have several ways of detecting rape. Once rape is detected, it is reported to the police. For instance, the WAJU has set up a special unit that deals with rape cases. Also, rape victims are sent to nearby health centers for treatment and collection of physical and other evidence. For younger victims, including toddlers, rape is usually identified after people notice the child crying from pain or blood oozing from his or her private parts. Immobilized rape victims, especially in cases where the victim was either forced or tricked to ingest intoxicants and/or suffered violent physical abuse, are found and returned to their families. The inability of rape victims, mostly young girls, to walk properly tends to reveal that they have been raped. Rape cases that end in **pregnancy** also pave the way for the detection of rape. Some victims themselves, mostly teenagers, report the incidence of rape to their families, usually their mothers, who in turn lodge complaints with the police.

Through the lens of court cases, we can discern some of the ridiculous reasons given by rapists for their acts. The reasons range from ones based on **patriarchy** to ones bordering on depravity. But underlying all the reasons for rape are warped patriarchal values. In most cases, the perpetrators see their victims as objects that should be exploited to satisfy their sexual urges. Some rapists blame their victims for the offense, while others insist that they could not control their sexual urges. Yet some rapists maintain that they did not know why they engaged in rape and even blame unseen forces, including the work of the devil. Rapists have also blamed **alcohol** as the reason for engaging in rape. Some of the reasons have an air of casualness symptomatic of assumed patriarchal rights to female sexuality; for example, some rapists claim that they only wanted to enjoy sex with their victims. In South Africa, the strange mythical belief that having sex with a virgin is a cure for **HIV/AIDS** has been blamed for the scourge of rape. In Ethiopia and Egypt, the latter until recently, rape paved the way for marriage: **virginity** is prized, and once a rape victim loses it, she is forced to marry the perpetrator.

The media have also offered some reasons for the scourge of rape. Some commentators have claimed that the provocative appearance of girls accounts for some rape cases, while others have asserted that rapists are mentally ill. Growing unemployment and its consequent idleness and confusion, according to some observers, have provided the fuel for violence, including rape. Also, rapid urbanization and the weakening of the extended family have been used to explain rape. For one thing, urbanization brings about anonymity, and for another, the weakening of the extended family causes individualism. In both cases, individuals are able to hide behind social masks to engage in crimes, one of which is rape. Globalism, the foreign tourist industry, and the spread of foreign cultures have also contributed to the rape epidemic in Africa.

The demographics of rape reflect how class and status affect disclosures of rape. Most of those accused of rape or identified as rapists belong to the lower rungs of society. This does not mean that highly placed men do not commit rape. Rather, the evidence shows that powerful men are able to get away with rape. For their part, influential women hardly report being raped because of the stigma attached to rape and the patriarchal tradition that blames the victim. Most of the reported cases of rape occur in the rural backwater; rape cases that come to light in the urban areas tend to occur outside the core residential areas of the rich and powerful.

How rape is criminalized varies among African countries. What is common is that in all cases the police and courts are involved, but it is the ineffectiveness of these institutions that is the problem. Ghana's Criminal Code can be used as a case study. The Ghanaian Criminal Code makes provisions for "defilement," defined as "carnal knowledge of any female under fourteen years of age, with or without her consent. Defilement is a second-degree felony punishable by imprisonment for a period ranging from 12 months to 10 years. The application of this law is, however, weakened by Section 102 of the Criminal Code. This provision provides a defense that the accused rapist had reasonable cause to believe a female between the ages of 10 and 14 was above 14 years of age. In contrast, rape is a first-degree felony and is punishable by not less than 3 years' imprisonment and a fine. The maximum sentence is life imprisonment. Most African countries, for example, Kenya and Ethiopia, like Ghana do not criminalize marital rape, nor do they define rape as any act other than forced vaginal sex. In fact, in the case of Kenya, the victim must prove the degree of penetration. While such laws are informed by indigenous patriarchal practice, they are also the products of colonial laws.

Some rural communities attempt to solve rape cases through the use of indigenous arbitration panels consisting of community elders. Judgment includes formal rebuke of the rapist and his payment of compensation to the victim and her family. This type of intervention does not serve as a deterrent and may even encourage rapists to continue. Some rape cases are settled out of court after the rapist has compensated his victim. Women activists have called for the abandonment of such practices.

The effects of rape are the least discussed subject in the media and popular discourses. Emotional, psychological, and physical trauma are at best implied but never the subject of focus. Most of the reports describe toddlers, babies, and teenagers who experienced bleeding from broken hymens or had blood oozing from their private parts. The physical assaults that accompany rape are only mentioned to indicate the violent tactics employed by rapists but not how such assaults affected the victims.

Several solutions have been suggested as a means to eradicate the rape epidemic. Perhaps the most common recommended solution is the imposition of severe sentences on rapists. Many have proposed even more severe punishment for rapists who are infected with HIV/AIDS. Calls have been made to establish **rape crisis centers** to meet the emotional and physical needs of rape victims. The education of girls has been identified as an important factor in curbing rape. Groups such as the Federation of African Women Educationists (FAWE), a nongovernmental organization (NGO), support female education as a means of empowerment. In South Africa and Nigeria, the African National Congress (ANC) Women's League and the Women's Rights Watch are, respectively, active in the campaign against rape. The pulpits of various churches draw attention to rape. For example, the Christian Council of Ghana has called for combined efforts of churches and other organizations to end **sexual harassment** and rape. Teachers, especially females, have also been urged to form antirape task forces to counsel against rape and violence against women. Women's groups all over Africa—for example, the Ghana National Commission on Women and Development, Kenya's Coalition of Violence against Women, and Women in Nigeria—are politicizing and internationalizing rape and other forms of violence against women. As a result of internal and external pressures, African governments have become involved in eliminating violence against females, including rape. In Egypt, for example, internal pressures forced the government to scrap the law known as Article 291, a legal anomaly that allowed a rapist to escape punishment if the rapist legally married his victim. Sources of support and activism against rape outside Africa have included Amnesty International and the World Health Organization.

In recent times, African women have become empowered and conscientized. The

African media, women's groups, NGOs, churches, and academic institutions are working to improve the conditions and status of women. All of these groups have the elimination of rape on their agenda and have called on victims of rape to come forward. In spite of this, the greatest threat to women is patriarchal ideology that justifies gender and social inequalities by making rape seem natural. *See also:* **"Blaming the Victim" Syndrome; Genocide; Wartime Rape.**

Suggested Reading: December Green, *Gender Violence in Africa: African Women's Responses* (New York: St. Martin's Press, 1999); René Lefort, "Congo: A Hell on Earth for Women," *World Press Review Online*, http://www.worldpress.org/Africa/1561.cfm; Binaifer Nowrojee, *Violence against Women in South Africa: The State Response to Domestic Violence and Rape* (New York: Human Rights Watch, 1995); Lloyd Vogelman, *The Sexual Face of Violence: Rapists on Rape* (Johannesburg: Ravan Press, 1990).

KWABENA O. AKURANG-PARRY

AGAINST OUR WILL. The first, and still most comprehensive, examination of rape in world history, **Susan Brownmiller**'s bestselling study *Against Our Will: Men, Women and Rape* was published in 1975, at the height of the modern women's rights movement. A popular rather than strictly scholarly account, it was nonetheless an ambitious volume. Geographically and temporally vast in scope, *Against Our Will* relies on an extensive array of sources to document rape's history in a variety of contexts, including wars, riots, revolutions, and **pogrom**s, from antiquity to the present.

According to Brownmiller, rape is a natural product of patriarchal social relations in which males are schooled in the arts of dominance, while females are taught to submit. She rejects the view of rape as fundamentally sexual, construing it instead as an act of violence deployed by men to maintain their preeminence in the prevailing gender hierarchy. Brownmiller's theoretical posture is most aptly conveyed in her controversial assertion that rape "is nothing more or less than a conscious process of intimidation by which *all men* keep *all women* in a state of fear." Although this interpretation resonated with many readers, women in particular, it was widely seen as hostile, extremist, and antimale, over time providing much grist for the mill of women's rights opponents. Brownmiller made a number of other provocative statements on the subject—for instance, describing marriage as a dangerous bargain whereby women accepted the dominion of one man as protection against rape by the many—but these were generally consistent with the radical feminist thinking of the day.

Critical reaction to *Against Our Will* ran the gamut from enthusiastic praise to vitriolic attack. On the one hand, the book was commended for its breadth, passion, and consciousness-raising impact. On the other, it was criticized for universalizing the experiences of white, middle-class women at the expense of those of other classes and colors. Some charged Brownmiller with outright racism, taking issue, for example, with her contention that lynching victim Emmett Till—a 14-year-old black visiting his great-uncle's cabin in Money, Mississippi, in late August 1955—and his white murderers shared a view of women as objects of sexual conquest. *Against Our Will* has also been censured for establishing too rigid a divide between sex and violence, thus oversimplifying complex relations of power in which both are implicated, and finally, for inadvertently perpetuating the fallacy that rape is something that happens "out there" rather than "at home," where in fact the vast majority of such assaults take place.

Whatever its deficiencies, *Against Our Will* remains a pioneering study. Through its compelling presentation of rape as a fundamental social problem, it helped to consolidate its place on the public agenda. Along with works like Kate Millett's *Sexual Politics* (1970) and Germaine Greer's *The Female Eunuch* (1970), *Against Our Will* stands as a key text of second-wave feminism and Brownmiller's most enduring contribution to the cause of women's rights to date. *See also*: **Feminist Movement; National Organization for Women (NOW); New York Radical Feminists; Rape, Causes of; Rape History in the United States: Twentieth Century.**

Suggested Reading: Susan Brownmiller, *In Our Time: Memoir of a Revolution* (New York: Random House, 1999).

LISA CARDYN

ALCOHOL. Most statistics converge on the conclusion that a sizable proportion of rape incidents involve alcohol. The percentages of rapes committed under the influence of alcohol range from 26 to 90 percent. Such high figures are most obviously due to alcohol's role in overcoming sexual inhibition. Convicted rapists who were drunk at the time of the incident admit having felt more powerful owing to alcohol. Yet although this cause-effect relationship seems straightforward and intuitively obvious, the exact correlation between alcohol abuse and rape is more complicated. It is hard to ascertain whether alcohol can be a single factor prompting sexually abusive behavior. Alcohol may merely be an accompanying element in incidents where perpetrators have an inherent tendency to be aggressive, as some studies show that a large number of **sex offenders** have a record of other nonsexual crimes. Besides, part of the statistics of alcohol-related rape can be explained by the fact that many drunken offenders are motivated by the common false notion that alcohol mitigates the rapist's criminal liability.

The offender is not always the only intoxicated party in a rape. Many rapes occur as a result of a common misconception that a drunken woman "invites sex." This reasoning serves as a twisted rationalization for sexual aggression, and it inevitably makes women more prone to being victimized. Alcohol is also known to contribute to rape by reducing a woman's reluctance to have sex; it clouds judgment and considerably limits her ability to assess risk. A woman under the influence of alcohol will often miss telltale signs of a potential assailant's sexually driven behavior. In fact, as many males admit, mindful of alcohol's effects, they have offered alcohol or drugs in order to obtain a woman's sexual **consent**. Numerous studies confirm that large percentages of women who experience sexual aggression are often themselves intoxicated. But intoxication jeopardizes victims regardless of their sex. This became obvious in the sex scandal in the Catholic Church revealed in 2002, where some priests were said to have resorted to alcohol in order to cajole their underage male victims into having sex. Although the magnitude of the scandal may never be revealed entirely, a number of specific allegations regarding alcohol have already been made. One victim accused Ronald Paquin, a priest defrocked after several other accusations, of intoxicating and drugging him and a friend and attempting to abuse them sexually afterward.

Alcohol-induced rape has been known since time immemorial, as it is recorded in the earliest myths of antiquity. A principal figure in Greek **mythology** that symbolizes this form of sexual craving is Satyr, associated with the god of wine, Dionysus (Bacchus). Satyr was depicted as a woodland creature fond of drinking and raping nymphs. In real life, too, drinking and sexual abuse, often forced on children, were not unheard of in ancient times, but because such acts were considered religious in nature, they rarely bore the **stigma** of any wrongdoing.

More recently in history, massive military conflicts have occasioned countless cases of brutal **gang rapes**, most often committed by soldiers emboldened by alcohol. But here, too, despite the frequency and notoriety of drinking, it is hard to explain rape solely in terms of the rapists' intoxication. Raping women of an invaded land has traditionally been understood as part of military conquest, whatever the invading soldiers' state of mind. A case in point was the Soviet counterattack campaign against Nazi Germany in 1945, during which hundreds of thousands of women, not only German, were raped in the wake of the advancing Red Army. Many of the rapists were drunk, but any theory imputing the havoc they have wrought solely to drinking is not credible. Among other important factors behind sexual abuse in the time of war are constant battlefield stress, a lack of fear of retribution for rape, and prolonged sexual inactivity, which gives rise to sexual frustration, conditions easily exacerbated by alcohol consumption.

Alcohol's role in overcoming natural inhibitions and in turn leading to sexual aggression is cited as one of the reasons behind the Islamic Prohibition of alcohol. Similarly, an aversion to the general corruption was among the forces underlying the American Prohibition of 1919–1933. Based on similar premises, a number of other attempts have been made in the past to outlaw the consumption of alcoholic beverages, the earliest ones being in ancient China, Aztec society, and in feudal Japan. However, most countries that have attempted to ban alcohol have repealed their austere prohibition laws, which have been maintained only in a few Muslim states.

Nowadays adverse effects of alcohol consumption are fought through various forms of **rape prevention** policies. Special regulations are issued on U.S. college campuses, where most sex crimes have involved alcohol and drug abuse, and acquaintance rape is the most common crime committed in college. One measure aiming at preventing this problem is the stipulation that acquaintance rape, even that committed in drunkenness, is tantamount to and carries the same consequences as a rape by a stranger.

Alcohol-related rape has also received special attention in the air force. Currently a report is being produced by the General Counsel Working Group studying 56 alleged sexual assaults by Air Force Academy cadets since 1993, almost half of which were committed under the influence of alcohol. The report discusses breaches in procedures for guarding against sexual assault.

Among the most recent rape incidents involving alcohol was the gang rape of a 16-year-old girl on August 25, 2002. Six U.S. soldiers stationed at Fort Drum were charged with third-degree **sodomy** and endangering the welfare of a child. The rape occurred at a party, and the perpetrators admitted having been under the influence of alcohol. The six soldiers were arrested, then released on bail, and their cases are currently pending grand jury action. *See also*: **Campus Rape; Date Rape/Acquaintance Rape; Sexual Assault, Drug-Facilitated; U.S. Military.**

Suggested Reading: Antonia Abbey, "Acquaintance Rape and Alcohol Consumption on College Campuses," *Journal of American College Health* 39 (January 1991): 165–169; Antony Beevor, "They Raped Every German Female from Eight to 80," *The Guardian*, May 1, 2002.

KONRAD SZCZESNIAK

ANAL SEX. Anal sex is a penetration of the rectum through the anus, by a penis or another mechanical means, most often for achieving sexual gratification or in foreplay. As an experience, therefore, it is comparable to a vaginal penetration, despite the anatomical differences between the vagina and the rectum.

Historically, the practice of anal sex for sexual gratification can be traced back to such "love" manuals as the Kama Sutra in India, which describes the steps leading to a complete satisfaction of the couple as an alternative to vaginal penetration. In ancient Greece anal sex is also related to bodily pleasure, since homosexual relations were socially accepted and regarded as a higher level of spirituality between men, especially between older men and boys.

Sigmund Freud, the founder of modern psychoanalysis, described anal sex as most often related to the sadomasochistic ritual of submission and dominance. He further connected this practice with certain character traits in adults, namely, extreme neatness (orderliness), parsimony, and obstinacy.

Forced anal sex can produce a rupture and bruising of the tissue of the anal area, with all the consequences that a vaginal rape might have, for example, hemorrhage. While in no immediate danger of unwanted **pregnancy**, the female victim—as well as the male one, for that matter—is still in danger of contracting venereal diseases or **HIV/AIDS**. As in vaginal rapes, the psychological trauma is equally difficult to overcome. *See also*: **Male Rape; Oral Sex.**

Suggested Reading: Sigmund Freud, "Character and Anal Eroticism," in *The Standard Edition of the Complete Psychological Works*, vol. 9, trans. and ed. James Strachey (London: Hogarth Press, 1991); William Armstrong Percy, *Pederasty and Pedagogy in Archaic Greece* (Champaign: University of Illinois Press, 1996); Steven G. Underwood, *Gay Men and Anal Eroticism: Tops, Bottoms and Versatiles* (Binghamton, NY: Harrington Park Press, 2003).

ROSSITSA TERZIEVA-ARTEMIS

ANCIENT LAW CODES. The codification of laws by which civilizations expressed their beliefs and regulated social order goes back to antiquity. Ancient laws were usually based on *lex talionis*—an eye for an eye, or blood justice. In general, these ancient laws delineate the mores of patriarchal and hierarchical societies that placed the interests of free men above that of their wives, concubines, and slaves. As rape scholar Susan Brownmiller notes, "Written law in its origin was a solemn compact among men of property, designed to protect their own male interests by a civilized exchange of goods or silver *in place of force* wherever possible" (18). It remained acceptable to capture brides from other settlements during battles because this was deemed a natural bonus of war, but it became unacceptable to abduct or rape females from within one's own tribe or city because it disrupted the status quo. Thus it became the custom and then the law for fathers to be paid for their daughters in the form of bride prices.

Rape of a virgin, then, became a crime that damaged the property of her father—devaluing the price he could achieve for her as a bride. This view can be seen in the Babylonian Code of Hammurabi, which dates from about 1780 B.C.E. According to Hammurabi's code, **virgins** were considered innocent if raped, but their attackers were executed. However, a married woman who was raped was considered to be guilty of adultery. Both she and her rapist could be executed by being thrown in the river, although her husband had the right to save her, *if* he wished to do so.

Other ancient codes produced similar laws on rape. The Code of the Nesilim (Hittites), c. 1650–1500 B.C.E., noted that a man would be killed if he raped a woman a distance from her house, but if he raped her within her house, she was deemed culpable and could be executed. It was assumed that the woman did not scream or show much **resistance**, bringing others to her rescue, and therefore she must have consented to have sexual intercourse with him.

Besides outlining the penalties for a variety of laws, including the raping of virgins, married women, and slaves, these ancient law codes listed the punishments for other sex-related crimes. The Code of Assura, c. 1075 B.C.E., indicated that a soldier would be castrated if he had sex with a fellow soldier. The Code of the Nesilim proscribed various penalties for having intercourse with animals. **Bestiality** was considered to be a capital crime if committed with some animals but not all. *See also*: **Abduction (Kidnapping); Bible, Old Testament; Rape Law; Religion.**

Suggested Reading: Susan Brownmiller, *Against Our Will: Men, Women and Rape* (New York: Fawcett Columbine, 1975); Internet Ancient History Sourcebook, http://www.fordham.edu/halsall/ancient/asbook.html.

MERRIL D. SMITH

ARMIES. *See* **U.S. Military; War Crimes; Wartime Rape.**

ART. The art history of rape stretches from ancient Greek paintings of gods abducting mortals to contemporary feminist images of brutal attacks. Reflecting the broader rape discourse of their eras, early artists represented nonconsensual sex as romantic and heroic, whereas more recent artists show rape as violent and terrifying. Similarly, the strategies for depicting rape have shifted from subtle signs of the victim's unwillingness to overt representations of penetration and physical assault.

Most images of rape in the history of Western art illustrate well-known literary traditions and act as metaphors of love or power and as voyeuristic opportunities. Ancient Greek legends, for example, are filled with nonconsensual sex, such as the story of Ganymede, in which the god Zeus, having fallen in love with the beautiful boy, transformed himself into an eagle, carried him off, and raped him. To illustrate the myth, artists including Rembrandt van Rijn (1606–1669) portrayed the moments before the rape, with the beautiful body of the surprised boy displayed before the strong, rapacious bird. The literary history of the Roman civilization is likewise filled with stories of forced sex including Rome's foundation legend, a rape narrative that artists such as Nicolas Poussin (1594–1665) illustrated under the title *Rape of the Sabine Women* (*see* **Rape of the Sabine Women**). The paintings and sculptures show Rome's founding fathers abducting their neighbors' wives to impregnate with the city's future citizens. The women appear fearful, disheveled, and resistant as they are carried away by rapists represented as strong and virtuous. The rape and suicide of the Roman heroine Lucretia similarly made a regular appearance in art from antiquity to the nineteenth century, either illustrating the attacker overpowering his supine victim or displaying the woman's voluptuous body after the assault as she plunged the knife in her chest. In these and other cases, the paintings and sculptures of rape were created by men for men and evince little or no compassion for the victims or concern for the physical violence of rape. Since the purpose of these images was to demonstrate virtues of strength and power, artists avoided representing the sex act, permitting abduction, dishevelment, and the victim's resistance to stand for the rape itself.

Rape also appears in scenes of war, but unlike the images derived from literary sources, these works generally do not heroicize the rapist. Instead, rape is offered as part of an array of vile—but expected—behaviors committed by undisciplined soldiers. French printmaker Jacques Callot (1592–1635) and Spanish artist Francisco de Goya (1746–1828) created some of the most brutal images of rape before the 1960s. Callot's *The Miseries of War* (1633) and Goya's *The Disasters of War* (1810–1815) both show soldiers raping and killing female noncombatants. Both artists employ a frank code of symbols to suggest the imminent rape, representing a dressed and armed man seizing a dressed or nude woman or lying on top of her. Callot and Goya display sympathy for the female victims as part of their general horror at the cruelty civilians endured during wars, using pose, facial expression, and fearful gestures to communicate the victims' terror.

The change rape's images underwent in the hands of late-twentieth-century feminists was hinted at by German artist Käthe Kollwitz (1867–1945), whose work focuses attention away from the literary and historical contexts and onto the act's violence and its devastating effect on the individual woman. The 1960s rise of feminism completed the transformation. Today British artist Sue Coe (1952–   ) confronts the viewer directly with a horrific rape scene in *Rape, Bedford* (1984), in which the deathly body of the female victim is held motionless by two men while another rapes her. Cuban artist Ana Mendieta (1948–1985) made an equally powerful protest against rape with a 1973 performance in which she assumed the role of the victim, displaying her own bloodied, half-nude body for the audience. These women and other feminist artists active today prefer to confront their viewers directly with their disgust and anger, rejecting the heroic tradition and the subtle symbolism employed by earlier artists in favor of realistic and expressive depictions of rape.

As in other areas of cultural production, the images of rape have changed dramatically since the early paintings of gods abducting beautiful youths. The change can be attributed not only to differing perceptions of rape from era to era but also to the increasing visibility of women artists. A topic for painters that was once a metaphor of power and virtue is today, due to feminist influence, a critical comment on violence against women. *See also*: **Media; Mythology; Rape of Lucretia; Theater; Wartime Rape.**

Suggested Reading: Margaret D. Carroll, "The Erotics of Absolutism: Rubens and the Mystification of Sexual Violence," in *The Expanding Discourse: Feminism and Art History*, ed. Norma Broude and Mary D. Garrard (New York: HarperCollins, 1992); Yael Even, "The Loggia dei Lanzi: A Showcase of Female Subjugation," in *The Expanding Discourse: Feminism and Art History*, ed. Norma Broude and Mary D. Garrard (New York: HarperCollins, 1992); Natalie Boymel Kampen, ed., *Sexuality in Ancient Art: Near East, Egypt, Greece, and Italy* (Cambridge: Cambridge University Press, 1996); Diane Wolfthal, *Images of Rape: The "Heroic" Tradition and Its Alternatives* (Cambridge: Cambridge University Press, 1999).

KELLY DONAHUE-WALLACE

ASIA. *See* **Comfort Women; Okinawa Rape Case; Rape of Nanking.**

ASIAN AMERICANS. *Asian American* is a term used in the United States to describe a wide range of identities and ethnic groups with vastly different cultures and experiences. It is therefore advisable to examine the specific culture that an individual identifies with in order to create culturally competent models of care, research, and understanding, rather than to rely on generalizations that result in the homogenization of various ethnic groups. Groups that may fall under the heading of "Asian American" include the following: Chinese, Japanese, Korean, South Korean, Indian, Vietnamese, Filipino/a, Pakistani, Bangladeshi, Sri Lankan, Nepalese, Laotian, Thai, Taiwanese, Malaysian, and Cambodian.

The United States homogenizes these categories into the single identity marker "Asian American" and uses the term to describe demographics related to all members of these ethnic groups, regardless of particular cultural identity or, generally, immigration status. Thus, when the U.S. Bureau of Statistics reports that "1 out of every 1,000 Asian Americans report being sexually assaulted," it is often unclear what those particular statistics mean. This condensation of statistics, along with U.S. stereotypes of Asian American women as being hypersexualized, docile, and obedient, and tied to the community and thus unable or unwilling to speak about rape, contributes to the many barriers to care and reporting faced by **survivors** of **sexual assault** that identify as Asian American.

According to the Asian American Pacific Islanders Domestic Violence Resource project, Asian Americans face several other challenges in reporting rape that contribute to the low amounts of available data and qualitative studies regarding sexual assault for their particular ethnic groups. These issues include a lack of culturally competent services, the predominant belief within many Asian American and Pacific Island cultures that bringing private matters into the public arena (e.g., **law enforcement**, health centers, mental health counseling) will bring shame to one's **family**, language barriers, and documentation problems surrounding immigration.

Most reports of Asian American sexual assault are embedded within studies on **domestic violence** or intimate partner violence, though some Asian American feminist anthologies also include specific narratives of women who have been sexually assaulted or who are survivors of domestic violence. Predominant studies include the work of Project AWARE (Asian Women Advocating Respect and Empowerment), a study funded by the Asian American Domestic Violence Resource Center that acts as a needs assessment study for survivors in the DC area. Similarly, the Asian Family Violence Report of the Asian Task Force against Domestic Violence has completed a similar study in Massachusetts. These two reports estimate that family violence, including sexual assault, is a major problem within Asian American communities and take pains to underscore the importance of ethnic breakdown when studying any group. The Project AWARE study (2003) estimated that approximately 35 women in their study of 178 participants in the Washington, DC area experienced forced sexual encounters "occasionally, frequently, or very frequently." The Executive Summary of the Asian Family Violence Report indicates that 69 percent of survey participants (a sample of which included perpetrators and survivors) had experienced physical abuse as children, and this correlated to incidents of both physical and sexual violence within various communities. Additionally, cultural beliefs about the role of women and men within familial contexts provided rationale for family violence, which most often included **marital rape**. Further contributing factors included concepts of familial shame, internalization of "the Model Minority" stereotype, and threats related to one's immigration status.

The process of immigration and one's immigration status (documented or un-documented) can also pose a risk for sexual assault. Vietnamese women immigrating to the United States as late as 1985 report being subjected to rape and pillage at the hands of pirates feeding off of boats bound for America. Particularly in Vietnam, these sexual assaults are further compounded by high rates of sexual assaults in asylum camps and cultural stigmas attached to leaving one's marriage, even if the situation is violent. Often, Vietnamese women are subject to rape within marriage, flee to asylum camps where they may again be assaulted, leave for America, and are assaulted again by pirates on the journey to America. Once in the United States, culturally competent services are difficult to find, and many Vietnamese women will not discuss the circumstances of their rape, fearing rejection by their family for airing personal problems in public. Similar problems in immigration are reported by Korean and some Chinese survivors.

Finally, the U.S.-bred stereotypes of Asian American women as exotic, hypersexualized, and submissive also contribute to the objectification of these women and thus make them highly susceptible to sexual assault. Initial steps in almost any strategy of dominance include dehumanization, and because Asian American women are often perceived as quiet and subservient, it becomes easy for their bodies to become the objects of assault. Additionally, pornographers in the United States capitalize on what is known as "Asian Fetishes," an apparent fetishization of Asian American women and their sexual practices. Often, these erotic or pornographic images are exceptionally violent and show repeated acts of forced intercourse. These images and the predominant historical notion of Asian American women as prostitutes may contribute to violence against Asian American women.

Asian American feminists of all cultural backgrounds are actively seeking to break apart these stereotypes and break silences about the abuse and violence within their lives. Chinese American songwriter Magdalen Hsu-Li writes about the experience of sexual assault on her album *Fire*, and several women work in violence advocacy groups, participate in outreach, and have contributed to feminist-based anthologies around issues of sexual violence. *See also* **Interracial Rape; Massie Case; Pornography.**

Suggested Reading: Asian Women United of California, *Making Waves: An Anthology of Writings by and about Asian American Women* (Boston: Beacon, 1989); Shamita Das Dasgupta, *A Patchwork Shawl: Chronicles of South Asian Women in America* (New Brunswick, NJ: Rutgers University Press, 1998); Karen McDonnell and Shamira Abdulla, "Project AWARE," Asian Pacific Islanders Domestic Violence Resource Project, Washington, DC, 2003, http://chnm.gmu.edu/dvrp/docs/aware.pdf; Marianne Yoshiola, "Asian Family Violence Report: A Study of the Chinese, Cambodian, Korean, and South Asian Communities in Massachusetts" (Cambridge, MA: Asian Task Force against Domestic Violence, 2003).

CHRISTINA BOREL

ATHLETES. With increased and unprecedented reports of athletes at every level from high school to professional involved in abusive behavior against women, rape has become a topic of critical concern. It is presumed that sports culture mirrors society, and since violence is so prevalent, it should come as no surprise that athletes are not only involved in abusive behavior against women, but athletes are more likely to be involved in social violence than nonathletes, according to Wechsler and colleagues. In recent decades, several professional athletes have been accused of rape. There are great debates as to why athletes seem committed to negative activities and behavior and feel drawn to aggressive action against women. Much **media** attention has been given to cases involving athletes, such as Mike Tyson, Mark Chmura, and Kobe Bryant—to name just a few.

Are athletes out of control? Are they just spoiled jocks who have lost touch with reality? Or is this phenomenon merely a reflection of what society has become? Some theorists argue that athletes make the mistake of believing that they are stars (celebrities) who are beyond the realm of society's laws. They sexually assault women because they are not held to the same standards as everyone else.

In contrast, athletes and their supporters contend that because of their stardom, athletes are more likely to be scrutinized or falsely accused than nonathletes and that there is no difference in their behaviors. Still other theories hold that athletic aggression is the key to an athlete's success and that this aggression carries over to relationships with women, where it becomes difficult to separate the hostility and control anger. As violence becomes a way of life, the athlete engages in antisocial behavior.

Among athletes, there is a climate of "privilege" that has been conveyed to infer special treatment associated with their athletic skills. Then, too, there is a general feeling that they are not held to the same standard as everyone else. As a result, crimes such as assault, **domestic violence**, and rape seem to go unpunished or are not punished harshly.

Generally, there are many who blame sports (literally) for the sexual violence against women. They put forth the concept that the (sport) activity is a demonstration of manhood and that it spawns attitudes and frequent occurrences where females are looked upon as objects and considered conquests. Rape, they believe, is its by-product.

While sports, in and of themselves, do not make athletes likely to rape women, it is likely that the way sports are organized to influence masculine identities may lead some male athletes to rape. Yet, overall, even a negative association within the sports culture as part of an athletic team usually does more good than harm.

Whether the theories are true or not, many can agree that athletes are placed on a pedestal in American society. Fame often precedes that sense of invincibility that begins early in childhood, when an athlete's ability first becomes apparent. Psychologists and sociologists alike believe that this heightens the sense of privilege that is the breeding ground for most of their off-field behavior and the direct abuse against women.

With communities/institutions outraged by athletes' involvement in **sexual assaults**, authorities are confused as to how to resolve the problem. Victims often find their complaints are not treated seriously. **Gang rape** cases have been dismissed to "group sex," and women are pressured to drop charges. In some cases, women seeking redress are frequently silenced for the sake of an institution.

These institutions have begun to address the problem. Brochures, seminars, and films are being used to heighten athletes' sensitivity to rape and other violence, but more stringent measures are called for. While most women have faith their attackers will be caught, they have less faith that their attackers will be prosecuted. Many attacks are committed by friends/dates, and in a court of law, sexual assault is difficult to prove, and many violators are set free. *See also*: **Celebrity Rapists; Glen Ridge (NJ) Rape Case; Rape Trials.**

Suggested Reading: Jeffery R. Benedict, *Athletes and Acquaintance Rape*, vol. 8 of *Sage Series on Violence against Women* (Thousand Oaks, CA: Sage Publications, 1998): Ronald Berger and Patricia Searles, *Rape and Society: Readings in the Problems of Sexual Assault* (Boulder, CO: Westview Press, 1995); Pamela Carrol, Steve Chandler, and Dwayne Johnson, "Abusive Behavior of College Athletes," *College Student Journal* 33 (1999): 1–7; K.A. Douglas, J.L. Collins, C. Warren, et al., "The National College Women Sexual Victimization Survey, National Institute of Justice (NIJ)," *Journal of American College Health* 46.5 (December 2000): 55–66; A. Parrot and L. Bechofer, *Acquaintance Rape: The Hidden Crime* (New York: John Wiley and Sons, 1991); Cheryl Rigel, *Criminal Victimization 1996: Changes 1995–96 with Trends 1993–1996* (Washington, DC: Bureau of Justice Statistics, 1996); H. Wechsler, A. Davenport, G.W. Dowdall, B. Molykens, and S. Castillo, "College Binge Drinking and Alcohol-Related Injury and Violence," *Journal of Public Health* 85 (1995): 921–925.

FRED LINDSEY

B

BATTERED WOMEN. The term *battered women* refers to women who are **victims of domestic violence**. Domestic violence is defined as violence between members of a household, usually spouses. In contrast, the term *spousal abuse* refers specifically to any type of abuse—physical, sexual, or psychological abuse—inflicted on one spouse by the other and highlights the intimate nature of the relationship of a batterer and his victim. Though not all women within battering relationships suffer sexual abuse, some are subjected to **marital rape**. This may include any sexual activity that is forced or coerced from a wife by her spouse. Similarly, not all victims of marital rape endure what is considered a battering relationship.

Approximately 1.5 million battered women seek assistance from social welfare and legal organizations each year; there are probably many others, who never come forward for help. Though studies reveal that no two battering relationships are identical, batterers across ethnicities, social classes, and nation–states do exhibit similar patterns. Experts find that physical abuse is generally accompanied by mental, economic, and psychological abuse to create an environment in which the batterer has an inordinate amount of power and control over his victim's autonomy. Today in the United States service providers educate battered women about what is known as the "Cycle of Violence," which begins with a Tension Building phase, leads to an Explosion of a violent incident, and often results in a Hearts and Flowers phase, in which batterers show remorse and vigorously apologize. The combination of nonphysical abuses with both bodily injury and the threat of physical force, and even death, produces a context of intimidation and terror in which battered women may choose to stay confined for fear of death.

Forced sexual activity within an intimate-partner relationship is a relatively new crime in the United States. From the seventeenth century through much of the 1980s in both the United States and Britain, it was a legal impossibility for a husband to be charged, prosecuted, or convicted of raping his wife. With the advent of the women's movement in the 1960s and 1970s came the abolishment of the "spousal exemption," or the exclusion of husbands who sexually abused their wives, from the prosecutorial process. Today, in most states, husbands can be prosecuted for raping their wives. However, where marital rape is concerned, legal processing remains difficult, because **rape myths** persist among the population and among victims themselves. Usually, before any legal action can be taken, victim-survivors must view their partners' coerced sex acts as criminal. Qualitative data and clinical case studies suggest that some women, for a variety of reasons, are reluctant to name forced sexual violence within marriage "rape."

Social services and legal assistance for battered women have steadily grown in North America since the 1970s to include shelters, court advocates, and special **family** violence sections of police stations and state attorney's offices. Irrespective of the multitude of agencies available to aid women in battering relationships, researchers concur that the chief legal service available to battered women is the protective order, or a court injunction mandated by judges that prohibits a person from harassing, threatening, and even approaching another specified person. But research indicates that wife rape is often not documented in affidavits for protective orders and that service providers in shelters are still reluctant to talk to battered women about sexual violence. *See also*: **Sexual Coercion.**

Suggested Reading: Raquel Kennedy Bergen, *Wife Rape: Understanding the Response of Survivors and Service Providers* (Thousand Oaks, CA: Sage, 1996); David Finkelhor and Kersti Ÿllo, *License to Rape: Sexual Abuse of Wives* (New York: Holt, Rinehart & Winston, 1996); Judith Lewis Herman, *Trauma and Recovery: The Aftermath of Violence—from Domestic Abuse to Political Terror* (New York: Basic Books, 1992); Andrew Klein, "Re-abuse in a Population of Court-Restrained Male Batterers: Why Restraining Orders Don't Work," in *Do Arrests and Restraining Orders Work?* ed. E.S. Buzawa and C.G. Buzawa (Thousand Oaks, CA: Sage, 1996), 53–73; Sharon Lamb, "Constructing the Victim: Popular Images and Lasting Labels," in *New Versions of Victims: Feminists Struggle with the Concept*, ed. S. Lamb (New York: New York University Press, 1999), 108–138; S. Sally Merry, "Spatial Governmentality and the New Urban Social Order: Controlling Gender Violence through Law," *American Anthropologist* 103 (2001): 16–29; Diana Russell, *Rape in Marriage* (Indianapolis: Indiana University Press, 1990); Shonna Trinch, "The Advocate as Gatekeeper: The Limits of Politeness in Protective Order Interviews with Latina Survivors of Domestic Violence," *Journal of Sociolinguistics* 5 (2001): 475–506; Shonna Trinch, "Managing Euphemism and Transcending Taboos: Negotiating the Meaning of Sexual Assault in Latinas' Narratives of Domestic Violence," *Text* 21 (2001): 567–610.

SHONNA L. TRINCH

BESTIALITY. In its narrowest sense, bestiality involves intercourse, either vaginal or anal, with a nonhuman animal; but bestiality can also include oral-genital contact of any kind between humans and animals, as well as the insertion of digits or objects other than the penis into the vagina, anus, or cloaca. Acts of bestiality highlight interesting aspects of the definition of rape. Is rape something a human does to another human? Or is bestiality a form of rape? It is known that women have been raped by abusers who force sex with animals, or force animals upon women. But is bestiality a form of forced sex itself? Recently this claim has been advanced by animal advocates.

Forms of bestiality include *opportunistic* or *safety-valve sex* in which the animal is viewed as an available sex object who provides sexual release in the absence of a human partner; *fixated sex* involves persons who see animals not as mere stand-ins but as love objects and exclusive sexual "partners"; in *domineering sex*, batterers, rapists, and pornographers arrange or force sex between a human and an animal in order to exploit or to humiliate the human, most often a woman.

Proximity allows for sexual access. This is why cats, dogs, sheep, cows, hens, rabbits, goats, mules, ducks, rabbits, horses, boars, bulls, and fishes are more frequently used, rather than gorillas, chimpanzees, and other animals.

With the growth of the Internet, bestiality has achieved a new visibility and a defense that it is a benign act, but the issue of perspective remains: What does the animal experience? Further, bestiality, like rape, raises questions of **consent**. In human-animal relationships, the human being has control of many—if not all—of the aspects of an animal's well being. Relationships of unequal power cannot be consensual. Bestiality is the model case of *circumventing consent*, on the one hand, while confusing *affection for consent*, on the other. *See also*: **Computers and the Internet; Pornography**.

Suggested Reading: Carol J. Adams, "Bestiality: The Unmentioned Abuse," *Animals' Agenda* 15 (January 1996): 29–31.

CAROL J. ADAMS

BIBLE, OLD TESTAMENT. The Hebrew Bible (Old Testament) is a canon of 24 books that chronicle the laws and history of a monotheistic Jewish **religion** as far back as 1400 B.C.E. The biblical laws concerning rape are unequivocal. Exodus 22: 15–16 decrees that if a man seduces a **virgin** for whom a dowry has not been paid, and lies with her, he must pay a dowry for her to be his wife. If her father refuses to give her to him, he must still pay him the equivalent dowry set for virgins. Furthermore, in Deuteronomy 22:29 where this scenario recurs, the text adds that because the man has violated a virgin, he can never divorce her. The law becomes merciless when the rape has occurred in the open country where the girl could not be heard and saved (Deuteronomy 22:25–27). In this case, the man is put to death, and the girl is spared.

Threats of rape are found in the narratives about Sarah (Genesis 20; 26), Avishag (1 Kings 1), Jeremiah (Jeremiah 20:7) and the cities of Jerusalem and Samaria (Ezekiel 16; 23). Interestingly, only three actual rapes of women are depicted in the entire corpus: the rape of Dinah, Jacob's daughter (Genesis 34), the rape of the anonymous concubine in Gibeah (Judges 19–21), and the incestuous rape of Tamar, King David's daughter (2 Samuel 13).

Genesis 34 is a tale of intrigue, deception, sexual violence, and **ethnic cleansing**. It begins by introducing the victim Dinah, who is visiting with the daughters of the land. Shechem, son of Hamor, Prince of the Land, saw her, took her by force, and raped her. Schechem—who feminist scholars identify as a "sexual gratification rapist" (Scholz, 142)—continued to desire Dinah and proposed to marry her. When Jacob heard that his daughter was violated, he decided to wait silently for his sons to return from the fields. Dinah's brothers were enraged upon hearing the news because "this was an outrage in Israel—a thing not to be done." On his son's urging, Hamor went to ask Jacob's blessing for the marriage between Dinah and Shechem. He also offered complete integration and intermarriage between his people and Jacob's tribe, along with a large dowry for Dinah. Jacob's sons demanded that all the city's males be circumcised as a condition for such a union. (Male circumcision became a practice among the Jews during the days of Abraham the patriarch, Jacob's grandfather.) The people of Shechem complied and circumcised all of their males. On the third day when the men were still in pain, Dinah's brothers, Simeon and Levi, attacked the city and slew all the males. They rescued Dinah from Shechem's house, confiscated the Hivite livestock, looted their houses, and captured the children and women.

The horrific rape of the concubine in Gibeah (Judges 19–21) commences as well by introducing the victim, a nameless concubine. She deserted her husband, a Levite from the hills of Ephraim, and returned to her father's house in Bethlechem. Her husband followed her "to woo her and win her back." After staying a few nights in her father's home, the Levite and his concubine decided to travel back. The narrative describes the period as harsh and dangerous—"in those days . . . there was no king in Israel; everyone did as he pleased." Therefore, the traveling companions were cautious in choosing a place to spend the night. Eventually, they were invited to stay with an old man in the Benjaminite city of Gibeah. The Gibeonites came pounding on the door and insisted "to know" (sexually violate, humiliate) the visiting Levite. The old man refused, and instead the Levite offered his concubine. The woman was gang-raped and tortured all night. The next morning she was found dead at the old man's door. As soon as the Levite arrived home, he "picked up a knife . . . cut her up limb by limb into twelve parts" and scattered them throughout the Land of Israel. This outrage led to a full-fledged civil war between the tribes of Israel and their kinsmen the Benjaminites. The war resulted in the eradication of Gibeah and the remaining Benjaminite cities.

The third rape transpires in the royal family of King David. The victim Tamar, King David's daughter, was raped by her half brother Amnon, who deceived and lured her into his bedroom. Two years later Tamar's brother Absalom retaliated and killed Amnon.

Understanding rape as an acute social problem, feminist interpretation of these exigent texts—or as feminist scholar Phyllis Trible names them, "texts of terror"—focuses on the rape **victims** and their predicament rather than on the patriarchal perspective. The biblical narratives leave the readers bewildered with regard to the fate of the two named victims. The object of male discourse, Dinah does not speak for herself. Tamar, on the other hand, is given a voice during the rape; yet forlorn and in mourning she disappears into Absalom's household, never to be mentioned again. Despite their relevance and their contribution to a more holistic examination of the biblical society, contemporary rape theories are still overlooked in biblical scholarship. *See also*: **Literature, World and American; Patriarchy; Religion.**

Suggested Reading: Tikva Kensky Frymer, *Reading the Women of the Bible* (New York: Schocken Books, 2002); Susanne Scholz, *Rape Plots: A Feminist Cultural Study of Genesis 34* (New York: Peter Lang, 2002); Phyllis Trible, *Texts of Terror: Literary-Feminist Readings of Biblical Narratives* (Philadelphia: Fortress Press, 1984).

DINA RIPSMAN EYLON

BIG DAN'S TAVERN CASE. Around 9:00 P.M. on the evening of March 6, 1983, a young woman entered a New Bedford Falls, Massachusetts, tavern, bought a pack of cigarettes, and sat down at the bar to have a drink. When the 21-year-old mother of two got up to leave, she was grabbed, hoisted on top of a pool table, and repeatedly raped by a group of men. The bar remained open during the two-hour ordeal while the men shouted and cheered, encouraging each other to "Do it! Do it!" No one, including the bartender, called for help. Sometime after midnight the bruised and half-naked woman stumbled out of the bar. A passing motorist came to her aid and summoned police. Six men were charged with aggravated rape. Big Dan's Tavern, quickly thrust into the national spotlight, voluntarily closed its doors several days later.

Groups quickly rallied, in support of both the **victim** and the defendants. Nearly 2,500 marched in front of city hall, carrying banners stating, "Rape Is Not a Spectator Sport." Meanwhile the Committee for Justice helped raise bail for the defendants.

Newspaper accounts reported that the crime was causing great pain to the community. Once characterized by its thriving whaling industry and flourishing textile mills, by 1983 New Bedford was described as economically and psychologically depressed. Its 98,000 residents—60 percent of whom were of Portuguese descent—suffered from one of the highest unemployment rates in the state. Intense **media** scrutiny, much of it focused on the ethnic backgrounds of the defendants who were Portuguese immigrants, resulted in the trial being moved to a nearby town. Called into question were not only the character of the victim—who was also Portuguese American—but the character of the bar and indeed that of the whole town as well. Many believed that the entire Portuguese American community was being indicted.

To avoid the defendants implicating each other, the **prosecution** and defense agreed to hold two separate trials: Four men would appear in court in the morning and the other two in the afternoon. Courtroom proceedings were translated into Portuguese for the non-English-speaking defendants and witnesses.

In March 1984, the monthlong trial yielded four convictions of rape, including prison sentences ranging from 6 to 12 years. A crowd of 2,000 railed against the court's decision, while more than 7,000 participated in a candlelight vigil, blaming the verdicts on anti-Portuguese sentiment. The victim, reportedly exhausted and living in fear, moved to Florida with her two children, where she died in an automobile accident in December 1986.

The legacy of the rape case continues. "Big Dan's" was first in a 1999 *Boston Globe* newspaper series titled "Crimes of the Century." The article recalled the brutality of the assault that elicited national outrage. Accusations that the victim socialized with the men prior to the attack and possibly provoked the crime prompted discussions regarding the degree to which women could be held accountable for their own rape. But as Katharine Baker, a law professor quoted in the *Globe* article asserted, this watershed case dictated that "once a woman says no, the advances that follow are the actions of a felon," adding unambiguously that it was "so bad that everyone could look at it and say that wherever the line is, this crosses it."

Big Dan's also is remembered for the unprecedented attention it garnered, primarily through live coverage of the trial by the Cable News Network (CNN). Daily broadcasts, which repeatedly announced the young woman's name to 2.5 million nationwide viewers, fueled controversy and resulted in other media sources dropping their policy of shielding a rape victim's name.

A television movie, *Silent Witness*, aired in 1985, and Jodie Foster's portrayal of the victim in the 1988 feature film *Accused*, "inspired" by the events that took place in Big Dan's Tavern, earned her an Academy Award. *See also*: **Films, U.S.; Gang Rape; Rape Shield Laws.**

Suggested Reading: Lisa M. Cuklanz, *Rape on Trial: How the Mass Media Construct Legal Reform and Social Change* (Philadelphia: University of Pennsylvania Press, 1996); Thomas Farragher, "Widely Watched Mass. Trial Reshaped Society's Attitude toward Rape Victims," Crimes of the Century: Big Dan's: First in a Series, *Boston Globe*, October 18, 1999.

CHRISTINE CLARK ZEMLA

BLACKSTONE, SIR WILLIAM (1723–1780). Among the most influential interpreters of the English common law, English jurist and writer William Blackstone is best known today as the author of the classic four-volume treatise *Commentaries on the Laws of England* (1765–1769). In these volumes, Blackstone considered several principles relating to the common law of rape that were soon incorporated into the nascent legal system of the United States.

Blackstone's exposition of *coverture*, and the doctrine of marital unity underlying it, has been fundamental to the development of American rape law. Blackstone's widely cited formulation "by marriage the husband and wife are one person in law" sustained a range of gender-based disabilities. Most crucially, under coverture, a woman, upon marriage, relinquished control of her property as well as her body, both of which became her husband's lawful possessions. Although Blackstone does not address the issue directly, his authoritative delineation of women's *feme covert* status lent further support to the common law's long-standing nonrecognition of rape in marriage (a concept that had earlier been expounded by **Sir Matthew Hale** in *The History of the Pleas of the Crown*).

Blackstone's discussion of rape is marked by a skepticism of women's motives that is highly reminiscent of Hale. According to the *Commentaries*, "rape" is defined as "carnal knowledge of a woman forcibly and against her will," the essential elements of which were codified in U.S. statutory law. So thoroughly did this approach permeate American law that its residue remains apparent two and a half centuries later. Yet as feminist critics have in recent decades remarked, this conception of rape derives from the perpetrator's perspective, while that of the victim is conspicuously elided. Eschewing detailed proscriptions on the crime itself, Blackstone focused instead on the requisites of appropriate feminine response, imposing the greater burden on raped women in order to protect potentially innocent men from the threat of lying accusers.

Through his celebrated *Commentaries*, Blackstone had a profound effect on the **prosecution** of rape and the treatment of its **victims** in American law and society. In particular, his naturalization of the metaphor of marital unity, his disproportionate emphasis on male victimization, and his manifest suspicion of rape claimants redounded to the detriment of generations of women, at once invigorating traditional stereotypes of female behavior and discouraging evenhanded prosecution of the crime. *See also*: **Rape Law.**

Suggested Reading: Sir William Blackstone, *Commentaries on the Laws of England*, 4 vols. (reprint, Facsimile of the First Edition, with an introduction by Thomas A. Green, Chicago: University of Chicago Press, 1979).

LISA CARDYN

"BLAMING THE VICTIM" SYNDROME. Blaming the Victim Syndrome refers to the pervasive tendency to blame a victim or to hold her responsible in some way for having been raped. Concepts of female sexuality over time have influenced the cultural definition of rape. In the Middle Ages, women were prized for their virginity, fertility, and ability to increase **family** prosperity through marital contracts. Thus, rape was viewed as a crime against women's male guardians. As women became politically and legally autonomous, however, the issue became more complex. Shifting sexual mores, particularly in the twentieth century, which encouraged women to embrace their sexuality, sharpened the dichotomy between the "good girl" and the "bad girl." Unfortunately, the judicial system has traditionally characterized rape **victims** as bad girls and has either blamed them for the crime or has discounted their claims altogether. This disregard for victims has its origins in the enduring male myths of rape.

One of the most enduring **rape myths** is the belief that a woman cannot be raped against her will. This idea has its origins in science and the law. In regard to science, medieval physicians and scientists believed that women had to achieve orgasm in order to conceive a child. Therefore, if a woman was raped and authorities later discovered her pregnant, then her accusations were discounted, and she bore the blame for her condition. Although the medical theories surrounding female orgasm and **pregnancy** began to wane in the seventeenth century, medical literature continued to doubt the veracity of women's claims of rape.

The legal ideology of this myth has a much longer and more complex history and continued well into the twentieth century. Beginning in the thirteenth century in English common law, if a woman was raped, the law required her to immediately go to the local authorities and make her accusation. Local officials subjected her to an inspection, and if sufficient evidence existed, then charges were brought against her rapist. As the American legal system derives from English common law, the notion of sufficient evidence made its way into American law, where it remained until the 1970s. The biggest problem with placing the burden of proof on rape victims lies in the way in which this provision characterizes women; by treating women's rape claims as suspect from the beginning, these laws perpetuated the notion that women are not trustworthy. In fact, until the creation of special victims' units and the increased use of female police officers in investigating **sexual assault** complaints, rape had the highest rate of spurious claims as a result of male officers' distrust of victims' stories.

The myth does not end with the police. When rape victims enter the courtroom, defense attorneys challenge their claims again. Until the 1970s, if a woman did not have corroborating evidence such as bruising, vaginal tears, or an eyewitness, then prosecutors could not even bring the case to trial. However, if the case went to court, defense attorneys often went to great lengths to demonstrate to juries the difficulty of raping a moving target. In one instance, a lawyer attempted to insert a pencil into the opening of a spinning cola bottle as proof that a woman cannot be raped against her will. Such courtroom antics, while effective with juries, serve only to redirect the blame for rape toward the victims.

In addition to blaming women for not successfully fighting off their attackers, the legal system has effectively placed women on trial for their past sexual history. Before the implementation of **rape shield laws,** and even afterward, defense attorneys have questioned victims regarding their sexual habits, style of dress, and behavior with the opposite sex. This line of questioning is intended to convince juries that the victim asked to be raped by placing herself in a dangerous situation or by dressing provocatively, leading her attacker to believe that she was interested in having sexual intercourse. Rape victims often ask themselves these same questions, and the courtroom experience intensifies the guilt that they feel, particularly as the legal system tends to favor the accused.

Rape is often described as a crime easy to claim and difficult to prove. By supporting this mentality, the legal profession and lawmakers have placed the blame for rape squarely on the victims. The old dictum that "good girls don't get raped" continues to affect rape **survivors**, furthering the notion that the victim somehow contributed to the crime. Feminists have attempted to abolish these notions through the redefinition of rape as a crime of male power over women, rather than as a sexual offense rooted in passion and desire. It is their hope that the politicization of rape will remove the blame from the victims and return it to the offenders. As gender ideologies remain inextricably tied to sexual behavior, women continue to bear the burden of blame for rape. *See also*: **Blackstone, Sir William; Clothing; Rape Law.**

Suggested Reading: Susan Brownmiller, *Against Our Will: Men, Women and Rape* (New York: Simon and Schuster, 1975); Karen J. Maschke, ed., *The Legal Response to Violence against Women* (New York: Garland Publishing, 1997).

CATHERINE MAYBREY

BOSNIA-HERZEGOVINA. The war in Bosnia (1991–1995) was a genocidal campaign carried out by the Yugoslav People's Army (JNA) and by Serbian irregular and paramilitary forces against the country's Muslim residents. The war was brought about by the breakup of Yugoslavia. While rape takes place in almost every war, the Bosnian conflict was unique for the role rape played in efforts to eradicate Muslims in the country. Whereas rape is usually secondary to the actions of the military, in the Bosnian war the degradation of Muslim women was one of the primary aims of the conflict. Raping them was part of the genocidal campaign against Muslims, euphemistically called "**ethnic cleansing.**" Rape was used to systematically humiliate and terrorize Muslim and Croatian women. The exact number of incidents is unknown, though European investigators stated that 20,000 women were raped in 1992. The estimates of those killed, men and women, range from 150,000 to 250,000. As author Beverly Allen has attempted to explain, the perpetrators of these heinous acts implied some twisted logic by which the act of rape would cancel out the **victim**'s cultural identity. If the victim became impregnated, she would be detained long enough to ensure that she could not abort her fetus and the offspring would be considered nothing less than "a little Serb soldier."

Since Muslim women typically do not have sex before marriage, the physical and emotional trauma of rape brought with it the strong possibility of rejection from society, living without marriage, and childlessness. However, the rapes were not limited to these women, as girls below the age of 12 and women over the age of 60 were also assaulted. Sex crimes were also carried out against Bosnian men in the detention camps, who were forced to commit sexual acts on each other.

A brief review of the history of the Balkans is necessary to explain the tensions among the different ethnic groups since these tensions date back to the time of the Ottoman Empire. The Islamic Ottoman Turks defeated Serbia in the battle of Kosovo in 1389. This humiliating event is often alluded to in Serbian nationalistic propaganda. Bosnia, too, became part of the Ottoman Empire, but not until many years later. Many Bosnians voluntarily became Muslims in the fifteenth and sixteenth centuries, but Bosnian Muslim culture maintained a notable distinction from much of the Islamic world, as evidenced in its architecture as well as its customs and lifestyles.

In March 1992, Bosnia declared independence. Although Muslims, Serbs, and Croats joined in calling for peace, the JNA and Serbian paramilitary units began attacks immediately. The Bosnian Muslims and Croats were quickly overwhelmed. Attacks in the Serbian war against Bosnia took on a loose pattern. Because they controlled the army, the Serbs had a near monopoly on weapons, especially artillery. The Yugoslav army would bombard defenseless areas for days, then Serbian paramilitary forces would be sent in. The paramilitary groups were made up of Serbian ultranationalists, criminals, and the unemployed. When these forces arrived, they would round up and execute the non-Serbian leaders. In some instances, such as in Srebrenica, nearly all the Muslim men were executed and then buried in mass graves. In other cases, Muslim and Croatian men of fighting age were sent to detention camps, where thousands of them died as a result of being tortured, beaten, and starved. With the men gone, the women were then at the mercy of the Serbs.

Thousands of these women were raped. The irregular forces often held Muslim women captive for weeks or months in "rape camps" while they were repeatedly sexually assaulted. The war was marked by the inability or unwillingness of the United Nations and the international community to recognize and stop the atrocities in Bosnia. Repeated exposure of these crimes in the **media** finally forced authorities to acknowledge the problem. UN peacekeepers were sent to Bosnia but were unable to stop the violence. In December 1995, the Dayton Agreement was signed. This peace agreement recognized the international boundaries of Bosnia and Herzegovina and provided for two roughly equal governments: a Bosnian Muslim-Croat Federation of Bosnia and Herzegovina and the Bosnian Serb Republika Srpska. The International Crime Tribunal for the former Yugoslavia (ICTY) was created to prosecute war crimes there. As of 2004, a few of the perpetrators of rape, torture, and enslavement have been convicted, but others such as Serbian president Slobodan Milosevic are still being tried before the tribunal or are appealing decisions. As of March 2004, Milosevic was about halfway through his trial, but the United States was still pressing Serbia to turn over 16 indicted war criminals to the United Nations tribunal. *See also*: **Comfort Women; Genocide; MacKinnon, Catharine A.; War Crimes.**

Suggested Reading: Beverly Allen, *Rape Warfare: The Hidden Genocide in Bosnia-Herzegovina and Croatia* (Minneapolis: University of Minnesota Press, 1996); Fact Sheet on ICTY, http://www.un.org/icty/glance/procfact-e.htm (a listing of the status of war criminals indicted by the ICTY); Human Rights Watch, http://www.hrw.org/press/2001/02/serbia 0222.htm; Rape as a Crime against Humanity, http://www.haverford.edu/relg/sells/rape.html; Andras Riedlmayer, *A Brief History of Bosnia-Herzegovina*, http://www.kakarigi.net/manu/briefhis.htm; Alexandra Stiglmayer, *Mass Rape: The War against Women in Bosnia-Herzegovina* (Lincoln: University of Nebraska Press, 1994).

ERIC SKINNER

BOSTON STRANGLER. Albert DeSalvo (1931–1973), known as the Boston Strangler, confessed to 11 of 13 rape-killings that took place in the Boston area between June 14, 1962, and January 4, 1964. The first killing attributed to DeSalvo was that of Anna Slesers, a 55-year-old woman found raped with an unknown object, strangled with her bathrobe belt, and positioned to expose her vagina to those entering the apartment. The next five victims fit the same pattern as the Slesers killing: Caucasian women between the ages of 65 and 87 who had allowed the assailant into their homes, raped with no semen present, strangled with one of their own items, and often positioned to shock. The seventh killing, of a 21-year-old African American student, Sophie Clark, ended suspicions that the strangler was a "mother killer." Following the final murder, of 19-year-old Mary Sullivan, who was raped with a broom handle and positioned with a greeting card at her feet, Massachusetts Attorney General Edward Brooke took over the investigation. State detectives focused on Albert DeSalvo, a married father of two charged with attempted rape. DeSalvo admitted to being the Green Man, responsible for raping women in four states while wearing green work pants. He soon confessed to 11 of the Boston murders, possibly in an effort to claim reward money for his family. DeSalvo provided details of the crime scenes and convinced his defense attorney, F. Lee Bailey, of his guilt, though forensic experts expressed doubts that one man committed all of the killings. No physical evidence linked DeSalvo to the murders, and witnesses could not identify him. DeSalvo stood trial only for the Green Man crimes and received a life sentence. Sent to Walpole State Prison in 1967, he was murdered in the infirmary. *See also*: **Foreign-Object Rape; Serial Rape and Serial Rapists.**

Suggested Reading: Gerold Frank, *The Boston Strangler* (New York: New American Library, 1988).

CARYN E. NEUMANN

BROWNMILLER, SUSAN (1935–). What helped bring discussions of rape from inside the women's liberation movement to mainstream audiences was the publication of writer and feminist activist Susan Brownmiller's widely read *Against Our Will: Men, Women and Rape* in 1975. This controversial bestseller is a significant text of American feminism; it detailed the political uses of rape, revising the popular conceptions of rape from a crime of lust to a means of enforcing **patriarchy.** As Brownmiller so famously wrote, rape is "nothing more or less than a conscious process of intimidation by which *all* men keep *all* women in a state of fear."

Brownmiller was born and raised in Brooklyn and attended Cornell University. She was introduced to activism through her experiences with the Congress on Racial Equality (CORE) 1964 Freedom Summer, registering southern black voters, and became involved in the **feminist movement** through consciousness-raising groups. In 1969 she was a founding member of the **New York Radical Feminists (NYRF)** and helped organize Speak-Out Against Rape in 1971.

Published in 1975, **Against Our Will** argued that both the possibility and actuality of rape are pervasive, culturally condoned tools of oppression that men use to establish their manhood. Brownmiller drew on psychoanalysis, literature, sociology, law, and **mythology** in providing one of the first histories of rape. She analyzed rape from the Old Testament through feudalism as a crime against men's ownership of women as property, and modern perceptions of rape as a crime of passion and a violation of chastity. She then discussed contemporary issues such as racism, **prison rape,** and **homosexual rape** in terms of sexual violence as an exercise of power.

The most sustained feminist critique of Brownmiller's writing came from black feminists, who were quick to critique Brownmiller's analysis of rape as a means of intimidation that knows no race distinctions, arguing instead that racism is an essential component of rape of women of color. Brownmiller's retelling of the Emmett Till rape case was especially problematic for many feminists because it reinscribed racist stereotypes. These critiques of Brownmiller argued for more specific examinations of rape in particular social, cultural, and economic contexts.

After the publication of *Against Our Will*, Brownmiller stayed active in the feminist movement, known largely for her anti-**pornography** writings such as "Let's Put Pornography Back in the Closet," originally published in *Newsday* in 1979. Brownmiller's other major books are *Femininity* (1984) and her history/memoir of her experiences in the feminist movement, *In Our Time: Memoir of a Revolution* (1999). *See also*: **Race and Racism; Rape, Causes of.**

Suggested Reading: Susan Brownmiller, *Against Our Will: Men, Women and Rape* (New York: Fawcett Columbine, 1975); Susan Brownmiller, *In Our Time: Memoir of a Revolution* (New York: Dial, 1999).

ANDREA LOWGREN

C

CAMPUS RAPE. Campus rape is a **sexual assault** that is associated in some way with a college or university. In many cases, the **victim** or perpetrator is a student at that institution of higher education (IHE); in other cases, the assault occurs on or near the campus.

Accurate statistics on campus rape are difficult to obtain, because many women do not report their assaults to the IHE or the police. Various studies conducted over the past two decades have produced a wide range of estimates: One study numbers the **victims** as 12 percent of college women; another says 78 percent. Nationwide, the age group with the highest number of rape victimizations is 16–24, which coincides with the traditional age bracket for college women. The most generally accepted statistic reports that one in four female college students experiences campus rape. The average victim is an 18-year-old woman.

Campus rape falls into two general categories: stranger rape and acquaintance rape. Stranger rape is perpetrated by someone entirely unknown to the victim. Acquaintance rape includes any person the victim knows, from a casual acquaintance such as a classmate or friend to a boyfriend or spouse. **Date rape** and party rape are more specific categories of acquaintance rape based on the context of the relationship. Date rape occurs during a dating relationship, ranging from a first date to a committed relationship. Party rape includes situations where the victim and perpetrator are strangers but part of the same social situation.

Campus rape occurs most often in dormitories, off-campus housing, or fraternity houses. Many assaults occur during or after parties, and one or both of those involved have usually consumed **alcohol**. Eight out of 10 campus rapes are acquaintance rapes, and 57 percent involve a date. The assailants generally ignore the woman's verbal and physical protests and use verbal coercion and, at times, physical force or the threat of force. Although the experiences are psychologically traumatic, the victims rarely reveal their assaults, with only about 5 percent reported to the police and 58 percent revealed to anyone at all. Few of the victims of campus rape seek counseling after being raped. Some rape victims drop out of school or transfer to another university.

Campus rape is underreported for several reasons. First, many victims believe that they are at fault for the assault, perhaps because of drinking, accepting a date, or being at the man's residence. Second, many women do not report their assaults in the fear that they will be subjected to further pain and humiliation at the hands of the college authorities or police. They fear the authorities will not take their assault seriously or will consider them responsible. Also, some students do not report rapes because they do not want their parents to know. And finally, some victims do not even realize that their experience can be considered rape.

Every college or university responds to reports of campus rape differently. Victims are usually presented with two options: pursue criminal charges or use the campus judicial system. Criminal **prosecution** is time-consuming and requires strong evidence; in addition, many prosecutors do not believe they can win cases of acquaintance rape and decline to press charges; thus campus justice may be the only option available to the victim. Advocates of campus justice say their method is swift, sensitive, and private and may allow for more assailants to be found guilty than does criminal prosecution. However, campus justice has numerous drawbacks. The most serious punishment for assailants is expulsion; and many who have been found guilty receive lighter sentences, such as community service or probation. Cases are handled in a variety of settings; some IHEs suggest rape charges be adjudicated with mediation, while others prefer disciplinary hearings. The methods used in disciplinary hearings vary widely. Some hearings involve lawyers, student or faculty advocates, and other witnesses, while others may include just the victim, assailant, and a few administrators. Hearings may be open or closed to the public; however, open hearings generally prove more traumatic for the victim. Some IHEs have tried to protect the privacy of the assailant by claiming that the Federal Education Records and Privacy Act forbids disclosure of the assailant's punishment to the victim and community at large. However, the 1992 Ramsted Amendment requires that both parties be notified of the outcome of a hearing, thus protecting the victim's rights. Critics of campus justice note the conflict of interest that occurs when IHEs advise rape victims to use campus justice rather than press criminal charges, for many IHEs have preferred to protect their reputations and avoid potential lawsuits from the accused rapists if they are expelled. More recently, some victims of campus rape have turned to civil litigation to adjudicate their cases. This process lends greater control to the victim, who is merely a witness in criminal or campus judicial proceedings; the assailant, if found guilty, pays financial compensation rather than receiving prison time.

Colleges and universities have used a variety of strategies to address and prevent campus rape. Many IHEs have now created clear policies about unacceptable sexual behavior that include strict penalties and have educated all members of the academic community, including faculty and staff. Acknowledging that most campus rapes are not committed by strangers, many students receive acquaintance rape education both at freshman orientation and throughout their college years. Women are alerted to the dangers of supposedly nonrisky settings, such as dorm rooms, especially when alcohol is present, and taught specific tactics against verbal and physical coercion and aggression by male acquaintances. Men are educated about what constitutes rape and the importance of verbal **consent**. Some IHEs reinforce risk reduction education at meetings in dormitories and Greek houses and in seminars for student organizations, especially athletic teams and fraternities. When an assault does occur, the strategy most often recommended is for all policies and penalties to be swiftly and uniformly enforced, which sends the message to potential rapists that campus rape will not be tolerated. *See also*: **Campus Security Act (Clery Act)**; **Rape Prevention; Sexual Assault, Drug-Facilitated.**

Suggested Reading: Nina Bernstein, "With Colleges Holding Court, Victims Can Learn Bitter Lessons," *New York Times*, May 5, 1996; Carol Bohmer and Andrea Parrot, *Sexual Assault on Campus: The Problem and the Solution* (New York: Lexington Books, 1993); Mary Koss, "Rape on Campus: Facts and Measures," *Planning for Higher Education* 20 (Spring 1992): 21–28; Sally K. Ward, Kathy Chapman, Ellen Cohn, Susan White, and Kirk Williams, "Acquaintance Rape and the College Social Scene," *Family Relations* 40 (January 1991): 65–71.

ROBIN E. FIELD

CAMPUS SECURITY ACT (CLERY ACT). The Jeanne Clery Disclosure of Campus Security Policy and Campus Crime Statistics Act (1998), amended the Crime Awareness and Campus Security Act of 1990, is commonly referred to as the Students' Right-to-Know Act, the Jeanne Clery Act, and the Campus Security Act. The legislation, named in memory of brutally raped and slain Lehigh University freshman **Jeanne Ann Clery**, requires all federally funded colleges and universities to publicly disclose information on campus crime and security policies. The act ensures access to information but is distinct and separate from the **prosecution** of the assailants, crime protection programs, and victim support services.

The legislation stipulates four mandatory requirements for the schools: to maintain a daily log of all reported and alleged crimes, timely notification of crimes that threaten campus safety, publication of a consolidated security report, and notification to all students of the existence of that report. The report must be published by October 1 of each year and is commonly available on the institutional Web site. It must include program and policy statements, including where to report crimes, security policies, access to facilities, procedures for **victims** of sexual offenses, and the jurisdictional authority of campus police. The most recent three years of statistics are reported for eight types of crimes: forcible and nonforcible sexual offenses, criminal homicide (**murder** and manslaughter), aggravated assault, hate crimes, robbery, arson, burglary, and vehicle theft. A forcible sexual act is one committed against the will of the victim or where the victim is not capable of **consent**, and includes rape, **sodomy**, fondling, and sexual assault with an object. A nonforcible sexual act is unlawful sexual intercourse, where the victim is below the legal age of consent (**statutory rape**) or where the laws prohibit marriage between the two (**incest**). Numerous agencies publish statistics collected under the act, including the schools and the Office of Post-Secondary Education (U.S. Department of Education). The implementation of the legislation, and the resultant increase in the disclosure of information on campus crime and security policies, has been credited with increasing student safety on campuses throughout the United States.

Critics of the act, such as the American Council on Education, claim a lack of clarity in the interpretation and implementation of the act, due to the numerous statute amendments. The **National Organization for Women (NOW)** suggests the contradiction inherent in a university, which needs to attract new students and funding, in publicizing crime statistics. NOW claims campus administrators counsel students against reporting rape to the civil authorities, then deal with this violent crime as an administrative matter within the university. This claim is supported with the fact that a minimal number of rapes are statistically reported, yet over 20 percent of postsecondary women students have been raped or forced into nonconsensual sexual acts. *See also*: **Campus Rape; Rape Statistics.**

Suggested Reading: American Council on Education, "Campus Crime," *Easing a Costly Burden: The Higher Education Committee Responds to the FED.UP Initiative*, June 21, 2001, Sect. III (c); *From Understanding to Compliance: Your Campus and the Clery Act* (Long Beach: Office of Chancellor, California State University, Long Beach, 2002); for institutions implementing the Jeanne Clery Act, a sample reference guide and video are both available from http://www.calstate.edu/clery.

LAURIE JACKLIN

CASTRATION. Castration is a practice of body mutilation by the removal of the testes. Although castration in the traditional, surgical sense is gradually being consigned to history, it is still recorded nowadays as a form of punishment for rapists and child molesters, as a religious ritual, or as a symbolic act of subduing an enemy in a time of war.

The rationale behind castration as it is applied to **sex offenders** is that it results in the reduction of testosterone levels, which means diminished libido and reduced deviant sexual activity. According to studies conducted in a number of European countries, between the years 1929 and 1959, less than 10 percent of convicted rapists recommitted sexual offenses after castration, whereas recidivism rates for noncastrated males are estimated to be as high as 60 percent. It could therefore be effective both as punishment and treatment, but disciplinary surgical castration is nowadays viewed as highly inhumane and is no longer practiced legally in the Western world.

In this situation, medical research is conducted in an effort to produce a satisfying alternative. Chemical castration through the administration of drugs has recently been tested on convicted sexual offenders. Drugs in application nowadays, such as medroxyprogesterone acetate (MPA), lower blood levels of testosterone, which in turn reduces a male's erectile ability and tends to bring beneficial behavioral effects. Many experts venture to opine that MPA appears effective, as recidivism rates among disturbed males who underwent treatment drop visibly. But as critics point out, this form of prevention has limited effectiveness, especially in the case of pedophiles. Although castrated offenders are physically unable to penetrate their victims, many nevertheless still demonstrate sexual anxiety and are likely to abuse children in other ways. Moreover, as other critics argue, castration in any form is unconstitutional.

The legal status of castration has varied from society to society. After hundreds of years of castration being an-eye-for-an-eye-style punishment for sexual crimes in ancient Rome, especially for adultery, Emperor Hadrian regarded it with extreme repugnance and declared that it was a crime on a par with **murder**. Similarly, a prohibition against castration was added to the original six Talmudic commandments. But in other cultures it was endorsed as an official form of punishment for a range of crimes, as was the case of ancient China's laws of Han. Castration was also the common sentence for rape and adultery in ancient India, Egypt, among the

Huns, and in medieval Europe. Not infrequently, it was also a fate befalling homosexuals, both because homosexuality itself was commonly considered a sexual crime and because homosexuals were believed to be more reliable as guards of the chastity of women in harems. Castration for this purpose was endorsed by the Shariah, the Court of Islamic Law. Because sexual relations between individuals of uneven social stations were deemed unacceptable, castration was often used to punish the one of inferior status. A familiar example is the fate of American slaves accused of raping white women. In the twentieth century, castration was reinstituted for a few decades in several European countries as a sentence for sex offenders.

Apart from a history of being judicial punishment and treatment, castration is not infrequently resorted to, extrajudicially, as a form of vengeance. In 1936, a Tokyo geisha Sada Abe, 31, was apprehended on charges of having castrated her unfaithful lover in his sleep. Perhaps the best-known case of castration committed in a desire for vengeance is recounted in the work of the medieval French philosopher Pierre Abelard describing his tragic love affair with his young pupil Héloïse. Abelard had been entrusted with Héloïse's education by her uncle Fulbert, one of the clergy of the Notre Dame cathedral in Paris. Héloïse and Abelard fell in love, had a son, and were married secretly. Soon Abelard was castrated at the instigation of Héloïse's enraged relatives, clearly reassured in their vindictiveness by strong religious convictions and a grotesque sense of morality.

In fact, castration in religious contexts is fairly common. The myth of Attis, a beautiful youth who castrated himself, gave rise to a fanatical cult whose devotees, called *galli*, performed an orgiastic dance culminated in self-castration. Nowadays, in the Western world, self-castration for religious reasons is performed by fanatics driven by the extreme belief that carnal pleasures are sinful, and potential temptation should be eliminated. Religion-related castration is also practiced in parts of the United States and Mexico as a holdover of the widespread ascetic movement that emerged in Europe during the Middle Ages. *See also*: **Prosecution; Rape Laws.**

Suggested Reading: Gary Taylor, *Castration: An Abbreviated History of Western Manhood* (New York: Routledge, 2000); Peter Tompkins, *The Eunuch and the Virgin: A Study of Curious Customs* (New York: Bramhall House, 1962).

KONRAD SZCZESNIAK

CELEBRITY RAPISTS. As men famous first by name and then by crime, celebrity rapists have stirred up controversy for many types of **sexual assault: date rape, statutory rape,** use of date rape drugs, and **gang rape.** Celebrity rapists include **athletes,** movie stars and entertainment moguls, business tycoons, and politicos from prominent families. Since celebrity rapists have money, power, and influence, their clout may cloud the public's and the press's opinion of the accusations against them and their accusers, as well as influencing the evidence, trial process, and as some critics say, justice.

Celebrity rape allegations, trials, and convictions are publicized in a mad **media** frenzy. Kobe Bryant, a forward for the Los Angeles Lakers, is facing a hotly contested upcoming trial for raping a hotel employee at the Cordillera Lodge & Spa in Denver, Colorado, on June 13, 2003. Bryant has insisted that he had consensual sex with the woman. Pretrial hearings concerning issues such as whether to admit the alleged victim's sexual past have taken months. In March 2004, she asked the judge to set a trial date, noting that she had received hundreds of death threats. Pop entertainer Michael Jackson has been formally charged with sexual assault of a child. In March 2004, a grand jury convened to determine if there was enough evidence to indict him for child molestation. With each celebrity case, journalists, fans, women's rights advocates, and armchair detectives engage in heated public discussion over the merits of the charges.

With so many accusations surrounding celebrities so often, some have begun to wonder if raping women is part of the lifestyles of celebrity men. Many athletes are accused of sexual misconduct, and some have gained a reputation for it. Mike Tyson, a heavyweight prizefighter, for instance, has been accused of rape at least twice and convicted once. In 1992 Tyson was sentenced to six years in prison and served three years before being released on parole. Angry at getting caught, he told reporter Greta Van Susteren for *USA Today*, "I just hate her [the victim's] guts. . . . Now I really do want to rape her."

Along with professional athletes, famous Hollywood personalities, business tycoons, and members of prominent political families have graced police blotters for rape charges. Fugitive Max Factor heir Andrew Luster was captured in Mexico recently nearly a year after fleeing from a rape conviction for poisoning and raping three women. Roscoe "Fatty" Arbuckle, a silent film star, was accused of raping, brutally sodomizing with a bottle and broken glass, then killing a woman in 1921. He was acquitted. Sometimes Hollywood men's legendary reputations are elevated with rape allegations. Errol Flynn was acquitted for statutorily raping two girls in 1942, but the scandal increased his popularity. Similarly, the Kennedy name is often casually linked to rape. William Kennedy Smith, nephew of Massachusetts Senator Edward Kennedy, was charged in 1991 with rape in Palm Beach, Florida, and acquitted. Years earlier, Michael Kennedy, Robert Kennedy's son, was accused of raping his children's underage babysitter.

Some other prominent celebrities have beaten statutory rape charges as well. Stars accused of raping young women include R&B artist R. Kelly, who was recently indicted on 21 counts of child **pornography** after he taped himself having sex with underage girls. Director Roman Polanski fled the United States in 1977 after admitting to having sex with a 13-year-old girl at the home of actor Jack Nicholson. After a plea bargain was dismissed, Polanski fled to Europe hours before he was to be sentenced to up to 50 years in prison. Polanski has not returned to the United States.

Many stars, such as Rob Lowe, have pled to lesser charges. Lowe was sentenced to 20 hours of community service to avoid criminal charges after taping himself in sex acts with a 16-year-old in 1988. Still, many Hollywood celebrities never face charges for questionable under-age relationships.

Some conjecture links celebrity culture—a cult of personality that props up the famous to larger-than-life proportion—and rape culture—a prevalent social acceptance of persistent violence against women. It is always news when celebrities are having sex. Sex, stardom, and felonies, and the compounded combination of them, sell newspapers. When a celebrity is accused of rape, the media feasts on a buffet of salacious details, and the public reacts with dissonant fascination and disbelief. It is understandable: A hero, by definition, can't be a criminal. And vice versa. A glimpse at media news coverage, Web blogs, and op-ed columns reveals a pattern of typical commentary on both the accused and the accuser.

Media coverage of the accused celebrity typically focuses on his accomplishments as a star and his presumed moral character. Discussion of celebrities' character seem to fall into three categories: (1) Celebrities, too, sadly, are human (and thus just as likely to rape), (2) celebrities are model citizens (and thus unlikely to rape anybody), and (3) celebrities are demigods who are used to extra special privileges (and thus much more likely to rape and understandably so). Most significantly, fans often pledge unfaltering support and claim that the allegations are "out of character." As if knowing him personally, fans often profess, "He's not that kind of guy." Sometimes celebrities attempt to preemptively try their case in the court of public opinion by reaching out to their fans with elaborate press conferences to showcase their wives and families. It is common for press commentaries to rationalize that with so much at stake—family, fortune, and reputation—nobody would act that stupidly. Besides, op-eds sometimes report, celebrities do not need to take sex by force because they have beautiful wives and millions of young women adoring them voluntarily. Ultimately, they portray the sex as consensual, or imply that the victim asked for it, shifting the media focus from the accused celebrity to the accuser.

In celebrity rape cases, the press often puts the alleged victim on trial. Vilified characterizations of alleged **victims** are thrown around by the pubic to discredit them: accusers become accused liars, sluts with a past, golddiggers, and home wreckers. Nationwide discussion turns the celebrity into the victim—evidenced by op-ed outcries that these men are easy targets preyed upon and falsely accused by opportunistic women hungry for fame and attention and lovelorn stalkers who will make up anything to get close to their idols. Overall, concern for the victim is slighted. Fans say they feel deceived and let down, and lament the loss of their idol, as if rape accusations reveal a monster hiding underneath the squeaky-clean surface appearance.

Media stories abound with accused celebrities not because rape is a big story but because the man is famous. Celebrities probably do not rape more; we just hear about it more. As a result, media coverage of celebrity rapists may adversely affect justice in rape cases for a few reasons. For one, critics claim that celebrities are subject to intense public scrutiny and less likely to receive a fair trial. Excessive publicity is seen as a witch-hunt. The extensive media coverage might obscure the fact that all those accused are presumed innocent until proven guilty by a court of law. However, the media hype of celebrity rapists might prevent justice for the victim. Celebrities are less likely to be charged, much less convicted. It has been noted that many celebrities accused of rape never face charges, let alone see the inside of a courtroom. In recent years there have been many celebrity rape charges that have been quickly dismissed. In 2003 the Florida Marlins went to the World Series, but little was made of the fact that their catcher Ramon Castro was released on bond, charged with rape the previous year. The Oakland Raiders' kicker Sebastian Janikowski was acquitted on charges of possessing **gammahydroxybutyrate (GHB)**, commonly known as the "date rape drug" in 2001. Shielded by a lucrative entertainment industry, few celebrities are successfully prosecuted in the courts, and they rarely face internal sanctions on their eligibility to play, make a movie, or run for office. Ultimately, media coverage of celebrity rapists leaves the impression that rape in general is not as serious as it is, does not happen as often as it does, and occurs between relative strangers. *See also*: **Rape Trials.**

Suggested Reading: Jeffrey R. Benedict, *Public Heroes, Private Felons: Athletes and Crimes against Women* (Boston: Northeastern University Press, 1997); Jackson Katz, "When You're Asked about the Kobe Bryant Case," 2003. http://www.jacksonkatz.com/bryant.html.

SARAH L. RASMUSSON

CENTRAL PARK JOGGER. After 9:00 P.M. on April 19, 1989, a group of at least 40 youths went on a rampage in Central Park in New York City. According to all reports, these youths set out to mug, rob, scare, and beat anyone who crossed their paths. Records show that the youths robbed and beat up a homeless man, accosted a couple on a tandem bicycle, and assaulted two male joggers. The attacks were so extensive and so vicious that the term "wilding" was coined to explain their behavior. A 28-year-old investment banker, later known as the Central Park Jogger, became the focus of attention and the symbol of the unprovoked attacks. This well-educated, middle-class white female was raped, beaten, and left for dead. When the unidentified jogger was discovered, she was gagged and unconscious, her left eye had been torn from the socket, she exhibited symptoms of severe brain damage, and she had lost at least three-fourths of her blood. Neither the officers who found her nor the medical team who treated her believed that she would survive. Identified only by a distinctive ring she wore, the jogger remained in a coma for 12 days and woke with no memory of the attack.

Police arrested five teenagers, all either black or Latino, and charged them with the attack. Four of the youths confessed on videotape, providing graphic descriptions of their actions. The Central Park Five served from 7 to 11 years in prison. In December 2002, Matias Rayes, then in prison for murder and serial rape, confessed to the crime. DNA evidence collected at the time of the crime identified him as the rapist. The cases against Kharey Wise, Kevin Richardson, Antron McCray, Yusef Salaam, and Raymond Santana were overturned, and they sued New York City for $250 million. The New York Police Department was cleared of wrongdoing and continues to believe that the youths were involved in the attack in some way, citing detailed evidence given at the time of the crime. Prosecutors, however, believe that Rayes acted alone.

For 14 years after the attack, the victim was known simply as the Central Park Jogger. She had been known by the pseudonym "Paula Harris" during the trial, and most white **media** had protected her identity, as well as that of her current boyfriend. While tension over the trial was at its height, the black press had announced both names, claiming that she had been raped and beaten by the boyfriend. In early 2003, Trisha Meili, then 42, announced that she is the Central Park Jogger in an autobiography detailing the horrors of her experience and the ways in which she had reclaimed her life. Meili is still unable to accomplish multitasking, has some memory, balance, and coordination problems, and has permanently lost her sense of smell. *See also:* **Gang Rape; Memoirs.**

Suggested Reading: Trisha Meili, *I Am the Central Park Jogger: A Study of Hope and Possibility* (New York: Simon and Schuster, 2003); Timothy Sullivan, *Unequal Verdicts: The Central Park Jogger Trials* (New York: Simon and Schuster, 1992).

ELIZABETH R. PURDY

CHILD RAPE. Around the globe, societies have tended to view childhood as a unique stage of life and have generally viewed children as innocent beings in need of special protection. To that end, from ancient times to the present, many societies have acted to try to safeguard children from rape and other forms of sexual degradation, though they might define sexual degradation differently from era to era and from place to place. One way societies have tried to protect young girls is through laws that designate a statutory age of **consent**. Such laws prohibit men from having sexual relations with females under a specified age on the legal theory that they are too young and immature to make informed decisions and, therefore, are incapable of giving a legal consent. Historically, the age of consent was set somewhere between 10 and 13 years, depending on the era and the culture, and tended to coincide with female puberty, which was also the age at which a female could marry without parental permission. Child rape laws punished men who had sexual relations with females younger than the designated age of consent on par with the crime of rape, even if the girl consented and the man used no force. While societies appear to have been less interested in protecting male youths from sexual exploitation, many of the ones that had laws against **sodomy** used them to punish the adult participant while not holding the male minor criminally liable.

Though past societies were concerned about the sexual degradation of children, especially females who have suffered the brunt of sexual violence, people of modern times have become highly immersed in the issue of child rape. The modern **media** have played a role in raising awareness that there is a problem and that its scope is global. Yet there are critics who charge that the popular media has been as much a part of the problem of child rape as the solution. Some critics have asserted that the media relate stories of child abuse in the passive voice, as if the problem has no discernable source and is unavoidable, and that they depict the tales in such a lurid and sensationalistic fashion they ultimately titillate more than they inform. Others have claimed that popular mediums, especially of the entertainment variety, have sexualized children in potentially dangerous ways.

Individuals as well as governmental and private organizations engaged in promoting the safety and welfare of children are working toward solutions to the age-old problem of child rape. They have much to overcome. There are cultures that do not view sexual relations with children as harmful or exploitative. There are places in the world where poverty is so pervasive and parents so desperate that they send a child out to earn money from **prostitution**, and it is the family's only means of survival. There are businesses that purchase young girls from their parents and sell them into sexual **slavery**. Some cultures retain folkloric traditions that assert that sexual relations with a virginal female will cure the afflicted of sexually transmitted diseases, including **HIV/AIDS**. There are underage children who willingly trade sexual favors for food, shelter, necessities, or even spending money.

The solutions to preventing and stopping child rape are as difficult as the problem is complex. Governmental agencies of several nations and nongovernmental associations are making an effort ultimately to stop child rape. The World Congress against the Commercial Sexual Exploitation of Children and the United Nations Children's Fund have tried to address the myriad fundamental problems that lead to sexual violence against children and to conduct research not only to pinpoint its causes and prevalence but to clarify such seemingly obvious points as what constitutes a child and what constitutes a rape. Some groups define a child as any person under the age of 18, but others hold that the age should be 16 or even 12 years. Further, the rape laws of many nations are in need of some reform. A number of countries have rape laws that preclude the criminal prosecution of men who rape boys as well as of those who use objects such as coke bottles or knives rather than their genitals to commit the crime.

The governments of some nations have demonstrated a lack of concern for the issue of child rape within their borders, while others have a host of problems that officials deem in more immediate need of their attention. South Africa has experienced a rash of child rapes since the end of the apartheid era, as many as 100 reported cases a month in some townships, and the government does not have the resources to stem the tide. Thailand has a well-known problem with child prostitution, an industry upon which its tourism is dependent. The Thai government has recently raised the age of consent and now more strongly enforces the laws against prostitution. Eastern European countries have seen dramatic increases in the trafficking of young girls as prostitutes and sex slaves to the West, and Belgium has experienced a spate of child murders in connection with the **pornography** industry. Some countries have come to understand that their citizens play a role in the sexual exploitation of children in other lands and have passed legislation in response that allows them to prosecute their citizens if they commit child rape while abroad, even if their actions are legal in the country of destination. *See also*: **African Women and Girls; Asian Americans; Trafficking in Women and Children.**

Suggested Reading: James Kincaid, *Erotic Innocence: The Culture of Child Molesting* (Durham, NC: Duke University Press, 1998); Angeliki E. Laiou, ed., *Consent and Coercion to Sex and Marriage in Ancient and Medieval Societies* (Washington, DC: Dumbarton Oaks Research Library and Collection, 1993); Karen Mahler, "Global Concern for Children's Rights: The World Congress against Sexual Exploitation," *International Family Planning Perspectives* 23.2 (June 1997): 79–84; Michelle Oberman, "Turning Girls into Women: Reevaluating Modern Statutory Rape Laws," *Journal of Criminal Law and Criminality* 85.1 (1994): 15–79.

MARY BLOCK

CLERGY, COUNSELING BY. Members of religious organizations such as churches, synagogues, or mosques may seek out a member of the clergy for counseling after being raped or after a **family** member has been raped. They are usually seeking emotional and spiritual support to cope with the trauma of rape as well as helpful religious resources. There are many spiritual needs and questions that clergy could be asked to address. Clergy may be called upon to describe God's response to the victim or the perpetrator and God's general concern about the crime of rape.

Reassurance of God's love and concern can be a crucial source of comfort that those seeking counseling may need. Clergy may be asked questions like: "Why did God allow the rape to happen?" Counseling might be requested to address confusion about whether or not religious tradition fully supports a person who has been raped or somehow holds the victim partly responsible, perhaps because of the sexual nature of this kind of violence.

For women who have been raped, certain religious attitudes about sexuality may encourage feelings of shame. For instance, stories about women who sexually tempt men and incite men's desire to be sinful are part of Christian and Hebrew scriptures. These stories support religious views that hold women responsible for men's lustful and "sinful" sexual conduct toward them. These blaming attitudes may create shame, guilt, and confusion for women **victims.** Similar issues that might be addressed include religious teachings about forgiveness of the perpetrator; a wife's obedience to her husband and **marital rape;** sex outside of marriage and **date rape;** homosexuality and rape of a gay man or lesbian. Whenever religious teachings known to someone who has been raped could increase their anguish, counseling by clergy may be sought to find alternative religious understandings.

As leaders, clergy teach not only about ancient scripture and traditions but also about contemporary values. They may sometimes uphold attitudes that encourage shame and silence about rape within the distinctive cultural groups they serve. When counseling a woman who has been raped by a man, some black clergy could be mainly concerned about protecting the public image of black men from racist stereotyping; some Muslim clerics could be primarily concerned with protecting the honor of the males in her family; certain Jewish clergy might not believe her because they assume that rape does not happen in the Jewish community; some white clergy could see protection of family privacy and the white victim's reputation as the main priority. However, contrary to these examples, clergy from these same groups may be extremely critical of maintaining shame and silence about rape. Based upon their understanding of the need to take risks and speak out about racism, black clergy could be especially affirming of the rape victim speaking out. Drawing from the strong emphasis on respecting women in their tradition, Muslim clerics could be primarily concerned with supporting the victim. Jewish clergy might emphasize the woman's sacred worth and the shamefulness of the perpetrator's defiling acts, rather than blaming the victim (*see* **"Blaming the Victim" Syndrome**). White clergy might focus on feminist theological ideas empowering women to hold perpetrators accountable. Balancing their roles as both community leader and counselor to individuals in crisis, clergy will differ on how to conserve particular cultural values without doing so at the expense of the person who has been raped.

There are ethical concerns about the responsibilities of clergy in counseling situations. In several religious traditions clergy have a unique obligation to maintain strict confidentiality. But should clergy be legally mandated to report it to authorities if, for example, a teenager confides that she or he has been raped by a family member? What if a perpetrator of rape confesses to clergy? Should the confidence be violated? For some, clergy have a moral obligation to society to break confidentiality when told about acts, or threat, of physical harm. For others, because of their moral obligation to the counselee and sacred vow to God, under no circumstances should clergy violate the confidentiality entrusted to them.

In the aftermath of rape there are many reasons why counseling by clergy is sometimes sought by victims and their families. Counseling offers emotional and spiritual support and teaches important cultural values about rape. In response to their **religion**, the broader society, and the person they are counseling, clergy make important choices about how to play a trustworthy and constructive role. *See also:* Clergy, Sexual Abuse by; Rape Counseling.

Suggested Reading: Mary D. Pellauer, Barbara Chester, and Jane Boyajian, eds., *Sexual Assault and Abuse: A Handbook for Clergy and Religious Professionals* (1987; New York: HarperCollins, 1991).

TRACI C. WEST

CLERGY, SEXUAL ABUSE BY. It is a violation of professional ethics for any person in a pastoral role of leadership or pastoral counseling (clergy or lay) to engage in sexual contact or sexualized behavior with a congregant, client, employee, or student (adult, teen, or child) within the professional (pastoral or supervisory) relationship. It is wrong because sexual activity *in this context* is exploitative and abusive.

Ministerial violation of boundaries involving sexualization of a relationship can take place in the ministerial relationship or the counseling relationship, as well as the staff supervisory or mentor relationship. When the minister sexualizes the ministerial or counseling relationship, it is similar to the violation of the therapeutic relationship by a therapist. When the minister sexualizes the supervisory or mentor relationship with a staff member or student, it is similar to **sexual harassment** in the workplace, and the principles of workplace harassment apply. When a child or teenager is the object of the sexual contact, the situation is one of **pedophilia** or child sexual abuse, which is by definition not only unethical and abusive but criminal.

For example, in 2002 the crisis of sexual abuse of children by Roman Catholic priests, which had been simmering for years, finally came to a boil. The Boston Archdiocese became the subject of intense scrutiny by the **media** and numerous civil lawsuits filed by adult survivors of childhood abuse by priests. Cardinal Bernard Law, who led the Boston Archdiocese, was pressured to resign. The media reported a long-standing pattern of cover-up and institutional protection of priest pedophiles. A multimillion-dollar settlement with **survivors** was finally reached. The U.S. Conference of Catholic Bishops issued a new policy and established a National Review Board to monitor diocesan compliance with the new policy.

Although the experience of the Roman Catholic Church in the United States is not unique, it is illustrative of the historic difficulty of religious institutions to screen, supervise, and if necessary, suspend abusive religious leaders. Every tradition is confronted with the fact of abusive leaders who take advantage of the vulnerability of their followers whether children, teens, or adults.

Sexual contact by clergy and pastoral counselors with congregants/clients undercuts an otherwise effective ministerial relationship and violates the trust necessary in that relationship. It is not the sexual contact per se that is problematic but the fact that the sexual activity takes place within the ministerial relationship. The crossing of this particular boundary is significant because it changes the nature of the relationship, and the potential harm that it causes is enormous.

The behaviors that occur in the sexual violation of boundaries include, but are not limited to, sexual comments or suggestions (jokes, innuendoes, invitations, etc.), touching, fondling, **seduction**, kissing, intercourse, molestation, rape, and other sexual behavior. There may be only one incident or a series of incidents or an ongoing intimate relationship over time.

Sexual contact by ministers or ministerial counselors in ministerial, professional relationships is an instance of professional misconduct that is often minimized or ignored. It is not "just an affair," although it may involve an ongoing sexual relationship with a client or congregant. It is not merely adultery, although adultery may be a consequence if the minister/counselor or congregant/client is in a committed, marriage relationship. It is not just a momentary lapse of judgment by the minister or counselor. Often it is a recurring pattern of misuse of the ministerial role by a minister or counselor who seems to neither comprehend nor care about the damaging effects it may have on the congregant/client.

Although the vast majority of ministerial offenders in reported cases are heterosexual males and the vast majority of victims are heterosexual females, it is clear that neither gender nor sexual orientation excludes anyone from the risk of offending (ministers/counselors) or from the possibility of being taken advantage of (congregants/clients) in the ministerial or counseling relationship.

There are four basic ethical principles involved in instances of sexual abuse by clergy:

It is a violation of role. The ministerial relationship presupposes certain role expectations. The minister/counselor is expected to make available certain resources, talents, knowledge, and expertise that will serve the best interests of the congregant, client, staff member, or student intern. Sexual contact is not part of the ministerial, professional role.

It is a misuse of authority and power. The role of minister/counselor carries with it authority and power and the attendant responsibility to use this power to benefit the people who call upon the minister/counselor for service. This power can easily be misused, as is the case when a minister/counselor uses (intentionally or unintentionally) his/her authority to initiate or pursue sexual contact with a congregant, client, or anyone he/she supervises. Even if it is the congregant who sexualizes the relationship, it is still the minister/counselor's responsibility to maintain the boundaries of the ministerial relationship and not pursue a sexual relationship.

It is taking advantage of vulnerability. The congregant, client, employee, or student intern is by definition vulnerable to the minister/counselor in multiple ways; she/he has fewer resources and less power than the minister/counselor. When the minister/counselor takes advantage of this vulnerability to gain sexual access to her/him, the minister/counselor violates the mandate to protect the vulnerable from harm. (For Jews and Christians, the protection of the vulnerable is a practice that derives from the Jewish and Christian traditions of a hospitality code.)

It is an absence of meaningful consent. Meaningful **consent** to sexual activity requires a context of not only choice but also mutuality and equality; hence meaningful consent requires the absence of fear or the most subtle coercion. There is always an imbalance of power and thus inequality between the person in the ministerial role and those whom he/she serves or supervises. Even in the relationship between two persons who see themselves as "consenting adults," the difference in role precludes the possibility of meaningful consent.

The violation of ministerial or teaching boundaries by the sexualization of a ministerial relationship is a common problem for all religious traditions (Buddhist, Christian, Jewish, Native American, Muslim, etc.). There are unethical and exploitative religious and spiritual leaders in every tradition. The misconduct of a few undercuts the integrity of all religious and spiritual leaders as it violates the trust necessary for a healthy and meaningful ministerial relationship. *See also* **Child Rape; Clergy, Counseling by; Religion; Sexual Coercion.**

Suggested Reading: Marie M. Fortune, *Is Nothing Sacred?* (Cleveland, OH: Pilgrim Press, 1988); Marie M. Fortune, *Sexual Violence: The Unmentionable Sin* (Cleveland, OH: Pilgrim Press, 1993).

MARIE M. FORTUNE

CLERY, JEANNE ANN (1966–1986). On April 5, 1986, freshman Jeanne Clery slept in her campus dormitory at Stoughton Hall, Lehigh University (Bethlehem, Pennsylvania). A stranger, fellow-student Josoph Henry, entered the dormitory through a series of doors, all propped open by pizza boxes, and burglarized her room. He violently beat, raped, sodomized, then strangled Clery to death in order to avoid her identifying him later. Henry was convicted and sentenced for numerous offenses, including rape, first-degree **murder**, indecent and aggravated assault, and involuntary deviate sexual intercourse.

In 2002, Federal District Court Judge Anita Brody set aside Henry's death sentence, arguing that instructions to the jury had been confusing. The Northampton County Court had 180 days to decide on another sentencing hearing or to sentence Henry to life imprisonment. On September 1, 2002, the court sentenced him to life in prison. There is no caveat of "with" or "without" possibility of parole.

From the time of his original conviction and sentencing (1987), Henry spent 15 years on death row.

Parents Connie and Howard Clery launched a $25 million civil suit of negligence against Lehigh University. They attributed her death to the lack of disclosure of information about violent crimes and breaches of security on the campus; for instance, the school had 181 reports of propped-open dormitory doors during the period immediately preceding Clery's murder. The suit cited the failure of security and negligence in warning students of dangers on the campus and raised the legal issue of the university's responsibility and obligation for student safety. Lehigh repeatedly denied the claims but eventually settled out of court. Clery's family used the settlement to establish Security on Campus, a nonprofit activist organization devoted to increasing campus security, victim assistance, and public access to crime statistics at higher education institutions throughout America. The activist group also lobbied for other federal laws, including the Campus Sexual Assault Victims' Bill of Rights (1992) and Campus Sex Crimes Prevention Act (2000). *See also*: **Campus Rape; Campus Security Act (Clery Act).**

Suggested Reading: Security on Campus (and Jeanne Clery's story), http://www.securityoncampus.org/; Spalding University, Louisville, KY, *SCSD Safety Awareness* 2.2 (Fall 2002).

LAURIE JACKLIN

CLOTHING. While the subject of clothing typically generates discussions about **rape myths**, which serve to "blame the victim" (*see* **"Blaming the Victim" Syndrome**), clothing is being appropriated increasingly as a means of empowerment for **victims**.

The most common association of clothing with rape involves rape myths. For example, accusations about the way a woman dresses can easily fall into the "she asked for it" myth. A woman is understood (by courts, religious groups, or society in general) of bearing at least partial responsibility for her rape if her clothing is regarded as skimpy or questionable in nature. This argument assumes that if a female dresses in a provocative manner, then she is a "bad girl" who is looking for any kind of sexual activity, and therefore she is assumed to be a willing participant in any sexual act. The clothing a victim wears also becomes relevant in rape myths that seek to provide reasons for the sexually aggressive behavior of men. This myth claims that men cannot control their sexual urges and that therefore a woman's choice of dress may provoke an uncontrollable response in men that could lead to a forced sexual act. Feminist theorists and psychologists have noted that both of these myths influence and are influenced by a culture that constructs women as submissive sexual objects and men as aggressive **sexual predators** in their gender and sexual roles. While there is a move to make new generations more cognizant of these dangerous gendered stereotypes, many feel that these ideologies are so engrained in our culture (from movies to music videos to religious beliefs) that victims of rape are taught from a very young age to blame themselves for any sexual crime that may occur.

Mention should be made of some empowering uses of clothing. First, on a logistical level, women's clothing is a source of incriminating data about the assailant (semen or hair). Second, the Clothesline Project uses clothing as a means of healing and empowerment for **survivors** and of education for the public. Begun in Massachusetts in 1990 and now existing on an international level, victims design shirts that express their own suffering and survival; the shirts periodically hang in public settings to increase public awareness. *See also*: **"Blaming the Victim" Syndrome; Rape Myths.**

Suggested Reading: Martha R. Burt, "Rape Myths," in Mary E. Odem and Jody Clay-Warner, eds., *Confronting Rape and Sexual Assault*, Worlds of Women, No. 3 (Wilmington, DE: SR Books, 1998).

JILL GORMAN

COERCED SEX. *See* Sexual Coercion.

COMFORT WOMEN. Between 1932 and 1946, thousands of women, mostly Korean and Chinese, were captured and imprisoned in "comfort stations" where they were repeatedly raped by Japanese soldiers and sailors. This sexual **slavery** violated numerous international laws. Yet little has been done to punish those responsible. Comfort women have lived in silence with the physical and emotional consequences of their abuse. Only recently have **survivors** called upon their own governments and Japan to make amends for this terror and sexual violence.

The first stations opened in the spring of 1932 in Shanghai, as a response to the raping of local women by the Japanese army and navy. Military rapes, particularly in Nanking in 1937–1938, were thought to reflect poorly on Japan and to make the conquered Chinese more difficult to control. The troops, however, saw sexual license as one of the few benefits of military life that was harsh, brutally disciplined, poorly provided, and constantly under the specter of combat and death. To boost troop morale and maintain order among the Chinese, the Japanese high command instituted the comfort system.

Comfort stations were built everywhere Japanese troops went, including the front lines. The "girl army" was under the direct control of the military. The army and navy built or took buildings for use as stations and supplied provisions for the women prisoners. The military set the hours, rules, prices, and hygiene standards for the brothels. Management of comfort stations was taught at the army's accounting school. The military also issued "Guidelines for Conducting Medical Examinations of Prostitutes and Serving Women" and provided the doctors who examined the women each week. Hopeful that comfort women would help prevent the spread of disease, Brigade Headquarters constantly warned soldiers to check prostitutes' health certificates, use condoms and Secret Star Cream disinfecting lubricant, and carefully wash their genitals after intercourse. Still, because the troops were rarely examined, the system did not control the spread of venereal disease.

Between 50,000 and 200,000 women staffed more than 1,000 comfort stations. While the majority were Korean or Chinese, Taiwanese, Filipina, Indonesian, Vietnamese, Indian, Dutch, and Australian women were also enslaved. Some Japanese prostitutes served as comfort women, but the troops preferred the "tighter fit" of captured women. The vast majority of them were between 14 and 18 years old. Most came from poor families and were illiterate. Some were deceived by promises of good jobs, others were taken from their families in payment of debts, and more were simply kidnapped by force. The Japanese argued that women were willing to serve, but the number of volunteers in the girls' army was quite small. Even if a woman chose to accompany the troops, it was a decision rooted in economic deprivation and fear for the welfare of her **family** who were terrorized by local police.

Captured women were kept in small rooms, which, at best, were furnished with a bed, blankets, and disinfectant liquid. At worst, a mat was placed on a dirt floor. Women were forced to have sex with as many as 30 men a day. Chafed and raw, sex was excruciating, but women were required to be gentle and welcome each man. The fact that the soldiers called comfort women "public toilets" suggests how brutally they must have treated them. Few women ever had a day off. They even worked when infected. The army issued each soldier two condoms a month, but when these wore out, the women were expected to wash and reuse prophylactics. When these failed, **abortion** and surgical sterilization were forced on women. For the most part, medication was reserved for military personnel, so sick women suffered and died without treatment.

Women fiercely resisted this sexual slavery. Some killed themselves; others cut off their hair, refused to bathe, or tried to appear ugly so men would not want them. Despite armed guards, some tried to run away, but not knowing the language in a strange land, and with no way to return to their own country, this was futile. **Resistance** resulted in beatings, starvation, and threats to one's family. This compelled most women to acquiesce.

As Japan neared defeat, soldiers who fought to the death demanded nightly sexual service. When units engaged in mass suicide to avoid surrender, the comfort women were expected to join in and were murdered if they refused. Although there was concern that the system would reflect poorly on Japan, when the Allies requested comfort stations for their own use, Japan supplied them. These operated for the benefit of U.S. soldiers until March 1946, when they were closed because too many American soldiers contracted venereal disease. At that time, comfort women were abandoned. No effort was made to return them to their countries, and few women had money with which to travel.

The consequences of this sexual servitude were extreme. Women suffered from the aftereffects of venereal disease. There were also psychological injuries like **post-traumatic stress disorder**, depression, alienation, fear of sex, and self-loathing. Their culture prized male heirs, but many comfort women were left sterile. Asian Confucianism upheld female purity as a virtue greater than life. This perpetuated the belief that any comfort woman who did not kill herself from shame was an abomination. Thus, women were afraid to speak of their experiences and suffered in silence.

Only after 1988 did Asian feminists rise up to protect sexual exploitation. Former comfort women lobbied the International Commission of Jurists and the United Nations Human Rights Commission. Their activism led to the United Nation's 1998 report, which argued that sexual violence against women must be prosecuted as a crime against humanity. While these **war crimes** continue, they are now punished. The International Criminal Tribunals for the former Yugoslavia and for Rwanda issued many indictments on charges of **torture** and **genocide** for crimes involving the sexual violence against women. Lawsuits brought by former comfort women have, however, been rejected. *See also*: **Bosnia-Hergezovina; Nazis; Prostitution; Trafficking in Women and Children.**

Suggested Reading: George Hicks, *The Comfort Women* (New York: Norton, 1994); Yoshimi Yoshiaki, *Comfort Women*, trans. Suzanne O'Brien (New York: Columbia University Press, 2000).

MARY LINEHAN

COMPUTERS AND THE INTERNET. The growth of computer technology and widespread access to the Internet has created numerous new opportunities for criminal behavior, especially in the area of sex crimes. Three areas of computer and Internet technology that facilitate sex crimes are chat rooms, newsgroups/Web sites, and computer graphics/video.

Online chat rooms allow computer users to exchange information in real time; they are also used as places for individuals to meet for the purposes of dating or finding partners for sexual activity. Group conversations attract larger numbers of participants who can break off to other rooms or use email for more private interactions. Participants have the option to engage in online sexual banter and play, which reaches various levels of intimacy. Since participants do not see each other, their personal identities are protected; there is no way to prevent individuals from lying about their ages, genders, or interests. Other forms of chat occur in virtual reality. These sophisticated social forums are part fantasy, part role-play, part public street corner, and part complex social laboratory. They have a transfixing power over certain types of participants; a simulated online rape of one participant by another has actually been documented as a psychologically traumatizing experience.

A widely publicized problem with chat rooms is the threat posed to children who make online contact with adults; a number of **media** reports have documented instances in which children were abducted by pedophiles who befriended them in chat rooms. While such incidents are uncommon, they are devastating in terms of the physical and psychological harm inflicted on the **victims**. As a result, the National Center for Missing and Exploited Children has established a list of precautions that include limited online time for children and close parental supervision. Similarly, teenagers are suspectible to online overtures from adults to meet offline, often subjecting the teens to **statutory rape** or other forms of **sexual assault**. But the problem is not limited to children; anyone who makes offline contact with an online acquaintance can become a victim of criminal sexual acts.

Newsgroups are Web sites that allow users to post and view messages on a variety of topics; they differ from chat rooms in that they do not operate in real time. But like chat rooms, they are locations that can be used for exchanging child **pornography** and information leading to the sexual exploitation of women and children. There are numerous examples of child pornography rings that use sophisticated computer techniques to avoid detection; a group named the Wonderland Club uses a code developed by the Soviet KGB to encrypt all of its communications.

A variety of other nonnewsgroup Web sites also sexually exploit women and children by disseminating information and distributing pornography. The sex industry includes a number of large, legal businesses that operate sophisticated Web sites charging subscription fees that bring in millions of dollars per year. Tens of thousands of free pornography sites bring in smaller amounts of money from banner advertisements for larger sites and related businesses. Many of these same Web sites also offer access to streaming pornographic videos that can be viewed using Web browser plug-ins.

The most egregious Web sites market images and videos of rape and **torture**. Slave Farm, a Web site registered in Denmark, claims to have the "world's largest collection of real life amateur slaves" and encourages men to "submit a slave to the picture farm." Images include women being subjected to sexual torture, bondage, and fetish sadism. The site also allows visitors who pay subscription fees to give real-time commands to women who perform sexual acts in front of Web cameras. A number of images (even those that are available for free) show badly injured women with cuts, burns, bruises, welts, and bleeding wounds.

A Web site registered in Moscow advertises itself as "the best and most violent rape site on earth." Subscribers are offered 30,000 hardcore pornographic images, 500 online video channels, and 100 extended-length videos, almost all of them depicting rape. To induce subscriptions, visitors to the site can download 12 segments of a 13-megabyte video showing a hooded man raping a woman in an office.

In the third category, advancements in computer hardware and software have made it possible to create lifelike human images or to manipulate photographs of actual humans. Using a scanner and relatively inexpensive software, anyone can scan a picture of a child and alter it to make it appear as though the child is posing nude or engaging in sexually explicit conduct. Using another type of software, computer users can create three-dimensional animated images of humans without scanning photographs. While such software is currently very expensive and the resulting images are easily distinguished from actual persons, it is expected that it will soon become very difficult to tell the difference between actual and virtual figures, and the associated costs will also drop. Even though no actual children are involved, Congress saw fit to pass legislation prohibiting computer-generated child pornography.

Sexually explicit material is not a new phenomenon, but individuals have never had such open access to such a large body of extreme images. Consumers of violent pornography once had to go outside their immediate communities to make their purchases and often needed intermediaries to help them find their preferred products. Today, the Web gives them immediate access to violent pornography in their own homes. At no time in history has there been such an advanced rate of distribution of sexually explicit material. *See also*: **Child Rape; Pedophilia; Prostitution; Trafficking in Women and Children.**

Suggested Reading: Blake T. Bilstad, "Obscenity and Indecency in a Digital Age: The Legal and Political Implications of Cybersmut, Virtual Pornography, and the Communications Decency Act of 1996," *Santa Clara Computer & High Technology Law Journal* 13 (1997): 321–384; Donna M. Hughes, "Symposium on Sexual Slavery: The Trafficking of Women and Girls into the United States for Sexual Exploitation, The Use of New Communications and Information Technologies for Sexual Exploitation of Women and Children," *Hastings Women's Law Journal* 13 (2002): 127–146; Vincent Lodato, "Computer-Generated Child Pornography: Exposing Prejudice in Our First Amendment Jurisprudence?" *Seton Hall Law Review* 28 (1998): 1328–1364.

GREGORY M. DUHL

COMSTOCK ACT. In March 1873, the U.S. Congress passed the first national obscenity law to include the category of contraceptives. The new law was named after its most vocal supporter and primary author, Anthony Comstock. Comstock, a social purity reformer supported by the New York Young Men's Christian Association (YMCA), linked birth control and **abortion** to social problems such as **pornography** and **prostitution**, claiming that all of these "vices" posed a risk to the health and well-being of American citizens. The Comstock Act made it illegal to import or circulate any "obscene, lewd, or lascivious book, pamphlet, picture, paper, print or other publication of an indecent character, or any article or thing designed or intended for the prevention of contraception or the procuring of abortion, nor any article or thing intended or adapted for any indecent or immoral use or nature." These restrictions made it illegal to distribute birth control information, medical literature on the subject, or actual contraceptive devices through the U.S. postal system, even to **victims** of rape.

Comstock himself served as the first special agent of the United States Post Office from 1873 till his death in 1915. Although the legislation initially targeted dissemination of information related to abortion and contraception, Comstock expanded the purview of the law to censor materials as varied as artwork, the poetry of Walt Whitman, and pamphlets advocating free love and reproductive freedom for women. Those found guilty of violating the Comstock Act faced jail terms (up to 10 years) and fines (set at a maximum of $5,000). In theory, federal law suppressed birth control and abortion information from being distributed through the U.S. postal system. In addition to this federal legislation, a number of states passed antiobscenity statutes further restricting sales and possession of "obscene" materials, including contraceptives and abortifacients.

While the Comstock Act symbolized expanded federal control over reproductive choice, Congress did not significantly expand funding for the postal service in order to ensure that these measures could be adequately enforced. Historian Andrea Tone argues that these restrictions did not eliminate the dissemination of contraceptive information and products. Contraceptive entrepreneurs developed creative strategies to safely advertise and market their products, and established companies continued to sell contraceptives to doctors, druggists, and mail-order houses without interference from Comstock. Despite such selective prosecutions and the unwillingness of the federal government to wholeheartedly support its enforcement, the Comstock law represented federal commitment to defining and controlling "obscene materials" through censorship of the U.S. mail. Provisions of the law remained in effect until the 1960s when a series of court cases nullified restrictions on birth control information. *See also*: **Free Love Movement.**

Suggested Reading: Nicola Beisel, *Imperiled Innocents: Anthony Comstock and Family Reproduction in Victorian America* (Princeton, NJ: Princeton University Press, 1997); Comstock Act, ch. 258, 17 Stat. 598 (1873); Andrea Tone, "Black Market Birth Control: Contraceptive Entrepreneurship and Criminality in the Gilded Age," *Journal of American History* 87 (2000): 435–459.

REGAN SHELTON

CONCEPTION. *See* Pregnancy.

CONSENT. Consent is an issue that constitutes the very essence of rape prosecutions. If a woman consents to sexual relations with a man, she cannot accuse him of rape. Consent means to agree to or approve of what is done or proposed, or to give one's permission. The law recognizes two kinds of consent. An *express consent* is one that is directly given, either verbally or in writing, and clearly demonstrates an accession of the will of the individual giving it. An *implied consent* is indirectly given and is usually indicated by a sign, an action or inaction, or a silence that creates a reasonable presumption that an acquiescence of the will has been given.

The legal standards for a valid and invalid consent are fairly clear and well defined. An individual must be mentally and physically capable of granting consent. The consent must be informed; that is, the person giving the consent must understand and be knowledgeable as to what he or she is consenting. It is vital that the consent be voluntary and given wholly of a person's free will. Typically, the law invalidates a consent that is uninformed, has been given in ignorance, or has been obtained through force, fraud, coercion, or duress. There are exceptions to these general legal principles, however, and they primarily occur in **rape law**.

The concept of consent in rape law has changed over time. Defendants can use a consent defense if they are charged with crimes such as assault, battery, trespass, and theft, but rape was the only one where courts demanded physical **resistance** as proof of nonconsent. At common law, rape could only be committed if sexual intercourse occurred in the absence of the woman's consent and where it was against her will. A mere verbal expression of dissent did not suffice to prove nonconsent in rape cases, though it did in other crimes that allowed a consent defense. The absence of consent is still vital to the crime, but since the mid- to late 1980s, courts have begun to allow women to prove a mere involuntary submission to the act. Where common law mandated proof that a woman resisted to the utmost of her ability, modern case law is slowly starting to hold that such overt and continued physical and verbal resistance is not required if it would be futile or where it would result in more serious bodily harm. The utmost resistance standard has been replaced with a reasonable resistance rule. The woman's resistance is still scrutinized in **rape trials**, and she must still resist in earnest, but courts are now more likely to consider the totality of circumstances surrounding the act rather than focusing almost exclusively on the woman's behavior.

In theory, modern rape law does not require that a woman do more than her age, strength, health, and all the attending circumstances reasonably support. Complainants need not physically or verbally express their lack of consent so long as they demonstrate it and do so in such a manner that it can readily be implied from their behavior. Also, modern courts have allowed rape convictions in cases where a woman initially gave her consent and then withdrew it. However, she must retract the consent before penetration occurs, or there is no rape. Further, the law recognizes that some women cannot give a legal consent to sexual intercourse. The test is whether the complainant can understand the nature and consequences of the sexual act and is determined by her ability to exercise reasonable judgment in comprehending what is being done to her. She must understand that she can refuse to participate. Females under a specified statutory age cannot consent to sexual relations. Women of unsound mind or who are physically or mentally incapacitated cannot consent if they are unable to give an informed consent. However, intercourse obtained through fraudulent or deceptive practices amounts to rape only if a state's statute includes fraud as an element of the crime. In the absence of a statute, modern courts rely on the common law, which mandates that the intercourse be achieved through force. Generally, if a woman is capable of consenting and she does so, she cannot charge a man with rape if he beguiled her into acquiescing, even if she otherwise would have refused him. *See also*: **Child Rape; Mental Disabilities, People with; Rape, Definitions of; Seduction; Sexual Coercion; Statutory Rape.**

Suggested Reading: Susan Estrich, *Real Rape* (Cambridge: Harvard University Press, 1987); West Group, *Corpus Juris Secundum: A Contemporary Statement of American Law*, vol. 75 (St. Paul, MN: Author, 2002).

MARY BLOCK

CONTRACEPTION. *See* Abortion; Morning-After Pill.

COUNSELING. *See* Rape Counseling.

COX BROADCASTING CORPORATION V. COHN. In *Cox Broadcasting Corporation v. Cohn*, 420 U.S. 469 (1975), the right to privacy came into direct conflict with the right of the free press. In August 1971, the 17-year-old daughter of Martin Cohn was raped and murdered, and six youths were arrested and brought to trial. According to Georgia law (26-9901), it was a misdemeanor for members of the press to publicly identify rape **victims**. During the trial, a reporter for WSB-TV, owned by Cox Broadcasting Company, identified the victim through examination of public records and announced her name on Atlanta's Channel 2 news. The victim's father sued for monetary damages, arguing that his right to privacy had been violated. The Georgia Supreme Court upheld the law, and Cox Broadcasting Corporation appealed to the U.S. Supreme Court, claiming protection under the First and Fourteenth Amendments.

When the case was argued in 1975, the Court was asked to deal with conflicting constitutionally protected rights. The Court had officially recognized the *implicit* right to privacy only a decade before in *Griswold v. Connecticut*, 381 U.S. 479 (1965). The First Amendment right to a free press, however, is *specifically expressed* in the Bill of Rights. The Supreme Court has historically been reluctant to infringe on this right. The Fourteenth Amendment had been passed in 1868 to limit state interference with constitutional rights.

The Supreme Court overturned Georgia's law, deciding that since the information was rightfully made public, the reporter had a right to identify the victim. Justice White wrote in his decision that the news **media** had a societal responsibility to inform the public about government proceedings. Since the reporter acted lawfully, the station could not be charged monetary damages. *See also*: ***Michigan v. Lucas***; **Rape Shield Laws; Rules of Evidence.**

Suggested Reading: Joel B. Grossman and Richard S. Wells, *Constitutional Law and Judicial Policy Making* (New York: Longman, 1988).

ELIZABETH R. PURDY

CREDIBILITY. Credibility indicates the degree to which something or someone is worthy of belief or confidence. As such, it is a key element in the outcome of legal proceedings, especially regarding sexual crimes. The credibility of both the **victim** and the perpetrator often rests on the plausibility of the reported crime as well as the character of the individuals involved. Fundamentally, the issue revolves around the truthfulness of the account and believability of the victim.

Regarding the crime itself, the accuracy of the report, the reliability of the witnesses, and the likeliness of the tale are all called into question. The victim's ability to repeat the tale without alteration suggests a factual basis, while prevarication tends to discredit the victim. Objective matters, such as verifying logistical details, provide a foundation that proves either reliable or unstable. In many instances, it is possible to determine whether or not the people involved were indeed in the places they claimed to be at the time they claimed to be there. The value of the eyewitnesses, though, may be diminished by inconsistencies in their tales, an unwillingness to participate, or the defamation of their characters.

Even when eyewitnesses accurately place the victim and the perpetrator at the scene, however, it is less common to have witnesses to the attack itself, as sexual crimes are often committed in isolation. Physical evidence, then, provides another avenue for determining the likelihood of the tale. Gathering such evidence requires that the victim submit to a medical examination within a specified time period after the attack. For various reasons, including embarrassment, shame, and fear, many victims do not turn to medical or legal authorities immediately afterward.

Although the notion of credibility deals with facts, without hard evidence, prosecuting a sexual crime is often reduced to a he-said-she-said scenario. Consequently, secondary definitions of credibility, ideas of having or deserving credit, come into play, and evaluating character becomes crucial. The character of the accused usually holds a minor role in assessing the situation. Previous arrests or convictions can weigh heavily. A history of abuse or violence many also tip the scales against the accused. On the other hand, a respected position in society or a clean record may lead people to doubt the accusation and champion the accused person's innocence.

The victim's character, however, is almost always scrutinized. Initially, there are judgments concerning the circumstances surrounding the crime. Members of society and even officers of the court may find themselves imposing the moral ought, comparing the victim's story to preconceived ideas of how people ought to behave and mentally doling out suitable consequences for rebelling against these traditions. Then the events connected to reporting the crime, such as a time lapse between the attack and the report or the victim's behavior during the course of the investigation, are analyzed. Finally, the victim's personal history and reputation are dissected in an effort to determine whether or not the story is credible. Ultimately, many victims feel that the outcome rests on people's willingness or inclination to believe them rather than on a blind administration of justice. *See also*: **Rape Shield Laws.**

Suggested Reading: Rudi Williams, "Psychiatrist Discusses Abuse, Harassment, Violence against Military Women," *American Forces Press Service*, May 15, 2003, http://www.defenselink.mil/news/May2003/n05152003_200305154.html.

GREGORY M. DUHL

D

DATE RAPE/ACQUAINTANCE RAPE. *Acquaintance rape* is most broadly defined as any situation in which the requisite elements of the crime of rape are satisfied (i.e., to force a woman to engage in intercourse against her will and without her **consent**) and the victim and the rapist know one another. This prior relationship between the parties—which can range in degree of familiarity from fellow classmates who have never spoken to one another to a couple involved in a long-term relationship—is the only difference between acquaintance and stranger rape scenarios, though the two have been treated quite differently by both the public and the criminal justice system. *Date rape* is a subset of acquaintance rape, though the two phrases are often used interchangeably, which refers to a rape scenario in which there is some sort of romantic relationship between the two parties. Date rape is a particular problem on college campuses, where it frequently occurs in situations involving **alcohol** and/or "date rape" drugs. High school students are also at risk, and concerns about teen dating violence are now being addressed in school assemblies and on Web sites such as VAWnet (http://www.vawnet.org).

Approximately one in four women in the United States will be **victims** of rape or attempted rape at some point during their lives. Over three-quarters of those assaults will occur between people who know each other. According to a study by the National Institute of Justice, "criminal reporting by victims of acquaintance rape remains well below the actual incidence of the crime, which appears to be high" (Epstein and Langenbahn, 65). However, some people have challenged these figures. In particular, **Katie Roiphe**, in *The Morning After: Sex, Fear, and Feminism*, takes issue with the statistic that one in four women will be a victim of rape as well as the *Ms. Magazine* study Robin Warshaw's book *I Never Called It Rape* is based upon. Roiphe argues, "If I were really standing in the middle of an epidemic, a crisis, if 25 percent of my female friends were being raped, wouldn't I know it?" (52).

Yet even if **survivors** do come forward to report these assaults, an acquaintance rapist is most likely to be charged and tried only when the following additional conditions are met: a prompt report to the police, the existence of witnesses who can testify to similar crimes committed by the suspect, physical injury to the survivor, and corroboration of the individual's story. This differential treatment of survivors of acquaintance rape, as contrasted with stranger rape, has been documented and corroborated by a number of researchers studying different components of the criminal justice system. The thoroughness of a police investigation, the decision whether or not to prosecute a charge, the likelihood that the defendant will be convicted, and the likelihood of incarceration have all been shown to vary significantly along acquaintance rape/stranger rape lines.

Susan Estrich, a professor at the Law Center of the University of Southern California, for example, illustrates how the law distinguishes between the "aggravated, jump-from-the-bushes stranger rapes and the simple cases of unarmed rape by friends, neighbors, and acquaintances" in her groundbreaking book on **rape law** *Real Rape*: *How the Legal System Victimizes Women Who Say No*. As Estrich compellingly demonstrates, the distinctions drawn by both the public and the criminal justice system between acquaintance rape and stranger rape simultaneously define and limit the dimensions of the problem.

> If only the aggravated cases are considered rape—if we limit our practical definition to cases involving more than one man, or strangers, or weapons and beatings—then "rape" is a relatively rare event, is reported to the police more often than most crimes, and is addressed aggressively by the system. If the simple cases are considered—the cases where a woman is forced to have sex without consent by only one man, whom she knows, who does not beat or attack her with a gun—then rape emerges as a far more common, vastly underreported, and dramatically ignored problem. (10)

The intersection between these competing dimensions of the problem is where the current debate regarding rape law is being waged.

But the laws themselves are only part of the story. The larger part of the story, particularly with respect to acquaintance rape, is how the police, **prosecution**, defense attorneys, and courts/juries will apply the laws to a particular set of facts. As both the National Institute of Justice's study and the research cited in Cassia Spohn and Julie Horney's book illustrate, the distinctions drawn between date rape/acquaintance rape and stranger rape—which cause one to be taken more seriously than the other and therefore prosecuted much more frequently—are made not by the legislatures' drafting statutes but by the individuals in the justice system charged with interpreting and enforcing them. So until the larger public and individual perceptions concerning date and acquaintance rape change, statutory reform can only go so far. *See also*: **Campus Rape; Forcible Rape; Fraternities; Sexual Assault.**

Suggested Reading: Laurie Bechhofer and Andrea Parrot, eds., *Acquaintance Rape: The Hidden Crime* (New York: John Wiley & Sons, 1991); Carol Bohmer, "Acquaintance Rape and the Law," in *Acquaintance Rape: The Hidden Crime*, ed. Andrea Parrot and Laurie Bechhofer (New York: John Wiley & Sons, 1991); Mark Cowling, *Date Rape and Consent* (Aldershot: Ashgate Publishing, 1998); Joel Epstein, and Stacia Langenbahn, "The Criminal Justice and Community Response to Rape," in *Issues and Practices in Criminal Justice* (Washington, DC: U.S. Department of Justice, Office of Justice Programs, National Institute of Justice, 1994); Susan Estrich, *Real Rape: How the Legal System Victimizes Women Who Say No* (Cambridge: Harvard University Press, 1987); Leslie Francis, ed., *Date Rape: Feminism, Philosophy, and the Law* (University Park: Pennsylvania State University Press, 1996); Katie Roiphe, *The Morning After: Sex, Fear, and Feminism* (Boston: Little, Brown, 1993); Cassia Spohn and Julie Horney, *Rape Law Reform: A Grassroots Revolution and Its Impact*

(New York: Plenum Press, 1992); Robin Warshaw, *I Never Called It Rape: The Ms. Report on Recognizing, Fighting and Surviving Date and Acquaintance Rape* (New York: Harper and Row, 1988).

STEPHANIE L. SCHMID

DATE RAPE DRUGS. *See* listings by drug names.

DESALVO, ALBERT. *See* Boston Strangler.

DEUTSCH, HELENE (1884–1982). Trained in psychiatry at the University of Vienna, Psychoanalyst Helene Deutsch studied psychoanalysis with **Sigmund Freud** and became a member of his inner circle. She was the head of the Training Institute of the Vienna Psychoanalytic Society from 1924 to 1935, when she moved to Boston. She is best known for her influential thesis that female psychology is characterized by masochism and passivity. This led her to insist that rape **fantasies** are common among women.

Deutsch followed Freud, who had argued that there was an inherent masochistic trend in femininity. Like Freud, Deutsch traced this to anatomy: When little girls realize that they do not have a penis, their active stance toward the world turns inward. Mature female sexuality is, in this formulation, vaginal only; Deutsch saw this as passive and represents the sexual act as one that is, at least initially, unpleasant for women. Menstruation and childbirth are also female experiences that Deutsch associated with pain and suffering. She concluded that normal womanhood requires the capacity to take pleasure in pain.

For Deutsch, women's rape fantasies can express fears about sexuality, but they are often erotic. She noted that because they represent real female sexuality, "rape fantasies often have such irresistible verisimilitude that even the most experienced judges are misled in trials of innocent men accused of rape" (*Psychology of Women*, 256).

Her theories influenced popular understandings of rape. They were disputed by her contemporary Karen Horney, who argued that masochism in women be understood culturally and not simply in terms of anatomy. Later feminists, for instance, **Susan Brownmiller** (1975), who called Deutsch "a traitor to her sex," have criticized Deutsch's theory for contributing to myths about women and rape. *See also*: *Against Our Will.*

Suggested Reading: Susan Brownmiller, *Against Our Will: Men, Women and Rape* (New York: Fawcett Columbine, 1975); Helene Deutsch, *Psychology of Women*, 2 vols. (New York: Grune and Stratton, 1944–1945); Helene Deutsch, "The Significance of Masochism in the Mental Life of Women" (1930), in *The Psychoanalytic Reader*, ed. R. Fliess (New York: International Universities Press, 1969).

SARA MURPHY

DISABLED VICTIMS. *See* Victims.

DISSOCIATIVE IDENTITY DISORDER (DID). Previously known as multiple personality disorder, dissociative identity disorder (DID) develops in response to an extreme trauma such as rape. To survive the abuse, people disconnect their minds from what is done to them. Approximately 1 in 100 people have some form of DID, but the disorder is not yet well understood.

DID is now considered to be a fairly common reaction to repeated physical, emotional, or sexual abuse in childhood. Victims of long term incest, for example, frequently develop DID as a survival technique. Over time, it may prove so effective that a victim may use it to "escape" any threatening situation. In addition, when those with DID experience a situation that reminds them in some way of their previous abuse and trauma, it may trigger a reaction of some sort, such as flashbacks, panic attacks, or self-destructive behavior.

Everybody has different aspects to their personality, but in DID this takes an extreme manifestation. The boundaries between personality parts are very rigid, and the personalities are very distinct. Often, a child personality carries the secret of rape. To be diagnosed with DID, a person must have two or more distinct personalities who can control behavior. These personality states cannot be due to a medical condition or inebriation, and they must leave the individual unable to recall important personal information. Indeed, the DID sufferer may lose track of time and forget what happened while dissociating. While this "splitting" into "alters" is vital in surviving the initial trauma, when it begins to interfere with daily life, therapy is helpful.

Therapy is long term, and its goal is to help the client function effectively in the here and now, while dealing with a painful past. The client chooses between two equally viable treatment options. One fuses the alters so they cease to exist as separate parts; the other creates "co-consciousness" where each part works in awareness and cooperation with the other. Medication will not cure DID, but it can work with therapy in helping clients manage other conditions that can afflict those with DID: night frights, hearing voices, panic attacks, depression, eating disorders, chemical dependence, body memories, or severe headaches. *See also*: **Incest**; **Posttraumatic Stress Disorder (PTSD)**; **Rape Trauma Syndrome**.

Suggested Reading: Deborah Bray Haddock, *Dissociative Identity Disorder Sourcebook* (Chicago: Contemporary Books, 2001).

MARY LINEHAN

DNA COLLECTION AND EVIDENCE. DNA evidence is a type of physical, scientific evidence used in investigating, solving, and prosecuting criminal cases, including cases of rape. When **law enforcement** agencies and attorneys properly utilize DNA evidence, it is like a "silent witness" that helps to identify or eliminate certain suspects. Deoxyribonucleic acid (DNA) is a string of coded genetic information found in cell nuclei, which determines individual hereditary characteristics. It is like a genetic blueprint and is identical in every cell of an individual. The use of DNA evidence in criminal investigations and prosecutions centers on the theory that no two human beings, except for identical twins, have exactly the same DNA, although this theory has not yet been absolutely proven. DNA evidence falls into the category of class characteristic evidence because it cannot be forensically identified with a specific individual to the exclusion of all others. DNA reports and the resulting court testimony can only give the probability of finding two people with the same DNA pattern in the random population, a probability that can be extremely high or low, based on the frequency of that particular DNA pattern. The types of physical evidence useful in providing DNA samples are among the most commonly found and the most crucial in the majority of **sexual assault** investigations.

Nobel Prize–winning scientists James Watson and Francis Crick discovered the structure of DNA in the 1950s. Since its beginning, DNA analysis has had a major impact on the conduct of criminal investigations and litigations. Many sexual assault cases lack identifying evidence like latent fingerprints but often contain trace evidence like semen, hair, blood, and other class characteristic evidence from which scientists can extract DNA. This evidence is one of the primary targets of evidence collection in rape cases. DNA evidence is also valuable because it is less likely to be detected and destroyed by the perpetrator than fingerprints, which are easily eliminated through the use of gloves or careful wiping of surfaces at the crime scene. DNA is also invaluable to criminal investigators because of its durability. Researchers have extracted DNA from the bones of long-dead individuals to help solve old criminal cases. DNA analysis will become ever more valuable in the future as scientific advances promise to someday allow scientists to match DNA evidence to a single individual with absolute certainty.

The primary sources of DNA evidence in sexual assault cases are the victim, the crime scene, and any known suspects. In order for DNA evidence to be useful, investigators need both a DNA sample recovered from the victim or the crime scene and a DNA sample from the suspected perpetrator of the crime. Without both samples, an investigator cannot determine a particular individual's likelihood or elimination as a suspect. Although medical examination of the rape victim is of primary importance, investigators should not neglect the possibility of DNA evidence recovery at the crime scene as well. Responding officers and investigators must properly recognize and collect potential evidence at the scene in order for a forensic laboratory to be able to extract and analyze any available DNA.

In rape cases, investigators should consider the victim the focal point of the crime and of the search for evidence. The medical personnel who treat rape victims can either greatly facilitate or impair the courtroom use of evidence. Direct involvement of police personnel in medical evidence recovery depends on location, funding, personnel availability, and training. Police presence during the medical treatment of rape victims can greatly aid in questions of evidence chain of custody and integrity that may be required for trial testimony, but their presence is a highly controversial issue due to questions of sensitivity toward the victim. Medical personnel or law enforcement investigators should also conduct an evidence search involving any potential suspects as soon as possible in order to avoid loss or destruction of evidence. Suspects will also need to provide known DNA samples for comparison to DNA recovered from the crime scene.

The use of preassembled sexual assault evidence collection kits, often called **rape kits**, has become increasingly popular. These kits provide for the systematic collection and documentation of physical evidence, including DNA evidence, that can corroborate sexual activity and associate the suspect with the victim. Different kits use different evidence recovery methods and procedures, depending on the age and sex of the person or whether that person is the victim or the suspect. Most kits are designed for use with a female victim and a male suspect. The types of evidence collected include **clothing**, body hair, body fluids, fingernail scrapings, and debris collection. The kits also ensure that medical personnel collect physical evidence in keeping with proper medical, forensic, and legal requirements. Their development and use is one benefit of planning and liaison between law enforcement and the medical community.

The relevance and admissibility of physical evidence depend on its recognition, utilization, collection, packaging, and preservation. Successful use of DNA evidence requires proper technique, administration, organization, attitude, and funding. The entire process of handling evidence materials from the start of the crime scene to its presentation in court must be efficient, uncontaminated, and well documented. The protection of possible evidence should begin immediately after the victim contacts a law enforcement agency to report the rape. Evidence integrity can be affected by anyone coming in physical contact with the evidence, including the victim, responding officers, investigators, crime scene technicians, medical personnel, forensic laboratory examiners, and attorneys. The consequences of DNA evidence contamination may include the introduction of misleading evidence, confusion, and serious questions as to the evidence's effectiveness. Contamination can also impair DNA evidence to the point that prosecution or exoneration of a particular suspect is no longer possible.

The process of DNA analysis begins when evidence reaches the laboratory. Adequate funding is essential due to the expense of completing the analysis. Many law enforcement agencies throughout the country have a backlog of rape kits that have not been analyzed due to lack of funds. DNA analysis can be completed on hair root cells, blood, and semen. Urine, perspiration, seminal fluid, and saliva do not contain DNA, but DNA can be extracted from seminal fluid and saliva if certain types of cells are present. The two most common methods of analysis are designated restriction fragment length polymorphism (RFLP) and polymerase chain reaction (PCR). Both of these processes were developed by a team of genetics researchers led by Alec Jeffreys, the inventor of genetic fingerprinting, at the Lister Institute of the University of Leicester in England in 1984. PCR analysis is particularly beneficial because it can be completed with more minute quantities of DNA and with body fluid samples that have degraded.

After scientists analyze the DNA, they create an image of the DNA fragment that resembles a supermarket bar code. This image is then compared with a similar image created from DNA samples taken from a known suspect. If the samples do not match, the known suspect is eliminated. If the samples match, the scientist will then determine the probability that the suspect's DNA pattern could have randomly matched the DNA pattern recovered from the crime. Scientists determine probability by comparing the DNA pattern with those patterns stored in computer databases around the world. The probability of such a match will vary depending on the rarity or commonality of the found DNA fragments. The lower the probability of a random match, the more likely it is that the suspect committed the crime.

Since DNA evidence cannot link a suspect to a crime with absolute certainty, courts will only allow expert testimony concerning the probability of a random match. DNA evidence can support or contradict the testimony of participants or witnesses and can greatly increase the chances for **prosecution** or exoneration, but only if such evidence is uncontaminated and clearly understood. DNA evidence is also useful in disproving false confessions and in linking **serial rapes** to a single perpetrator. In a few cases, scientists have even used DNA evidence from a victim's parents and from blood recovered at the crime scene to prove the victim's murder when her body was unable to be recovered. Advances in DNA technology provide greater forensic insight but also provide greater challenges for its use in prosecution as it becomes harder for the layperson to understand. Attorneys must present DNA evidence and explain its purpose in a clear manner. Any weaknesses or problems in evidence collection or analysis will allow opposing attorneys to challenge its admissibility and reliability. The use of DNA evidence in the courtroom will become increasingly prevalent as DNA analysis becomes more sophisticated, especially when scientists are able to conclusively link DNA samples to a single individual. *See also*: **Physicians/Medical Professionals; Profiling.**

Suggested Reading: Colin Evans, *The Casebook of Forensic Detection* (New York: John Wiley and Sons, 1996); Robert R. Hazelwood and Ann Wolbert Burgess, *Practical Aspects of Rape Investigation: A Multidisciplinary Approach* (Boca Raton, FL: CRC Press, 1995); F.E. Inbau and A.A. Moenssens, *Scientific Evidence in Criminal Cases* (Mineola, NY: Foundation Press, 1978); David Owen, *Hidden Evidence: Forty True Crimes and How Forensic Science Helped Solve Them* (Buffalo, NY: Firefly Books, 2000).

MARCELLA TREVIÑO

DOMESTIC VIOLENCE. The American Psychological Association (APA) presents domestic violence as a pattern of abusive behaviors including a wide range of physical, sexual, and psychological maltreatment used by one **family** member against another, often to maintain that person's misuse of power, control, and authority. Domestic violence include abuse between members of a family who are not intimate, such as elder abuse, abuse of and by children, and abuse between other family members such as siblings, cousins, or in-laws. Abuse shows patterns of interconnection, with men who batter partners often abusing children as well (APA). Domestic violence applies to homosexual as well as heterosexual relationships, and to violence from females as well as from males, although the latter is more common.

Domestic violence may be criminal and includes physical assault (use of a weapon, hitting, shoving, etc.), sexual abuse (unwanted sexual activity, including rape), stalking, and terroristic threats. Other forms of domestic violence are not usually considered criminal but are still abusive. These include emotional control, such as continual insults and derogatory name-calling, and intimidation, such as preventing the person from contacting friends or family or from taking a job. Domestic violence can involve depriving a person of financial resources and depriving a person of rights, such as physical freedom or medical care. It can include threats, such as the threat of deportation.

According to the National Violence against Women Survey (Tjaden and Thoennes), 1 out of 4 U.S. women has been raped or physically assaulted by an intimate partner, while 1 out of 14 U.S. men report rape or physical assault. The American Psychological Association estimates that the lifetime prevalence of physical assault toward women in an intimate relationship is one in three. If other forms of domestic violence such as emotional abuse were to be included, the estimated rates of occurrence would be much higher.

Female **victims** of domestic violence, as compared to male victims, are more likely to need medical attention and to spend more days in bed (National Research Council). Differences between racial and ethnic groups in experience of domestic violence have been reported, but these differences are hard to interpret because of differences in willingness to report and because differences in educational and economic status are often not reported. There are indications that more educated abusive men, when compared with less educated abusive men, are more likely to use verbal and emotional abuse rather than physical abuse.

Consequences of domestic violence include physical injury, illness, and death. It has been estimated that 30 to 40 percent of women seen in U.S. hospital emergency rooms have symptoms that are related to domestic violence. In addition, victims show emotional consequences, which can include **posttraumatic stress disorder**, depression, anxiety disorders, and other disorders. The financial costs in medical and lost labor costs is staggering; direct medical costs alone have been estimated at $1.8 billion each year (Wisner et al.). There are also consequences for children who observe domestic violence; witnessing violence is a risk factor for children's long-term physical and mental health problems, including substance abuse; for their being victims of abuse; and for their own later perpetrating domestic violence.

Victims of domestic violence do not show consistent personality factors. The only consistent risk factor is being a woman. Women may stay in violent relationships for a variety of reasons, including fear of retribution to themselves and their children, financial need, and because of the cycle of violence in which some abusive men become loving and vow change after the abuse.

Alcohol use has been frequently associated with domestic violence, but perpetrators of domestic violence do not form a cohesive group. Studies suggest a typology of abusers. A small group of abusers have antisocial attitudes and exhibit violence in many situations; another group shows psychopathology involving dysphoria or borderline psychological problems and high levels of violence toward their partners; a third shows less psychopathology, violence only within the family, and cultural and educational factors are likely to play a role in their acceptance of violence as appropriate.

Programs to prevent domestic violence focus on educational outreach: to victims; to children through programs in the **schools** about communication and expression of anger; and to professionals such as legislators, physicians, mental health personnel, police, and judges. Programs provide shelter and treatment programs for women, including homeless women and women from varied cultural backgrounds. Treatment programs for men can be psychoeducational, such as the Duluth model, or psychotherapeutic, or some combination of the two. Many programs also provide a focus on substance abuse. *See also:* **Battered Women; Incest.**

Suggested Reading: American Psychological Association, *Violence and the Family: Report of the American Psychological Association Presidential Task Force on Violence and the Family* (Washington, DC: Author, 1996); V. Felitti, R. Anda, D. Nordenberg, D. Williamson, A. Spitz, and V. Edwards, "Relationship of Childhood Abuse and Household Dysfunction to Many of the Leading Causes of Death in Adults," *American Journal of Preventive Medicine* 14.4 (1998): 245–258; A. Holtzworth-Munroe and G.L. Stuart, "Typologies of Male Batterers: Three Subtypes and the Differences between Them," *Psychological Bulletin* 116.3 (1994): 476–497; G.T. Hotaling and D.B. Sugarman, "A Risk Marker Analysis of Assaulted Wives," *Journal of Family Violence* 5.1 (1990): 1–13; National Research Council, *Understanding Violence against Women* (Washington, DC: National Academy Press, 1996); P. Tjaden and N. Thoennes, *Full Report of the Prevalence, Incidence, and Consequences of Intimate Partner Violence against Women: Findings from the National Violence against Women Survey*, report for grant 93-IJ-CX-0012, funded by the National Institute of Justice and the Centers for Disease Control and Prevention (Washington, DC: NIJ, 2000); L. Walker, *The Abused Woman: A Survivor Therapy Approach* (Washington, DC: American Psychological Association, 1994); C.L. Wisner, T.P. Gilmer, L.E. Saltzman, and T.M. Zink, "Intimate Partner Violence against Women: Do Victims Cost Health Plans More?" *Journal of Family Practice* 48.6 (1999): 439–443.

MARGARET GIBBS

DOUBLE STANDARD. *See* Sexual Double Standard.

DROIT DU SEIGNEUR. The *droit du seigneur*—also referred to as *droit de cuissage*, *marquette*, or *jus primae noctis*—refers to the right of an aristocratic lord to have forced sexual relations with a woman living on his domain during the first night of her marriage. Rather than allow sexual relations with his new bride, the groom would offer his lord a gift. Historians have generally agreed that this "right" was merely legend and probably never existed in practice. Early modern chroniclers ascribe the origins of the practice to pagan lords who required a marriage payment from their dependents. But the term itself, far from originating in the Middle Ages, only emerged in sixteenth-century juridical debates concerning relations between lords and peasants in rural European society.

The term remains nonetheless powerful. The *droit du seigneur* symbolizes sexual dependence between a male master and female servant. It concerns sexual power, which itself signifies social and political dominance. If the *droit du seigneur* has had any resonance in popular culture, it most likely derives from its use in eighteenth- and nineteenth-century literature, where the lord's first night is mentioned in writings of famous eighteenth-century authors such as Voltaire or in Pierre Augustin Caron de Beaumarchais's *The Marriage of Figaro* (1784). In these works, the master-servant sexual theme provides an avenue for social criticism of the inegalitarian society of the period.

The term *droit de cuissage* (along with *harcèlement sexuel*) has returned to the modern French lexicon amid government legislation against **sexual harassment** in the workplace.

Suggested Reading: Alain Boureau, *The Lord's First Night: The Myth of the Droit de Cuissage*, trans. Lydia G. Cochrane (Chicago: University of Chicago Press, 1998); Frances Eleanor Palermo Litvack, *Le Droit du Seigneur in European and American Literature* (Birmingham, AL: Summa Publications, 1984).

CHRISTOPHER CORLEY

DRUG-INDUCED RAPE PREVENTION AND PUNISHMENT ACT OF 1996. The Drug-Induced Rape Prevention and Punishment Act criminalized the intent to commit a violent crime (including rape), wherein the perpetrator provides a controlled substance to an unsuspecting victim. While distributing controlled substances was already a federal crime (Controlled Substances Act), this legislation targets the problem of **date rape** drugs. Flunitrazepam is named in the act, as the effects of this drug cause unknowing **victims** to become so submissive that they are an easy target of a rapist. Those convicted of distributing even a single dose face sentences of up to 20 years in prison, and the penalties for possession include both fines and 3 years' imprisonment.

Flunitrazepam, with a brand name **Rohypnol**, is commonly called Roofie, Mexican Valium, and R-2. A benzodiazepine (tranquilizer), with up to 10 times the strength of Valium, Rohypnol is a quick-acting sedative, marketed in many countries as a remedy for insomnia and as a preanesthetic. Rohypnol is not approved for either medical or therapeutic use in the United States, and possession, distribution, and manufacture of the drug are illegal. At the time of the enactment of the legislation, this low-cost sedative quickly dissolved in liquid without any trace of taste, color, or odor. It chemically induces drowsiness, confusion, and amnesia, renders the user unconscious, impairs judgment, and when mixed with **alcohol**, is potentially lethal. The Drug Enforcement Administration (DEA) raised specific concerns about the impairment of mental judgment and anterograde amnesia, whereby the user forgets all events while under the influence of the drug. Many victims of Rohypnol-facilitated rape do not realize that they have been assaulted until they are beyond the 60-hour maximum time wherein the ingested drug can be detected in the human body.

The DEA and legislators were concerned about the growing use of date rape drugs, such as Rohypnol and **gammahydroxybutyrate (GHB)**, as the pattern of illegal drug use changed in the 1990s. Frequently associated with Rave parties, the use of these inexpensive drugs, along with MDMA (3,4-methylenedioxymethamphetamine, street name **Ecstasy**), grew in popularity. Since the enactment of this legislation, manufacturer Hoffman-LaRoche reformulated Rohypnol so that it takes much longer to dissolve and changes the color of the liquid to blue. However, even with these changes to the chemical properties of the drug, the medical and legal profession caution that newer illicit date rape drugs continue to be stealth in their detection, and are formulated to be even more efficient and quick-acting. *See also*: **Sexual Assault, Drug-Facilitated.**

Suggested Reading: Drug-Induced Rape Prevention and Punishment Act of 1996, 21 U.S.C., sec. 841 (b)(7); Office of the Attorney General, "Memorandum for All United States Attorneys—Drug-Induced Violent Crime Prosecutions," September 23, 1997, http://www.usdoj.gov/ag/readingroom/drugcrime.htm; U.S.A. Drug Enforcement Administration, "DEA Briefs & Background, Drugs and Drug Abuse—Drug Descriptions, Rohypnol (Flunitrazepam)," http://www.dea.gov/concern/flunitrazepamp.html.

LAURIE JACKLIN

DWORKIN, ANDREA (1946–). Prominent feminist scholar, writer, and activist. While participating in an antiwar protest in New York in 1965, Dworkin was arrested and spent four days in the Manhattan Women's House of Detention, where she was strip-searched and sexually brutalized by male doctors. Later, as a young married woman living in Amsterdam, Dworkin was threatened, physically beaten, and terrorized by her husband. That experience inspired Dworkin to devote herself to ending oppression against women. Dworkin explains that her book *Woman Hating* (1974) was written because "I wanted to find out what had happened to me and why. I knew only that it was impersonal." In that book, Dworkin first advanced the theory that "[w]e are, clearly, a multisexed species which has its sexuality spread along a vast fluid continuum where the elements called male and female are not discrete." After escaping from her abusive husband, Dworkin returned to the United States and began a career as a scholar, writer, and activist. Her book *Intercourse* (1977) examined the way in which sexuality is constructed as domination. The so-called dominance theory of Dworkin, along with scholar **Catherine MacKinnon,** was the foundation for model antipornography ordinances that they drafted for Minneapolis and Indianapolis. Those ordinances sought to link **pornography** to tangible harm to women, thereby giving rise to a legal claim that their civil rights had been violated. Dworkin's work is provocative and often controversial. Her critics claim that she is antimale and antisex. Dworkin is a prolific writer, the author of numerous essays and articles as well as several books of nonfiction and fiction, including *Right Wing Women* (1983); *Ice and Fire* (1987); *Pornography: Men Possessing Women* (1989); *Mercy* (1992); *Scapegoat: The Jews, Israel, and Women's Liberation* (2000); *Heartbreak: The Political Memoir of a Feminist Militant* (2002). *See also*: **Prostitution; Roiphe, Katie; Steinem, Gloria.**

Suggested Reading: Martha Camallas, *Introduction to Feminist Legal Theory* (New York: Aspen Publishers, 1999); Andrea Dworkin Web site: http://www.igc.org/Womensnet/dworkin.

BRIDGET J. CRAWFORD

E

ECSTASY. 3,4-methylenedioxymethamphetamine (MDMA), or Ecstasy, is the most widely recognized name for a popular "club drug." Pharmaceutically, Ecstasy is a synthetic drug that is similar in action to amphetamines (categorized as stimulants) and to mescaline (a hallucinogen). Consequently, it produces both stimulant and psychedelic symptoms. Hence, the sale of brightly lighted ornaments at "Raves." Ecstasy appears to be an addictive substance producing many of the problems usually encountered with cocaine. While Ecstasy is not considered to be a "hard drug" by most of its youthful users, a number of researchers think that it is actually more dangerous than either heroin or cocaine.

While Ecstasy is generally ingested orally in the form of tablets or capsules, some users crush the pills into a powder that can be snorted, smoked, or injected. Since the amount of MDMA differs with each pill, it is difficult for the user to know just how much is being consumed at any one time. The combined stimulant and psychedelic effects reach a peak after approximately two hours but may continue to generate symptoms for as long as six hours or even longer. At one time, MDMA was utilized as an appetite suppressant in weight control. It was also prescribed as a medication to enhance close interpersonal relationships that were suffering from difficulties in establishing intimacy. It is this special quality of Ecstasy that is associated with inappropriate sexual contact and **date rape**.

The pleasurable effects of taking Ecstasy include increased self-confidence and a feeling of acceptance and closeness to others. The user has a strong desire to touch and be touched by others, even by complete strangers. It is easy to comprehend the popularity of Ecstasy with youth, especially at parties, nightclubs, and Raves. Moreover, a predator in date rape situations doesn't have to use a drug such as **Rohypnol** to render the **victim** unconscious; he or she only has to wait until the victim makes the first overture. Ecstasy facilitates sexual contact that might otherwise seem high risk.

The direct effects of taking Ecstasy include an increase in heart rate and the development of hypertension (high blood pressure), a heightened sense of energy and alertness (often associated with amphetamines), as well as lowered appetite. While the energizing effect enables the user to dance for hours, it can also result in malignant hyperthermia (extremely high body temperature) and dehydration (thus, the need for water). Eventually, the heart and kidneys are strained to the point of failure. Typical responses to Ecstasy also include a sense of euphoria, muscle spasms, jaw clenching, and tremors. Infant pacifiers are used to reduce the pressure on the teeth. When Ecstasy is combined with **alcohol**, the adverse effects are even more devastating than when Ecstasy is used alone. Chronic and heavy use of Ecstasy can lead to the development of sleep disorders, confusion, memory loss, attention deficits, chronically elevated levels of anxiety, and aggressive and impulsive behavior. Clearly, critical thinking processes and judgment are impaired. Serotonin depletion (reduction of an essential neurotransmitter) can account for long-term behavioral changes. *See also*: **Gammahydroxybutyrate (GHB)**; **Ketamine**; **Sexual Assault, Drug-Facilitated**.

Suggested Reading: Club Drugs.org, http://www.clubdrugs.org; Ronald Hitzler, "Pill Kick: The Pursuit of 'Ecstasy' at Techno-events," *Journal of Drug Issues* 32 (2002): 459–466; Susan J. Landers, "Club Drugs More Agony Than Ecstasy for Young People," *American Medical News* 44 (2001): 39–42; Partnership for a Drug-Free America, http://www. drugfreeamerica.org; Dori Rogers, "Ecstasy Overdose," *Nursing* 32 (2002): 112–117; Substance Abuse and Mental Health Services Administration's National Clearinghouse on Alcohol and Drug Information, http://www.health.org; Brian Vastag, "Ecstasy Experts Want Realistic Messages," *Journal of the American Medical Association* 286 (2001): 777–780.

JUDITH A. WATERS AND SHARON A. DROZDOWSKI

EJACULATION. Technically, ejaculation in males is the expulsion of seminal fluid out of the urethra during sexual climax. It is a rather complex process requiring the coordination of glands and muscles with activation from the brain and spinal chord. Orgasm occurs in two stages. Immediately prior to ejaculation, the various components of semen are expelled from the seminal vesicles and prostate into the posterior urethra near the prostate. As the seminal fluids collect, the urethra expands, and males have a feeling they are about to ejaculate; some do have premature ejaculation at this time, but the semen is not yet present in the urethra.

The second stage, ejaculation, involves two sphincters. The urethral sphincter between the urethra and the bladder contracts to seal off entrance to the bladder, keeping urine from mixing with semen and preventing semen from flowing into the bladder. The external sphincter relaxes, permitting the semen to be propelled by the contraction of smooth muscles in the urethra and of striated muscles in the pelvic floor with the other seminal fluids through the urethral opening in the penis in a series of four or five spurts, at intervals of eight-tenths of a second, with decreasing force. If the ejaculation takes place into free space, it might be propelled half a yard or so from the body.

This is then followed in males by a refractory period, during which for most males further erotic stimulation provokes no response. The length of this period varies according to the individual, usually between 30 and 90 minutes, but a small minority can have multiple orgasms since they do not experience the typical refractory period.

Some females also ejaculate, although there is considerable debate among experts over the extent and what constitutes the ejaculate. As with males the ejaculate is discharged from the urethra, sometimes with sufficient force to propel it away from the human body. There seem to be two kinds. One, a low-volume opalescent fluid (about a teaspoon), appears to be a secretion from the paraurethral or Skene's glands, homologous to the male prostate, and has prostatic acid phosphatase, a chemical believed previously to be secreted only by the male prostate gland. The high-volume secretion is more controversial and seems more likely to be urine. Regardless of what it might be, some studies have shown that as many as 40 percent of females report experiencing such ejaculation. Females do not experience the refractory period that males do.

In cases of rape, semen collected from the female's vagina or the anus of either sex can be analyzed for DNA and help in apprehension of the criminal. For this reason, some rapists are now using condoms to prevent analysis. *See also*: **DNA Collection and Evidence.**

Suggested Reading: F. Addiego, E. Belzer, J. Comoli, W. Moger, J. Perry, and B. Whipple, "Female Ejaculation: A Case Study," *Journal of Sex Research* 17 (1981): 13–21; E. Belzer, B. Whipple, and W. Moger, "A Female Ejaculation," *Journal of Sex Research* 20 (1984): 403–406; A.K. Ladas, B. Whipple, and J.D. Perry, *The G Spot and Other Recent Discoveries about Human Sexuality* (New York: Rinehart & Winston, 1982); William H. Masters and Virginia Johnson, *Human Sexual Response* (Boston: Little, Brown, 1966).

VERN L. BULLOUGH

ELDERLY VICTIMS. *See* Victims.

ESTRICH, SUSAN. *See Real Rape.*

ETHNIC CLEANSING. Although the practice is centuries old, ethnic cleansing as a phenomenon came into its own during the waning years of the twentieth century. The term *ethnic cleansing* is a literal translation of the Serbo-Croatian term *etnicko ciscenje* and has become synonymous with the term **genocide.** Ethnic cleansing is defined as when one ethnic group expels members of other ethnic groups from a geographic area in order to create ethnically pure enclaves for members of their ethnic group. During this involuntary displacement of people groups, often the members of the displaced group are savagely raped and tortured in a systematic fashion.

If there was an archetypal model for ethnic cleansing, then it would stem from the example of the Nazi experience during the Third Reich. In an effort to create *Lebensraum,* or "living space," Adolf Hitler began an expansionist drive to create a greater Germany during his reign of terror. Based on a platform of racial superiority, Hitler promoted the notion of the German people as the embodiment of the Aryan race. As such, he allowed Dr. Josef Mengele to conduct eugenics experiments on those he deemed racially inferior. During the eugenics experiments, German officers would forceably rape young women in order to breed a new super race. Countless women were used as breeding tools for the Third Reich, in addition to enduring the horrors of the concentration camps before the implementation of Hitler's "Final Solution" in which Hitler would authorize the extermination of 6 million Jews. The end of World War II saw the end of the Nazi eugenics experiments, but not of the ideas of ethnic cleansing.

The geopolitical landscape saw dramatic changes in the 50 years following World War II. During the Cold War, ethnic tensions that had been fueled by centuries of turmoil were quelled under the boots of dictators. One such dictator was Marshall Josip Broz Tito, who held Yugoslavia's ethnically diverse communities together under an iron fist. After his death and the subsequent collapse of the Soviet Union, Slobodan Milosevic emerged as the president of Serbia. Under Milosevic's reign, Serbia began a campaign for expansion into the region of the former Yugoslavia known as Kosovo. Like their counterparts in the Rwandan genocide of Tutsis, Serbian forces marched across the former Yugoslavia washed in the blood of dead Muslims and Albanians. Milosevic's forces ordered one of the bloodiest massacres of civilians in Srebrenica, which left over 7,000 dead and countless others victims of rape and **torture**. The North Atlantic Treaty Organization (NATO) and UN peacekeepers ended the violence and created the International Criminal Tribunal for the former Yugoslavia (ICTY) to prosecute members of the Serbian forces who engaged in rape, genocide and other **war crimes**. As of March 2004, Milosevic was among those facing the tribunal. *See also*: **Bosnia-Herzegovina; Nazis.**

Suggested Reading: *Erasing History: Ethnic Cleansing in Kosovo*, report released by the U.S. Department of State, Washington, DC, May 1999, http://www.state.gov/www/regions/eur/rpt_9905_ethnic_ksvo_toc.html; International Criminal Tribunal for the former Yugoslavia Web site, http://www.un.org/icty/; Stefan Kühl, *The Nazi Connection: Eugenics, American Racism, and German National Socialism* (Oxford: Oxford University Press, 2002); Drazen Petrovic, "Ethnic Cleansing—An Attempt at Methodology," *European Journal of International Law* 5.3 (1994), http://www.ejil.org/journal/Vol5/No3/art3.html.

OJAN ARYANFARD

EVIDENCE. *See* DNA Collection and Evidence; Rules of Evidence.

F

FAIRY TALES. Children receive early lessons on **gender roles** through reading and listening to fairy tales. The cultural construction of gender, as seen through Western fairy tales, emphasizes female obedience and passivity. When characters deviate from these ideals, they invariably receive some sort of punishment. On the surface, these stories appear to simply reflect the perceived gender roles of earlier centuries; however, the tales have a deeper meaning when examined through the lens of sexuality. In this context, fairy tales indicate acceptance of male sexual aggression, including rape, and place the burden of chastity solely on women.

Although modern-day readers usually think of fairy tales as stories designed for children, the original versions of such tales as Little Red Riding Hood were written to amuse adults and instruct those approaching adulthood. Charles Perrault's *Tales of Times Past with Morals* (1697) includes such stories as Little Red Riding Hood, Cinderella, Sleeping Beauty, and Tom Thumb. These tales are filled with allusions to life in the court of Louis XIV, and they are told in the style that was fashionable in the popular salons of the time. Educated readers then would have understood the story of Little Red Riding Hood, for example, to be a sexual parable warning young women to guard their virtue—vitally important during this time because a prospective bride's bad sexual reputation could jettison the plans for a wedding. Since fortunes were made and status acquired through marriages arranged by parents, a young woman had to remain chaste, even when a charming "wolf" sweet-talked her. In Perrault's version of the story, the pretty young woman with the red hood undresses and gets into bed with the wolf who is disguised as her grandmother. The wolf, who has already eaten the grandmother, climbs on top of Little Red Riding Hood and eats her, too. It has been noted that when a young woman lost her virginity, the popular slang phrase of the time was "She'd seen the wolf." Thus, Perrault made the point that young women must guard and protect their chastity very clear to his readers. In case the message still was not clear, an illustration showed the wolf climbing on top of a young woman—not a child—who is in a bed and who is reaching up to touch his snout.

By the nineteenth century when the Brothers Grimm published their adaptation of the story, Little Red Riding Hood had become a willfully disobedient child who ignored her mother's instructions and gave in to her desire to explore the woods. Again, the wolf eats the girl, but this time she bears even more responsibility for her "rape" because she disobeyed her mother's orders to stay on the path. The transformation of Red Riding Hood from a naive girl to a disobedient child governed by passions is indicative of changes in perceptions of gender that occurred during the nineteenth century. Fairy tales of the nineteenth century emphasize the need for order and for strong morals; as middle-class women spent more time unsupervised in public spaces, authors felt the need to inculcate the values of obedience and chastity, lest women fall prey to "wolves" in the guise of men.

Perrault would not have considered Little Red Riding Hood to be a story of rape because at the time his book was published, rape was not a crime against the woman who was raped but rather a crime against her father. In both the Perrault and the Grimm Brothers versions, however, Little Red Riding Hood did not conform to appropriate female standards. Therefore, she was responsible for what happened to her. In this way, it is similar to still widely held **rape myths** in which women who talk to strangers or who go out alone and unprotected are often said to be "asking for it."

As well as promoting the concept that women should be obedient and take responsibility for keeping their virtue intact, the most popular Western fairy tales portray ideal women as beautiful and completely passive—and in need of men to rescue them. Sleeping Beauty and Snow White both sleep until their princes awaken them. Cinderella is treated like a slave by her stepmother until she meets her prince. These fairy tales, and others like them, have entrenched in the cultural consciousness a patriarchal perspective on female sexuality and the dangers of female autonomy. Acceptance of male dominance and fear of female sexuality pervade the tales and perpetuate the notion that female sexuality must be guarded or else violence and chaos will ensue. However, fairy tales are changeable and adapt to the times and cultures in which they are being told. Contemporary versions of fairy tales include strong heroines who are capable of saving themselves, sexy women who *want* to attract wolves, and even stars of pornographic films. *See also*: **Literature, World and American**; **Mythology**.

Suggested Reading: Catherine Orenstein, *Little Red Riding Hood Uncloaked: Sex, Morality, and the Evolution of a Fairy Tale* (New York: Basic Books, 2002); Jack Zipes, *The Trials and Tribulations of Little Red Riding Hood* (South Hadley, MA: Bergin & Garvey, 1983).

CATHERINE MAYBREY AND MERRIL D. SMITH

FAMILY. The family of a rape **survivor**, friends, and coworkers are often referred to as co-survivors because they themselves are affected and not infrequently deeply traumatized by a **sexual assault**. But despite the shock the family inevitably experiences, they should bear in mind that they constitute an essential factor in the recovery process, and they are invested with a role and power to help the rape **victim** overcome the trauma. Being aware of the role of the family in supporting a rape victim is all the more important in light of what **rape statistics** seem to indicate—everybody should be prepared to face, at some point, the need to show compassion and offer help to a rape victim, whether a family member, friend, or a colleague.

Rape victims are driven by a diffident hope of understanding, and the decision to turn for support in such a critical situation is painful enough in itself. This makes the victim especially vulnerable, and family members to whom a rape survivor reaches out for help are entrusted with a responsibility to offer compassion, rather than succumbing to myths about the victim's behavior and blaming her for the incident. Victimizing a survivor further is not only downright irrational, but it cruelly aggravates an already dramatic situation and intensifies the victim's sense of helplessness. Moreover, offering support is more than a merely tacit responsibility of a healthy and loving family. This expectation, at least with regard to children, is addressed by documents issued during international conferences on population and development, which shape UN policies. The Cairo +5 Conference declaration (1999) comprehensively underscores "the central role of families . . . in educating their children and shaping their attitudes . . . to enable them to make responsible and informed choices and decisions regarding their sexual and reproductive health needs."

The powers of kinship make family members capable of significantly relieving the victim in a number of ways, and some approaches that the family is recommended to take in crisis situations are uncontroversial and undoubtedly beneficial for both the victim and co-victims. Being concerned listeners and allowing the victim to share the grief makes it possible to break the barriers of isolation and helplessness that haunt the victim after an assault. This, in turn, is an important step toward overcoming the devastating fear of the perpetrator that persists as a result of the violence or the threat of violence used in a rape. As some experts point out, to help a victim cope with fear, the family should emphasize and be grateful for the very fact that a raped person survived the assault, because it is a sign of the victim's brave and sensible behavior. Finally, on the formal level, the family proves an invaluable support in court when the victim decides to press charges.

Family can also be the environment responsible for sexual assaults. But because spouses accused of **marital rape** claim the intercourse in question was consensual, it is hard to obtain reliable statistics on rape within the family. Spousal rape is not any less grave than sexual assaults on nonrelatives. An especially serious offense within the family is sex forced on children—in addition to sexual assaults by parents or siblings being prohibited by law as incestuous, they have a traumatic effect on the child's psyche. *See also*: **Incest; Stigma.**

Suggested Reading: *Key Actions for the Further Implementation of the Programme of Action of the International Conference on Population and Development* (Cairo +5) (1999), http://www.un.org/documents/ecosoc/cn9/1999/ecn91999pc-crp/rev1.pdf; R. Levine, *When You Are the Partner of a Rape or Incest Survivor: A Workbook for You* (San Jose, CA: Resource Publications, 1996); Alan W. McEvoy and Jeff B. Brookings, *If She Is Raped: A Guidebook for Husbands, Fathers, and Male Friends* (Holmes Beach, FL: Learning Publications, 1991).

KONRAD SZCZESNIAK

FANTASIES. Fantasies are imaginary projections, oftentimes involving hidden desires or fears. They are part of the workings of the human mind and find expression in cultural practices such as **literature** and film. In their revision of psychoanalysis and sexology, feminist critics in the 1970s engaged various forms and functions of sexual fantasies, focusing on the problematic use of the term *rape fantasy*. Likewise, female authors of the time produced narratives of rape-revenge or fictions that involve rape fantasies. Both feminist thinkers and female authors insisted that just as male **castration** anxieties do not suggest that men wish to be castrated, so-called rape fantasies do not prove that women crave sexual violation. Arguing that men, not women, entertain rape fantasies in order to legitimate the aggression that culture deems inherent to male sexuality, feminists also acknowledged that women's sexual fantasies frequently involve a dynamic of domination and submission. However, these fantasies need to be seen as products of a historically grown discourse on sexuality that has tended to project women's sexual desire in contexts of sexual violence, thereby suggesting that women enjoy such aggression.

Locating a fundamental gender difference in male activity versus female passivity, psychoanalyst **Sigmund Freud** identified sadism and mastery with masculinity, masochism and submission with femininity. His beliefs were reinforced by **Helene Deutsch**'s *The Psychology of Women* (1944), which takes masochism as a key to female character and assigns fantasies about rape and **prostitution** a pivotal place in women's psyche. Deutsch's claim that female libido and pain are interdependent has been refuted by sexologist **Alfred Kinsey**'s studies on female sexuality as well as by psychoanalyst Karen Horney. Horney did not doubt that women fantasize rape but argued that such fantasies are a product of traditional female acculturation rather than a symptom of some essential aspect of femininity and female desire. Along with Horney, psychoanalyst Wilhelm Reich furthermore assumed that rape fantasies function as a means to diminish women's guilt feelings with regard to their sexual desires and practices. Such views reflect traditional assumptions about female sexuality and attest to the interdependent cultural construction of sexuality and sexual violence. Since women have always remained marginal to the construction of sexuality, any attempt to enter into the struggle over sexual definition, be it by way of women's **pornography** or rape fantasy fictions, involves interrogations of traditional gender identities, sexualities, and power relations. *See also*: **Rape Myths**.

Suggested Reading: Margaret Atwood, "Rape Fantasies," in *Dancing Girls and Other Stories* (Toronto: McClelland and Stewart, 1977), 101–110; Molly Haskell, "The 2000-Year-Old Misunderstanding: Rape Fantasy," *Ms.* (November 1976): 84–86, 92–98.

SABINE SIELKE

FEMINIST MOVEMENT. The feminist movement can claim political roots that stretch back many years. During the twentieth century, the political impact of the feminist movement has been significant, for example, in the United Kingdom in relation to women's right to vote in elections. The feminist influence on how we understand rape is a key factor in understanding how we conceptualize the phenomenon of rape, both in academic and popular arenas. This influence stems largely from the developments in feminism from the 1970s onward.

Prior to the 1970s, rape as a political issue was largely ignored. Those interested in the problems of society (such as Karl Marx or **Sigmund Freud**) had little to say about the position of women in general or about the sexual abuse of women by men in particular. The 1970s can be considered a kind of watershed in how we understood society, as there was a change in how those in advanced industrialized nations (such as the United States and the United Kingdom) understood themselves in relation to society. Up until the late 1960s and 1970s, explanations for the social aspects of life tended to be restricted to traditional understandings of the political Left (collectivists) and the political Right (individualists). From the late 1960s and 1970s onward, more critical social understandings began to emerge. The earliest radical perspectives to emerge were those related to social class and ethnicity. Following these, feminism emerged in the early 1970s and demonstrated that society is patriarchal. Or in other words, our social culture is structured in a way that gives men more power than women, resulting in the oppression of women by men. The feminist movement built up and continues to hold a significant degree of political influence. It aims to draw attention to social issues that impact on women's lives, such as health care, reproduction, and the environment. One of the most important issues that feminism has commented on consistently since the 1970s is the issue of sexual violence.

Anne Edwards, a contemporary feminist academic, describes the feminist movement's attitude toward male sexual violence during the 1970s as "two-wave." In the earlier half of the 1970s, rape was seen as a separate issue from other forms of men's abuse of women. Rape was perceived as playing a relatively minor role in women's oppression, in comparison to the influence that male control of social institutions (such as education) had on women's lives. A culture of victim blaming was common, and a main priority for the feminist movement was to highlight that rape was men's responsibility. But during the 1970s the feminist perspective on sexual violence developed. In the later period, rape became understood as just one example of the general pattern of male abuse of women, and ideas of what rape actually is changed. Violent rape was still the focus, but it was not seen as the only manifestation of sexual violence. Some feminists argued that heterosexual sex itself was an abusive, male-controlled political institution. The argument behind this view is that rape exists where women do not give **consent** to intercourse. If women live in a male-controlled society, then they are not able to give free consent. Therefore, if women are not able to consent, all heterosexual sex can be considered a violation. This viewpoint that all heterosexual sex is violative is not supported by all feminists, and there has been continued debate about the issue (not least by feminists who happen to be happy as heterosexuals). But the point remains an important one for those interested in understanding rape, because it was at this point that rape stopped being seen as an unusual phenomenon. Rape came to be seen as only one aspect of a broader and everyday pattern of male violence toward women.

Since the 1970s, feminism has had a significant impact on how we understand what rape is and how best to deal with this social problem. The contribution of individual feminists varies because the feminist perspective incorporates so many other political perspectives. Within the feminist movement, one may encounter liberal feminists, radical feminists, Marxist feminists, and poststructural feminists, to name but a few. Feminists have one common interest: the ways that women are systematically oppressed by a patriarchal society and the impact of this oppression on women's lives. But the debates within feminism are often as fierce as those between feminists and their detractors. Indeed, one of the reasons why the feminist perspective is so useful is that feminist ideas emerge from conflict and debate, which means that their explanations tend to be very thorough and well tested.

The feminist perspective has unintentionally dominated both popular and academic discussions of rape and **sexual assault**—compared to the mainstream, feminists have found rape a more interesting topic and therefore have discussed this topic more than anyone else. Without the feminist perspective, we would have a more limited understanding of the social context of sexual assault. Feminism identified rape as a blind spot in our understandings of society and has brought this issue to our attention. However, the feminist movement has its own blind spot. Now that rape has been firmly established on the political agenda, it is possible to look more critically at how feminism has helped us to understand rape. Many within the feminist perspective appear to be unconditionally committed to the idea of masculinity as always problematic and to the idea that sexual violence is by definition a thing that men do to women. Topics such as **domestic violence** between lesbian partners and **male rape** pose significant problems for the feminist perspective, which have yet to be resolved. *See also*: **National Organization for Women (NOW); Patriarchy; Rape History in the United States: Twentieth Century.**

Suggested Reading: Anne Edwards, "Male Violence in Feminist Theory: An Analysis of the Changing Conceptions of Sex/Gender Violence and Male Dominance," in *Women, Violence and Social Control*, ed. J. Hanmer and M. Maynard (London: Macmillan, 1990), 13–29; C. Smart, "Feminist Approaches to Criminology or Postmodern Woman Meets Atavistic Man," in *Feminist Perspectives in Criminology*, ed. L. Gelsthorpe and A. Morris (Bristol: Open University Press, 1992), 70–84.

RUTH GRAHAM

FILMS, FOREIGN. One of the earliest films to depict a rape was Spanish director Luis Buñuel's first short film, *Un chien andalou* (An Andalusian Dog, 1929), a 20-minute surrealist essay co-scripted with his friend, the artist Salvador Dali. The movie was an avant-garde essay about desire, love, and death. The first scenes are shocking: a woman's eye is cut with a knife, and then a man who cannot control his desire assaults that same woman. In another 1920s film, the woman was the aggressor. *Asphalt* (1928) was a silent movie directed by German filmmaker Joe May. In this film, a woman seduces a policeman and forces him to love her physically.

Rape began to be shown more explicitly and violently in the 1960s. Swedish filmmaker Ingmar Bergman's *Virgin Spring* (1960) adapted a legend from the fourteenth century about a spring that emerged where a young girl was raped and killed. The **victim**'s father gets revenge by killing the three brothers who committed the crime. Polish director Roman Polanski's first English-language movie, *Repulsion* (1965), starred Catherine Deneuve as a young woman alone in an apartment, haunted by a repetitive vision of her own rape by an unknown hidden man. It is unclear what part is reality or phantasm. Polanski's psychological horror movie illustrates the common feeling of being observed by somebody who is waiting to attack when you are most vulnerable.

In Luchino Visconti's *The Damned* (1969), a young Nazi opportunist, played by Helmut Berger, forces his mother to make love to him. Visconti's violent but melodramatic film depicts the rise of fascism through one morally corrupt **family**. Stanley Kubrick's *A Clockwork Orange* (1971) takes a comic approach to an extremely violent rape scene. In *Last Tango in Paris* (1972), Italian director Bernardo Bertolucci shows a woman (Maria Schneider) raped twice in an empty apartment by an aging Marlon Brando; she seems to more or less accept the situation. In this unconventional movie, rape is shown as the beginning of a perverse relationship.

In *Salo: The 120 Days of Sodom* (freely adapted from Sade), Italian director Pier Paolo Pasolini shows an institutional ritual of rape made by fascists during World War II; for Pasolini, it was a way to show that only the most perverse and powerful fascists could **torture** and rape in a purely sadistic way.

Although German filmmakers have also made films about the Holocaust or fascism that include scenes of rape, such as *The Tin Drum* (directed by Volker Schlondorff in 1982, from Günther Grass's novel), in which there are two violent rape scenes, there are many movies by German filmmakers that are not Holocaust related but that do include rape scenes. For example, a mysterious and unusual movie directed by Eric Rohmer from a novel by Heinrich von Kleist, *The Marquise von O* (The Marquise of O, 1976), involves an eighteenth-century widow who becomes pregnant for no possible reason. She publishes an add in a local newspaper, asking for the father to acknowledge and present himself. We learn at the very end of the movie that a soldier raped the woman while she was unconscious, during a battle in the Russian war.

Some films have focused on the rape of children. The 1931 movie *M* by Fritz Lang is an intense story of a serial killer who seduced, raped, and killed young girls. The police cannot find him; it is the mafia and beggars who ultimately hunt him down. In Luis Buñuel's film, adapted from Octave Mirbeau's novel *Journal d'une femme de chambre* (Diary of a Chambermaid, 1964), Buñuel indicates in an almost poetic, though tragic, fashion that a child was raped and killed. The director does not show the violent scene, but indicates it occurred by showing snails moving on the girl's motionless body, isolated in the woods.

There are many other French films that include rape scenes. A French film made by Walérian Borowzyk, *Immoral Tales* (Contes immoraux, 1974), explores the violent mix of eroticism and rape and had huge success. In an obscure thriller, *Catherine et compagnie* (Catherine and Company, dir. Michel Boisrond, 1975), Jane Birkin rapes a man tied in his bed. In *La Dérobade* (The Evasion, dir. Daniel Duval, from Jeanne Cordelier's novel, 1979), a film about **prostitution**, hookers are often raped. But the French film that raised many questions was *L'amour violé* (Love Violates, dir. Yannick Bellon, 1977), in which a sometimes emotionless woman tries to identify one of the four men who raped her and calls the police. The theme of revenge is also present in French blockbuster *L'Été meurtrier* (One Deadly Summer, dir. Jean Becker, 1983), where a young and sexy woman tries to find the man who raped her mother, in other words, her biological father. A controversial French film that was banned in France, *Baise Moi* (Rape Me, 2000) is a violent and provocative film by Virginie Despentes. It depicted many rape scenes where sometimes men were victims of dangerous and murderous women.

In contrast, some Canadian films have shown rape scenes in an almost casual way. *The Rape of a Sweet Young Girl* (Le Viol d'une jeune fille douce, dir. Gilles Carle, 1968) depicts a collective rape shown almost as a joke; so the same thing goes in *Taureau* (Bull, dir. Clément Perron, 1973) and *Gina* (dir. Denys Arcand, 1975). But another Canadian movie, produced by the National Film Board (NFB) of Canada, *Mourir à tue-tête* (A Scream from Silence, 1978), by Anne-Claire Poirier, is a mix of deconstructive fiction and documentary about a nurse who is raped by an unknown man. The individual story becomes generalized in the film's second half. The director explains that there is always a **secondary rape**, made by policemen, physicians, husbands, and friends who ask for details. The film also gives a universal portrait of rape and brutalization of women through countries, civilizations, and ages, including mutilations made to young girls in African countries. Although it contains some generalizations about men ("Any man in the crowd could be a rapist"), this radical movie remains among the best of all movies about rape.

Male rape of both men and boys has been portrayed in a number of Canadian films. For example, in the Canadian drama *Night Zoo* (dir. Jean-Claude Lauzon, 1987), a prisoner is raped by another man. In 1992, a controversial movie and miniseries *The Boys from St Vincent* (by John N. Smith) told the true story of young boys who were sexually abused in a Newfoundland orphanage during the 1950s. The film was released at the time when the case was in court.

Wartime rape has also been a theme for Canadian filmmakers. Atom Egoyan, for example, shows rape as a crime of war in his recent *Ararat* (2001), a movie about the Armenian **genocide** by the Turkish army. Documentaries, too, explore wartime rape. *Nés de la haine* (Born of Hatred, 2002) is a Canadian film directed by Raymonde Provencher. It is about the thousands of women who were raped during recent conflicts in **Bosnia-Hergezovina**, the Balkans, or Rwanda and who consequently gave birth to children.

Directors from all over the world have made films about rape. *Bandit Queen* (1994), a film by Shekar Kapur, is a less-than-accurate portrayal of the life of Phoolan Devi, India's real Bandit Queen. It is filled with rape scenes beginning with the rape of Devi as a child bride. Spanish director Pedro Almodovar has included rape scenes in several of his films. In *Pepi, Luci, Bom* (1980) a woman seeks revenge on her rapist. In his film *Kika* (1993), a woman is raped by an actor, and the scene is aired on Spanish TV as a weird reality show. In *Talk to Her* (2002), a hospital attendant takes care of a young woman who is in a coma. He rapes her, and when the child is born, the mother awakes. This controversial story raises the question: Did rape cure the comatose woman?

Having to face new issues and forms of censorship, feature films show the levels of violence that a society (audiences and censors) can tolerate in the representation of rape. *See also*: **Film, U.S.; Literature, World and American; Pornography.**

Suggested Reading: Derek Jones, ed., *Censorship: A World Encyclopedia*, 4 vols. (Chicago: Fitzroy Dearborn Publishers, 2001); Anton Kaes, *M* (London: British Film Institute, 2000); André Loiselle, *Mourir à tue-tête* (A Scream from Silence) (Trowbridge, Wiltshire, England: Flicks Books, 2000).

YVES LABERGE

FILMS, U.S. Since the beginning of film history, American movies have included scenes of rape and sexual violence. An early example from the silent era can be seen in D.W. Griffith's famous *Birth of a Nation* (1916). This movie, based on Thomas Dixon's novel *The Clansman*, includes a dramatic scene in which a beast-like black man is intent on raping a virginal white woman, depicting in visual form the fears of many white southerners during this time. Griffith portrays the Klansmen, who come to the young woman's rescue, as heroes, reflecting the views of many post-Reconstuction Southerners. However, many people rejected this view and protested the film. Oscar Micheaux made a daring response in *Within Our Gates* (1919), the first feature film directed by an **African American**. This movie tells the story of a black woman who is nearly raped by a white man, following the lynching of her parents.

Interracial rape is the focus of a number of American films. For example, Robert

Mulligan directed *To Kill a Mockingbird* (1962), with an Academy Award–winning screenplay by Horton Foote, based on Harper Lee's Pulitzer Prize–winning novel about race relations in a small southern town. Atticus Finch, played by Gregory Peck, defends a black man accused of raping a white woman. In the more recent film, *A Time to Kill* (1996), directed by Joel Schmacher and based on a John Grisham book, rape, race relations, and the courtroom once again intersect, as a white lawyer defends a black man who tried to gain revenge after two white men raped his daughter.

The degree to which an American film could show, or even allude to, rape, interracial or not, has varied depending on when it was filmed. The Hollywood scandals of the 1920s, followed by the introduction of "talkies," led to the censorship of movies by state censorship boards. The Movie Production Code, first adopted in 1930, was seen as a way that movie studios could self-police their work. It outlined strict prohibitions against showing nudity or anything that might be considered "immoral." Nevertheless, many movies slipped by the code in the early 1930s. One of these was *The Story of Temple Drake* (1933), the film version of William Faulkner's controversial novel *Sanctuary*. Temple Drake is a promiscuous woman, the daughter of a Southern judge. She is picked up, then kidnapped by the leader of a gang of gangsters. After he rapes her, she kills him. Temple Drake later confesses to the murder and admits that she enjoyed the rape. After 1934, few movies such as this were made for the next couple decades. Pressure from religious leaders and the threat of federal censorship forced movie studios to enforce the Production Code, also known as the Hays Code, from William H. Hays (1879–1954), who cowrote these rules. However, by the 1960s, the social climate had changed, the Production Code was no longer being enforced, and it was eventually replaced with the movie rating system.

In the 1960s and 1970s, several U.S. films depicted brutal rapes. *Straw Dogs* (1971), a film by Sam Peckinpah, is filled with graphic violence. It aims to portray the violence lurking just beneath the surface of civilization. The film is set in Cornwall, where an American professor has settled with his British-born wife to escape the conflicts of U.S. society. After a series of menacing actions, the town bullies eventually **gang rape** his wife. James Boorman's *Deliverance* (1972) also questions the idea of what lies just beyond civilized society and people. The plot concerns four men who decide to take a break from city life to canoe down a river in the backwoods of Georgia. In addition to its famous "Dueling Banjoes" music, the film is often remembered for its brutal scene in which two of the men are attacked by backwoodsmen, and one of them is raped.

Although made in 1989, Brian De Palma's *Casualties of War* also looks at this time of upheaval in American society. However, he examines the war in Vietnam. The movie focuses on the gang rape of young Vietnamese women by American soldiers and the aftermath of **war crimes**.

Also in the 1980s, director David Lynch explored what lies beneath the veneer of middle-class American society. In the disturbing *Blue Velvet* (1986), Lynch probed at the horrors lurking underneath the surface of the quintessential American town, which includes rape, sadomasochism, and sexual compulsion. These are themes he later developed in his television series *Twin Peaks* (1990–1991).

As the **feminist movement** moved rape into public discourse, some movies began to look more closely at the **victims** and **survivors** of rape. *The Accused* (1988), based on a true story of a gang rape, examines how women are often accused of "asking to be raped," because they dress a certain way or dare to be in a particular place. There were also films in which women sought revenge on their attackers, such as *Extremities* (1986) and *Thelma and Louise* (1991). More recently, *Boys Don't Cry* (1999) recounts the true-life story of Brandon Teena (born Teena Brandon), who was born female but lived life as a male and was beaten, raped, and ultimately murdered when her secret was discovered. *See also*: **Films, Foreign; Literature, World and American; Popular Culture; Southern Rape Complex.**

Suggested Reading: Matthew Bernstein, ed., *Controlling Hollywood: Censorship and Regulation in the Studio Era* (New Brunswick, NJ: Rutgers University Press, 1999); Susan Brownmiller, *Against Our Will: Men, Women and Rape* (New York: Fawcett Columbine, 1975); Ruth Petrie, ed., *Film and Censorship: The Index Reader* (London: Cassell, 1997).

YVES LABERGE AND MERRIL D. SMITH

FORCIBLE RAPE. Forcible rape is the "carnal knowledge of a female forcibly and against her will. Assaults or attempts to commit rape by force or threat of force are included; however, **statutory rape** (without force) and other sex offenses are excluded." This 2001 definition by the FBI Uniform Crime Reporting Program also excludes **male rape.** Other sources that have recognized that rape is not only male to female have broadened their definitions to include adult males and children of both sexes. A Missouri sexual offense statute states "a person commits the crime of forcible rape if such person has sexual intercourse with another person by the use of forcible compulsion. Forcible compulsion includes the use of a substance administered without a victim's knowledge or **consent** which renders the victim physically or mentally impaired so as to be incapable of making an informed consent to sexual intercourse."

The question of force is problematic because the threat of harm is strong enough to frighten the victim into acceding without physical resistance. In the case of statutory rape, even if the minor gives consent, it is not acceptable under the law. The age of consent differs from state to state and ranges from 12 to 18. Sexual intercourse with a person who is mentally deficient, unconscious, or incapable of giving consent is also sometimes considered statutory rape.

The word *force* and the term *without her consent* have been written into certain laws, but the boundaries are fuzzy because definitions vary. In one study, a distinction was made between forcible rape and rapes where girls were seduced first and then attacked (Amir). Force can be used at any stage in a rape, from a logistical advantage such as ambush to overt aggression if a perpetrator does not obtain verbal consent. Unlike any other crime, in forcible rape, the burden is on the victim to prove it occurred.

It is estimated that in 1998, 67 of every 100,000 females in the country were reported rape victims; however, it was also estimated that only 1 in 10 rapes was reported (Ruth, 233). From that information, one can conclude that validity and reliability of statistics are confusing at best. Although national statistics include assault and attempts, other studies only count rapes that were completed. Other reasons for underreporting are that the victim fears future attacks or publication of her identity. In certain crimes where there are multiple offenses, forced rape occurrences are included.

Because male rape most frequently occurs in prison populations or in other male populations, such as male religious orders, it has been downplayed. Male rape within prisons, if reported, is classified as either assault or sexual offense. The victims of priests and members of the **clergy** have been silent because frequently they are so young and shamed that they do not understand what has happened or are afraid to report the abuse. Sometimes they wait a lifetime before reporting it. In addition, until recently, the church has failed to rid itself of perpetrators by refusing to accept complaints. *See also*: **Rape, Definitions of; Rape Law; Rape Statistics; Sexual Assault.**

Suggested Reading: Menachim Amir, *Patterns in Forcible Rape* (Chicago: University of Chicago Press, 1971); Susan Brownmiller, *Against Our Will: Men, Women and Rape* (New York: Bantam, 1976); FBI Uniform Crime Report 2001, http://www.fbi.gov/ucr/cius_00/00crime2_4.pdf; Missouri House Bill 1656, http://www.house.state.mo.us/pr/Monitor/Archive2002/Mon4-25.doc/; Sheila Ruth, *Women's Personal Lives: The Effects of Sexism on Self and Relationships in Issues in Feminism* (Mountain View, CA: Mayfield, 1995).

LANA THOMPSON

FOREIGN-OBJECT RAPE. Foreign-object rape refers to the placement of an object into the vaginal, rectal, oral, or other orifice of an individual. Examples abound in cinema and literature. In the movie *True Confessions* (dir. Ulu Grosbard, 1981), loosely based on the real-life "Black Dahlia" case, the rapist stuffs a church candle into a young girl's vagina after raping and killing her, following the making of a pornographic film. One extreme cinematic example occurs in *A Clockwork Orange* (dir. Stanley Kubrick, 1971) where a woman doing yoga in a leotard is attacked, then raped with a huge phallic sculpture. In the book *The Painted Bird*, written by Jerzy Kosinski in 1965, a Polish woman, severely traumatized as a result of **gang rape** when young, is known as "Stupid Ludmilla." She seduces a man who strikes and bites her. When a group of women witness the attack, instead of pulling him off, they attack her further and shove a bottle filled with cow manure into her vagina. When it will go no further, they kick it, shattering the glass inside her. A 1920s newsstory tells of an aspiring actress forced to suffer the sexual advances of a drunk, morbidly obese man. When he finds himself too intoxicated to complete the act, he rapes her with a wine bottle. She dies three days later from a ruptured bladder.

Fiction or nonfiction, these narratives are studied by psychologists and forensic psychiatrists in order to understand the motivation for, and provide an explanation for, such brutal behavior. According to collected statistics, it is fairly common. In one study of 418 victims, only four cases reported penetration with a foreign object, although 40 percent reported digital penetration (Grossin et al.). Some say that the object represents a virile penis for the perpetrator who would otherwise be impotent. Others explain that raping with objects further humiliates the victim while amplifying the power of the attacker. The choice of object could be opportunistic or symbolic. If the rape is followed by **murder**, the object, as part of the crime scene, can provide information about the perpetrator.

A variety of legal definitions abound in the United States with regard to foreign-object rape. In some states, rape with a foreign object is classified as **sexual assault**. In New York State, digital rape (using a finger) is included in the foreign-object definition. In Pennsylvania, foreign-object rape is considered deviate sexual intercourse. In Georgia, "aggravated sexual battery" is the name given to foreign-object rape.

Internationally, there is variation as well. The definition of rape in the Turkish code of law is extremely limited compared with definitions accepted in international humanitarian law. There, rape with a foreign object and forced **oral sex** are not defined as rape, and documented instances of sexual assault on women have included rape by high-pressure hoses.

Statistics are difficult to obtain with regard to rape with a foreign object. In one study done on 30 men classified as sexual sadists, foreign-object penetration was the least common sexual activity of the four studied (anal, forced fellatio, vaginal, and foreign-object). However, the majority of the men subjected their **victims** to three of the four acts (Hazelwood, Dietz, and Warren). The decision a victim makes to report rape with a foreign object, or assaults involving oral or digital sex, is difficult to make, just as reporting other types of rape varies with the victim's acknowledgment of the crime and motivation to undergo the stresses involved in the legal process. *See also*: **Glen Ridge (NJ) Rape Case.**

Suggested Reading: Amnesty International Australia, "Defending Women's Human Rights," http://www.amnesty.org.au/women/action-letter14.html; Cecile Grossin et al., "Analysis of 418 Cases of Sexual Assault," *Forensic Science International* 131 (2003): 125–130; Robert R. Hazelwood, Park Elliot Dietz, and Janet Warren, "The Criminal Sexual Sadist," *FBI Law Enforcement Bulletin* (February 1992); Arnold S. Kahn et al., "Calling It Rape: Differences in Experiences of Women Who Do or Do Not Label Their Sexual Assault as Rape," *Psychology of Women Quarterly* 27.3 (September 2003): 233–242; Jerzy Kosinski, *The Painted Bird* (Boston: Houghton Mifflin, 1965).

LANA THOMPSON

FRATERNITIES. Fraternities are societies that are open to male college students in Canada and the United States who are invited to join. These societies are often associated with certain forms of social behavior such as excessive secrecy and solidarity among members. Fraternities have been of some considerable interest to those researching rape, and rape in the context of college or university life is an important aspect of the phenomenon in general. It allows examination of a population that is perceived to be particularly vulnerable (on the part of female students) and particularly sexually predatory (on the part of male students). It also helps to understand that **sexual assault** is not simply an issue of disturbed individuals. Instead, rape can be seen as an extreme form of a more general pattern of (often gendered) sexual violence, which is supported by the more "everyday" aspects of social culture. Because of these issues, the growing tradition for studying U.S. college campus culture in the context of sexual assault is to be expected.

The interest in fraternities and rape indicates an interest in explaining why rape happens. Explanations for why rape happens vary. Some see rape as an issue of individual psychopathology, regarding rapists as relatively rare and as deviant from the normal psychology of the general population. Others see rape as not just the responsibility of the individuals involved but also as a reflection of our social or cultural values. In other words, the rapist's perspective or opinions are conceptualized as an extension of normal values, rather than as intrinsically different from the norm. Indeed, some argue that when rapists are asked about how they feel about their crimes, they often draw on everyday cultural beliefs to justify their sexual violence. For example, everyday beliefs about acceptable sexual behavior (such as women "leading men on") may be used to justify rape. These "**rape myths**" are sometimes used to explain why rape happens. They have important consequences for how **survivors** are perceived (and whether they as **victims** end up being seen as responsible for the rape) and for how rapists are dealt with when identified (for example, through "treatment/therapy" or punishment/penalty). Those who argue that social culture has a role to play in the causes of rape have therefore shown more interest in studying that social culture. The role that fraternities play in encouraging a culture of sexual violence is a topic that falls into this interest in the social aspects of rape.

The social culture associated with fraternities has been identified as problematic from a **rape prevention** perspective. This is because there are several key characteristics of fraternity culture that can be considered "rape supportive," such as secrecy, loyalty to the fraternity, and the established use of strategies to ensure sexual access to young women—for example, the strategic use of **alcohol** to make victims more willing to submit to sex or less able to resist rape. The incidences of rape that take place within this culture may vary, from a systematic **gang rape** to the more ambiguous **sexual coercion** in the context of dating. The important point is that all of these sexual abuses take place against a social backdrop that sees sexual coercion as acceptable, even desirable, masculine behavior. Contemporary researchers in this field, such as Martin and Hummer, have addressed this issue specifically. They have argued that campus fraternity culture encourages the overriding of ethical decision making and also encourages a commitment to a particularly competitive form of masculinity where women are seen as a sexual commodity. In addition to the analysis of fraternity social culture, there is also work on the "everyday" sexual coercive behavior in the college population, such as emotional blackmail. Again, this work appears to be associated with college populations in the United States. Both within and beyond the United States, college populations appear to hold the attention of those interested in discovering why rape happens. The question of why these populations hold such popularity is an interesting one and could help to open up the research agenda on rape to a more critical evaluation that is long overdue. *See also*: **Campus Rape; Rape, Causes of.**

Suggested Reading: J.A. Allison and L.S. Wrightsman, *Rape: The Misunderstood Crime* (Newbury Park, CA: Sage, 1993); P.Y. Martin and R.A. Hummer, "Fraternities and Rape on Campus," in *Violence against Women: The Bloody Footprints*, ed. P.B. Bart and E.G. Moran (Newbury Park, CA: Sage, 1993), 114–131; C.L. Muehlenhard and C.S. Rodgers, "Token Resistance to Sex: New Perspectives on an Old Stereotype," *Psychology of Women Quarterly*, 22.3 (1998): 443–463.

RUTH GRAHAM

FREE LOVE MOVEMENT. The free love movement was born from the historical shifts brought about by the industrial revolution and the rise of the middle class. Spanning more than a century, people of various intellectual backgrounds embraced the growing movement: utopian socialists, anarchists, feminists, and sex radicals. Beginning in the 1820s, free lovers embraced the idea that love should be the basis for sexual relations, not marriage and not reproduction. While free lovers experimented with different living arrangements and challenged restrictive laws, they also were the first to contemplate institutionalized rape.

Free lover advocates and writers such as Mary Nichols and Victoria Woodhull turned their attention to **marital rape**. Both were from New York City, representing the shifting opportunities that city life offered for women. Nichols emerged onto the free love scene in the 1840s and 1850s. Although married, she deserted and then divorced her first husband. While Nichols questioned the institution of marriage, she also turned her attention to sexual relations and marital rape. Nichols vehemently criticized violence against women that occurred in marriage because of the law. Men controlled their wives' properties. But they also controlled their bodies, since by law, men were entitled to sexual relations with their wives regardless of their wives' desires. Woodhull was a suffragist, but like Nichols, she was also a free love supporter. Like Nichols, Woodhull condemned the concept of wifely duty whereby husbands were entitled to have sex with their wives regardless of their wives' sexual and/or reproductive desires. In 1834, Woodhull wrote, "Of all the brutalities of the age, I know none so horrid as those sanctioned and defended by marriage. Night after night there are thousands of rapes committed" (Stern, 8).

Both Nichols and Woodhull recanted their free love ideas later in life. However, both women discussed and acknowledge a dirty little secret in **family** life and jurisprudence: the existence of marital rape. Their early writings served as a guide to future arguments regarding violence against women in the form of institutionalized rape in the home. *See also:* **Rape History in the United States: Nineteenth Century.**

Suggested Reading: Hal D. Sears, *The Sex Radicals: Free Love in High Victorian America* (Lawrence: Regents Press of Kansas, 1997); John C. Spurlock, *Free Love: Marriage and Middle Class Radicalism in America, 1825–1860* (New York: New York University Press, 1988); Madeline Stern, ed., *The Victoria Woodhull Reader* (Weston, MA: M&S Press, 1874).

ELAINE CAREY

FREUD, SIGMUND/FREUDIAN THEORY. Psychoanalyst Sigmund Freud (1856–1939) wrote little explicitly about rape. However, because psychoanalysis is fundamentally concerned with human desire and aggression, at least two arenas of Freud's work can be isolated in which sexual violence is a strong theme: his early discussion of "the **seduction** hypothesis" and his later attempts to apply psychoanalysis to society.

Freud began his career by working with hysterical patients in Vienna. In the late nineteenth century, hysteria was a commonly diagnosed illness. As the name, from the Greek word for "womb," suggests, most of those diagnosed with hysteria were female and exhibited a wide range of symptoms: tics, pains, anxiety, depression, fainting spells, coughing, and paralysis. The prevalent understanding of hysteria was that it was caused by some hereditary factor, but in the early 1890s Freud came to believe, on the basis of information given him by his patients, that it was caused by a trauma of childhood sexual abuse, usually by fathers. The memory of an early **sexual assault** would, in this view, be revived by an apparently innocent event, and in the effort to repress the traumatic memory, the hysterical patient would develop her symptoms. But, by 1897, Freud came to reject his "seduction hypothesis," believing instead that the stories of early sexual abuse his patients had told him were in large part fantasy.

This shift in Freud's work has been very controversial. Jeffrey Masson, a former project director of the Freud Archives in London, accused Freud of burying the truth about his patients' experiences of **incest** and assault for reasons of self-interest and career advancement. The recovered-memory movement followed Masson in seeing Freud's self-reversal as part of a cover-up of the pervasive problem of incest. Feminists have often agreed, arguing that rather than take seriously what his patients were telling him, Freud's post-1897 treatment of women patients reinforced cultural stereotypes of women as liars, especially when it came to rape and sexual assault.

Yet the case is complex. Freud never denied the existence of child sexual abuse; what he rejected was the idea that it was the cause of *all* instances of hysteria. At the same time, the stereotype that women's and girls' accounts of sexual abuse, especially incest, are "fantasy" or outright lies was certainly not challenged by Freud's retraction of the seduction hypothesis.

Freud never returned, in any depth, to actual instances of rape or sexual assault, but his later attempts to apply psychoanalysis to broad questions of culture and society allude to sexual violence in ways that, while not obvious, are nonetheless important. In *Totem and Taboo* (1913), he hypothesized about the founding of society by applying insights from psychoanalysis to nineteenth- and early-twentieth-century anthropological research. He supposed a primal tribe led by one all-powerful chieftain, who controls all the tribe's women. After the chieftain's envious sons unite to **murder** their father, they are consumed with guilt for their murderous act. As a result, they internalize the dead father's power to restrict and order their society. This installation of order in the tribe entails a form of monogamy because the sons recognize that, in order to keep from becoming rivals of one another and entering into another cycle of violence, the women must be distributed among them. For Freud, the key moment in this anthropological story was the parricide and the way in which the sons' guilt feelings lead to the institution of conscience and social order. Another important theme might be seen here: the "possession" of the tribe's women by a violent patriarch. The violence before the murder of the father is his violence toward the women of the tribe. In Freud's story, as is the case in many other stories in Western civilization, sexual violence functions as a foundational event that is later forgotten or occluded.

Freudian theory became influential in the middle of the twentieth century, affecting how sexuality, aggression, and women were understood by clinicians, criminologists, and the public. Some of Freud's theories were revolutionary, but his views on women and female sexuality were shaped by Victorian ideologies. Psychoanalysis gave the stamp of science to cultural stereotypes, often to the detriment of understandings of sexual violence. Freudian theory tended to associate femininity with passivity and masochism, contributing to victim blaming. In analyses of **sex offenders**, Freudians were led to blame overbearing mothers for men's violence, rather than examining other factors. In the 1970s, the feminist antirape movement criticized the detrimental impact Freudian thought had made on women and understandings of rape. *See also*: **Deutsch, Helene**.

Suggested Reading: Sigmund Freud, "The Aetiology of Hysteria," in *The Standard Edition of the Complete Psychological Works of Sigmund Freud*, 24 vols., ed. James Strachey (London: Hogarth Press, 1953–1973), 3: 119–122 [hereafter cited as *SE*]; Sigmund Freud, "Letter to Wilhelm Fleiss, September 22, 1897," *SE*, 1: 259–260; Sigmund Freud, *Three Essays on the Theory of Sexuality*, *SE*, vol. 7; Sigmund Freud, *Totem and Taboo*, *SE*, 13: 1–161; Peter Gay, ed., *The Freud Reader* (New York: Norton, 1989); Jeffrey Moussaief Masson, *The Assault on Truth: Freud's Suppression of the Seduction Theory* (New York: Harper, 1985).

SARA MURPHY

FRIEDAN, BETTY (1921–   ). The mother of the second wave of the **feminist movement**, author and feminist Betty Friedan changed the views of women in the United States with the publication of *The Feminine Mystique* in 1963. Although written from the point of view of an educated, unfulfilled suburban housewife, Friedan had been a social activist for a number of years. Her work built upon ideas grounded in the Left, union work, and the civil rights movement. By the 1950s, her work already showed a growing criticism of the status of women.

Friedan was born in 1921 in Peoria, Illinois. Always an intelligent child, primary and secondary school were not easy places for Friedan; she was viewed as too bookish. When she went to Smith College, Friedan discovered a whole new world that offered her respect and opportunities. While at Smith College and after, she embarked on a journalism career that took her from student newspapers to union newspaper writing. After college, she met and married ex-GI Carl Friedan.

While married to Carl, Friedan worked as a freelance writer for different women's magazines. She also began work on *The Feminine Mystique* while living the life of a New York suburban housewife. In the early 1960s, rape, particularly marital rape, was not considered an important social or feminine issue. Although biographers have elaborated on the violence that plagued the Friedan marriage, Friedan avoided discussions of marital violence or rape in her own writing. Instead, she focused on the educated suburban housewife's sense of alienation in *The Feminine Mystique*.

The Feminine Mystique spoke to the experiences of a number of women. Building on the success of the book, Friedan formed the **National Organization for Women** (**NOW**). Yet it is significant that *The Feminine Mystique* did not discuss rape. It took time for rape to become an important issue in the feminist movement. By the time it did, Friedan's more conservative views of the early 1960s no longer reflected the viewpoint of the women's movement, which shifted in the late 1960s and 1970s. Other women emerged as leaders who addressed other issues such as rape and **domestic violence**. Thus, Friedan found herself at the margins of a movement she helped establish, replaced by younger women who addressed issues that Friedan avoided. *See also*: **Steinem, Gloria.**

Suggested Reading: Betty Friedan, *The Feminine Mystique* (New York: Laurel Press, 1984); Judith Hennessee, *Betty Friedan: Her Life* (New York: Random House, 1999); Daniel Horowitz, *Betty Friedan and the Making of the Feminine Mystique: The American Left, the Cold War, and Modern Feminism* (Amherst: University of Massachusetts Press, 1998).

ELAINE CAREY

G

GAMMAHYDROXYBUTYRATE (GHB). Gammahydroxybutyrate is a central nervous system depressant that was first used in the 1960s as an anesthetic and later as a body-building supplement. Although illegal due to the serious adverse effects that can even lead to death, GHB has become a recreational or "club drug." It is popular at "Raves," the all-night dance parties that are often held at beach communities. The attraction of GHB is due to two potent sources: the experience of euphoria associated with GHB and the increase in sex drive. As a "**date rape** drug," GHB reduces inhibitions, relaxes muscles, and produces amnesia. The intoxicating effects usually begin within 10 to 20 minutes following ingestion and can last up to four hours. Date rape drugs can be easily put into an open drink so that the potential victim for the **sexual assault** is completely unaware of the act. With respect to gathering evidence for a charge of rape, GHB cannot be detected by most hospital urine or blood toxicology screens.

GHB, a drug whose street names include "liquid Ecstasy," "Grievous Bodily Harm," and "Georgia Homeboy," is available in a liquid form for drinking or a white powder for smoking and snorting. In its liquid form, GHB is odorless, colorless, and has a slightly salty taste that is easily masked in a mixed drink. It is somewhat less expensive than either **Ecstasy** or **ketamine**. Since GHB is a central nervous system depressant, ingestion can result in slurred speech, blurred vision, dizziness, nausea and vomiting, numbness, convulsions, unconsciousness, and coma. When consumed with **alcohol**, it is even more dangerous than when consumed alone.

Despite the illegal status of GHB, it is relatively easy to obtain. The recipe and the ingredients are actually available on the Internet. One of the ingredients, 1,4-butanediol, is sold legally in health food stores as a dietary supplement. The other ingredients that are used to produce GHB are industrial solvents that have been neutralized. GHB can be manufactured in someone's garage or basement by a person with no training in chemistry and a lack of knowledge of quality control.

The larger the dose of GHB, the greater the risk for negative consequences.

Higher doses can actually lead to coma and cardiac or respiratory arrest. For those who want to stop using the drug, withdrawal can also be lethal. Low doses of GHB produce euphoria, an "out-of-body" high, increased sex drive, memory loss, and hallucinations. Since the effects of GHB wear off in two hours, the user is in constant need of more of the drug to prevent withdrawal symptoms. Withdrawal symptoms include insomnia, tremors, confusion, disorientation, delirium, nausea, and vomiting. *See also*: **Rohypnol.**

Suggested Reading: Club Drugs.org, http://www.clubdrugs.org; Jaime Diaz, *How Drugs Influence Behavior: Neuro-behavioral Approach* (Upper Saddle River, NJ: Prentice Hall, 1997); Harold E. Doweiko, *Concepts of Chemical Dependency*, 5th ed. (Pacific Grove, CA: Brooks/Cole, 2002); Kathiann M. Kowaksi, "Club Drugs: Nothing to Rave About," *Current Health* 2.28 (2002): 6–12; Partnership for a Drug-Free America, http://www.drugfree america.org; Joseph H. Pittman, "What You Need to Know about GHB," *Nursing* 32 (2002): CC6–CC7; Richard Sadovsky, "Gamma-hydroxybutyrate and Withdrawal Syndrome," *American Family Physician* 54 (2001): 1059–1062; Substance Abuse and Mental Health Services Administration's National Clearinghouse for Alcohol and Drug Information, http://www.health.org.

SHARON A. DROZDOWSKI AND JUDITH A. WATERS

GANG RAPE. Gang rape is sexualized violence involving two or more assailants. It is nothing new; it appears in the **Bible** (Judges 19–20) in the tale of the Ephraim Levite's concubine. Gang rapes are more common than people think. They are a frequent occurrence in war and with gangs. In Renaissance Florence, one-third of all reported heterosexual rapes and many homosexual rapes were gang rapes.

Gang rapes are employed as a method of punishment, social control, bonding, and as a rite of passage. For example, soldiers rape women as a way of humiliating their opponents and disrupting their society. They also increase the ties between the assailants. Another example involves the gang rapes performed by young apprentices in southern France in the fifteenth century. These rapes tied the men together, punished women deviating from the social norm, and were a rite of passage into manhood. Gang rape sometimes serves a religious purpose. Among the Xinguano peoples of central Brazil, the Kauka ritual involves men playing music on sacred flutes. If a woman sees the performance, she is gang raped, which is attributed to the spirit Kauka operating through the men.

Gang rapists do not necessarily always commit an assault with any of these consequences in mind, and it is important to distinguish the act of violence and the conscious goals from the resultant effects for all involved. The intentions of each individual rapist may vary. In some cases, the assault is the result of a group decision; in others, it is initiated by a leader or small group of those involved. Sometimes, it is a crime of opportunity; in other cases, the **victim** has been sought out. Some participate willingly, while others are coerced.

Gang rapes are even more difficult to prosecute than rapes involving only one assailant (but when successfully prosecuted will usually result in a harsher punishment). This is because the assailants may provide alibis for each other or offer differing versions of events, making it hard for the authorities. Victims of such attacks are often reluctant to report it because they fear reprisals from more than one person. When gang rape is a form of initiation for either an assailant or victim, silence is the price of inclusion. *See also*: **Fraternities; Glen Ridge (NJ) Rape Case; Wartime Rape.**

Suggested Reading: Catharine A. MacKinnon, "Rape, Genocide, and Women's Human Rights," in *Violence against Women: Philosophical Perspectives*, ed. Stanley G. French, Wanda Teays, and Laura M. Purdy (Ithaca, NY: Cornell University Press, 1998), 43–54; Cecilia McCallum, "Ritual and the Origin of Sexuality in the Alto Xingu," in *Sex and Violence: Issues in Representation and Experience*, ed. Penelope Harvey and Peter Gow (New York: Routledge, 1994), 90–114; Jacques Rossiaud, "Prostitution, Youth, and Society in the Towns of Southern France in the Fifteenth Century," in *Deviants and the Abandoned in French Society: Selections from the Annales Economies, Societes Civilisations*, ed. Robert Forster and Orest Ranum, trans. Elborg Forster and Patricia M. Ranum (Baltimore: Johns Hopkins University Press, 1978), 1–46.

TONYA MARIE LAMBERT

GAYS AND LESBIANS. Gays and lesbians are men and women who are involved in intimate sexual and emotional relationships with members of the same sex. The more clinical term *homosexual*, coined in 1869, has fallen out of popular usage. While *gay* describes homosexual men and *lesbian* refers to homosexual women, the term *gay* by itself is at times inclusive of both men and women.

In the latter half of the twentieth century, gays and lesbians have identified themselves as such to each other, their families, and the general public in record numbers in efforts to challenge the oppression they faced for being homosexual. This movement for civil rights has achieved rapid success since its widely recognized beginning in the New York City Stonewall Riots of 1969. This challenge to police harassment and brutality marked a turning point and rallying cry for the budding movement, though organizations such as the Mattachine Society for gay men and the lesbian Daughters of Bilitis were formed over a decade earlier in San Francisco.

Gay men and lesbians, long stigmatized by accusations of immorality, perversion, and antisocial behavior, won their first great national victory when the American Psychiatric Association removed homosexuality from its list of mental disorders in 1973. Both great advances and restrictions marked the next 30 years. Increasing numbers of corporations, universities, and municipalities grant domestic partner benefits, limited protection from employment discrimination, and hate crime laws aimed to restrict harassment and violence. Conservative right-wing political groups galvanized unprecedented numbers in their ranks, largely by claiming gays and lesbians threatened the family structure, social conventions, and religious values that many hold dear.

The most significant legal victory for the gay and lesbian community was the Supreme Court's 2003 ruling in *Lawrence and Garner v. Texas*, which overturned the **sodomy** laws protected by the same Court's 1986 *Bowers v. Hardwick* decision. *Lawrence and Garner v. Texas* will have implications ranging far beyond the rarely enforced sodomy laws, as the *Bowers* ruling was used to support discriminatory policies against gays and lesbians in areas as wide ranging as child custody, housing, employment, and health care.

While the fates of gay men and lesbians are tied together through discriminatory laws and cultural attitudes, as well as some shared community, their experiences, sense of identification, and sustaining social structures are often quite distinct. Much more so than gay men, lesbians were likely to come out later in life, identify as bisexual, or return to romantic involvement with men. Lesbians in contemporary America are much more likely to live in rural communities and noncoastal states than gay men. The women who did follow the demographic tendency of gay men to migrate to major urban centers live outside of the gay neighborhoods, in the suburbs and surrounding towns. Their main connection to the lesbian community is not public gay space but rather the social institutions of the women's movement, including bookstores, athletic leagues, and informal networks. The power of heterosexism and homophobia link gay men and lesbians more than any inherent commonality.

The issue of rape in the gay community is a sensitive one. Though lesbians have worked to end domestic and sexual violence against women since the **feminist movement** targeted the issue in the 1970s, the lesbian community has struggled to deal with women-on-woman violence. Mythic gender roles make it hard to comprehend the motives and behaviors of violent women. These ideas work against gay men as well, framing gay rape as an act perpetuated by gay men against unwilling heterosexuals, rather than the much more typical situation of heterosexual men attacking gay men. Like the lesbian community, the gay male community, defending itself against the violence aimed at it by heterosexuals, has been slow to look at the abusive behaviors of its own members. *See also*: **Gender Roles; Homosexual Rape; Male Rape.**

Suggested Reading: John D'Emilio, *The World Turned: Essays on Gay History, Politics, and Culture* (Durham, NC: Duke University Press, 2002); Urvashi Vaid, *Virtual Equality: The Mainstreaming of Gay and Lesbian Liberation* (New York: Anchor Books, 1995).

JENNIFER MANION

GENDER ROLES. *Gender* is a term that entered into the discussion of human sexuality in the mid-twentieth century. It was introduced by John Money to describe the difference between male and masculinity or female and femininity. Gender was defined as the constellation of mental and behavioral traits that to a greater or lesser degree differ between males and female, regardless of how those differences might arise. Children, at least as soon as they begin to talk, are known to establish a gender identity distinguishing themselves from the opposite sex. Although they understand a gender identity early on, they do not necessarily have a gender constancy, and a little girl could imagine she might later be a boy, or vice versa. The overwhelming majority of children, however, ultimately develop a gender identity consistent with their biological sex.

Gender role refers to the traits and characteristic expected of males and females in a particular society. This, at least partly, is a process of development, a social construction, in which individuals incorporate the behaviors and characteristics of a culturally defined gender role into their own personalities. Both women and men have departed, in some cases quite radically, from the gender roles of 100 years ago. Definitions of gender role vary not only in time periods but from society to society.

Gender role socialization occurs throughout childhood and adolescence as the child is influenced by parents and **family**, peer groups, and institutions such as **schools**. Girls in the past were usually encouraged to be more nurturing than boys, while boys have been inculcated to be self-reliant. Father and sons have tended to have more rough-and-tumble play than fathers have with their daughters. Boys are told big boys don't cry, while girls are permitted to do so.

Individuals, however, vary to the extent in which they incorporate the expected behaviors into their own personalities, and they may accept or reject them outright, or incorporate some of both into their gender role. In some cases, individuals seemingly develop two separate personae, as those transvestites do who believe that cross-dressing allows them to express their feminine side more easily.

Some of the more militant early feminists believed that gender role was entirely a social construct. They urged parents to modify the way they treated their children by avoiding stereotypical attitudes and play activities. While there were some successes reported, most parents found that their children, in spite of their efforts, stuck to stereotypical toy preferences and activities. Still there have been societal changes, as witnessed by the growth of women's athletics programs in schools and colleges. Active participation in sports, formerly one of the distinguishing characteristics of boys, have become much more common to both sexes.

One of the difficulties that parents had in making a gender-neutral environment is due to the fact that they are not the only ones involved in inculcating gender attitudes in children. Television and peer groups are at least as influential, if not more influential, and as society changes, so do education and gender roles.

All that can be said for certain is that the development of gender characteristics, including gender role, is probably multifactorial, and something that is not fully understood. The most active efforts in the past to create new gender roles and identities have involved intersex children and those who accidentally lost part of their genitals in early childhood. Challenges to surgical intervention in the past have led to challenges by adult intersex individuals, as well as by those whose genitals were surgically modified. Gender roles are certainly less restricted than they were in the immediate past, but what the ultimate result will be is still not clear, since any final answers are still lacking.

Those crossing gender lines are particularly vulnerable to rape in the United States, where the macho culture is hostile to them. Many males regard effeminate gay men, butch lesbians, and transgender individuals as challenges to their masculinity. It is part of the popular male folklore in large sections of American society that a lesbian could be "cured" by meeting a real man. This also seems to be the case with individuals who are discovered to be transgendered. In the case of effeminate males, the belief that they are asking for penetration is enough for some to rape them. In this sense, rape can perhaps be justified in the rapist's mind as essential for the preservation of society. It keeps women in their place and prevents any challenge to what macho men regard as the proper order in society. *See also*: **Gays and Lesbians.**

Suggested Reading: J. Calapinto, *As Nature Made Him* (New York: HarperCollins, 2000); J.S. Hyde, *Psychology of Gender: Advances through Meta-Analysis* (Baltimore: Johns Hopkins University Press, 1986); G.P. Knight, R.A. Fabes, and D.A. Higgins, "Concerns about Drawing Casual Inferences from Meta-Analyses: An Example in the Study of Gender Differences in Aggression," *Psychological Bulletin* 119 (1996): 410–421; John Money and Anke Ehrhardt, *Man & Woman, Boy & Girl* (Baltimore: Johns Hopkins University Press, 1972); Kenneth J. Zucker, "Intersexuality and Gender Identity Differentiation," *Annual Review of Sex Research* 10 (1999): 1–69.

VERN L. BULLOUGH

GENOCIDE. According to the 1948 Convention on genocide (78 U.N.T.S. 277) in force since 1951, this "crime of crimes" can be committed by killing members of a national, ethnical, racial, or religious group, causing serious bodily or mental harm to those members, deliberately inflicting on them conditions of life calculated to bring about its physical destruction in whole or in part, or imposing measures intended to prevent births or even by forcibly transferring children of the group to another group. To reach the level that becomes necessary for the acts to be qualified as genocide, they must be performed with *intent* to destroy the group, totally or partially. Nowadays, genocide, whose definition has become part of customary international law and an imperative norm, is one of the crimes under the scope of the recently created International Criminal Court. According to its particular characteristics, it may be committed not only during hostilities in an armed conflict but also in times of peace.

The definition of genocide requires the identification of two elements that are central to its legal nature: on the one hand, the objective aspect (*actus reus*) consisting of the practical commission of the material acts; on the other, the subjective or moral aspect of the offense (*mens rea*), which is translated as the specific intention—*dolus specialis*—behind the facts.

Since the process of destruction of a target group is expressly not limited to physical extermination, **sexual assaults** could be also sometimes regarded as genocide. Among the various sex crimes that may be considered genocide, if these conditions are met, rape is one of the most widespread. Rape is broadly conceived, in contemporary jurisprudence, as the sexual penetration of the victim's vagina, mouth, or anus by any body part or object, generally committed by force, threat, coercion, or other unlawful conduct. However, in spite of its gravity, it was only in the Statutes of the International Tribunals from Yugoslavia and Rwanda that some of the gender-oriented attacks committed against women were first explicitly included and punished. In these ad hoc courts, however, rape is only dealt with as a crime against humanity.

Nevertheless, and even if legal instruments do not explicitly state so, it is clear that forced penetration, resulting intentionally or unintentionally in the death of the victim, may fall under the scope of genocide, if it becomes part of a systematic plan with the ulterior motive of destroying the group to which that victim belonged. Rape can only be an offense described as genocide if it takes place in the context of a manifest pattern of similar conduct directed against the group, or if it could itself effect such destruction.

Some publicists agree that sexual violence should be included in the categories of actions that may constitute genocide. As far as the protected groups are concerned, the Rwandan Tribunal has mentioned—referring to the local massacre in 1994—that the definition of the crime should be extended and interpreted as including other similar groups, as long as they are stable. Even if women may not form a protected group, genocidal rape is possible every time the social structure of a community is broken based on arguments of **ethnic cleansing**; the imposition of measures intended to prevent births of a particular group, in fact, is clearly one of the behaviors that constitute genocide. It is possible to affirm that systematic, violent, or repeated rapes committed against a specific sector of the population (even if only a single member of the protected group is harmed) may be considered a genocidal act; the explanation often found for this focuses on the fact that it is demonstrated that sexual violence causes both serious bodily and mental harm to those who suffer it. *See also*: **Bosnia-Herzegovina; War Crimes.**

Suggested Reading: Kelly D. Askin, *War Crimes against Women: Prosecution in International War Crimes Tribunals* (The Hague: Kluwer Law International, M. Nijhoff Publishers, 1997); Dorean Koenig and Kelly D. Askin, *Women and International Human Rights Law* (Ardsley, NY: Transnational Publishers, 1999); L. Kuper, *Genocide: Its Political Use in the Twentieth Century* (New Haven, CT: Yale University Press, 1982); Catharine A. MacKinnon, "Rape, Genocide and Women's Human Rights," *Harvard Women's Law Journal* 17 (1994): 5–16; N. Robinson, *The Genocide Convention: A Commentary* (New York: Institute of Jewish Affairs, 1960).

EMILIANO J. BUIS

GENOVESE, KITTY (1935–1964). While 38 witnesses ignored her screams for help, Catherine "Kitty" Genovese was raped and stabbed to death in a case that became symbolic of the refusal of Americans to get involved. Genovese, a bar manager, had just ended her shift and returned to her Kew Gardens, Queens, New York City apartment at 3:15 A.M. on March 13, 1964. Genovese locked her car door and began the 20-foot walk to her apartment. She immediately noticed Winston Moseley, a married business-machine operator with no criminal record, walking quickly toward her. Genovese ran, but Moseley caught up to her underneath a street light at the end of the parking lot and stabbed her with a knife. Genovese screamed for help, with her shrieks heard by several residents of nearby buildings. One man opened his window, observed the struggle below, and shouted at the attacker. Moseley walked away, and the man closed his window. Genovese, bleeding heavily, staggered to her building and held the concrete wall. Five minutes later, Moseley returned to stab her again. Genovese screamed again. Lights in the buildings went on again, but no one called the police. Moseley ran away but returned a third time at 3:25 A.M. and followed a trail of blood to find Genovese. He cut off her bra and underwear, raped her, stole $49 from her purse, and fatally stabbed her before fleeing. The entire event lasted 32 minutes. The one call made to the police came after Genovese's death, and police arrived within 2 minutes. To a nation shocked by their apathy, Genovese's neighbors explained that they had not wanted to get involved. Moseley, who simply wanted to kill someone, received a death sentence that was later reduced to life imprisonment.

Suggested Reading: A.M. Rosenthal, *Thirty-eight Witnesses: The Kitty Genovese Case* (Berkeley: University of California Press, 1999).

CARYN E. NEUMANN

GEOGRAPHIC PROFILING. Also called criminal geographic targeting (CGT), geographic profiling, invented by Dr. Kim Rossmo, is a mathematical-algorithm technique for calculating the most probable area of residence of serial criminals. Although initially dismissed as overly optimistic, it has earned legitimacy and respect after helping the police solve a number of formidable cases of serial crimes.

Geographic profiling is based on the assumption that serial criminals do not act in entirely random ways. Whether they are engaged in serial arson, robbery, or rape, criminals follow several fairly specific principles. First, to protect their anonymity, criminals keep a "buffer zone" in their immediate neighborhood, where they tend not to operate. On the other hand, they do not venture very far from home either, because too great a distance from the base reduces their sense of security.

This latter tendency is further specified by a proportion principle saying that the graver the crime, the farther from the base it is planned. Believing these facts to define any offender's geographic "modus operandi," Rossmo and his team translated them into a computer algorithm whose function is to compare the location points of crime sites. The algorithm uses geographic coordinates fed into the computer to draw the so-called "jeopardy surface"—a region on the police map where the offender most likely resides.

This technique is most helpful in solving crimes believed to have been perpetrated by the same individual, such as an elusive serial rapist, or in single crimes after which the offender leaves traces in many other locations, for example, by making taunting phone calls to the police. Profiling narrows down the investigation area and, with a reduced number of suspects, makes it possible to examine DNA samples, something that would be difficult without the investigative focus enabled by geographic profiling. Among its great advantages is its ability to locate even very systematic offenders who took great pains to cover their traces and not to leave a discernible pattern. One of the most spectacular achievements of geographic profiling was its role in apprehending the notorious South Side rapist who for more than a decade terrorized women in Lafayette, Louisiana. *See also*: **DNA Collection and Evidence; Profiling; Serial Rape and Serial Rapists.**

Suggested Reading: Bruce Grierson, "The Hound of the Data Points," *Popular Science* (April 2003), http://www.popsci.com/popsci/science/article/0,12543,435555,00.html.

KONRAD SZCZESNIAK

GLEN RIDGE (NJ) RAPE CASE. After baseball practice on March 1, 1989, 13 Glen Ridge, New Jersey, **athletes** gathered at the home of twins Kevin and Kyle Scherzer. Joining them at the popular basement hangout was their former classmate, a 17-year-old mentally retarded girl. Unlike many previous get-togethers, this one had a specific purpose. One of the boys began to take off his pants. Six of them looked around nervously and left. Of the remaining 7, several watched while the others sexually assaulted the girl, fondling her breasts, coercing acts of **oral sex,** and penetrating her vagina with a broom and baseball bat.

The victim, described as having the intellectual and emotional maturity of a second-grader, also loved sports. Despite her transfer to a nearby school, she continued to play basketball for Glen Ridge High. Particularly fond of one of the boys, she was lured to the basement with a promise that he would meet her later that day. She mistakenly believed she was finally being accepted as one of the "jocks." Following the assault, she returned to the baseball field and anxiously paced, waiting for the date who would not appear. Eventually she returned home and, as instructed, told no one about her basement encounter.

Word spread quickly, however. The group bragged about their exploits and planned a repeat "performance," this one to be videotaped. Perhaps some residents of Glen Ridge—a small, upper-middle-class suburb, with attractive homes and well-manicured lawns—would not be surprised. The boys had a long, well-documented history of sexual misconduct. One of them masturbated openly at school, while others had had sex without telling their partners they were being observed. Still, many wondered if the rumors were true. Several weeks passed before a reluctant student informed school officials.

The story broke nationwide two months later: Five popular New Jersey athletes were arrested for raping a mentally retarded teen. Two more arrests followed. Ultimately, four faced charges of first-degree rape. All were freed on bail until the trial began in 1992. The widely publicized, six-month courtroom drama yielded four convictions. Found guilty of a misdemeanor, Bryant Grober received probation and community service. The Scherzer twins and Christopher Archer received prison sentences of up to 15 years, although Kyle Scherzer's sentence was later reduced. In a move that provoked a national outcry, the judge allowed the boys to remain out of jail until they exhausted their appeals. In 1997, the convictions were upheld, and the boys—by now, young men—entered a campus-style youth correctional facility. They could be assigned to this type of facility because they were first-time offenders and because the judge was able to classify them as "young-adult-offenders." At the time of the rape, Archer was almost 17, and the Scherzer twins were 18.

Kyle Scherzer was released in December 1999; Christopher Archer was released in August 2001, and Kevin Scherzer was released in November 2002. In October 2003, a federal appeals court granted their lawyers permission to proceed with a new appeal. Although they are no longer in custody, a favorable ruling (based on faulty trial procedures) would help to erase the **stigma** of conviction and prevent them from having to register as **sex offenders** under **Megan's Law.**

The events of March 1989 have been chronicled by two books and a television movie. Many observers hold the town partly responsible for this crime, witnessing the widespread support for their heroes of the playing field. They believe an exaggerated emphasis on sports, coupled with a refusal to hold young boys accountable for their actions, fostered a "boys will be boys" attitude, creating the backdrop for the Glen Ridge rape. *See also*: **Athletes; Foreign-Object Rape; Gang Rape; Gender Roles; Voyeurism.**

Suggested Reading: Peter Laufer, *A Question of Consent: Innocence and Complicity in the Glen Ridge Rape Case* (San Francisco: Mercury House, 1994); Bernard Lefkowitz, *The Glen Ridge Rape and the Secret Life of the Perfect Suburb* (Berkeley: University of California Press, 1997).

CHRISTINE CLARK ZEMLA

H

HALE, SIR MATTHEW (1609–1676). A renowned seventeenth-century English judge and legal scholar, Matthew Hale is remembered today primarily as the author of *The History of the Pleas of the Crown* (1736), a pathbreaking survey of the law and procedure of capital offenses. It was here that Hale set forth his influential summation of the development of English **rape law**.

Within the U.S. legal system, Hale's influence can be seen most clearly in two realms: first, in the suspicious stance toward female complainants generally and second, in the assertion of the legal impossibility of rape in marriage. While terming rape "a most detestable crime," Hale famously warned that "it is an accusation easily to be made and hard to be proved, and harder to be defended by the party accused, tho never so innocent." Hale's assertion of traditional stereotypes of gendered behavior shifted attention away from rape's actual **victims** to underscore men's supposed vulnerability to unscrupulous women, thus reorienting the locus of injury to the hypothetically wronged male. Versions of this caveat, often verbatim, appeared in jury instructions issued in jurisdictions throughout the country until the late twentieth century, when they were gradually eliminated.

Hale was also the principal expositor of the common law's **marital rape** exemption. Drawing on the notion of implied **consent** to spousal intercourse, he observed that "the husband cannot be guilty of a rape committed by himself upon his lawful wife, for by their mutual matrimonial consent and contract the wife hath given up herself in this kind unto her husband, which she cannot retract." Marriage was therefore a contract, an essential component of which was the wife's agreement to perform sexual services when called upon to do so. Hale was the authority most widely invoked by U.S. courts in support of the historical foundation for the spousal exemption, which remained in force until the 1970s, when feminists inaugurated the movement for rape law reform.

Hale's principal legacy for rape history lies in these two statements, which together served both to articulate and perpetuate cultural suspicion regarding women's allegations of sexual abuse within and outside of marriage. *See also*: **Rape**

History in the United States: Seventeenth Century; Rape History in the United States: Eighteenth Century; Rape History in the United States: Nineteenth Century; Rape History in the United States: Twentieth Century; Rape Law.

Suggested Reading: Sir Matthew Hale, *The History of the Pleas of the Crown* (1736; Facsimile of the first edition, introduced by P.R. Glazebrook, Abington, United Kingdom: Professional Books, 1987); [J.M.R.], "Sir Matthew Hale," in *The Dictionary of National Biography*, vol. 8, ed. Sir Leslie Stephen and Sir Sidney Lee (1908–1909; reprint, London: Oxford University Press, 1949–1950).

LISA CARDYN

HISPANICS/LATINOS. The terms *Latino* and *Hispanic* are commonly used in the United States to refer to people of Latin American, Caribbean, Mexican, or Spanish ancestry. These words are ethnic labels that do not signify nationality, as there are more than 23 nations from which people identified as such may come. When these words are used to refer to groups of people living within what is now considered to be the geopolitical borders of the United States, there is generally some assumption that people share certain social characteristics and cultural aspects. Broadly speaking, Latino culture is visible through artifacts, language, religion, customs, **clothing**, and foods. And typically, when we think of culture, we recognize that certain groups possess common beliefs, values, attitudes, and ways of knowing and learning.

Historically, the U.S. government has used the term *Hispanic* as an official designator to refer to people from these regions, who have the right to some type of legal residency in the United States. More recent censuses, however, have employed both *Latino* and *Hispanic* as ethnic labels for members of these groups. But the people themselves vary in their preference for *Latino* over *Hispanic*, and vice versa, and many reject overarching labeling, since the experience of Puerto Ricans, for example, differs from the experience of Nicaraguans, Argentines, or Spaniards.

The U.S. Census Bureau for 2000 reports that more than 35 million Latinos/Hispanics live within the borders of the United States, making up about 12.5 percent of the total U.S. population of 248,709,873 people. Though Mexican Americans make up the largest group with some 20 million inhabitants within the United States, there are also sizable populations of Puerto Ricans (nearly 3.5 million) and Cubans (1.2 million). Recent immigration has also brought Latinos from the Dominican Republic, Guatemala, Nicaragua, El Salvador, Ecuador, and other Central and South American countries (approximately 10 million people).

Latinas have a long history of having suffered sexual violence. It is well documented that Spanish soldiers abducted and raped Indigenous women during their conquest and subjugation of Amerindian peoples and their lands. Often, the Spanish phrase *la violación de las Indias*, or "the rape/violation of the Indies/female Indians," is used to express how, through European men's sexual violence, most of what is now known as Latin America and the Caribbean and the people who inhabited it fell under Spanish control and domination. The word *violación* carries the double meaning of rape/violation, and the feminine phrase *las Indias* can mean either the West Indies or Indigenous, Amerindian women. One historical study of the eighteenth-century Spanish expansion into California highlights the tension created between the Spanish Catholic Church and the Spanish army, precisely because of the sexual violence and rape of Californian Indians by Spanish soldiers. According to the author of the study, Antonia Castañeda, clergymen wrote to Spanish government officials about their difficulties in convincing the Indigenous population to convert to Catholicism, when Spanish soldiers were stealing Indigenous women and raping them. Feminists argue that as a result of the Western tradition in which women are seen as belonging to (in the sense of property and territory) their fathers and husbands, wartime abducting and raping of "enemy women" is symbolic of both physical domination of the land and of the group inhabiting it, as well as the emasculation of "enemy men" who are supposed to be able to protect what is theirs.

Today, as is the case for women of other ethnic and racial backgrounds, Latinas continue to be victimized by sexual violence. Though there has not been a great deal of research on sexual violence and Latina women in the United States, much of the literature that does exist suggests that Latina women are less likely to disclose sexual violence than their non-Latina counterparts. However, the data analyzed thus far cannot locate the reason for the disparity in reporting rates between women of different ethnic groups. In other words, it is not clear whether (1) Latina women suffer less sexual violence than women from other groups, (2) Latina women are not as inclined as women from other social and ethnic groups to consider certain coercive sexual acts to be acts of sexual violence, or (3) Latina women are more reluctant than are other women to disclose sexual violence. When the last two reasons are given to explain the phenomenon of Latinas' low reporting rates, researchers also implicate Latino culture as prohibiting women from speaking about sex in general, let alone sexual violence. Presumably for Latina women, all things sexual are thought to be sociocultural taboos. In some studies, aspects believed to be unique to Latino culture are put forth as explanations for Latinas' reticence on the sexual violence. Such cultural attributes include *familism*, or the importance Latinos supposedly put on the **family** and its ability to give lifelong, transgenerational support to its loyal members, and what are often assumed to be the rigidly prescribed and dichotomous gender roles for men and women of **machismo** and *Marianismo*, respectively. Machismo is the cultural concept that men have the responsibility of protecting and providing for their family, and Marianismo is the expectation that women are to emulate the Virgin Mary, a sacred mother who knows how to endure suffering for the good of others. But some experts suggest more systemic or social reasons for Latinas not reporting, such as their low socioeconomic status in the United States and their sensitivity as women of color to the structural and racist biases within U.S. prosecutorial and U.S. law enforcement agencies that will subject Latino men to unequal and unfair treatment as compared to their Anglo counterparts. *See also*: **Native Americans**.

Suggested Reading: Antonia Castañeda, "Sexual Violence in the Politics and Policies of Conquest: Amerindian Women and the Spanish Conquest of Alta California," in *Building with Our Hands: New Directions in Chicana Studies*, ed. Adela de la Torre and Beatriz Pesquera (Los Angeles: University of California Press, 1993), 15–33; Ernesto de la Vega, "Considerations for Reaching the Latino Population with Sexuality and HIV/AIDS Information and Education," *SIECUS Report* 18 (1990): 1–8; Georgiana Low and Kurt Organista, "Latinas and Sexual Assault: Towards Culturally Sensitive Assessment and Intervention," *Journal of Multicultural Social Work* 8 (2000): 131–157; Suzanne Oboler, *Ethnic Labels, Latino Lives: Identity and the Politics of (Re)presentation in the United States* (Minneapolis: University of Minnesota Press, 1995); Luciana Ramos-Lira, Mary Koss, and Nancy Felipe-Russo, "Mexican American Women's Definitions of Rape and Sexual Abuse," *Hispanic Journal of Behavioral Sciences* 21 (1999): 236–265; Shonna Trinch, "Managing

Euphemism and Transcending Taboos: Negotiating the Meaning of Sexual Assault in Latinas' Narratives of Domestic Violence," *Text* 21 (2001): 567–610.

SHONNA L. TRINCH

HIV/AIDS. Sometime in the mid-twentieth century, the human immunodeficiency virus (HIV) took hold and soon developed into the global epidemic of acquired immunodeficiency syndrome (AIDS). Rape is one of the methods by which this fatal disease is transmitted. In 2003, the World Health Organization estimated that 43 million people were HIV-positive, with 70 percent of those living in sub-Saharan Africa. AIDS remains the deadliest of the sexually transmitted diseases (STDs), which include gonorrhea, chlamydia, syphilis, crabs, genital warts, pelvic inflammatory disease, and scabies. While earlier hopes for a cure have faded, efforts to halt the further spread of AIDS through various preventive measures have been crippled by engrained fears, prejudices, and misconceptions regarding sex, gender, and sexuality. Scientists now believe that Congolese chimpanzees contracted a nonlethal form of the virus from eating monkeys, and while the mechanisms whereby it passed from nonhuman primates to humans remains unclear, the virus spread through international travel, intravenous (IV) drug use, and blood transfusion. Despite these facts, conspiracy theories linking AIDS to everything from the Central Intelligence Agency to polio vaccines, have persisted. Because of conspiracy theories and compulsions to "blame" AIDS on unpopular or socially disadvantaged groups such as gay men, racial minorities, the poor, and women, most organizations have remained reluctant to name rape as a crucial means of transmitting AIDS, although it clearly is.

In part, since testing methods and the nature of the disease complicate linking exposure to rape, the Centers for Disease Control lists "heterosexual sex" rather than rape as the main model of transmission, obscuring how rape, the most graphic form of sexist domination, is not only a devastating crime but also a death sentence for millions of female victims of this "femicide." However, statistics from South Africa, which has one of the highest rates of rape and HIV infection and AIDS in the world, prove the correlation. There, where men usually refuse to wear condoms, and cultural mores normalize male infidelity, **prostitution**, and the belief that sex with a **virgin** "cures" AIDS, Human Rights Watch reports that 50 percent of schoolgirls endure **sexual assault**. The presence of untreated STDS, which often cause open sores and lesions, worsens women's already heightened vulnerability to HIV infection. The World Health Organization estimates a 30 percent higher risk of HIV and STD transmission through rape than consensual sex, since the force involved in rape can often lead to cuts and abrasions but also because women are terrified of seeking treatment after a rape, especially if the perpetrator is an acquaintance or **family** member. In sixteen African countries, 10 percent of the population is now infected. In Rwanda, rape increased dramatically during and after the **genocide** in 1994, and now 22 percent of women between the ages of 25 and 29 are HIV-positive. Some African governments, worried about provoking the hostility of men, who too often regard rape as a birthright and a "natural need," avoid honest discussion about how AIDS, which can be termed biological sexism, is spread because of the violent, irresponsible, and domineering behavior of heterosexual men. However, their human rights violations have literally become the deadliest virus in the world.

Africa might only appear especially bleak because that continent has monitoring systems lacking in other parts of the developing world. For example, East Asia has an enormous sex trade, intravenous drug use, economic instability, traditional sexism, and mobile populations. The area has probably already witnessed an explosion of HIV/AIDS that most governments, indifferent to the plight of women and terrified of losing Western economic investment, minimize or deny. The same holds true for China, whose government recently admitted to 800,000 HIV infections, even though the real figures are much higher. Like most other developing countries, the Chinese government will soon be forced to choose between denial and the maintenance of the sexist status quo, on the one hand, and economic collapse, on the other. The Indian subcontinent, like the nations of the former Soviet Union, face similar choices regarding whether or not they will eliminate the male sexual privilege that, in the form of wanton rape and blaming and stigmatizing women they have infected with HIV, currently drives the epidemic.

Women are the predominant but not exclusive victims of rape, which, in various manifestations, currently drives the global AIDS epidemic and that has resulted, whether directly or indirectly, in the "feminization" of this fatal disease. Rape has always occurred in prisons and juvenile detention facilities, but the problem has worsened because of overcrowding and understaffing. The endemic dishonesty of state and federal governments over nonconsensual sex in prison now makes them accomplices in attempted murder. In the United States, 2 million now serve behind bars and millions more pass through each year, and HIV is 5 to 10 times higher than in the general population. **Male rape** victims are usually young, nonviolent, first-time offenders seen as "new meat." Often the targeted **victims** must accept sexual **slavery** and prostitution. As in the developing world, where police officers often rape women for "misconduct," prison staff use rape as punishment and seldom hold perpetrators accountable. In contrast to stereotypes, heterosexual men commit most rapes against other men, which reveals that "macho" cultures conceptualize sex as power. Male **survivors** often feel like they have been stripped of their "manhood" and remove the **stigma** associated with homosexual and female identity by getting their revenge on women and children. In this fashion, the cycle of sexism, homophobia, rape, and HIV/AIDS perpetuates itself.

More than 20 years into the AIDS epidemic, the picture looks far worse than most would have predicted 10 years ago. Ironically, the spread of AIDS to women, who are now the subpopulation most affected by the disease, has made the prevalence of rape impossible to ignore. It has also made evident that male sexist domination is not merely a bad idea but also a literally deadly matter that is eradicating entire cultures, halting economic progress, and posing a direct threat to the continuance of human civilization. In rural Africa, the sight of dying young women and orphaned children has become commonplace. In South Africa more than 8,500 women under the age of 18 were raped in the first six months of 1999. Unless dramatic action aimed at ending the cultural, economic, and political disenfranchisement of women does not occur in the near future, the damage already done will pale in comparison with what lies ahead. The advent of the AIDS epidemic now means that rape can no longer be silenced, denied, or minimized if cultures around the globe hope to survive. *See also*: **African Women and Girls; Prison Rape; Trafficking in Women and Children.**

Suggested Reading: "The Basics on Rape Behind Bars," *Stop Prisoner Rape*, http://www. spr.org; "HIV/AIDS," *Human Rights Reports*, 2003, http://www.hrw.org; "HIV/AIDS," World Health Organization, Annual Reports 2003, http://www.who.int/en/.

CORINNE E. BLACKMER

HOLOCAUST. *See* Ethnic Cleansing; Genocide; Nazis; War Crimes.

HOMOEROTICISM. Homoeroticism is a practice that holds the same-sex relationship as both spiritually and sexually most satisfying. In common language it is often synonymously used with "homosexuality." As a scientific discourse today, homoeroticism has been a subject of **gay and lesbian** studies.

In ancient Greece the homoerotic relationship was highly regarded as a true spiritual connection of men, first as minds and then as bodies, where older men were patrons of younger boys in their social initiation. As such, homoeroticism was considered more than a mere sexual gratification of bodily needs but rather a rite of passage and spiritual growth.

Homoerotic relationships, while never extinct from Western social life, were certainly hushed by society in later history. In many instances, homosexuals were severely persecuted, because they were wrongly understood as mentally, and therefore morally, unstable human beings. **Sigmund Freud**, the founder of modern psychoanalysis in the late nineteenth and early twentieth centuries, caused a revival in the scientific interest in the issues of homosexuality in males and females.

In a homoerotic relationship, partners face the same problems of violence, hate, and power that are often the leading forces in rape cases among heterosexuals. Violence can be exercised by homosexuals upon members of the same community, with the underlying issues of dominance and power between the "strong" and the "weak" parties in the conflict. On the other hand, because homoerotic relationships are not accepted by everyone, a rape can be committed by an ordinarily heterosexual perpetrator upon a homosexual victim, as a hate crime as well as a sexual one. *See also*: **Homosexual Rape; Male Rape.**

Suggested Reading: Judith Butler, *Gender Trouble*, Tenth Anniversary Issue (London: Routledge, 1999); Anne Fausto-Sterling, *Sexing the Body: Gender, Politics and the Construction of Sexuality* (New York: Basic Books, 2001); bell hooks, *Outlaw Culture: Resisting Representation* (London: Routledge, 1994); Martti Nissinen, *Homoeroticism in the Biblical World: An Historical Perspective* (Minneapolis: Augsburg Fortress Publishers, 1998).

ROSSITSA TERZIEVA-ARTEMIS

HOMOSEXUAL RAPE. Homosexual rape refers to coerced, nonconsensual sex between members of the same sex. This term has been used mistakenly to describe the sexual orientation of either the perpetrator or the victim. This is particularly the case for **male rape**, when a male perpetrator of another male is labeled homosexual because of the homosexual nature of the act. Studies have shown that heterosexual men, not homosexual men, usually perpetuate stranger rape between men. Though members of the opposite sex rape homosexual men and women, this does not constitute homosexual rape. One of the reasons homosexual rape has been harder to study and understand is that traditional definitions of rape do not easily lend themselves to same-sex situations. By defining rape as a sex act between people without freely given **consent**, legal systems can better address the range of sexual experiences that mark individual lives. Research into the causes, occurrence, and consequences of homosexual rape is minimal, but early findings have raised critical questions about the complex relationship between power, violence, **gender roles**, and sexuality.

Woman-to-woman **sexual assault** among strangers is still largely undocumented. That women can and do rape each other has been hard for many to believe. In a heterocentric, phallocentric society, even defining what constitutes sex between two women has been widely misunderstood outside of the lesbian community. Some believe sexual violence is a tool of **patriarchy**, the principle weapon with which men terrorize and control women, making it unlikely that women are capable of filling that role, or at least unclear why they would want to. The homosexual rape between women that is documented often occurs within a lesbian relationship. Homophobia, misinformation about lesbian sex, and disbelief that women hurt other women in relationships all contribute to the general silence that characterizes this issue. **Domestic violence** and **sexual assault** service agencies rarely provide the support and information needed by female **survivors** of homosexual rape, perpetuating their isolation and confusion.

Stranger rape between men is more common and better documented. Throughout American history, forced sex between men was characterized as **sodomy** but not rape. Early studies of male-on-male rape employed a similar model of analysis as that developed by feminists studying rape of women by men: Rape is about exerting power, not about sexual desire. Following this, it was held that rape between men was predominantly by heterosexual men against homosexual men. Gay men who cruise public places looking for casual sex partners are more susceptible to these kinds of attacks. One reason for the predominance of stranger rape over acquaintance rape between men was the focus of early studies—prisons, military, and other single-sexed but not explicitly gay situations. More recent studies focused on men in the gay community reveal a higher rate of rape between gay men than was previously thought. Male rape is dramatically underreported, by gay and straight men alike. Gay men often expect that they will be blamed for being raped, or worse yet, accused of enjoying it. Studies confirm that when the victim of male rape is homosexual, he is more likely to be blamed for the encounter than a heterosexual man in the same situation.

Sexual orientation is still an important variable to understanding the motivations behind and consequences of all forms of rape, including homosexual. Studies of college-aged students show that gay men and lesbians are more likely victims of sexual assault than their heterosexual counterparts. Sex is the significant factor when identifying the perpetrators—they are overwhelmingly male. Similarly, women are far more frequently raped than men. Perhaps one of the most interesting conclusions—or hypotheses—to this issue is the absence of a role for heterosexual women. Lesbian women who rape often rape their partners or ex-lovers—women who are gay and whom they know intimately. Heterosexual women do not use rape as a means of tormenting or demonstrating power over lesbians, in the way that men do. Though the label of *sexual abuser* or *pervert* is still used in political battles against gays and lesbians, it has not affected gay women nearly to the extent it has plagued gay men. Survivors of sex crimes whose lives do not fit heterosexual norms are regarded as having invited the unpleasant experience because of their own sexual deviance. Historically, consensual homosexual sex has been equated with other forms of nonconsensual sex. For centuries, homosexuality was listed side-by-side with **bestiality**, rape, and **incest** in the legal books. It might take another century or two to undo this association. *See also*: **Prison Rape.**

Suggested Reading: Darren L. Burt and Lesley R. DeMello, "Attribution of Rape Blame as a Function of Victim Gender and Sexuality, and Perceived Similarity to the Victim," *Journal of Homosexuality* 43.2 (May 2002): 39; Richie J. McMullen, *Male Rape: Breaking the Silence on the Last Taboo* (Boston: Gay Men's Press, 1990); Damon Mitchell, Richard Hirschman, and Gordon C. Nagayama Hall, "Attributions of Victim Responsibility, Pleasure, and Trauma in Male Rape," *Journal of Sex Research* 36 (November 1999): 369; Cheryl Brown Travis, ed., *Evolution, Gender, and Rape* (Cambridge, MA: MIT Press, 2003).

JENNIFER MANION

HOSPITALS AND NURSING HOMES. Hospitalized patients and disabled residents of long-term care facilities are dependent on health care providers for their safety. These special populations share a heightened risk of **sexual assault** due to their physical condition, the effects of prescribed medications, and/or mental impairments. The American Hospital Association listed 5,801 registered hospitals in its annual survey, *Hospital Statistics 2001*. In 1999, there were over 16,700 nursing homes providing either short-term convalescent care or long-term care for over 1.5 million patients. As the baby boom generation moves into retirement, there will be a growing need for long-term care residential facilities.

Sexual assault in health care facilities is an opportunistic crime. Patients, employees, and visitors have all been **victims** of sexual assault in hospitals and nursing homes. The offenders may be anesthesiologists, gynecologists, nurses, pediatricians, psychiatrists, other employees, fellow patients, or trespassers. Throughout the twentieth century, responses by professional associations and licensing review boards to complaints of sexual misconduct by health care practitioners tended to be ineffective. In 1983, Wisconsin became the first state to pass a law criminalizing professional sexual misconduct. Malpractice insurance carriers responded by developing exclusion of coverage clauses for sexual exploitation by medical professionals and by supporting financial caps on damages that could be awarded to victims of sexual abuse by health care providers.

The International Association for Healthcare Security & Safety conducts an annual health care facility crime survey. Its first survey in 1987 revealed that many hospitals were not tracking crime data. Several other factors make it difficult to obtain valid statistics on the frequency of sexual assaults in health care facilities. A patient's mental impairment and the absence of physical injury can make it difficult for anyone to know that a sexual assault has occurred. Health care professionals may succumb to peer pressure by refusing to report a colleague's sexual misconduct, discouraging patients from reporting sexual abuse or failing to impose effective penalties against offenders.

The medical consumer advocacy movement has successfully lobbied for safer conditions for patients in health care facilities. The Arc is a grassroots organization that supports the rights of the mentally retarded. The Accreditation Council for Services for the Mentally Retarded and Other Developmentally Disabled Persons was established in 1969. The United Nations General Assembly adopted the Declaration on the Rights of Mentally Retarded Persons in 1971, recognizing their right to protection from exploitation and abuse. Despite these measures, a national survey in 1991 revealed widespread complaints of **voyeurism**, fondling, and rape in hospitals with general psychiatric units or special units for adolescents, substance abusers, or elderly psychiatric patients.

The Joint Commission on Accreditation of Healthcare Organizations (JCAHO) is the nation's predominant accrediting body in health care. It began long-term care accreditation in 1966. Elma Holder, a social worker, founded the National Citizens' Coalition for Nursing Home Reform (NCCNHR) in 1975. NCCNHR helped write the Omnibus Budget Reconciliation Act (OBRA) of 1987, which regulates how nursing homes do business. OBRA established a Resident's Bill of Rights for nursing home patients, including the right to be free from physical and sexual abuse. Relatives of nursing home residents formed Nursing Home Monitors in 1995. This group supports "whistleblower" employees who lose their jobs for reporting nursing home abuse. The Health Care Financing Administration, now called the Centers for Medicare and Medicaid Services, first produced standardized national reporting of allegations of abuse and neglect in nursing homes in 1996.

The doctrine of "charitable immunity" once protected hospitals and similar institutions from liability when their employees committed acts of sexual misconduct. Now, however, courts are acknowledging a special relationship between hospitals and their patients, recognizing patients' right to protection from sexual abuse while they are incapacitated. Unfortunately, conflict of interest can influence health care providers to resist fixing the problems that lead to sexual abuse. In response to more stringent compliance laws of recent years, corporate lobbyists are seeking legislation to deregulate the nursing home industry and to limit medical malpractice and nursing home liability claims. If successful, these efforts could weaken the enforcement of federal quality standards for nursing homes and increase the vulnerability of people least able to protect themselves. *See also*: **Mental Disabilities, People with; Physicians and Medical Professionals.**

Suggested Reading: Ann W. Burgess and Carol R. Hartman, *Sexual Exploitation of Patients by Health Professionals* (New York: Praeger, 1986); General Accounting Office, *Nursing Homes: More Can Be Done to Protect Residents from Abuse*, GAO-02-312 (Washington, DC: U.S. General Accounting Office, March 2002), http://www.gao.gov/newitems/do2312.pdf; Gary Ilminen, *Consumer Guide to Long-Term Care* (Madison: University of Wisconsin Press, 1999); Pauline Trumpi, *Doctors Who Rape: Malpractice and Misogyny* (Rochester, VT: Schenkman Books, 1997).

BETTY J. GLASS

I

INCEST. Incest is the sexual abuse and rape of children by **family** members. While many forms of incest undoubtedly exist, by far the most common is the father-daughter relationship. Although incest has probably existed for as long as human history extends, the definition of incest and the social reactions to it have changed markedly over time. In preindustrial Europe, incest was primarily an ecclesiastical crime defined as unlawful marriage within prohibited degrees of consanguinity. Many historians believe that the modern definitions of incest only emerged in the nineteenth century, as conceptions of childhood and adolescence changed and as the state increasingly intervened in family life.

Ancient Hebrew and Greek civilizations were among the first to leave documents that reveal an "incest taboo," a social condemnation of sexual relations between family members. In medieval and early modern Europe, religious and political authorities defined incest primarily as unlawful marriage between blood relatives. Ecclesiastical legislation gradually included all relations between family members until the seventh degree. By the ninth century, prohibitions against incest extended to relationships of consanguinity, affinity, and even spiritual relationships created by godparenthood during baptism. Religious reformers in the sixteenth and seventeenth centuries were among the first to express anxieties about uncontrolled sexuality, but their concern did not stem from a desire to protect the child from abuse. Social and religious reformers detested incest because they believed sexual activities between close family members were dangerous and disorderly—the act transgressed the God-ordained distinction between human and animal life. One seventeenth-century journal, for instance, matter-of-factly records instances where adults fondled the genitals of a baby—the future King Louis XIII of France.

Before the latter half of the nineteenth century, incestuous activities were rarely vigorously pursued by authorities, most likely out of an aversion to interfere in the domestic exercise of paternal authority. In both Europe and the United States, cases came to the attention of authorities because the **victims** had become pregnant by their fathers, stepfathers, or uncles. Once in court, the law was not on the victim's side. Judges did not comprehend the helplessness of the incest victim, who was caught between devotion to a parent or guardian and the blatant disregard for the child's well-being. Preindustrial science claimed that a female could only become pregnant after achieving orgasm, and thus **pregnancy** was for the judges a sign of consensual sex. A failure to immediately report the incident also was received skeptically by the judges. Nineteenth-century judges in the southern United States were wary of incest accusations; they required explicit proof of sexual activity before reaching a decision. Sentences were generally light. While some perpetrators in Europe could be punished by death, most were publicly whipped and banished from their local towns.

Most historians note a dramatic shift in society's reaction to incest between 1880 and 1914, in both the United States and Europe. Although scholars cannot measure changes in incest activity itself, they argue that a more concerted effort was under way to protect children from sexual crimes. Western culture began to emphasize the innocence of childhood and increasingly worked to protect children from social evils. Governments became concerned about future generations of citizens. They instituted public schooling and adopted legislation designed to protect children. Children were perceived for the first time as having a right to protection. Volunteer organizations staffed by middle-class reformers emerged, such as the New York Society for the Prevention of Cruelty to Children. Reformers lobbied government for child protection laws and established networks of inspectors and caseworkers alongside the police force. In Britain, their work resulted in raising the age of **consent** from 12 to 16 years in 1885, and specific laws against incest finally emerged in the 1908 Punishment against Incest Act.

Prosecution remained extremely difficult. The nature of the crime made it difficult to identify. Spouses and close relatives hesitated to lodge complaints. Informal neighborhood enforcement often proved just as effective. Men who were identified as perpetrators by their peers were publicly humiliated and even beaten. Reformers sought, above all, to protect the morality of young girls, believing that social problems resulted from crimes committed against women that ruined their sexual virtue. Most volunteers were social elites who considered incest a problem of the poor, instigated by close living quarters and unscrupulous morals. Despite the new concern for the children, the volunteer societies were ill prepared to care for them. Most victims were placed in orphanages or child reform schools with juvenile delinquents.

Historians agree that the social concern and awareness about incest generally waned between the 1920s and the 1960s. Professional case workers, influenced by the psychiatrist **Sigmund Freud**, questioned the frequency of the crime and the victim's motivations for coming forward. Indeed, many accused the victim of seducing the parent. General perceptions of sexual crimes were reconstituted as a problem of old men unfamiliar with their female victims. Social workers concentrated less on crimes within the home than on delinquency and its consequences outside of the home.

In the last three decades of the twentieth century, awareness of incest and sexual abuse in general reemerged. Feminist groups, in particular, began speaking out against family violence in the 1970s and 1980s. From 1975 to 1985, incest accusations climbed astronomically, among all socioeconomic levels and ethnic groups. Social workers concentrated their attention on prevention of the crime through educational programs in the school systems. Psychiatrists had placed far more emphasis on understanding the mental problems and disorders among the abusers. By the 1990s, professionals helped victims recall earlier crimes committed against them that they had expunged from their memory because of the trauma involved. *See also*: **Child Rape.**

Suggested Reading: Leroy Ashby, *Endangered Children: Dependency, Neglect, and Abuse in American History* (New York: Twayne Publishers, 1997); Linda Gordon, *Heroes of Their Own Lives: The Politics and History of Family Violence, Boston 1880–1960* (New York: Viking Press, 1988); Louise A. Jackson, *Child Sexual Abuse in Victorian England* (New York: Routledge, 2000).

CHRISTOPHER CORLEY

INDENTURED SERVITUDE. In U.S. history, the system of indentured servitude began in the early seventeenth century when the Virginia Company recruited and transported English laborers to Jamestown. Servants who immigrated to America worked, according to the terms of an indenture contract, for four to seven years for their master and/or mistress. In exchange for servants' labors, employers paid for their travel expenses to America, agreed to maintain them during their term of service, and provided "freedom dues" upon the successful completion of the contract period. Though the system originated in Virginia, it quickly spread throughout the British colonies during the seventeenth and eighteenth centuries. Historians estimate that as many as one-half to two-thirds of the immigrants to the British colonies in the seventeenth and eighteenth centuries arrived as indentured servants. Most indentured servants were young single males; however, colonial recruiters increasingly targeted female servants to balance the sex ratio in the Chesapeake and to provide much-needed labor within planter households. By the mid-seventeenth century, one-third of the indentured servants arriving in America were women; most were under the age of 30.

Although indentured servitude was considered a labor system rather than a form of personal bondage (**slavery**), in reality the distinctions blurred. Both servants and slaves were considered dependents within the master's household, and both groups were subject to physical and sexual exploitation. Servants were not permitted to marry without the **consent** of their master or mistress. In the case of female servants, consent was rarely given, as marriage and potential pregnancies would complicate power relations and jeopardize the labor agreement. Servants also had little control over the conditions of their labor; treatment varied according to one's geographic region, the nature of the work expected of the servant, and the character of the master or mistress. Servants were subject to discipline from masters, including corporal punishment. A master or mistress could also sell the servant to another "owner" without the servant's consent. Servants who ran away, became pregnant, or otherwise deprived the master of their labor could be fined or have time added on to their indenture. A lack of control over one's labor and surroundings heightened the servant's status as a dependent within colonial society.

Still, there were crucial distinctions between servitude and slavery. Servitude was considered a voluntary and contractual process. Most servants were recruited from Great Britain and Germany and expected to improve their lives by escaping tenancy and overcrowded conditions in Europe. In the British colonies and during the early national period, indentured servants enjoyed the rights of Englishmen under the common law. This meant that they were entitled to adequate food, clothing, and shelter and generally received free time on Sundays. Unlike slaves, servants could legally own property and could complain to local courts for assistance if their masters treated them with cruelty or failed to comply with the terms of the indenture contract. However, the victim's access to legal redress was somewhat curtailed by the unequal social relationships pervasive in the colonial courtroom—a petitioner faced a judge and jury of masters rather than peers.

Female servants faced gender and sexual discrimination as bound laborers in colonial America. The rape of a servant by a master was difficult to prove in court, and many cases probably went unreported due to a servant's fear of the master's reprisals. Most female servants had left their families in Europe and had few relatives and friends who could provide protection for them in America. Even if a woman pursued her case in court, judges and juries could interpret cases of **sexual assault** and rape as consensual relationships, privileging a master's version of the event. Since masters controlled servants' movements and activities, servants were subject to sexual vulnerability and **sexual harassment**.

Female servants were in an especially vulnerable position as their work often took place within the household; women whose work involved child care, cooking, and cleaning found themselves on call at all hours of the day and night. Historian Sharon Block points out that women's attempts to negotiate with their masters could be misconstrued as consent or compliance. During the seventeenth and eighteenth centuries, most jurists assumed that conception could not occur if both parties did not achieve sexual satisfaction. According to this theory a rape could not result in **pregnancy**; conception entailed women's consent. A pregnant female servant received further penalty from her master/mistress who were deprived of the servant's labor as a result of childbearing. Thus pregnant servants often had additional time added to their period of indenture and/or fines levied against the father of the child who had to pay damages to the female's master or mistress. If the woman refused to name the father or if he could not be found, the fine was levied on the female servant. Female servants were also liable for medical and child care expenses resulting from pregnancy. In many cases, a servant's child could also be treated as an apprentice or indentured servant, perhaps removing him/her from the mother's care. Cases of illegitimate births were widespread in the Chesapeake region; in the late seventeenth century records indicate that 20 percent of the female servants living in one Maryland county were presented to the county court for bearing children out of wedlock.

Although rape was a capital crime in colonial America, masters or male members of the gentry class accused of rape generally saw their charges dropped to sexual assault or fornication (implying consent). If found guilty, they faced fines for their offense and were forced to sell the servant to another employer. Several studies, however, note that male servants accused of rape were more likely to be convicted and punished for the crime than were men of higher social standing.

Most servants worked for four to seven years under their labor contracts, although younger servants generally served longer contracts until they reached legal maturity. Servants generally worked six days a week for 10 to 14 hours per day. Upon completion of the period of indenture, a servant received his or her "freedom dues." These rewards varied according to the terms of the indenture; most servants received **clothing** and food; males also received rights to landownership as well as tools and livestock. Female servants generally received a small cash payment in lieu of land rights. Once freed, most female servants living in the Chesapeake area married and established households of their own. While a few former servants achieved material success and rose through the ranks of colonial society, most remained poor and continued to work as paid servants or tenants.

Indentured servitude declined over the course of the eighteenth century in the United States as servant prices rose, and planters increasingly relied on slave labor. Servants continued to work as laborers in the mid-Atlantic region, but by the 1830s most employers relied on wage laborers rather than indentured servants. Indentured servitude continues to exist in some parts of the world today. Human rights and labor organizations report cases of indentured servitude in the form of child and unpaid labor in countries such as Pakistan, Haiti, China, and Thailand.

Suggested Reading: Sharon Block, "Lines of Color, Sex, and Service: Comparative Sexual Coercion in Early America," in *Sex, Love, Race: Crossing Boundaries in North American History*, ed. Martha Hodes (New York: New York University Press, 1999), 141–163; Kathleen Brown, *Good Wives, Nasty Wenches and Anxious Patriarchs: Gender, Race and Power in Colonial Virginia* (Chapel Hill: University of North Carolina Press, 1996); David Galenson, *White Servitude in Colonial America: An Economic Analysis* (Cambridge: Cambridge University Press, 1981); Sharon Salinger, *"To Serve Well and Faithfully": Labor and Indentured Servants in Pennsylvania, 1682–1800* (Cambridge: Cambridge University Press, 1987).

REGAN SHELTON

INFANTICIDE. Infanticide is the killing of a newborn baby or an infant. In the United States, the crime is considered a homicide regardless of the age of the child. In the United Kingdom, France, Canada, Australia, and several other countries, infanticide is the killing of a newborn or infant under one year of age. Whether a form of population control, gender selection, or impoverished desperation, infanticide historically has been performed by young, single women who were either raped or seduced by males and then abandoned to cope with their **pregnancy** on their own.

The secret nature of infanticide and the sparse records concerning it do not readily allow historians to gauge its frequency and change over time. What can be traced, however, are the public attitudes toward infanticide. Many ancient societies allowed the father to decide whether the child should live or not. Roman Emperor Constantine I explicitly forbade this in the fourth century, but most legislation and enforcement of infanticide in the Middle Ages was left to the Catholic Church. Not until the sixteenth century did civil authorities explicitly prohibit the act. In 1556, King Henry II of France declared that all pregnancies out of wedlock must be declared to the public authorities. Failure to do so and miscarriage or subsequent death of the child were grounds for prosecuting the mother for **murder**. In England, King James I levied similar prohibitions in 1624. The punishment in both instances was death. These laws were copied in the American colonies and in several European countries. Until the mid-eighteenth century, judges strictly enforced the crime, and prosecutions were heavily weighted toward women.

By the late eighteenth and nineteenth centuries, judges and juries treated the defendants more leniently. In 1774, Massachusetts reduced the punishment for the death of an illegitimate child to a fine of $100 and imprisonment. In England and France, many juries began to acquit the female defendants. In the 1820s and 1830s, French courts admitted extenuating circumstances for **abortion** and infanticide. By the end of the nineteenth century, many defendants had successfully claimed that they were temporarily insane. The judges were sympathetic to these claims, believing that the women were **victims** both of male seducers and social evils. These beliefs underlay the changing definitions of infanticide and its penalty in the nineteenth century. By 1863 concealing a birth in France was a misdemeanor, and the death penalty for infanticide was abolished in 1901. The British Infanticide Act of 1922 (revised in 1938) changed the offense from murder to manslaughter. By the twentieth century many observers believed that mothers who killed their infants were in need of psychiatric help rather than prison.

The women most likely to commit infanticide through the early twentieth century were young, single, and poor. Many were domestic servants. They tried to hide their pregnancies for fear of dishonoring themselves, their families, and their employers. Many gave birth alone, without the aid of midwives, doctors, or **family** members, most frequently in latrines. They killed their babies by suffocating them immediately after birth, by drowning, or by abandoning the child in an isolated area. Although access to abortion in most Western societies has probably reduced the instances of infanticide, the characteristics of women most likely to commit infanticide have changed. Since 1990, several famous cases of young women who killed their babies by depositing them in toilets or on the highways have come to light. No longer is it a crime of the poor and isolated. Many women derived from middle-class families and were relatively well educated. Some of them remained in relationships with their partners. What has not changed, however, is the sense of shame and dishonor that these women felt about their pregnancies. *See also*: **Morning-After Pill.**

Suggested Reading: John Boswell, *The Kindness of Strangers: The Abandonment of Children in Western Europe from Late Antiquity to the Renaissance* (New York: Pantheon, 1988); Rachel G. Fuchs, *Poor and Pregnant in Paris: Strategies for Survival in the Nineteenth Century* (New Brunswick, NJ: Rutgers University Press, 1992); Peter C. Hoffer and N.E.H. Hull, *Murdering Mothers: Infanticide in England and New England, 1558–1803* (New York: New York University Press, 1981); Mark Jackson, ed., *Infanticide: Historical Perspectives on Child Murder and Concealment, 1550–2000* (Burlington, VT: Ashgate Publishing Company, 2002); Larry S. Milner, *Hardness of Heart/Hardness of Life: The Stain of Human Infanticide* (New York: University Press of America, 2000).

CHRISTOPHER CORLEY

INTERRACIAL RAPE. The term *interracial rape* refers to cases of rape that involve perpetrators and **victims** of different racial or ethnic descent. While interracial rape is statistically known to be the exception, not the rule, the term clearly underscores that the perception of and the discourse on acts of sexual violence are highly racialized. This holds particularly true for cultures that look back on a history of intense race conflict and racial discrimination. Accordingly, U.S. culture has coined such loaded concepts as "white-on-black" and "black-on-white" rape, which tends to recall particular eras in American history, most particularly **slavery** and postbellum culture. At the same time, the racialization of rape is an extension of a more general tendency within the history of sexual violence to register rape predominantly as a crime involving persons of unequal power relations. Defined for a long time as both an attack on a woman's and her **family**'s honor and as a kind of property damage, criminal courts have tended to limit themselves to cases in which parties of different classes, races, or ethnicities came into contact. Whether a case of rape receives high public visibility or is considered of little significance is therefore dependent on the relations of classes, races, and ethnicities within a particular culture at a particular historical moment. Historically, the rape of African American and lower-class women, for instance, registered only in rare cases, partly because sexual violence has for a long time been considered inherent to sexualities of **African Americans** and persons of lower-class status, partly because of the supposed insignificance of the "damage" done. Due to the legal status of slaves as chattel and property, the sexual violation of enslaved black women remained largely without legal retribution. To the contrary, during times of slavery the sexual violation of enslaved black women by their white owners became accepted as an institutionalized means of reproducing the slavers' property. The term *interracial rape* thus not only foregrounds the incongruence between acts of sexual violence, on the one hand, and the dominant narratives of rape cultures generate, on the other. It also underlines how ideas about gender, race, and class keep monitoring the perception and interpretation of actual sexual violence.

A paradigmatic example of how interracial rape continues to dominate the public perception and representation of sexual violence in American culture is the so-called **Central Park Jogger** rape case. Despite the fact that more than 30 rapes were reported during the same week in New York City, one of which involved the near decapitation of a black woman, the brutal rape of the 28-year-old white female jogger in April 1989 has preoccupied the **media** for years. Even though raped by a single perpetrator, until recently the woman, an investment banker, was assumed to have been the victim of a beating and **gang rape** by a group of black and Hispanic teenagers whom the news depicted as a "wolf pack." The case only reinforced the established, yet misconceived notion of rape as an encounter of strangers in public places. Moreover, media coverage did not center upon the gender issues involved in the sexual violation but interpreted the case as a conflict between two parties clearly distinguished by race, ethnicity, and class: on the one hand, whites to whom the violation of the young urban professional signified the loss of territory; on the other, African Americans who considered the treatment of the violators as yet another lynching campaign.

The discursive scene of the crime thus draws upon a whole cultural register generated in the course of late-nineteenth-century interracial conflicts and national identity formation. Specifically, it invoked what W.J. Cash in the early 1940s labeled the "**Southern rape complex**," according to which the presumed sexual violation of white beauty by black beast symbolized the "rape" of the South during Reconstruction (1865–1877) and legitimized retaliation through lynch violence. At the same time, this complex inflicted a fear of rape, which, like the threat of lynching, kept a subordinate group—American women in the process of fighting for suffrage—subjugated. Whereas the paradigm of rape and lynching has dominated the discourse on sexual violation, the victims of sexual violation themselves oftentimes receive little attention.

Capitalizing on interracial rape, American culture has tended to sexualize and criminalize interracial encounters and to inflect sexuality according to class, race, and ethnicity. At the same time intraracial and intraethnic sexual violence has oftentimes remained unmarked or insignificant. The predominant projection of the rapist as black or ethnic "other" has not only tended to draw attention away from cases of **sexual assault** involving white middle- and upper-class perpetrators, as feminist critics have underlined. From the 1970s on, African American feminists, in particular, have objected not only to the historical silencing of the sexual violence to which African American women have been subjected. In an act of self-criticism they also pointed to the denial, on the part of African American women, of intra-racial, that is, "black-on-black," sexual violence. Having been discriminated against on the basis of both race and gender, black women have frequently felt torn in their political loyalties, which leaned toward both black men in their fight against racism and women of different races and ethnicities in their struggle against sexism. Complicit with the dominant rhetoric of interracial rape, their tendency to pass silence on intraracial sexual violence has evolved the "cult of secrecy" and a "cul-ture of dissemblance," which can be seen to form black women's central strategy of coping and protecting "the sanity of inner aspects of their lives" (Hine, 294). This secrecy moreover tends to maintain both white supremacy at the expense of black people of both genders and the subjection of (white) female sexuality and personhood within white dominance. In turn, one may argue that the tendency to delete "black-on-black" rape from the cultural text has helped to evolve the lynch-ing of black men by white supremacy as a dominant figure of racial discrimination. This focus of the part of African American discourse on lynching, as opposed to rape, has in turn marginalized issues of (black) female sexuality and personhood. This explains why a sexual aggressor like boxer Mike Tyson may figure as a "vic-tim" of rape, while the actual rape victim, especially if she is of lower-class descent, may vanish from the scene almost entirely. *See also*: **Rape-Lynch Scenario.**

Suggested Reading: Angela Davis, "Rape, Racism, and the Myth of the Black Rapist," *Women, Race and Class* (New York: Random, 1983), 172–201; Darlene Clark Hine, "Rape and the Inner Lives of Black Women in the Middle West: Preliminary Thoughts on the Culture of Dissemblance," *Signs* 14.4 (1989): 912–920; Sabine Sielke, "The Rise of the (Black) Rapist and the Reconstruction of Difference, or: 'Realist' Rape," in her *Reading Rape: The Rhetoric of Sexual Violence in American Literature, 1790–1990* (Princeton, NJ: Princeton University Press, 2002), 33–74; Valerie Smith, "Split Affinities: The Case of Inter-racial Rape," in *Conflicts in Feminism*, ed. Marianne Hirsch and Evelyn Fox Keller (New York: Routledge, 1990), 271–287; Robyn Wiegman, "The Anatomy of Lynching," *Journal of the History of Sexuality* 3.3 (1993): 449–467.

SABINE SIELKE

K

KETAMINE. Ketamine is one of the "club drugs" that is most closely associated with **drug-facilitated sexual assault**. As a prescription drug, ketamine (tradename Ketalar) is an injectable anesthetic that has been used in hospitals and other medical facilities, such as pain management clinics, since 1970. It is a component of pain management programs for patients with chronic intractable pain such as one would experience from terminal cancer. However, most of the ketamine sold (90 percent) at the present time is for veterinary use.

Ketamine is usually ingested in a liquid form, snorted, or smoked as a white powder with marijuana or tobacco. It can also be injected intramuscularly. When ketamine is injected, the reaction may be almost immediate. When ingested orally, as would occur when a dose might be added to someone's drink at a club or party, the initial reaction may occur between 10 to 20 minutes, thus giving the perpetrator enough time to get away. When snorted, the reaction will occur between 5 and 10 minutes. The maximum effect peaks at anywhere between 1 and 6 hours. However, the effects can last up to 48 hours, therefore enabling **sexual predators** to take advantage of the **victim** and disappear without a trace.

Even low doses of ketamine (10–100 milligrams) can produce the following symptoms: poor attention and poor learning at the very least, followed by a dream-like state, hallucinations, hypertension, muscle rigidity, paranoia and aggressive behaviors, numbness, and paralysis. Chronic use can lead to psychological addiction and severe mental illness. One dose alone can produce severe psychological symptoms from which the individual may not recover. High doses of ketamine can cause delirium, amnesia-impaired motor function, depression, and potentially fatal respiratory symptoms.

The street names for ketamine include "Special K," "Vitamin K," and "Cat Valium." The popularity of ketamine increased in the 1980s when abusers found that reactions were similar to phencyclidine (PCP), a particularly dangerous drug that also produces dreamlike states and hallucinations. Ketamine can also be combined with **Ecstasy** and marijuana, producing a product called EKG on the streets. Some users prefer ketamine as opposed to other drugs and purchase it exclusively. *See also*: Alcohol; Gammahydroxybutyrate (GHB); Rohypnol.

Suggested Reading: "Ketamine: A Fact Sheet," Substance Abuse and Mental Health Association's National Clearinghouse for Alcohol and Drug Information, http://www.health. org/nongovpubs/ketamine/.

SHARON A. DROZDOWSKI AND JUDITH A. WATERS

KIDNAPPING. *See* Abduction (Kidnapping).

KINSEY, ALFRED C. (1894–1956). When his book, *Sexual Behavior in the Human Male* was released in 1948, people began to refer to author, scientist, and sex researcher Alfred Kinsey as "the Dr. Gallup of Sex." In 1953, Kinsey and the Institute of Sex Research at the University of Indiana published *Sexual Behavior in the Human Female*. The second volume did not yield that same success as the male volume; moreover, the Rockefeller Foundation withdrew its funding in 1953. Shortly after the funding collapsed, Kinsey died of a heart attack in 1956.

Kinsey examined human sexuality as a scientist. Like with his study of gall wasps, he collected numerous interviews and engaged in fieldwork throughout the Midwest, studying heterosexuals, homosexuals, couples, hustlers, **sex offenders**, and prisoners. Kinsey was viewed by those who worked with him and knew him as a talented interviewer. He changed his language, his body language, and his question format depending on the interviewee.

In his research on men, Kinsey turned a blind eye to certain questions, particularly **child rape**. An informant known as Mr. X provided Kinsey with information about child sexuality. Historian James Jones wrote that Mr. X, a career government employee, was also a career child molester who "masturbated infants, penetrated children, and performed a variety of sex acts on preadolescent boys and girls alike" (511). Although Kinsey believed that rape was wrong because it involved sex derived from force, violence, and coercion, he seemed unable or unwilling to distinguish the behavior of Mr. X as rape and molestation from a mutual sexual experience.

Even in death, Kinsey still caused a stir. Forty years after his death, Kinsey's work on the sexuality of boys and young men derived from the interviews with Mr. X came under fire. In 1995, Steve Stockman, in Galveston, Texas, initiated a bill to investigate Kinsey because of the funding he had received and the information he culled from Mr. X. However, the bill died in committee.

Suggested Reading: James H. Jones, *Alfred C. Kinsey: A Public/Private Life* (New York: W.W. Norton, 1997); Alfred Kinsey, Wardell Pomeroy, and Clyde Martin, *Sexual Behavior in the Human Male* (Philadelphia: W.B. Saunders, 1948); Alfred Kinsey and the Staff of the Institute of Sex Research, *Sexual Behavior in the Human Female* (Philadelphia: W.B. Saunders, 1953).

ELAINE CAREY

L

LAW ENFORCEMENT. Law enforcement agencies worldwide follow a variety of penal or criminal codes and sentencing guidelines. For instance, the contents of the New York Penal Code, the German Penal Code, the Penal Law of Israel,·and the Pennsylvania Crimes Code all differ slightly while addressing the same crimes. A crime may be defined by different terms in each state and country. There are various types and specific levels of the sexual offense known as rape. For instance, rape in the third degree is different from rape in the first degree. Rape is a felony in every U.S. state. A felony is an offense for which a criminal may be sentenced to more than a year in prison.

Law enforcement officials and prosecutors investigate rape thoroughly. They must narrow down the broad term of *rape* into its legal components. Thus, they explore whether or not a victim was mentally incapacitated or physically helpless during rape, whether there was forcible compulsion, how many crimes occurred surrounding the rape incident (e.g., **abduction/kidnapping**, aggravated sexual contact), and other issues.

Reporting a rape is frequently an unpleasant experience for **survivors**. In fact, the traumatic process of recounting the experience is often referred to as **secondary rape**. Women who have been raped might request to speak with a female police officer, but one may not be available at the time of a report, and in some places, there may not be one specialized to handle a rape case. Some rape **victims** have stated that police were insensitive, unsympathetic, or unreceptive. Still others have stated that law enforcement officials made harsh, psychologically damaging statements to them. There are even reports of bias against rape survivors; some assert that police are more ready to believe victims who struggled or who reported a rape immediately after its conclusion over victims who did not.

To combat this, officers in many places are given more sensitivity training than in past decades. In addition, some cities have organized all sex crimes into special victims units. Officers in these units are given special training, and the units have ties to rape counselors and others trained to gather evidence and prosecute sex crimes.

Police collect and compile basic data on the suspect, such as height, race, mode of operation, and previous arrest records. They work upon facts, information, and evidence received by the victim, as well as physical and medical evidence. The law enforcement and medical communities work together to collect rape evidence. At the hospital, medical personnel may use a **rape kit** to collect evidence. In some cases, such as the rape of a child not yet old enough to talk, the medical evidence is the entire case against a defendant.

When gathering a report, all police officers generally use the same principles. An officer is sent to the scene of the crime. The officer interviews the survivor at the scene, hospital, police office, or the individual's home. **Clothing** may be collected for evidence. Standardized questions help the officer remember to cover all areas and details needed for suspect apprehension and a possible trial. While it may seem to the survivor that repeated questions means that an officer doubts the account, repetition is common in attempts to document all details. Police make sure the survivor gets treatment for injuries. Further questioning may take place at a later time at police headquarters, where a sketch artist might work with the survivor to create a picture of the rapist. Testimony gathered helps officials piece together any pattern, which may match details from other rapes and lead to a suspect. Police will seek witnesses but will keep a rape victim's identity private as they do so. Even someone who saw the victim after the attack may have circumstantial evidence, such as testimony of the victim's demeanor, composure, injuries, or physiological state, such as shock.

A survivor cannot be forced to press charges. If the survivor does so, the investigation continues. A suspect is sought and must be identified. With a suspect in custody, the case is handed over to a prosecutor, who decides if the case is strong enough to go to trial. The district attorney has the final say on trying the case. In court, the survivor testifies as the primary witness against the attacker. Sometimes the entire process from the initial stages of reporting the crime to a rapist's sentencing can take several years. *See also*: **DNA Collection and Evidence; Prosecution.**

Suggested Reading: Helen Benedict, *Recovery: How to Survive Sexual Assault for Women, Men, Teenagers, Their Friends and Families* (Garden City, NY: Doubleday, 1985); Susan Brownmiller, *Against Our Will: Men, Women and Rape* (New York: First Ballantine Books, 1993).

ELIZABETH JENNER

LAWS. *See* Rape Laws.

LEGISLATION, ILLEGAL SEX ACTS. One of the areas of jurisprudence that has been controversial throughout history has been the element of law dealing with sexual intercourse and in turn the prohibition on specific sexual acts that have been deemed immoral and therefore illegal. In the Western legal tradition, the sexual acts that have been classified as illegal, such as homosexuality, **bestiality, incest,** adultery and necrophilia, are prohibited in large part as a result of theological prohibitions established in the Pentateuch, the first five books of the Judeo-Christian monotheistic tradition. With the advent of Islam in 622 C.E., many of the theological traditions and prohibitions within the Judeo-Christian tradition were also incorporated into the Islamic jurisprudential framework, included the prohibition against sexual acts considered to "go against the Natural Order."

English common law—the model for the Western legal tradition—does prohibit rape, bestiality, and incest, which carried over to the American constitutional system. However, the legal rules surrounding adultery and homosexual intercourse, which existed for centuries, have slowly eroded due to societal changes. In the context of the American judicial system, there has been a systematic change in both the perception of the law and the application of legal precedence toward consensual sex between unmarried persons, which had been decriminalized and deemed as being socially acceptable. In terms of legislation and the evitable interpretation of laws by the judiciary pertaining to sexual conduct, the "illegal sex acts" under the most scrutiny are those that are interwoven into the discussion regarding privacy and discrimination—namely, same-sex intercourse, which has been examined by landmark cases *Bowers v. Hardwick* (1986) and *Lawrence v. Texas* (2003).

The U.S. Supreme Court in *Bowers v. Hardwick* (1986)—the seminal Supreme Court decision that upheld a Georgia state law that criminalized homosexual activity—argued in the majority opinion that nation–states had long repressed homosexual acts throughout the course of Western civilization and that case precedence in Roman law, as well as the writings of **Sir William Blackstone** and the Baron de Montesquieu, supported the 1986 decision. As such, in regard to the issue of privacy, Justice Byron White argued in the majority opinion that even though homosexual conduct may occur in the privacy of one's home, illegal conduct, in the context of the Georgia law where **sodomy** was illegal, is not always immunized "whenever it occurs in the home." However, the 1986 decision would be challenged and overturned in the case of *Lawrence v. Texas*, where the Supreme Court would reverse itself and find in the majority opinion in the case of John Lawrence's conviction of a Class C misdemeanor for sodomy that Lawrence's conviction for adult consensual sexual intimacy was a violation of the due process clause of the Fourteenth Amendment. Following the ruling in *Lawrence*, the legal environment toward illegal sex acts changed dramatically, of which the repercussions are still being dealt with. With the exception of acts of rape and incest, all consensual sexual acts have been decriminalized, and as such, legislators are redefining the laws accordingly. *See also*: **Prison Rape; Rape Law.**

Suggested Reading: Sodomy Laws, www.sodomylaws.org/lawrence/lawrence.htm.

OJAN ARYANFARD

LEGISLATION, SEXUAL HARASSMENT. Sexual harassment is defined as any unwelcome conduct that is sexual in nature. Legislation prohibits sexual harassment in many social contexts including education, housing, and employment; however, most law revolves around two types of sexual harassment that have been recognized as illegal in the workplace: quid pro quo and hostile work environment. Quid pro quo consists of illegal acts in which **victims** are forced to submit sexually to others' demands or face negative consequences such as being denied requests for raises or promotions. A hostile work environment is defined as a workplace in which sexual language and behavior creates a perceived impediment to an individual fulfilling his/her professional responsibilities.

Federal sexual harassment law evolved out of the Civil Rights Act of 1964, as amended by Title IX of the Educational Amendment of 1972, the Equal Employment Opportunity Act of 1972, and the Civil Rights Act of 1991. However, federal courts were at first reluctant to find sexual harassment unlawful in the workplace under Title VII of the 1964 Act, in part because there was little legislative history to Congress' last-minute decision to prohibit gender discrimination in Title VII.

In *Meritor Savings Bank v. Vinson*, 477 U.S. 57 (1986), the U.S. Supreme Court found both quid pro quo and hostile work environment unlawful under Title VII, and since that time, victims of sexual harassment in workplaces of 15 or more employees have had a private right of action in federal court against alleged harassers. In a series of decisions in the late 1990s, the U.S. Supreme Court expanded the scope of employer liability for a supervisor's harassing conduct, even to certain situations in which the employer did not know of the supervisor's unlawful activities. Title VII of the 1964 Act, as amended by the Civil Rights Act of 1991, entitles aggrieved employees to different remedies, depending on the case. An employee might be entitled to an injunction enjoining the harassing conduct, reinstatement, back pay and benefits, damages for personal injuries (physical and emotional), punitive damages against the employer, attorneys' fees and costs, or an order requiring the company to reform its sexual harassment policies. All 50 states have civil laws, in some form or another, prohibiting sexual harassment in employment; however, the scope of the prohibited conduct and available remedies vary from state to state. Additionally, state laws often target smaller employers not reached by federal law.

In the 1990s, courts and legislatures started to look more closely at sexual harassment in social contexts other than employment. In *Franklin v. Gwinnett County Public Schools*, 503 U.S. 60 (1992), the U.S. Supreme Court ruled that sexual harassment in public **schools** is illegal under both Title VII of the 1964 Act and Title IX (which prohibits gender-based discrimination in schools receiving federal funds), passed as part of the Educational Amendment of 1972. All states have also enacted various forms of antistalking laws criminalizing persistent, harassing conduct that causes harassed individuals to suffer emotional distress and develop reasonable fears of physical injury or death. Some of those laws reach cyber stalking, or stalking that occurs over the Internet. While antistalking laws are not limited to stalking that is sexually motivated, much of the stalking that is prosecuted under those laws has a sexual animus.

Despite federal and state law prohibiting sexual harassment, the most aggressive sexual harassment policies are often adopted by nongovernmental entities. In employment and higher education, for example, employers and universities have incentives to develop their own sexual harassment policies and to self-police. Such proactive behavior makes them less susceptible to employees and students who allege not only that they were harassed but also that their employers or universities did nothing to prevent the harassment. *See also*: **Campus Rape; Campus Security Act (Clery Act)**.

Suggested Reading: Ernest C. Hadley and George M. Chuzi, *Sexual Harassment: Federal Law*, 3rd ed. (Arlington, VA: Dewey Publications, 1997).

GREGORY M. DUHL

LITERATURE, WORLD AND AMERICAN. Rape and sexual violence are recurrent and central tropes and motives of world literature from ancient myths to postmodernist fiction. Accordingly, the meaning of literary representations of rape has changed with the different forms and functions literature has taken in the course of its history. Greek and Roman **mythology** has repeatedly employed rape as a figure of transformation and a motor of change as, for instance, in the Philomela myth or the legends of the **rape of the Sabine women** and the **rape of Lucretia**. By contrast, realist literature from the nineteenth to the twenty-first century evolved rape as a dominant rhetorical figure of social, racial, and ethnic difference and as part of its moral and aesthetic agenda, which meant to renegotiate cultural consensus through literary effects of authenticity. Still literary texts, be they classic rape narratives or modernist poems featuring tropes of rape, such as W.B. Yeats's "Leda and the Swan," should not be taken as depictions that mirror social phenomena of sexual violence. Like other physical experiences, including pain and sexuality, rape tends to resist representation. Moreover, rape narratives and poems are first of all cultural representations that refer to, recall, and oftentimes mock or parody their own tradition and history of representation. The legend of the rape of Lucretia, for instance, is prominently recontextualized in Renaissance literature and culture, for instance, in William Shakespeare's *The Rape of Lucrece*, as well as in Rembrandt's paintings. Likewise the Philomela myth was reworked by the Roman poet Ovid, as well as in the fiction of many American authors, including John Irving and Maya Angelou.

Such intertextual references underline that literary representations of rape relate to real rape incidents in highly mediated ways only. They are primarily interpretations, readings of rape. Transposed into discourse, rape functions as a rhetorical device, an insistent figure for other social, political, and economic concerns and conflicts. In addition, as they have evolved in historically specific contexts, rape narratives interrelate with, produce, and subsequently reproduce a cultural symbology that employs sexual deviance for the formation of cultural identities. More specifically, rape narratives have been a major force in the cultural construction of sexuality, gender, race, ethnicity, class, and even national identity. As they seem to make sense of socially deviant behavior, they oftentimes limit our understanding of sexual violence, while producing norms of sexuality in the process.

American rape narratives in particular are highly overdetermined by a distinct history of racial conflict and a discourse on race. In the African American slave narrative, for instance, hints at sexual violation of enslaved black women functioned as part of the political agenda of abolitionism. The image of the hypersexualized black rapist, projected, for instance, by racist historical novels of Thomas Dixon, became a trope for "Negro rule" during Reconstruction, which in turn legitimized lynch violence against **African Americans**. Thus each national literary history evolves its own dominant rape narratives, which are historically and ideologically specific, even if they rely on widely established pretexts (such as myths) and functional patterns (such as the "othering" of sexual violence).

Literary texts are particularly revealing for an understanding of cultural representations of rape and their meaning because they embed instances of rape into supposedly conclusive stories and manage to "naturalize" sexual violence into consensual views on gender, sexuality, and the world at large. At the same time fictional, especially modernist and postmodernist novels such as William Faulkner's *Sanctuary* (1931), Toni Morrison's *Beloved* (1987), or Bret Easton Ellis's *American Psycho* (1991) do not render rape realistically but re-present, repoliticize, and thus reinterpret previous literary interrogations of rape and sexual violence. In this way they inscribe themselves into a tradition of readings of rape, a tradition they simultaneously remember, interfere with, and call into question. *See also*: **Art; Films, Foreign; Films, U.S.**

Suggested Reading: Nancy Armstrong and Leonard Tennenhouse, eds., *The Violence of Representation: Literature and the History of Violence* (London: Routledge, 1989); Frances Ferguson, "Rape and the Rise of the Novel," *Representations* 20 (September 1987): 88–112; Christine Froula, "The Daughter's Seduction: Sexual Violence and Literary History," *Signs* 11.4 (1986): 621–644; Lynn Higgins and Brenda Silver, eds., *Rape and Representation* (New York: Columbia University Press, 1991); Stephanie H. Jed, *Chaste Thinking: The Rape of Lucretia and the Birth of Humanism* (Bloomington: Indiana University Press, 1989); Sabine Sielke, *Reading Rape: The Rhetoric of Sexual Violence in American Literature, 1790–1990* (Princeton, NJ: Princeton University Press, 2002).

SABINE SIELKE

LYNCHING. *See* **Rape-Lynch Scenario.**

M

MACHISMO. Machismo is most commonly linked with Latin American and Latino constructions of masculinity, although it is evident in other cultures. The use and application of the term *machismo* is contradictory if not also complex. Although a stereotypical view of Latin masculinity and sexuality, it has historically been used by scholars as a gendered category of analysis of men and their relationships with women.

According to scholars, men exhibit a number of characteristics that serve as a basis of machismo. Machos are sexually virile and promiscuous. In regard to women, machos view women as passive, but they are also dangerous because their sexuality is the source of **family** and masculine honor. Machos respect the cult of **virginity** and prescribe it for the women of their family as the basis of their own masculine honor. However, other women, those outside the family, are for the taking. Young men are taught early "to be a man" and to become sexually active at an early age. Thus, the macho's sexual conquest as evident in his fertility and number of offspring is a source of power and prestige.

The contradiction in male and female sexuality and behavior contributes to masculine aggression and violence. Because the macho's goal is to pursue women and have many women, he may resort to rape, in and outside of marriage. The dishonoring and rape of women may be necessary for a man to maintain his machismo. Thus, the macho is portrayed and viewed as violent, lascivious, and dangerous.

Puerto Rican scholar, poet, and novelist Martín Espada argues that Anglos have used the stereotypical construction of Latino masculinity and machismo to repress Latino men in the United States (González, 87). Although the word *macho* is many times used as a pejorative term, contemporary writers have embraced the word and recreated it as a signifier of the positive aspects of Latino masculinity. Activist and poet Luis J. Rodríquez writes, "For us, macho does not mean the bully, the jock, the knucklehead. He is warrior, protector, defender, and lover. He is artist, hero, father, and elder" (González, 201). *See also*: **Hispanics/Latinos.**

Suggested Reading: Ray González, ed., *Muy Macho: Latino Men Confront Their Manhood* (New York: Anchor, 1996); Alfredo Mirandé, *Hombres y Machos: Masculinity in Latino Culture* (Boulder, CO: Westview Press, 1997); Rafael Ramírez, *What It Means to Be a Man: Reflections on Puerto Rican Masculinity* (New Brunswick, NJ: Rutgers University Press, 1999).

ELAINE CAREY

MACKINNON, CATHARINE A. (1946–   ). Feminist legal scholar, law professor, advocate, and a founder of feminist legal theory and litigation methods, Catharine A. MacKinnon has been a pivotal force in the movement to elevate women's status in law and society since the late 1970s, when her compelling insights into the nature and consequences of sexual inequality first gained notice. Best known for her path-breaking, often controversial work on **sexual harassment** and **pornography** (much of the latter with **Andrea Dworkin**), she has steadfastly endeavored to expose and remediate all forms of sexual violence against women. And while her positions on these and other issues continue to draw fire from multiple quarters, their influence on evolving legal conceptions of sex discrimination remains unmistakable.

MacKinnon's ideas are unified by a radical conception of entrenched male dominance and enforced female subordination, a pervasively eroticized hierarchical relationship that both sustains inequality between the sexes and facilitates the sexually assaultive practices that are among its most pernicious by-products. This is nowhere more apparent than in the case of rape. According to MacKinnon, "If sexuality is central to women's definition and forced sex is central to sexuality, rape is indigenous, not exceptional, to women's social condition" (*Feminist Theory*, 172). Emphasizing rape's socially constructed, deeply gendered character, she contends that "[t]o be rapable . . . defines what a woman is" (178). Law, with its relentlessly masculine stance, has exacerbated victims' plight, producing a climate in which rape, from women's point of view, is not "prohibited" but merely "regulated" (179).

MacKinnon has not confined her activities to the borders of the United States. Her most significant international involvement to date grew out of the systematic rapes perpetrated by Serbian forces in **Bosnia-Herzegovina** in the early 1990s. In response, she developed the claim that ethnically based mass rape intended to destroy a people was a genocidal act, a motivation further evidenced in the widespread practice of forced impregnation as part of a strategy of "**ethnic cleansing.**" These were central elements in a civil action brought in federal district court by MacKinnon and her colleagues against the former Serb leader Radovan Karadzic for command responsibility in sexual and other crimes committed against Bosnian and Croation women and children, a case that ultimately resulted in a $745 million judgment for the plaintiffs.

As these examples suggest, MacKinnon's efforts to advance the cause of sex equality have been vast in scope as well as impact. Together they bespeak a profound awareness of the continued vulnerability of women and girls to sex-based exploitation and an abiding commitment to working toward its elimination worldwide. *See also*: **Genocide.**

Suggested Reading: Elizabeth Amon, "Rape in Wartime: Letting the Victims Tell Their Stories," *National Law Journal*, September 18, 2000; Catharine A. MacKinnon, "Rape, Genocide, and Women's Human Rights," in *Mass Rape: The War against Women in Bosnia-*

Herzegovina, ed. Alexandra Stiglmayer (Lincoln: University of Nebraska Press, 1994); Catharine A. MacKinnon, *Toward a Feminist Theory of the State* (Cambridge: Harvard University Press, 1989); Fred Strebeigh, "Defining Law on the Feminist Frontier," *New York Times Magazine*, October 6, 1991.

LISA CARDYN

MALE RAPE. Male rape is an act of violence and a crime. It can include anal and oral penetration, **oral sex**, and other behaviors that illegally violate an individual's body by use of manipulation, coercion, or force. Any man can be a **victim** of **sexual assault** regardless of his age, physical ability, economic status, race/ethnicity, and sexual identity. Most men are raped by other men. A small percentage of men are raped by women, usually an acquaintance. In most cases, women use coercion and manipulation instead of physical force.

The 1999 Bureau of Justice Statistics reports that 9 percent of all rape happens to men. Although statistics vary, research indicates that more male rape occurs within the prison system. In their 2000 article in *The Prison Journal*, Cindy Struckman-Johnson and David Struckman-Johnson noted that 21 percent of male inmates who responded to a survey of seven midwestern prisons indicated that they had been raped or had experienced forced sexual contact at least once since they were incarcerated.

Although most male rape is perpetrated by men, it should not be considered "**homosexual rape**." While males who rape other males usually identify themselves as heterosexual, neither the biological sex nor the sexual identification of the rapist or the rape victim makes the act a sexual one. Sexual intercourse without mutual **consent** is always rape. Rape is not a pursuit of sex; it is about the attainment of power and control over another person or group.

Many men who are raped feel humiliated, ashamed, isolated, and alone. **Survivors** may fear that they will not be believed or that they will be blamed for not fending off the attacker and "stopping" the rape. Because of cultural ideas about male strength and sexuality, some people believe that "real" men do not get raped and that if a man is raped by another man, this will make him gay. Additionally, male survivors may interpret their rape as an act of sex and therefore believe they had a homosexual encounter. This can lead some men to question their sexual identity and even prevent them from telling someone about the rape for fear of being called homosexual.

Due to the **stigma** attached to being a male rape victim and the above-mentioned concerns, many men do not report rape or tell anyone about their experience. Coming forward as a victim and getting medical and social help may feel like a violation of the code of masculinity. When gay men are raped, their feelings of isolation and powerlessness can be even greater. Due to homophobia, the fear and/or hatred of homosexuality in oneself or others, they may not be "out" as gay to their **family** and community and fear a negative reaction. They may not live in a community with counseling and advocacy services for gay survivors, and in some states they can even be prosecuted under anti**sodomy** laws for having what is considered illegal sex.

Lack of reporting and community awareness creates a lack of visibility of male rape and reinforces the isolation and silence of all victims. Some men do not realize that they can anonymously call a **rape crisis center**, get a medical examination, and report acquaintance and stranger rape to the police because they believe that these services are only for female victims. While most services still focus on female survivors and violence prevention for women, men can and do access these services. There are increasingly more men involved in violence prevention efforts, as well as men's groups to address concerns of male survivors and male perpetrators of rape. A part of stopping male rape requires awareness, education, and more accessible services for male survivors. *See also*: **Anal Sex; Prison Rape; Rape Counseling.**

Suggested Reading: Bureau of Justice Statistics Web site, http://www.ojp.usdoj.gov/bjs/pub; Fred Pelka, "Raped: A Male Survivor Breaks His Silence," in *Rape and Society: Readings on the Problem of Sexual Assault*, ed. P. Searles and R.J. Berger (Boulder, CO: Westview Press, 1995); Michael Scarce, *Male on Male Rape: The Hidden Toll of Stigma and Shame* (New York: Insight Books, 1997); Cindy Struckman-Johnson and David Struckman-Johnson, "Sexual Coercion Rates in Seven Midwestern Facilities for Men," *The Prison Journal* 80.4 (2000): 379–390, http://www.spr.org/pdf/struckman.pdf. Joseph Weinberg, "Male Survivors of Incest and Other Sexual Assault (Part 1)," *Teaching Sexual Ethics* 4.1 (January 2000): 1–20.

HEATHER SCHMIDT

MARITAL RAPE. The word *rape* is derived from the Latin work *raptus*, which was used to define the act wherein one man damaged the property of another. The property, of course, was the man's wife or daughter. In the United States and England, wives were considered the property of their husbands under the legal concept of *coverture*, meaning that a woman was literally "covered" by her husband when she married. Thereafter, she ceased to have a separate legal existence. The reasoning went that since a wife was owned by her husband, he had inherent rights to her body. In most states a husband could beat his wife as long as the instrument used was no bigger than his thumb. Husbands also had legal unlimited access to their wives' bodies whenever they chose to exercise the right, regardless of a wife's personal desires. While *coverture* was no longer legally valid in most states after the mid-nineteenth century when the first Married Women's Property Acts were passed, husbands and the legal system continued to treat wives as sexual property. In Alabama, for example, even husbands who raped wives who left them and filed for divorce could not be prosecuted for rape. As late as 1992 a South Carolina man was acquitted of raping his wife, even though he had videotaped the rape. He successfully argued that she was tied to the bed on the videotape not because of rape but as part of their "usual" sexual practices.

The right of a husband to rape his wife has historically been protected by what became known as the marital or spousal exemption. The legal basis for the marital exemption has been traced to seventeenth-century England when Lord **Matthew Hale** declared, "But the husband cannot be guilty of a rape committed by himself upon his lawful wife; for their mutual matrimonial consent and contract the wife hath given up herself in the kind unto her husband, which she cannot retract" (Hale, 628). Using that line of reasoning, most states defined rape as "the forcible penetration of the body of a woman, not the wife of the perpetrator," making marital rape legal by definition.

States have been slow to retract marital exemption laws because marriage has been protected both traditionally and legally as a sacred and private institution. Supporters of marital exemptions have also claimed that vindictive wives could claim rape to repay husbands for real or imagined grievances and that marital rape would be almost impossible to prove in a court of law. A landmark study of 900 rape victims by Diana Russell in 1982 revealed that one out of every seven women who has ever been married has been raped by her husband at least once, and some women have been raped many times within marriage. Many of the women in Russell's study did not identify violent sexual acts within marriage as rape; yet they suffered typical rape trauma symptoms. Some **victims** of marital rape exhibit extensive physical and emotional problems for years after the marriage has been dissolved. It has been argued that the aftermath of rape by a sexual partner may be even more emotionally damaging than rape by a stranger because of the loss of trust in intimate relationships.

In 1975 in Oregon, John Rideout became the first man to be charged with raping his wife while still living with her. According to his wife Greta, Rideout was addicted to violent sex, which he frequently demanded several times a day. In October 1975, Greta Rideout ran away from her abusive husband, but he followed her and locked her in their apartment and beat her until she agreed to have sex with him. After he was acquitted of the rape charge, the couple reconciled but later divorced. Much criticism was directed at Greta Rideout throughout the trial, and it was frequently argued that she must have not been "raped" if she could return to the marriage. Studies on marital rape have shown that most wives who are raped are also battered, as was the case with Greta Rideout.

Unlike most rape cases where **prosecution** is often unsuccessful, in marital rape cases the conviction rate is around 90 percent. For example, in the case of *People v. Liberta*, a New York man raped his wife in front of their small son. Since the Libertas were living apart under court order at the time of the rape, the trial court determined that they were not "married," and the husband was not allowed to claim the marital exemption. Liberta appealed his conviction, arguing that New York's marital exemption was unconstitutional because it denied men who were not married the right to equal protection from rape laws. New York's highest court turned the tables on him and upheld his conviction, and it overturned the state's marital exemption law on the grounds that it denied equal protection to married women to be protected from rape in the same way that unmarried women were. The *Liberta* decision contended that none of the traditional legal arguments in support of marital exemption laws were valid.

Up until the last quarter of the twentieth century when the women's movement pushed for major changes in the legal status of women, most states retained marital exemptions from rape laws. In some states, this exemption was extended to common-law husbands and live-in partners. By 2003, all 50 states and the federal government defined marital rape as a crime punishable by law. Seventeen states and Washington, DC completely abolished the marital exemption, while other states retained some element of the exemption. In most states, married women who are raped by their husbands also have the right to bring civil suit and may recover medical and legal expenses, as well as damages for pain and suffering. *See also*: Battered Women; Rape Law.

Suggested Reading: Matthew Hale, *History of the Pleas of the Crown*, vol. 1 (Philadelphia: R.H. Small, 1847); Linda Ledray, *Recovering from Rape* (New York: Henry Holt, 1994); Mary E. Odem and Judy Clay-Warner, eds., *Confronting Rape and Sexual Assault* (Wilmington, DE: Scholarly Resources, 1998); Diana E.H. Russell, *Rape in Marriage* (New York:

Macmillan, 1982); Irving J. Sloan, *Rape* (Dobbs Ferry, NY: Oceana Publishing, 1992); Wellesley Centers for Women, "The Wife Rape Information Page," http://www.wellesley.edu/WCW/projects/mrape.html.

ELIZABETH R. PURDY

MASSIE CASE. One of the most socially divisive cases of the twentieth century is the rape of Thalia Massie on the Island of Hawaii. The daughter of a wealthy Washington couple and the wife of a naval officer, Massie was savagely raped by five men of Asian descent following a dinner party. The incident set off a firestorm of racial angst, which led to the **murder** of one of the accused rapists by Massie's husband.

In 1931, Massie and her husband Lt. Thomas Massie moved to Honolulu as part of her husband's deployment orders with the navy. On the night of September 11, 1931, the Massies attended a party at the Ala Wai Inn. Thalia Massie decided to leave the get-together early and walk home. According to her testimony, as she was walking home, five men, including a man named Joseph Kahahawai, forced Massie into their car and drove her to the secluded Ala Moana Park, where she was beaten and raped by the men. The commander of the 14th Naval District, Rear Admiral Yates Stirling, which encompassed all the naval forces in Hawaii, purportedly contacted the governor of Hawaii, Lawrence Judd, to have the case "vigorously prosecuted." However, as the court records illustrate, the five men gave conflicting testimony of the rape, and after days of deliberation, the jury was deadlocked. The judge declared a mistrial, and a second trial was scheduled.

Critics of the trial accused the jury of racial bias, and tensions ran high through the States as a result. Admiral Stirling petitioned President Herbert Hoover to declare martial law in Hawaii, as did the General Assembly of Kentucky. The events took a turn for the surreal when Massie's mother, Grace Fortescue, Lieutenant Massie, and two subordinates kidnapped Kahahawai and began to interrogate him to extract a confession for the rape, which he purportedly did give Massie. Massie shot Kahahawai, but he was caught by police as he and his accomplices were attempting to dispose of the body. Acclaimed defense attorney Clarence Darrow was retained for Thomas Massie's defense. He argued that Massie was temporarily insane. However, Massie and his accomplices were sentenced to 10 years, which was commuted by the governor to one hour to be served in his office. The Massie case presents a unique study of how the judiciary can be changed by political pressure, and it accentuates the need for impartiality. *See also*: **Rape Trials.**

Suggested Reading: Cobey Black, *Hawaii Scandal* (Honolulu: Island Heritage, 2002); Richard Borreca, "The Massie Case Brought Turmoil," *Honolulu Star-Bulletin*, October 15, 1999, http://starbulletin.com/1999/10/15/news/story7.html; Ronald T.Y. Moon, "The Case for Judicial Independence," *Honolulu Star-Bulletin*, July 24, 1999, http://starbulletin.com/1999/07/24/editorial/special2.html.

OJAN ARYANFARD

MEDIA. The subject of media and rape is complicated. To be sure, media attention raises public consciousness of any social issue. For example, as media attention has increased, women have been more willing to report rapes. However, the quality and the effects of media coverage have been assessed both positively and negatively by recent scholars.

Media attention in the past century has been intricately connected with the civil rights and **feminist movements**. Until the 1950s, media coverage of rapes was usually limited to those allegedly committed by **African American** men. During the civil rights movement, in an effort to increase public sensitivity to racist stereotypes, the media sometimes emphasized the innocence of the wrongly accused by "denigrating the **victim**." Feminist attention to rape in the 1970s was significant in creating public awareness of rape as an important social issue. This is demonstrated in the increase in stories focused on rape. In 1968 the *New York Times* published 18 stories about rape, and in 1973, it published 108. This coverage can be divided into three types: incident reports, episodic stories (which illustrated a specific woman's rape to demonstrate the political, legal, and social barriers involved in reporting and prosecuting a rape), and thematic stories (which examined one particular aspect of the **prosecution** process from the victim's point of view). A constructive and direct result of the press attention was a sudden increase in the amount of antirape legislation and social services for rape victims.

Media coverage of rape involves some controversial issues: the coverage of the trial, the identification of the victim, and the types of rape that the media cover. First, some feminist critics charge that the media purposefully provide stories saturated with "voyeuristic" and sensationalized details. Second, some question whether it is ethical for the media to publicly identify the victim. In the case of *Cox Broadcasting Corporation v. Cohn* in 1975, the U.S. Supreme Court ruled that news agencies have the constitutional right to publish victims' names. This public identification of victims is a contested topic. Some advocates argue that the ability to disclose victims' identities complicates a woman's resolve to prosecute rapists because of her fear of being placed "on trial" in the public eye or from public embarrassment. But others counter this argument by emphasizing that the "ideal" of having a silenced and unnamed victim contributes to a culture of shame and disempowerment for rape victims. In other words, silence equals another type of identity loss. To speak out about one's experiences would empower them and cause them to take control over the event itself. Third, some believe that the media plays a pivotal role in creating a public understanding and definition of what constitutes rape. For example, in the last decade, there has been a greater focus on "**date rape**" or "acquaintance rape." The effect, some have argued, is that more money has been directed to college campuses to the detriment of women's social centers and **rape crisis centers** in urban and poorer areas.

These controversies aside, most have found productive results from media coverage. A less optimistic view can be found in the work of Helen Benedict, who finds that the media fails in its coverage because it does not provide analyses of gender relations and sexist stereotypes that feminist research asserts is the root cause of rape. Instead, according to Benedict, the press treats rape as simply "unwanted sex," and in so doing, it perpetuates rape in two ways: one, either by offering an image of a victim who has tempted a man, or men, and in so doing effectively blames the victim or, two, by blaming racial or socioeconomic conditions when the accused falls into a "criminal stereotype."

While it is certain that the quality and merits of press coverage will continue to be debated, it is undeniable that the media has helped shape public attitudes toward and awareness of rape and will continue to do so. *See also*: **Advertising; Rape Shield Laws.**

Suggested Reading: Helen Benedict, *Virgin or Vamp: How the Press Covers Sex Crimes* (New York: Oxford University Press, 1992); Maria Bevacqua, *Rape on the Public Agenda: Feminism and the Politics of Sexual Assault* (Boston: Northeastern University Press, 2000).

JILL GORMAN

MEGAN'S LAW. On July 29, 1994, seven-year-old Megan Kanka was lured into the nearby home of **sex offender** Jesse Timmendequas, who promised her a puppy. Megan was brutally raped and murdered. Her parents did not know that Timmendequas and two other sexual offenders were sharing a house in their neighborhood in Hamilton Township, New Jersey. Timmendequas had twice been convicted of sexual abuse of children but had only served 6 years of a 10-year sentence. Megan's parents, Maureen and Richard Kanka, were outraged that they had not been notified and became outspoken advocates of community notification laws, founding the Megan Nicole Kanka Foundation. In 1994 Megan's Law was enacted in New Jersey. Following New Jersey's example, a number of states passed similar laws. Some states named laws after Megan Kanka, while others named their laws after victims of similar crimes in the particular state. When President Bill Clinton signed the federal version of Megan's Law, mandating community notification, in June 1996, he called for a national registry of sexual offenders. By 1998, all 50 states had passed some version of Megan's Law.

Most legislation based on Megan's Law requires three tiers of notification. Tier One is made up of "low-risk" offenders and calls for notification to law officers when a convicted sex offender moves into a neighborhood. Tier Two is classified as "moderate-risk" and mandates notification to places where children are likely to be, such as **schools**, day care centers, and parks, as well as to legal authorities. Tier Three is made up of "high-risk" offenders who have a strong likelihood of repeating the crime. In this case, sexual offenders may be required to distribute flyers and run ads in newspapers in addition to notifying school, communities, and the police. Most police departments have databases of known sexual offenders that can be accessed by parents or other interested parties, and most states now provide Internet access to sexual offender registries. Some states have passed laws that allow authorities to hold known sexual offenders who are likely to repeat their crimes in state psychiatric institutions even after criminal sentences have been served.

Parents and the police generally applaud Megan's Law, but critics of the law argue that it violates the rights of sexual offenders who have served their sentences. Even supporters agree that it only affects a small number of sexual offenders because most children who are sexually assaulted know the offender. Opinions on whether Megan's Law has been successful are divided. In March 1998, *U.S. News and World Report* reported that 22 percent of sexual offenders had repeated crimes before Megan's Law went into effect, and the number dropped by only 3 percent after enactment of the law. While the difference may seem small, it represents a number of children who were saved from being sexually assaulted by strangers. *See also*: **Child Rape; Pedophilia.**

Suggested Reading: "Megan's Law: Community Notification for the Release of Sex Offenders," *Criminal Justice Ethics* (Summer–Fall 1995): 3–5; Bonnie Steinbeck, "A Policy Perspective," *Criminal Justice Ethics* (Summer–Fall 1995): 4–8.

ELIZABETH R. PURDY

MEILI, TRISHA. *See* **Central Park Jogger.**

MEMOIRS. Memoirs of rape have come to form their own small, if growing, subgenre. Maya Angelou's memoir of childhood rape and its consequences was published in 1970, but most rape memoirs are more recent, indicating perhaps increasing openness about the subject.

A theme of many memoirs is that of breaking silence, with the goal not only of asserting oneself in the face of a crime that threatened erasure but also of helping others. Memoirists note that **victims** of rape often remain anonymous, but though anonymity can be protective, it also permits some myths about rape and rape victims to remain in place. Memoirists frequently trace the process of recovery, as it is linked to speaking about their experience. Philosopher Susan Brison titles her 2002 memoir *Aftermath* and takes up broader problems of trauma, memory, and violence. Many memoirists focus on recovery and discuss their experiences in psychotherapy and **self-defense courses**. Several memoirs chart experiences with the legal **prosecution** of their assailants.

While most memoirs focus on one woman's story, there are significant exceptions. In writing about the impact of his wife's rape on their **family**, Jamie Kalven points out that violence has secondary victims. Charlotte Pierce-Baker begins her collection of black women's memoirs and testimonies of sexual violence with her own story and draws attention to the so-far predominantly white, middle-class authorship of rape memoirs. She also makes clear that for women of color speaking about sexual violence still has different dynamics and historical resonance than it does for white women. *See also*: **Central Park Jogger; Child Rape; Rape Trauma Syndrome.**

Suggested Reading: Maya Angelou, *I Know Why the Caged Bird Sings* (New York: Bantam, 1983); Susan Brison, *Aftermath: Violence and the Remaking of the Self* (Princeton, NJ: Princeton University Press, 2002); Jamie Kalven, *Working with Available Light: A Family's World after Violence* (New York: Norton, 1999); Charlotte Pierce-Baker, *Surviving the Silence: Black Women's Stories of Rape* (New York: Norton, 1998).

SARA MURPHY

MENTAL DISABILITIES, PEOPLE WITH. People with mental retardation and other developmental disabilities are at a greater risk of sexual victimization. People with mental retardation are often unable to choose to stop abuse due to a lack of understanding of what is happening during abuse, a need of acceptance from their caregiver, or a dependent relationship with the abuser. People with mental retardation may not realize that sexual abuse is abusive, unusual, or illegal. Consequently, they may never tell anyone about sexually abusive situations. They are often fearful to talk openly about such painful experiences due to the risk of not being believed or taken seriously, and they typically learn not to question caregivers or others in authority. Sexual abuse consists of sexually inappropriate and nonconsensual actions, such as exposure to sexual materials (such as **pornography**), the use of inappropriate sexual remarks/language, not respecting the privacy or physical boundaries of a child or individual, fondling, exhibitionism, **oral sex**, and forced sexual intercourse.

More than 90 percent of people with developmental disabilities will experience sexual abuse at some point in their lives. The likelihood of rape is staggering: 15,000 to 19,000 of people with developmental disabilities are raped each year in the United States. Sexual abuse causes harmful psychological, physical, and behavioral effects. Individuals who experience long-term abuse by a known, trusted adult at an early age suffer more severe damage compared to those whose abuse is perpetrated by someone not well known to the **victim**, begins later in life, and is less frequent and nonviolent. Both cases require attention and can benefit from therapeutic counseling. Research suggests that those most likely to abuse a victim with developmental disabilities are those who are known by the victim, such as **family** members, acquaintances, residential care staff, transportation providers, and personal caretakers.

Signs of sexual abuse include:

- *Physical signs.* Bruises in genital areas, genital discomfort, unexplained **pregnancy**, sexually transmitted diseases, signs of physical abuse, torn or missing **clothing**.
- *Behavioral signs.* Avoids specific setting, avoids specific adults, substance abuse, withdrawal, excessive crying spells, regression, sleep disturbances, disclosure, poor self-esteem, noncompliance, eating disorders, resists exam, self-destructive behavior, headaches, seizures, learning difficulty, sexually inappropriate behavior.
- *Circumstantial signs.* **Alcohol** or drug abuse by caregiver or caregiver who exhibits excessive or inappropriate eroticism, previous history of abuse, seeks isolated contact with and has strong preference for children, pornography usage.

Experts conclude that the first step in reducing the occurrence of sexual abuse is recognizing the magnitude of the problem. Abusers typically abuse as many as 70 people before ever getting caught. Without reporting, there can be no **prosecution** of offenders or treatment for victims. Underreporting of sexually abusive incidents involving people with disabilities has in the past, and continues to be, a major obstacle in preventing sexual abuse. Reporting can be increased through educating individuals with disabilities and service providers, improving investigation and prosecution, and creating a safe environment that allows victims to disclose. Finally, employment policies regarding caregivers need updating. *See also*: **Consent; Hospitals and Nursing Homes.**

Suggested Reading: D. Sobsey, *Violence and Abuse in the Lives of People with Disabilities: The End of Silent Acceptance?* (Baltimore: Paul H. Brookes, 1994); "People with Mental Retardation and Sexual Abuse," *ARC's, Q&A,* http://www.thearc.org/faqs/Sexabuse.html.

FLAVIA NELSON

MICHIGAN v. LUCAS. In *Michigan v. Lucas*, 500 U.S. 145 (1991), the U.S. Supreme Court struck down a per se rule that the preclusion of evidence of a rape **victim**'s prior sexual relationship with a criminal defendant violates the defendant's Sixth Amendment rights. The Court held that preclusion could occur if it served legitimate interests and that decisions as to the appropriateness of preclusion when a defendant fails to comply with a valid discovery rule must be made on a case-by-case basis.

Michigan's "rape shield" statute prohibited defendants from introducing evidence of an alleged rape victim's prior sexual conduct. However, pursuant to a statutory exception, evidence of the victim's past sexual conduct *with the defendant* was not prohibited as long as the defendant filed a written motion to introduce the evidence within 10 days of arraignment. The trial court had the discretion to hold an *in camera* hearing to determine the admissibility of the defendant's evidence.

Lucas, who was charged with criminal sexual conduct, had not complied with the statute's notice requirements, but his lawyer nevertheless tried to present evidence at trial of a prior sexual relationship between his client and the alleged victim.

The trial court rejected that attempt. In reversing the trial court's decision, the Michigan Court of Appeals invoked a per se rule that the preclusion of evidence of a rape victim's prior sexual relationship with a criminal defendant was in violation of the defendant's Sixth Amendment protections.

In its majority opinion, the Supreme Court struck down that per se rule, explaining that a defendant's Sixth Amendment rights are not without limitation, and they may be set aside to accommodate other legitimate interests. The Court noted that the Michigan statute protected rape victims from surprise, harassment, and unnecessary invasions of privacy and gave prosecutors notice to investigate whether prior relationships existed. Without determining whether preclusion was justified in this particular case, the Court stated that the appellate court could not adopt a per se rule making preclusion unconstitutional in all cases and therefore sent the case back with instructions for the appellate court to decide whether the facts of the case showed that such preclusion had violated Lucas's Sixth Amendment rights. *See also*: *Cox Broadcasting Corporation v. Cohn*; **Rape Shield Laws; Rape Trials.**

Suggested Reading: Maria Bevacqua, *Rape on the Public Agenda: Feminism and the Politics of Sexual Assault* (Boston: Northeastern University Press, 2000).

GREGORY M. DUHL

MORNING-AFTER PILL. Classified as emergency contraception (EC) and used after intercourse, the morning-after pill is actually two pills taken in a series. The most common EC pills available in the United States are *Preven* and *Plan B*. Preven contains high dosages of hormones estrogen and progestin, but Plan B contains only progestin. Progestin-only pills are more effective, and the risk of nausea is lower. A dozen other brands are available with slightly varying hormone proportions, but their application does not differ from that of Preven or Plan B. One dose is administered within 72 hours of an unplanned conception, and a follow-up dose should be taken 12 hours later. The effectiveness of this birth control method depends on administration time. Although research indicates that the method remains effective even after the 72-hour window, specialists agree that the treatment is more successful the earlier it is initiated. The effectiveness rate within one day after coitus is as high as 99 percent.

Within the first three days of a **sexual assault**, medical care is critical. Besides obtaining information on EC options, patients should be examined for sexually transmitted diseases and injuries. Although Preven and Plan B have the Food and Drug Administration's approval (1998 and 1999, respectively), not all hospitals in the United States provide EC services to rape **victims.**

A debate about the legitimacy of the pill is fueled by questions about how it works, when it should be used, and who should take it. EC is endorsed by its advocates as a safe and effective solution to unplanned pregnancies resulting from unprotected sex, rape, and **incest**. A frequent argument in favor of EC is that it could prevent at least half of all **abortions** in the United States. However, antiabortion groups counter that since its exact mechanism is unknown, it is not clear whether the pill serves as prevention or abortion. Among theories about its functioning is that it prevents ovulation or stops fertilization. But there also remains the controversial possibility that the pill prevents an already fertilized egg from being implanted in the uterus, which would, in practice, mean abortion. Moreover, besides a number of side effects, such as nausea and weight gain, the use of oral contraceptives may be linked to a high incidence of blood-clotting disorders. EC is not recommended for women over 35, women with a history of high blood pressure, diabetes, clotting disorders, or women in advanced pregnancies. Nevertheless, EC remains a valuable resource for rape victims. *See also*: **Pregnancy**.

Suggested Reading: Janelle Brown, "High Noon for the Morning-After Pill," *Salon.com Life*, 2001, http://archive.salon.com/mast/feature/2001/06/20/pill; Anna Glasier, "Emergency Postcoital Contraception," *New England Journal of Medicine* 337 (October 9, 1997): 1058, http://www.healthunit.org/physicians/contraception/Emergency%20Postcoital%20 Contraception-NEJM.pdf; Nathan Seppa, "Non-Estrogen Morning-After Pill Works Best," *Science News Online*, 1998, http://www.sciencenews.org/sn_arc98/8_15_98/fob3.htm.

KONRAD SZCZESNIAK

MOVIES. *See* Films, Foreign; Films, U.S.

MULTIPLE PERSONALITY DISORDER. *See* Dissociative Identity Disorder.

MURDER. Murder is intimately related to rape and can manifest itself as a reaction to rape, as an element of the crime, and as punishment for it. Race often plays a central role in the relationship between rape and murder. Rape-murder has also become a common weapon in genocidal conflicts.

Murder can be committed in **self-defense** when a woman (or man) is threatened with **sexual assault**. Court practice has generally sanctioned the use of deadly force by men to prevent forcible **sodomy**, but it has not always applied the same standards to women. This difference results from the belief that violence is not appropriate behavior for women. In addition, traditional views of women as objects have reinforced the perception that violating a man's body is the more egregious offense. Furthermore, because **battered women** frequently have a history of intimacy with their attackers, the courts often treat their claims of self-defense from rape with skepticism. Women are thus held to higher standards than men to prove they reacted to a threat of imminent danger.

Murder can also be part of the crime of rape. Between 1976 and 1994, approximately 1.5 percent of all murder cases in the United States involved sexual assault or rape. Sexual assault that results in murder is a felony crime punishable by life in prison or the death penalty. The rape and subsequent murder of a person, usually a woman, is seen by American society as particularly heinous and subject to harsher punishment than each crime would be separately. In the majority of cases where the death penalty is imposed in rape-murders, the **victims** and offenders were strangers. National averages, however, indicate that most rape-murders are committed by acquaintances or **family** members. The severity of the death sentence suggests that rape-murders committed by strangers are perceived as more serious offenses than those committed by acquaintances.

In sentencing, rape-murder diminishes the significance of the rape itself. When a rape victim is murdered, she can no longer speak for herself, and thus her **credibility** is not questioned, even in cases where evidence of rape is inconclusive. Furthermore, in cases of rape-murder, stereotypical understandings of rape (that it is committed by a stranger, that it is interracial, that a woman must resist, etc.) are dismissed under the extenuating circumstance of murder. Thus, rape is seen as an aggravating factor in the commission of murder that makes the offender eligible for the death penalty.

Race plays a central role both in the punishments for rape-murder and in violent reactions to rape. In cases of rape-murder, more severe penalties are often imposed against a black offender whose victim was white, reinforcing the assumption that a black woman's rape-murder is somehow less serious than a white woman's. More rape-murders, however, involve white defendants than other types of murder, and rape-murder victims are more often white and female than murder victims in general. The perception that rape-murder is committed by an "underclass" may contribute to the endurance of racial (and economic) rape-murder stereotypes.

Race has also led to murder in reaction to rape. In racially charged atmospheres such as South Africa and the American South, accusations of rape, particularly of a white woman by a black man, could lead to violent retribution and the lynching of the suspected perpetrator. A "rape scare" in Natal, Africa, in the late nineteenth century, for instance, resulted in vigilante justice against those black men thought to have committed rape and sparked legislation making a white woman's rape a capital offense.

Finally, rape and murder frequently occur together during times of war. Women have been the targets of mass rape and murder throughout the violent genocidal conflicts of the twentieth century. During the 1937–1938 **Rape of Nanking,** for instance, thousands of Chinese women were raped and killed by Japanese soldiers. Similar atrocities occurred in Bangladesh and Serbia, among others, where women were held in camps, repeatedly raped, and murdered. The sexual assault and murder of women has also been used to attack male members of different ethnic groups. In such conflicts, women are seen as male property. Thus, rape-murder in genocides symbolically reinforces the impotence of one ethnic group and the dominance of the other. Rape as a weapon in war can have serious effects on its victims as well. The guilt, shame, and humiliation women experience as rape victims could lead them to commit suicide but also to murder any children who result from rape. *See also*: **Genocide; Rape-Lynch Scenario; Serial Rape and Serial Rapists.**

Suggested Reading: Anne Llewellyn Barstow, ed., *War's Dirty Secret: Rape, Prostitution, and Other Crimes against Women* (Cleveland, OH: Pilgrim Press, 2000); Phyllis Crocker, "Crossing the Line: Rape-Murder and the Death Penalty," *Ohio Northern University Law Review* 26.3 (2000): 689–723.

SHARON A. KOWALSKY

MY LAI. On March 16, 1968, Company C, 1st Battalion, 20th Infantry of the U.S. Army, conducted a search-and-destroy mission on the South Vietnamese village of Son My, which included the subvillage of My Lai. The soldiers, who had been told the village was an enemy stronghold, destroyed everything they found there. They murdered and raped villagers, killed cattle, destroyed food stores, and burned huts. Estimates of the number of women, children, and elderly murdered range from 175 to 400. The exact number of rapes committed is unknown; however, multiple rapes occurred, including vaginal, anal, oral, and **gang rape.**

The soldiers of Company C were told the assault would be a chance to repay the enemy for earlier casualties suffered by the unit. In fact, the soldiers mainly encountered unarmed villagers. More important, the leaders of the company had taken no disciplinary action against soldiers who had engaged in acts of violence, including rapes, countless times before. Several of the men were known to rape Vietnamese women at every opportunity, and at least one Company C soldier was given penicillin as a precaution against venereal disease every time the company went on a field mission.

A cover-up of the events at My Lai began almost immediately after the raid. The army reported the mission as a successful military operation. The soldiers of Company C were ordered not to discuss the assault on My Lai. One soldier, who planned to write his congressman about the incident, was ordered not to do so. Some of the film used by an army photographer accompanying Company C was confiscated, but he managed to keep the film from his personal camera, which contained photographs of the massacre. These photographs were later published in *Life* magazine to support stories of the incident.

Lieutenant William L. Calley, Jr., leader of 2nd platoon of Company C, was charged with the murder of "109 Oriental human beings" in September 1969. Calley was court-martialed in 1970, found guilty, and sentenced to life at hard labor. However, Calley's conviction created a public outcry among people who supported the war. In 1971, President Richard M. Nixon ordered Calley held under house arrest. Calley's sentence was reduced several times, and he was paroled in 1974. Captain Ernest Medina, commander of Company C, was tried and acquitted of all charges related to the raid. No one else was charged with **murder** or rape in the My Lai Massacre. *See also*: **U.S. Military; War Crimes; Wartime Rape.**

Suggested Reading: The American Experience, *Vietnam: In the Trenches, the My Lai Massacre*, PBS/WGBH, http://www.pbs.org/wgbh/amex/vietnam/trenches/mylai.html (1983, 1997), Michal R. Belknap, *The Vietnam War on Trial: The My Lai Massacre and the Court-Martial of Lieutenant Calley* (Lawrence: University Press of Kansas, 2002); Susan Brownmiller, *Against Our Will: Men, Women and Rape* (New York: Fawcett Columbine, 1975); Douglas Linder, *Famous American Trials: The My Lai Courts-Martial, 1970*, 1999, http://www.law.umkc.edu/faculty/projects/ftrials/mylai/mylai.htm.

ERIC SKINNER

MYTHOLOGY. Myth is a complex cultural construction that contains a sacred story and, therefore, is based on the irruption of a divine factor into human life. It is the retelling of a creation event, usually occurring in primitive times, and capable of explaining the world as a supernatural phenomenon. Since mythology is undisputedly linked to the original source of mankind, and to the primitive history of a society, it shall not surprise that sexual references are abundant in its genealogical descriptions.

The frequency of rape in classical times can be explained as an assertion of masculinity. In raping situations, women (or young men, depending on the case) are degraded as powerless creatures in front of the strength of a male attacker. In Greek and Roman mythology, rape is frequently presented through the imposition of inequality: Sexual physical violence is often shown between a god and a human, preferably a potent male god and a young **virgin** girl. Only a very few instances are revealed in which the rapist and the raped involved in this conduct are both divinities (Hephaiston and Athena, for example). The religious category of mythical constructions, as well as its social purpose in antiquity, does not allow finding examples of rape dealing exclusively with sex between humans.

The general inequality that lays at the basis of rape in myth is noticeable if one takes into account that most of the times the male god acting with aggressive impulse presents himself metamorphosed into a brute: This is the case of mighty Zeus attacking Europa as a bull, Leda as a swan, or Persephone as a snake; Poseidon as a bull raping Canace or as a dolphin forcing Melantho, and Apollo as a snake and a tortoise acting against Dryope. According to the mythical versions, these confused girls are usually placed in lonely environments lacking protection and where they will not be discovered right away. The masculine appearance under a bestial aspect is used in various plots as a way of causing the **victim** to get deceived before the commission of the sexual offense. The **seduction** of women by animals, in many of these moral stories, might be studied from a traditional view, according to which females are seen as passionate and sometimes attracted to the virility of animals (cf. Dryope or Leda).

Since the female perspective, as such, was feared to be a real threat to social structures, girls could be themselves metaphorically assimilated to beasts as well. In this sense, some myths deal with the transformation of young women, and not of gods, into animals: Taygete as a deer is raped by Zeus, and Psamathe as a seal is seized by Aeacus. Elsewhere, girls tend to be presented as real shape shifters, as it happens with Metis and Thetis when they are snatched by Zeus and Peleus, respectively.

In a few examples, however, some classicists and historians of **religion** perceive that this unbalanced interaction is left aside, due to the fact that man and woman are equally transformed into beasts just before the intercourse: It is the case of Zeus's rape of Asterie, which is committed when he becomes an eagle and she is a quail; also Theophane as a bird is raped by a ram, which is born from Poseidon's metamorphosis. Nevertheless, even in these situations, this apparent balance is really false, since the two categories of animals are always different enough, in size and behavior, as to justify the violent approach and the control of men over their victims.

The possible **consent** of women in these mythical rapes is ambiguous, and some authors suggest that females in myth, instead of being unwillingly attacked, are rather seduced or abducted. Scattered evidence does not supply any conclusive answer on this. It can only be stated that if myth becomes a way of consolidating social values, both in Greece and Rome, the recurrence of the topic of rape could demonstrate certain aspects intrinsically related to the ideology of classical societies: In male-oriented communities, feminine figures seem to be deeply attached to the origin of offspring, and manly gods need to be shown as imposing over nature and controlling humans. Thus, the analysis of rape in mythology can demonstrate how sexual attitudes ought to be identified in accordance to the principles and rules that form the necessary background for the persistence of a common morality, in particular, and of society, in general. *See also*: **Literature, World and American.**

Suggested Reading: Susan Deacy and Karen F. Pierce, eds., *Rape in Antiquity* (London: Duckworth, 1997); Lin Foxhall and John Salmon, eds., *Thinking Men: Masculinity and Its Self-Representation in the Classical Tradition* (New York: Routledge, 1998); Susan Deacy and Karen F. Pierce, eds., *When Men Were Men: Masculinity, Power and Identity in Classical Antiquity* (New York: Routledge, 1998); Angeliki E. Laiou, ed., *Consent and Coercion to Sex and Marriage in Ancient and Medieval Societies* (Washington, DC: Dumbarton Oaks Research Library and Collection & Harvard University Press, 1993); Rosanna Omitowoju,

Rape and the Politics of Consent in Classical Athens (Cambridge: Cambridge University Press, 2002); Ralph Rosen and Ineke Sluiter, eds., *Andreia: Studies in Manliness and Courage in Classical Antiquity*, Mnemosyne Suppl. 238 (Boston: Brill, 2003).

EMILIANO J. BUIS

MYTHS. *See* Rape Myths.

N

NATIONAL CRIME VICTIMIZATION SURVEY (NCVS). The NCVS was established in 1973, and it is one of two statistical programs the U.S. Department of Justice uses to measure crime. The purpose of the NCVS is to gather empirical data about both reported and unreported crimes suffered by **victims** and/or households. Because many crimes are never reported, this survey complements the Uniform Crime Reports collected by the Federal Bureau of Investigation and provides additional information on the number of crimes committed and the level of victimization in this country each year. Twice annually, approximately 45,000 U.S. households are surveyed and asked about their experiences with rape, **sexual assault**, robbery, assault, theft, household burglary, and motor vehicle theft.

The survey is a program of the Bureau of Justice Statistics (BJS), under the Department of Justice, but it is administered by the U.S. Census Bureau. The "National Crime Victimization Survey Resource Guide" notes that the four objectives of the survey are "(1) to develop information about the victims and consequences of crime, (2) to estimate the number and types of crimes not reported to the police, (3) to provide uniform measures of selected types of crimes, and (4) to permit comparisons over time and types of areas." These objectives, when fulfilled, provide researchers with data on victims, including information on age, sex, race, and whether or not they knew their attacker, and data on crimes, such as where and when they occurred and whether weapons were involved. These findings make it possible to better study crime in America.

The BJS publishes reports and statistical tables each year detailing the information collected by the NCVS. For example, the 2002 NCVS notes a slight decline in rapes and sexual assaults from the previous year. In 2001, there were 248,250 rapes and sexual assaults, and in the 2002, there were 247,730. But this is a big decline from the 485,000 rapes and sexual assaults reported in 1993. However, the NCVS does not interview children age 11 and younger. The 2002 report also notes that rape victims are more willing to report their attacks to the police than they were in years past. *See also*: **Rape Statistics.**

Suggested Reading: Maria Bevacqua, *Rape on the Public Agenda: Feminism and the Politics of Sexual Assault* (Boston: Northeastern University Press, 2000); "National Crime Victimization Survey Resource Guide," National Archive of Criminal Justice Data, http://www.icpsr.umich.edu/NACJD/NCVS; "New Reports Shows Dramatic Increase in Willingness to Report Rapes to Police," Rape, Abuse & Incest National Network (RAINN), http://www.rainn.org/news2002.html.

ARTHUR HOLST

NATIONAL ORGANIZATION FOR WOMEN (NOW). Founded in 1966 as a group dedicated to achieving women's equality, NOW gained international recognition during the 1970s as it relentlessly campaigned in support of the equal rights amendment to the U.S. Constitution. This struggle for economic equality validated NOW as a significant grassroots movement. In 2003, with more than 500,000 members, it is now the largest feminist activist organization in America, with a defined mission to eliminate all forms of sexism in society, so that women can achieve full equality with men. With a broad economic, political, legal, and social change agenda, NOW's stated priorities include antiracism, reproductive freedoms, abortion rights, constitutional amendments to guarantee equality, and the termination of all forms of harassment and violence against women (battering, murder, and all manifestations of the act of rape).

To agitate for social change to stop rapes throughout America, NOW employs a five-part strategy: direct action, legislative changes, electoral involvement, lobbying, and lawsuits/prosecutions. Mass demonstrations, such as the "**Take Back the Night**" marches throughout the country, raised awareness on the magnitude of the problem of rape. In lobbying for legislative changes, NOW's electoral strategy evolved from attempting to persuade elected officials to support their cause to direct involvement in electing men and women who support the goals of the feminist organization. With more sympathetic supporters throughout all levels of government, NOW has been instrumental in advancing a comprehensive framework for the definition of rape, as well as the recognition, **prosecution**, and perpetrator stigmatization of the crime. Legislation, such as the 1994 **Violence against Women Act**, was viewed as an important step to ensuring that rape is both recognized and prosecuted as a criminal act. As only a very small number of the rapes in the United States are reported, NOW believes in the importance of educating women to recognize and reject this form of violence in their lives. NOW's awareness programs help women to understand that any type of rape (by a husband, a date, or a stranger) constitutes a violent crime. For instance, while marriage implies **consent** for sex, the lobby group educates women that forced, nonconsensual intermarital sex is a crime. Additionally, this feminist movement directly mobilizes the membership to protest all violent attacks on women and to raise public awareness that rape is both a criminal offense and a socially unacceptable behavior. Therein, NOW disavows all societal myths that are sympathetic to the perpetrator, such as the idea that women dress in a provocative manner to encourage the rape—to NOW this is simply the rationalization of a criminal act.

In addition to their many activities to agitate for social change against rape, NOW works to provide resources to the women who are **victims**. As an early supporter of **rape crises centers** and women's shelters, the movement helps women react to, and recover from, rape. Assistance services for victims also extend to help in levying charges and prosecuting rapists in all sectors of society, even those traditionally closed to scrutiny from the general public. For instance, NOW determinedly criticizes the Department of Defense for continually ignoring and denying reported incidents of **sexual assault**, rape, and harassment and demands that the abuses within the U.S. Armed Forces are to be investigated by civilians from outside of the self-protective hierarchy.

After four decades of targeted activism, NOW understands that the struggle against rape, on behalf of all women, is not yet over. The organization cites statistics such as the facts that 20 percent of secondary school women are physically and sexually abused by a date, that only a minority of stranger and **date rapes** are reported annually, and that a significant problem still exists with **marital rape**. NOW continues with their five-point activist strategy to increase awareness and to decrease the incidents of rape, such that it will be widely recognized, charged, and prosecuted as a socially unacceptable and violent crime against women. *See also*: **Feminist Movement**.

Suggested Reading: American Medical Association, *Report 7 of the Council on Scientific Affairs: Violence between Intimates*, January 2000, http://www.ama-assn.org; Toni Carabillo, Judith Meuli, and June Bundy Csida, *The Feminist Chronicles: 1953–1993* (Los Angeles: Women's Graphics, 1993); National Organization for Women's Web site, http://www.now.org; Merril D. Smith, ed., "Introduction: Studying Rape in American History," in *Sex without Consent: Rape and Sexual Coercion in America* (New York: New York University Press, 2001).

LAURIE JACKLIN

NATIVE AMERICANS. Sexual violence was not unknown in Native North America prior to the European invasion, although rape was a rare occurrence in many societies. **Interracial rape** became a commonplace experience for Native American women and a rallying point for tribal resistance following the invasion of their homelands, however. While European and Anglo-American societies dismissed accounts of **sexual assault**, or wrongly attributed them to Native women's supposed licentiousness, Native people, particularly Native women, struggled to mitigate the effects of their rapes and to prevent further sexual violence.

While rape was institutionalized in a few Native societies, men rarely sexually assaulted women in most Native societies. Images of rape do not abound in indigenous art and material culture, and the oral and written historical record gives fleeting testimony to the occurrence of rape within many Native cultures. The prevalence or absence of sexual violence reflected the socioeconomic status of women. For example, in the matrilineal and matrilocal cultures of the East in which women not only determined clan membership but also grew and distributed corn, the staple crop, men seem to have rarely raped. On the other hand, in the patrilineal cultures of the Plains in which women worked processing buffalo hides hunted and owned by men, women were more likely to experience sexual violence. Among the Cheyenne, for instance, members of male warrior societies assaulted women, or "put them on the prairie," as part of their ritualized lifestyle. This escalation of sexual violence likely coincided with the emergence of the male-dominated hunting culture that developed following the introduction of the horse in the late seventeenth century. In other words, as women lost socioeconomic status, their vulnerability to sexual violence increased.

Because they considered rape to be an egregious violation, most Native societies harshly punished rapists. While the method and severity of punishment varied among tribes, most communities considered rape a crime against the **victim**, and the perpetrator was obliged to make peace with her and her kin. Thus, victims, often accompanied by their female kin or village women, meted out punishment collectively, or the **survivor** could accept payment as retribution. Most Native societies do not seem to have punished or ostracized the victim, but victims in cultures that valued **virginity** and chastity in women as an expression of familial honor, including many Plains tribes, could have suffered a loss in status.

European invaders and their American successors used rape as a means of conquest. Misinterpreting the ways that Native American women dressed and behaved as a solicitation, many European men assumed that Native American women were sexually available, even when the women refused their advances. European custom, labeling women as spoils of war, reinforced European men's belief in their access to Native women's bodies as a right of conquest. Accounts of Christopher Columbus's expedition to the Caribbean include mass rape in addition to mass **murder**. While matrilineal kinship systems accorded Native women in the East considerable sexual freedom, Englishmen often took advantage of Native women's sexual hospitality. In New France (Canada), too, traders and trappers often treated Native women's bodies as another commodity in the trade. In the American West, rape by American miners, traders, and soldiers became so rampant by the late nineteenth century that a Northern Paiute woman, Sarah Winnemucca Hopkins, wrote sexual violence into her autobiography as a key theme; she commented, "My people have been so unhappy for a long time they now wish to disincrease, instead of multiply. The mothers are afraid to have more children, for fear they shall have daughters, who are not safe even in their mother's presence." These sexual frontiers created gray areas in which Native women could use their sexuality for their benefit but also in which they could be horribly abused because of their sexuality. Among all the cultural diversity and particular local circumstances, the one constant was that very few white men respected a Native woman's right to say no to sexual intercourse.

While accepting many aspects of white culture, Native people did not adopt interracial rape into their worldview as appropriate behavior, and they continued to label rapists as sexual deviants and responded to mitigate and prevent rape in a variety of ways. Native people modified their seasonal cycle of hunting, gathering, and farming and their daily work patterns so that lone or small groups of women would not be likely targets for white men. Elders took closer care over adolescent girls. Native leaders appealed to European and American leaders to keep unwanted men away from their villages and camps. When communal and diplomatic solutions failed, Native men went to war to punish outsiders who violated their value systems, although because of common cultural rules forbidding warriors from engaging in sexual relations, Native men did not usually retaliate sexually. White female captives in the East remarked that they were not sexually assaulted by war parties, but some Plains warriors were reported to have raped white captives.

Rape has continued to affect Native American communities in disproportionately high numbers. In 1999, the Department of Justice reported that American Indians were victims of rape at 3.5 times the rate of other racial groups; Native Americans remain more impoverished than any other racial group. Moreover, unlike other racial groups, someone of another race assaulted 90 percent of Native American rape victims.

Rape has continued to be a prominent theme in the work of Native American artists and authors. In her memoir *Lakota Woman*, Mary Crow Dog addressed sexual interracial and intraracial sexual violence on a modern Indian reservation. In her 2000 film *Backroads*, Cree filmmaker Shirley Cheechoo gave powerful visual image to the destructive power of sexual violence in Native communities. While working in different mediums across centuries, Native women confirm the negative impact of rape and their continued resistance to it.

Suggested Reading: Mary Crow Dog, *Lakota Woman* (New York: HarperPerennial, 1990); Rayna Greene, "The Pocahontas Perplex: The Image of Indian Women in American Culture," in *Unequal Sisters: A Multicultural Reader in U.S. Women's History*, ed. Ellen Carol DuBois (New York: Routledge, 1990), 15–21; Sarah Winnemucca Hopkins, *Life among the Piutes* (New York: G.P. Putnam's Sons, 1883; reprint, Reno: University of Nevada Press, 1994); Carolyn Neithammer, *Daughters of the Earth: The Lives and Legends of American Indian Women* (1977; New York: Touchstone, 1996); Theda Perdue, "Columbus Meets Pocahontas in the American South," *Southern Cultures* 3 (1997): 4–21; Clifford E. Trafzer and Joel R. Hyer, eds., *Exterminate Them! Written Accounts of the Murder, Rape, and Enslavement of Native Americans during the California Gold Rush* (East Lansing: Michigan State University Press, 1999).

ROSE STREMLAU

NAZIS. Rape for the Nazis played a sinister role in what they wanted to achieve: namely, the humiliation and destruction of "inferior peoples" and the creation of a master race. Technically, it was forbidden for a German to rape a Jew according to the Nuremberg race laws of 1935. These race laws issued a harsh prohibition against what they called "race defilement." The Nazis feared that Germans who had sex with Jews would contaminate Aryan "blood." There were times, however, when these laws were broken.

The first major reports of Nazi mob rape were directed against Jewish women and occurred during *Kristallnacht*, or Night of Broken Glass, in 1938. The *Kristallnacht* became the model for the actions repeated in many towns once World War II began. During the war, the Nazis marched into Polish or Russian villages and looted homes, especially Jewish homes. Jewish girls were singled out for rape. They were often raped in front of their parents and siblings. If the girls resisted, they would be beaten. In general, all women were prey as the Nazis advanced into Poland, Russia, and elsewhere. During the Nuremberg **war crimes** tribunal after the war, the Russians reported, "Women and girls [were] vilely outraged in all the occupied areas" (Brownmiller, 55).

Surgeon-gynecologists of the Jewish ghettos regularly gave antitetanus shots to **victims** of Nazi rape. One Jewish doctor in Warsaw reported, "In one mirror shop in Swietokerska Street there was a mass raping of Jewish girls. The Germans seized the most beautiful and healthy girls in the streets and brought them in to pack mirrors. After the work the girls were raped" (Brownmiller, 52). Another affidavit told of a similar event that occurred on another street in Warsaw, where "40 Jewish girls were dragged into the house which was occupied by German officers. There . . . the girls were ordered to undress and to dance for the amusement of their tormentors. Beaten, abused, and raped, the girls were not released till 3 A.M." (Brownmiller, 52). Sala Pawlowicz, a survivor of the concentration camp Bergen-Belsen, writes in her **memoirs** of the Nazis making nightly swoops in her German-occupied Polish village of Lask in search of young Jewish girls.

German documents captured at the end of the war and presented at the Nuremberg war crimes tribunal in 1946 corroborated the regular use of rape as a weapon of terror. In some instances, German commanders used cases of rape against the Nazi secret police, or SS. In early 1940, a German army commander in Poland compiled a long list of complaints against the SS. One of the complaints filed involved two SS policemen who dragged two teenage Jewish girls out of bed. It was reported that one of the girls was raped in a Polish cemetery. Reportedly, the German army commander who wrote the report was upset over the "amateurish" way that the SS was attempting to deal with the "Jewish problem."

The Nazis also used rape as a means of military retaliation or reprisal. Accounts surfaced of punitive measures taken by the Germans in occupied France during the summer of 1944 because of the presence of French resistance fighters. One region of French resistance fighting was Vecours. Stories there told of a raid on the village of St. Donat. It was reported that "54 women or young girls from 13 to 50 years of age were raped by the maddened soldiers" (Brownmiller, 56). A raid in Nice in July 1944 also concluded with similar results.

Women in concentration camps were more often sexually humiliated as opposed to violated. In the concentration camps, women were at risk of being assaulted, but rape by Nazi officers was rare because of the prohibition of *Rassenschande*, or interracial sexual relations. Women in the camps were also often physically unattractive to the Nazis, and the officers were monitored more closely by their superiors than they were in urban areas.

Nazi rape was more likely to occur in towns and cities, as opposed to concentration camps. Towns and cities were more unregulated than the concentration camps, and they also provided more opportunity for the Nazis to take revenge on the population by means other than military warfare. The Nazis used rape for terror, retaliation, and sexual humiliation. *See also*: **Ethnic Cleansing; Genocide.**

Suggested Reading: Elizabeth R. Baer and Myrna Goldenberg, eds., *Experience and Expression: Women, the Nazis, and the Holocaust* (Detroit: Wayne State University Press, 2003); Susan Brownmiller, *Against Our Will: Men, Women and Rape* (New York: Simon and Schuster, 1975); Katherine Morris, ed., *Odyssey of Exile: Jewish Women Flee the Nazis for Brazil* (Detroit: Wayne State University Press, 1996); Carol Rittner and John K. Roth, eds., *Different Voices: Women and the Holocaust* (New York: Praeger, 1993).

DAVID TREVIÑO

NEW YORK RADICAL FEMINISTS (NYRF). Formed in the fall of 1969, the NYRF raised public consciousness about rape in the United States. Because the police, hospitals, and society in general tended to blame women for rape, NYRF sought to redefine public understanding of rape as a crime "against" women, not an offense women brought on themselves. On January 24, 1971, NYRF held the first "Speak Out on Rape" where women who had been raped told their stories, illustrating that rape could happen to any women, not just those who dressed too provocatively, led men on, or wandered down dark alleys. Media coverage of the speak-out publicized feminist perspectives on rape and recruited members to the growing antirape movement.

In April 1971, NYRF sponsored a conference about rape. From the experiences that women shared, NYRF realized that rape is a crime largely perpetrated by boyfriends and husbands. This revelation had a profound influence on American society where women had been taught to fear the stranger lurking in dark shadows but not the boy next door. NYRF inextricably tied the crime of rape to male domination, seeing rape as one more patriarchal weapon used to oppress women.

As a result of their early activism, NRYF published *Rape: The First Sourcebook for Women*, which outlined a feminist perspective on rape and an agenda for antirape activism. Members of NYRF, particularly **Susan Brownmiller**, became important public figures in the feminist antirape movement, and the group itself can be credited with helping to put this "hidden" crime on the public agenda.

Suggested Reading: Susan Brownmiller, *Against Our Will: Men, Women and Rape* (New York: Simon and Schuster, 1975); Noreen Connell and Cassandra Wilson, eds., *Rape: The First Sourcebook for Women* (New York: New American Library, 1974).

MICHELLE MORAVEC

NEWSPAPERS. *See* Media.

O

OKINAWA RAPE CASE. One of the most notorious sex scandals in the U.S. Military, the Okinawa rape took place in 1995 on the Japanese island of Okinawa. On September 4, 1995, three U.S. servicemen stationed in Okinawa abducted a 12-year-old local schoolgirl, bound her by duct tape, beat, raped, and abandoned her in a sugarcane field. In March 1996, both Navy Seaman Marcus Gill and Marine Private First Class Rodrico Harp were sentenced to 7 years of prison, while Marine Private First Class Kendrick Ledet's sentence was 6.5 years. All of the sentences were to be served in Japan. During the trial, the suspects pleaded guilty but gave conflicting reports as to who instigated the incident, accusing each other of coercing the **abduction**. At one point, Private Rodrico Harp recanted his confession, claiming it had been taken from him under duress.

The incident sent thousands of Japanese protesters to the streets. Their anger was further stoked by the Status of Forces agreement between the United States and Japan. Under this agreement, the United States is not required to release suspects to Japanese authorities until formal charges are presented. In the Okinawa rape case, too, the U.S. military chose not to immediately allow Japanese police to take the three suspects into custody. Although the suspects were regularly transported to the local authorities for questioning and were eventually convicted, the scandal turned into a political issue, with some Japanese politicians calling for the withdrawal of American troops from Japan.

Currently, similar incidents by the military personnel continue to deepen resentment toward U.S. presence in the region. In July 2001, U.S. Air Force Staff Sergeant Timothy Woodland was charged with raping a Japanese woman. Woodland admitted having sex with her but claimed their sexual relationship was consensual. The **victim** denied that, and in March 2002 a Japanese court found Woodland guilty and sentenced him to 32 months in jail.

Most incidents of this nature happen on the island of Okinawa, as over a half of U.S. military deployed in Japan are concentrated in Okinawa Prefecture. But U.S. Armed Forces must contend with an equally bad reputation in South Korea, where sex scandals have taken place, sparking anti-American protests in the streets. *See also*: **Tailhook Convention of 1991; Wartime Rape.**

Suggested Readings: Edward Desmond, "Rape of an Innocent, Dishonor in the Ranks," *Time*, October 2, 1995, 51–52; Justin McCurry, "U.S. Airmen Questioned about Okinawa Rape," *The Guardian*, June 30, 2001, http://www.guardian.co.uk/japan/story/0,7369, 514865,00.html.

KONRAD SZCZESNIAK

ORAL SEX. The National Women's Study definition of completed rape is "any nonconsensual sexual penetration of the **victim**'s vagina, anus, or mouth by an object or a perpetrator's penis, finger, or tongue that involved the use of force." By this definition, and numerous others, forced oral sex does constitute rape. Still, some women who have been screened as potential rape victims are not told that forcible oral sex should be included in the definition of rape and therefore fail to report such experiences to screeners. Many victims of oral sex rape are not just female but males as well, particularly underage males.

On pornographic Internet sites and magazines, there are numerous depictions of women being forcibly raped with oral sex. Most of the captions included with oral sex rape in such **pornography** depict women as sexual objects with no feelings. The men committing oral sex rape and the pornographers who write the captions and take the pictures treat women as dehumanized objects. Men who have committed oral sex rape see that type of sex in movies or magazines. They have sexual **fantasies** about it and want to mimic that action. Some pornographic magazines even advocate that men use their penises to silence women. The advice that men use fellatio to silence women amounts to advocating oral rape. This has motivated some people to accuse the **media** of inciting and causing violence like oral sex rape. Forced oral sex is a form of rape itself and should be treated as completed rape. *See also*: **Advertising; Anal Sex; Consent; Male Rape.**

Suggested Reading: James F. Hodgson and Debra S. Kelley, *Sexual Violence: Policies, Practices, and Challenges in the United States and Canada* (Westport, CT: Praeger, 2002); Laura Lederer, ed., *Take Back the Night: Women on Pornography* (New York; William Morrow, 1980); Diana E.H. Russell, *Dangerous Relationships: Pornography, Misogyny, and Rape* (Thousand Oaks, CA: Sage, 1998); Diana E.H. Russell and Rebecca M. Bolen, *The Epidemic of Rape and Child Sexual Abuse in the United States* (Thousand Oaks, CA: Sage, 2000).

DAVID TREVIÑO

P

PAGLIA, CAMILLE (1947–). A literary scholar, feminist critic, self-declared "Amazon feminist," and confessing Madonna fan, Camille Paglia has repeatedly engaged matters of sexuality and violence and is known particularly for her book *Sexual Personae* (1990) and her provocative interventions into feminist debates during the 1990s. Considering these debates too academic and predominated by a coy ideology of political correctness, Paglia has aimed to rethink the feminist agenda by revising cultural history and reclaiming **popular culture** as an alternative "streetwise" political practice. Her several essays on sexual violence and rape can be understood in the context of both her binary conception of cultural history—her clear-cut division between nature and culture—and her call for a sex-positive feminism that stresses personal agency and responsibility. Proposing a "revamped feminism," Paglia distances herself from liberal feminism's claim for equality before the law, from the cultural relativism of gender studies as well as from the so-called radical feminist perspectives of **Catharine MacKinnon** and **Andrea Dworkin,** whose rape crisis discourse and encompassing definition of rape Paglia rejects. Considering masculinity a (sexually) aggressive as well as creative force, and accepting the heterosexist sadomasochistic sexual dynamic projected by early sexology and part of psychoanalysis as the natural order of things, Paglia insists that women need to accept the "fundamental, unchanging truth about sex" and exercise self-awareness and self-control. Grounded in a polarized, universalizing, and ahistorical conception of gender, Paglia's critique of the feminist debate on sexual violence remains politically controversial.

Suggested Reading: Camille Paglia, "Now Law in the Arena" and "The Culture Wars," in her *Vamps and Tramps: New Essays* (New York: Vintage, 1994), 19–94, 95–126; Camille Paglia, "Rape and the Modern Sex War" and "The Rape Debate Continued," in her *Sex, Art and American Culture* (New York: Vintage, 1992), 49–55, 55–74; Camille Paglia, *Sexual Personae: Art and Decadence from Nefertiti to Emily Dickinson* (New York: Vintage, 1990).

SABINE SIELKE

PATERNITY TESTING. Paternity testing is a method of establishing the genetic relationship between a child and an alleged father. Apart from cases of pregnancies resulting from rape, where it is used to identify the offender, paternity identification testing is commonly sought by mothers trying to prove the fatherhood of men who refuse to pay child support.

Originally, parentage testing involved blood analysis, which involved comparing blood samples for the presence of antigens that determine a person's blood type. An advantage of this method was that it served to reliably exclude candidates for a father. If a child possessed antigens not found in a putative father's blood, that man would be excluded as being the child's biological father. But because an antigen can be found in many unrelated people, the presence of an antigen in the father's and child's blood is no guarantee of their actual genetic relatedness, and so this test's reliability is seriously limited.

Paternity testing has been significantly improved, thanks to the invention of DNA testing. This method is based on the fact that each parent contributes half of a child's DNA, and each half is a person's unique signature, different from anybody else's. If a man's DNA markers are found in the child, that man cannot be ruled out as that child's father. If their genetic patterns match, the probability that they are father and child is more than 99 percent.

DNA tests are relatively simple and can be performed at home or at a hospital. Samples are made by taking a swab of skin cells inside the cheek. They are shipped to a laboratory to be analyzed and compared to each parent's. Results are produced as either an inclusionary report (confirming the fatherhood) or an exclusionary report (ruling it out). *See also*: **DNA Collection and Evidence.**

Suggested Reading: Terrence Carmichael and Alexander Kuklin, *How to DNA Test Our Family Relationships?* (Mountain View, CA: AceN Press, 2000); James R. Wronko, "What Litigators Should Know about DNA Testing," *New Jersey Lawyer*, May 5, 1995, http://www.newjerseylawyer.org/articles/dnanjl.htm.

KONRAD SZCZESNIAK

PATRIARCHY. Patriarchy is a sociopolitical doctrine and cultural system that posits men above women. Thus the superiority of the male sex is a priori established by virtue of its physical attributes (i.e., strength, endurance) and intellectual abilities (i.e., decision making, ethical capacity).

In patriarchy, the superiority of men is passed from father to son in particular and from men to men in society in general. The social system, therefore, depends on the strong bonds between men as kinship and professional relations and less on the relation between men and women. Even the familial structure, despite its biological dependence on the female for procreation, puts down women as "the second sex."

Historically, patriarchy is well established, taking over from the tradition of matriarchy ("the cult of the mother") in the prehistoric societies. Some ancient myths describe the many ways in which female humans—as well as goddesses—were abused by gods because of the superiority of the gods. The ancient Greek **mythology** is an especially rich source of such examples: the kidnapping of Europa by Zeus, the elaborate rape of Leto, and others.

Another negative instance of a strong patriarchal tradition in the Middle Ages in Europe is the so-called *prima note* ("first night"), when on their wedding night some brides were deflowered by the father-in-law or the lord of the village. In this way the actual rapes achieved the status of a "rightful" act that supposedly established the laws and traditions of a tribe and helped the son in performing his marital function later.

The first subversive attempts to change the patriarchal order could be traced back to nineteenth-century Europe and the United States, when some women dared to defy patriarchy in search of social equality and political freedom. Despite the significant changes in the structure of certain cultures and many waves of the **feminist movement** in the Western countries from the 1960s and 1970s of the twentieth century until today, patriarchy is still a predominant form of sociocultural organization. For religious or other reasons, many countries strongly support hard-line patriarchy as the only viable social system, while the other countries struggle to continue the process of social, political, and economic emancipation of women. *See also*: *Droit du seigneur*; **Tribal Customs and Laws.**

Suggested Reading: Judith Butler, *Gender Trouble, Tenth Anniversary Issue* (New York: Routledge, 1999); Judith Butler, *The Psychic Life of Power: Theories in Subjection* (Stanford: Stanford University Press, 1997); Simone de Beauvoir, *The Second Sex* (New York: Vintage, 1997).

ROSSITSA TERZIEVA-ARTEMIS

PEDOPHILIA. *Pedophilia* originates from the Greek words *paidos*, meaning "child," and *philia*, meaning "love." Pedophiles are characterized by their sexual attraction to children. The first scientist to use the term was the German Austrian sexologist and physician Richard Krafft-Ebing. In his monograph *Psychopatia Sexualis*, published in 1886, pedophilia was defined as a psychosexual perversion, open to cure. To Krafft-Ebing, pedophilia could be caused by senility or other mental deficiencies. However, his British counterpart, Henry Havelock-Ellis, believed that pedophilia should be seen as an extreme version of normal masculine sexuality. The concept of pedophilia was rarely discussed in English before the 1950s. It is currently understood as a divergence of personality, caused by psychological damage in early childhood.

Sexual relations between adults and children have been condemned since antiquity for different reasons including religious, judicial, and psychological. Most pedophiles are men who seek contact with children, mainly boys in early puberty. Some wish to stimulate the child, some seek mutual stimulation, and others want to have intercourse with the child. Although they receive most of the press coverage, only a minority is fascinated by sadistic elements in their relation to children. During the last two decades, a growing awareness of the phenomenon has made it more difficult for pedophiles to realize their sexual urges. That is why easy access to child **pornography** and chat rooms on the Internet plays such a prominent role in stimulating the **fantasies** of pedophiles.

Despite the lack of reliable statistics, it is known that sexual relations between adults and children have always taken place. The first British and U.S. surveys of sexual child abuse date from the 1920s, but the Kinsey reports of the 1950s were the first to study the subject in a detailed and scientific manner. A comparative study of Anglo-American surveys covering the years 1940 to 1990 showed that the relative number of cases did not change during this time, despite variations in survey design. Between 10 and 12 percent of young women reported having been sexually abused as girls younger than 14. There were no comparable figures for boys. In contrast, the surveys of the 1990s have produced highly contradictory data, depending on basic differences in study populations and designs. In these surveys, the number of college students who claim to have been sexually abused as children varies from 15 to 30 percent; however, intercourse is only mentioned by 5 or 6 percent of the young informants in New Zealand, the United States, and England. The Scandinavian surveys show a similar picture. Official crime statistics, however, indicate a much lower incidence of sexual child abuse than that produced by these surveys. This suggests a large dark figure, especially for severe crimes in **family** settings. In addition, research is being done to determine what and how much individuals can actually recall from early childhood. To what degree the sexual abuse is caused by pedophiles and not by other kinds of sexual criminals is impossible to discern from the existing statistical sources. *See also*: **Child Rape; Computers and the Internet; Incest.**

Suggested Readings: V.L. Bullough, "History in Adult Human Sexual Behavior with Children and Adolescence in Western societies," in *Pedophilia: Biosocial Dimensions*, ed. J.R. Feirman (New York: Springer-Verlag, 1990), 69–90; David Finkelhor and Jennifer Dziuba-Leatherman, "Children as Victims of Violence: A National Survey," *Pediatrics* 94.4 (1994): 413–420; Philip Jenkins, *Moral Panic: Changing Concepts of the Child Molester in Modern America* (New Haven, CT: Yale University Press, 1998).

NING DE CONINCK-SMITH

PHYSICIANS/MEDICAL PROFESSIONALS. A vast array of medical professionals (nurses, physicians, psychiatrists, counselors, and so on) provide important services to help rape **victims** deal with the medical and psychological repercussions of rape, both immediately after the crime and as latent problems manifest over time. While the medical profession is generally applauded for providing these vital services, it is also criticized for its part in not recognizing the signs of unreported rapes and, in some instances, for being the perpetrator of the crime.

Medical professionals play a key role in assisting the **survivors** of rape to deal with the short- and long-term physical, sexual, and emotional repercussions. Both the American Medical Association (AMA) and the American Academy of Family Physicians suggest that, immediately following the assault, victims should first ensure that they are in a safe place, then immediately seek professional medical attention. Due to the specialized nature of the needed medical procedures, most rape crises support agencies and the AMA suggest that the survivors should seek this assistance at a hospital emergency room or a purpose-designed clinic. As the first point of contact, the medical profession plays two vital roles: first, in treating any injuries (physical, internal, and shock), trauma, **pregnancy**, and infectious diseases (sexually transmitted diseases and **HIV/AIDs**) contracted during the assault and, second, in collecting the evidence of the crime. Medical evidence should be extracted and preserved with a special-purpose **rape kit**, as this may be required in subsequent legal proceedings. Both the forensic evidence and the expert testimony of the medical professionals can play a vital role in future criminal trials. In addition to providing treatment for the physical injuries sustained during the rape, it is now recognized that early intervention and counseling can accelerate the emotional, mental, and psychological recovery of a survivor. There is a growing trend to combine emergency response teams of medical, counseling, and legal professionals to provide a more comprehensive form of treatment at the time of the crime. Psychological intervention by psychiatrists and counselors can help the victims deal with the **rape trauma syndrome** and **post traumatic stress disorder.**

While the immediate provision of multidisciplinary medical care signifies the start of the optimum treatment program for survivors, the AMA recognizes that the vast majority of rape victims (as high as 83 percent) never seek medical care. While there are many complex reasons for the silence of the victims, the profession is criticized for ignoring or missing the symptoms that a patient may have been victimized in the recent or distant past. Female victims of intimate violence, including rape, frequently experience more gynecological, neurological, and stress-related medical problems over time. The profession comes under criticism for the absence of resources and time allocated to identifying and correlating that a wide array of repeated medical complaints may in fact be symptomatic of a traumatic rape or repeated intimate abuse.

The physician-patient relationship is predicated on objectivity, a bond of trust, and an uneven association of power, with the doctor being deemed as the more powerful in the relationship. As early as the fourth century B.C.E., the Hippocratic oath expressed ethical opposition to any sexual encounters within the doctor-patient relationship. The current Code of Ethics of most professional medical associations, including the AMA, American Psychiatric Association, and American Osteopathic Association, explicitly states that sexual relationships are unethical between doctors and their current or former patients. Doctors who have either consensual or nonconsensual sexual encounters with patients may be disciplined by their medical association or by the state licensing board. Deemed as sexual misconduct, these acts are believed to be exploitative and harmful to the patient, to preclude medical objectivity, and to compromise treatment. Despite these ethical guidelines, studies show that an increasing number of physicians are charged with sex-related offenses with patients, including rape. State medical licensing boards discipline these physicians by suspending or revoking their medical licenses, and the perpetrator can also face criminal **prosecution.** The medical profession itself recognizes the ethical problem of sexual misconduct and rape by physicians and claims a no-tolerance policy. However, most professional organizations respond that physicians need more instruction on the appropriate boundaries in the doctor-patient relationship, and they cite the fact that ethics are not a core component of the curriculum at many medical schools. Despite this professional debate, in 1996, Idaho was the first state to introduce legislation that criminalizes all forms of sexual contact between a patient and a health care provider. Another controversy within the medical profession emanates from the tradition of medical students performing nonconsensual pelvic examinations on anesthetized women who are undergoing surgery for non-related medical procedures. While the frequency of this complaint has only recently received attention in the **media**, many female victims are now claiming that this invasive procedure constitutes rape while under general anesthesia.

While the conduct of a minority of the medical profession comes under ongoing criticism, the services provided by the majority of the health care professionals are vitally important in helping victims survive and recover from a rape. Organizations such as the AMA have implemented specific policies to ensure that all medical professionals, and especially those specializing in victim care, receive up-to-date information on the newest medical approaches to caring for the survivors of rape. *See also*: **DNA Collection and Evidence; Morning-After Pill.**

Suggested Reading: American Medical Association, *Strategies for the Treatment and Prevention of Sexual Assault* (Chicago: Author, 1995), http://www.ama-assn.org/ama1/pub/upload/mm/386/sexualassault.pdf; American Medical Association, Council on Ethical and Judicial Affairs, "Sexual Misconduct in the Practice of Medicine," *Journal of the American Medical Association* 266.19 (November 20, 1991): 2741–2745; A. Amey and D. Bishai, "Measuring the Quality of Medical Care for Women Who Experience Sexual Assault with Data from the National Hospital Ambulatory Medical Care Survey," *Annals of Emergency Medicine* 39.6 (June 2002): 631–638; D. Davis, "Pelvic Exams Performed on Anesthetized Women," *Virtual Mentor (The Ethics Journal of the American Medical Association)* 5.5 (May 2003), http://www.ama-assn.org/ama/pub/category/10220.html; C. Dehlendorf and S. Wolfe, "Physicians Disciplined for Sex-Related Offenses," *Journal of the American Medical Association* 279.23 (June 17, 1998): 1883–1888; C. Winchell, "Curbside Consultation— The Seductive Patient," *American Academy of Family Physicians* 62 (September 1, 2000): 1196.

LAURIE JACKLIN

POGROM. From the Russian word *pogromit*, meaning "outrage" and "havoc," the term *pogrom* describes an organized, often officially encouraged massacre or persecution of a minority group. Pogroms initially referred to organized violence against Russian Jews in the late nineteenth and early twentieth centuries. "Organized," in this context, means the violent actions were either state sponsored or state approved and usually ignored by the police or soldiers in the area. Typically, Jewish homes and businesses were looted, people were injured and sometimes murdered, and women were raped. Jewish families often hid their daughters in rolled-up mattresses or pickle barrels. Similarities to these Russian pogroms can be seen during the *Kristallnacht* pogroms in Germany in November 1938. These riots against the Jews were supposed to be the spontaneous actions of outraged Germans, following the assassination of a minor German official by a Jewish teenager whose family had been deported to a concentration camp in Poland. In reality, Nazi officials orchestrated the mob violence, which resulted in a vast amount of damage to Jewish property, as well as in the injuries and deaths of many Jews. Over several days, **Nazis** and Nazi sympathizers destroyed Jewish homes, businesses, and synagogues and raped, injured, murdered, and deported Jews throughout Germany.

Although it is still most commonly used in the sense of a riot directed against Jews, *pogrom* is now used sometimes to refer to the persecution and riots against any group of people. Pogroms occur most often in areas where strong racial, religious, or political differences are prominent among the population and there exists a minority scapegoat population. In the Gujarat area in India in 2002, for example, a pogrom was executed against Muslim people by Hindu extremists. Some research presents the pogrom in Gujarat as a violent riot, but one defining characteristic that clearly indicated a pogrom was that door-to-door targeted and organized violence took place. Hindu extremists moved from house to house, killing, raping, and looting the houses of Muslims. Also, the level of violence was extreme. Young girls were raped and then burned, and others were chopped to pieces with swords. Also, the police in the area did nothing to stop the mob of 1,000 murderers and rapists, but instead they patrolled areas outside of the incident, turning a blind eye to the massacre. *See also*: **Bosnia-Herzegovina; Rape of Nanking.**

Suggested Reading: Susan Brownmiller, *Against Our Will: Men, Women and Rape* (New York: Fawcett Columbine, 1975); Miranda Kennedy, "Report from Gujarat," *The Nation*, December 9, 2002, http://www.thenation.com/doc,mhtm1%03Fi=20021209&s=Kennedy 20021121; "*Kristallnacht*: The November 1938 Pogroms," United States Holocaust Memorial Museum, http://www.ushmm.org/museum/exhibit/online/kristallnacht/frame.htm.

ARTHUR HOLST

POPULAR CULTURE. In contrast to high culture, popular culture is considered to represent cultural practices generated by and for a general as opposed to an elite or educated audience. Popular culture includes folk and native art, as well as the **media**, music from pop to hip hop, visual representations such as **film** and advertisements, and certain literary genres such as pulp and detective fiction. Many cultures, though, have never made a clear-cut distinction between high and popular culture. Contemporary postmodern culture in particular tends to blur this binarism, generating a hybrid culture, which is distributed globally. Moreover, forms of popular culture may evolve as avant-garde cultural practices (e.g., pop art, punk music, and cyber culture) before they become appropriated into and reproduced by mass culture. *Popular culture* is thus a contested term that transports values, marks cultural territories, and like cultures themselves, is always in transition.

In contemporary popular culture, representations of rape and sexual violence seem rampant, recurring in the rap lyrics, visual arts, and cinematic texts from Sam Peckinpah's *Straw Dogs* (1971) to Jonathan Kaplan's *The Accused* (1988) and Quentin Tarantino's *Pulp Fiction* (1994). Rape and **incest** are hinted at, even in fashion photography. In line with traditional resentments against popular culture, which have partly been triggered by the dismissal of American mass culture by the Frankfurt School, this deployment of (sexual) violence in popular culture is frequently deemed to mirror social phenomena of violence. The exposure to movies, **pornography**, and pop songs with violent content is said to reproduce and thus to perpetuate real violence. Accordingly, mass products of popular culture such as films and CDs are rated and thus restricted to certain age groups.

In the United States the belief that representations of violence reproduce real violence was reinforced in the 1980s and 1990s by an intensified debate of prominent cases of rape, **date rape**, and **sexual harassment** within the media. This prominence of rape and sexual violence in popular culture seemed to suggest that American culture is a "**rape culture**." However, the term *rape culture* misleadingly hints that rape occurs more frequently in a culture that talks about rape intensively than in cultures that deny its existence. Instead of documenting the state of real rape, though, the deployment of rape in American popular culture bespeaks the status of rape as a central trope within the American cultural imagination. Accordingly, films, videos, and pop music do not present us with cases of real rape but with representations of rape that need to be interpreted with reference to the history of their own particular aesthetics. Thus the cultural effect of gangsta rap, for instance, cannot be reduced to its violence-prone, misogynist lyrics. It also needs to be interpreted as part of a tradition that thrives on ambivalence and parody. *See also*: **Advertising; Literature, World and American.**

Suggested Reading: Ray B. Browne and Pat Browne, eds., *The Guide to United States Popular Culture* (Bowling Green, OH: Bowling Green State University Popular Press, 2001); Marjorie Garber, Jann Matlock, and Rebecca L. Walkowitz, eds., *Media Spectacles* (New

York: Routledge, 1993); Adele M. Stan, *Debating Sexual Correctness: Pornography, Sexual Harassment, Date Rape, and the Politics of Sexual Equality* (New York: Delta, 1995); John Storey, *An Introductory Guide to Cultural Theory and Popular Culture* (Athens: University of Georgia Press, 1993).

SABINE SIELKE

PORNOGRAPHY. How one defines pornography depends to a degree on how one views it. Literally, the word *pornography* means "the graphic depiction of whores," though it is often translated as "writing about prostitutes." A useful definition that captures its historic function is offered by Gail Dines: "any product produced for the primary purpose of facilitating male arousal and masturbation" (Morgan, 306). Religious conservatives define pornography as immoral; antipornography feminists see pornography as about justice, not morality. Recently, pro-pornography academics have suggested that pornography is liberating, and so it is not about justice, or morality, but sexual freedom. This definitional conflict is at the heart of the problem of pornography—is it protected speech or a violation of human equality rights?

The relationship between pornography and rape is a complex, unsettling, and unsettled one and is a central aspect of the debate about what pornography is and what it does. Feminist Robin Morgan proposed in 1974 that "pornography is the theory, rape is the practice" (Lederer, 140). This argument holds that pornography perpetuates **rape myths** and thus facilitates the acceptance of rape myths (i.e., "women want it, their protests notwithstanding"), and consequently pornography fosters violence against women. In pornography, according to one of the most famous antipornography writers, **Andrea Dworkin**, "rape or battering cannot exist as violation of female will because they are viewed as expressions of female will" (140). Or as feminist legal scholar **Catharine MacKinnon** explains, "[P]ornography constructs what a woman is as what men want from sex" (Itzin, 461). These writers claim that pornography makes the inequality that exists between men and women sexy, and in making inequality sexy, it promotes and authorizes rape, battery, **sexual harassment, prostitution**, and child sexual abuse.

The problem in understanding pornography in general, and pornography's relationship to rape in specific, is that pornography exists as an "idea" for some—an idea about speech, about creative expression—but is experienced as an industry by others—from those who underwrite its production and profit from its consumption to those who are used in it. As an industry, it exists to be sold, and it exists to be bought. Its making requires the acts that are reproduced for consumption in various **media**—through the Internet, through videos, and through magazines. Thus, violence against the people appearing in pornography is one aspect of the making of pornography. Just as it becomes a model for recording sexual violence that some rapists, sex murderers, and soldiers in wars or genocides reiterate through filming their own exploits, so pornography that expresses violence in its depiction required violence in its production. Pornography can be seen as a record of harm in its making, harm specifically to women, children, and nondominant males; pornography is not words but a record of acts, and these acts constitute harm. For instance, anal intercourse is usually depicted without any use of a lubricant.

Unlike any other medium, pornography is not a depiction of some thing but exists to establish a sexual relationship with the material itself, a relationship that culminates in **ejaculation**. Thus, antipornography activists argue that masturbating to pornography is not *about* sex but in itself constitutes sex, sex with an object, and fosters sex that uses others, predominantly women, children, and nondominant men as objects for sex. Pornography is therefore viewed as harm to women, children, and nondominant men both in its production and its consumption.

Antipornography writers point to many instances of "copy-cat" crimes, in which a man copies pornography in his **sexual assault** of a woman: rapists who use pornography as a blueprint for violation; husbands who force their wives to enact scenes from pornography, including using animals to penetrate their partners. Some studies of the effect of pornography on male behavior have espied a causal link between pornography and aggressive behavior, between viewing pornography and men's increased levels of violence against women.

While pornography's clientele seems to have changed in the past 30 years, and pornography for female arousal has recently been produced, the basic model and preponderant pornographic offerings cater to men. How heterosexual couples use pornography also is subject to debate. Some see pornography as providing a form of sexual education or as expanding sexual possibilities; others see the use of pornography by heterosexual couples as something that the man requests, as a way of lowering his partner's defenses so that the acts in pornography can be reproduced sexually. This is a form of "grooming" behavior, a term that describes how a child sexual abuser uses various techniques, including showing pornography, to manipulate a child into accepting the sexual acts that constitute the abuse.

On the other hand, civil libertarians argue that pornography is fantasy, often a form of artistic expression that leads merely to "one-handed reading" (i.e., masturbation), that it is therefore speech, that as speech it is protected by the First Amendment of the Constitution, and that to be against pornography is to be against free speech. Those who hold this position argue that it is a mistake to collapse sexuality within a feminist discussion of "gender," that opposition to pornography limits sexual liberty, and in doing so, it is sexual minorities, such as homosexuals, who will be the first to be persecuted. Finally, those who defend pornography argue that those who work in pornography have consented, and so the making of pornography is not a form of sexual discrimination.

Antipornography activists point out that not all speech is protected (like yelling "fire" in a crowded theater) and argue that pornography is not speech but acts. Further, they respond that the approach to viewing pornography as speech was in place before pornography as we know it now existed—pornography that uses photographs, cameras, and other technology that records acts, not "ideas."

Can sexuality and sexual practices be separated from the construction of gender? Is sexuality an aspect of inequality? When an act is sexual, is it harder to see the harm that it represents? These are key aspects of the debate.

Suggested Reading: Carol J. Adams, *The Pornography of Meat* (New York: Continuum, 2003); Andrea Dworkin, *Pornography: Men Possessing Women* (New York: Perigree Books, 1981); Catherine Itzin, *Pornography: Women, Violence and Civil Liberties* (New York: Oxford University Press, 1993); Laura Lederer, *Take Back the Night: Women on Pornography* (New York: William Morrow, 1980); Robin Morgan, *Sisterhood Is Forever: The Women's Anthology for a New Millenium* (New York: Washington Square Press, 2003); Diane E.H. Russell, *Making Violence Sexy: Feminist Views on Pornography* (New York: Teachers College Press, 1993); Lynne Segal and Mary McIntosh, *Sex Exposed: Sexuality and the Pornography Debate* (New Brunswick, NJ: Rutgers University Press, 1993).

CAROL J. ADAMS

POSTTRAUMATIC STRESS DISORDER (PTSD). Posttraumatic stress disorder is a diagnosis used by the American Psychiatric Association (APA) to refer to an anxiety disorder that follows exposure to a traumatic event. The event can be something witnessed or experienced, but to meet criteria for PTSD, it must involve "actual or threatened death or serious injury, or a threat to the physical integrity of self or others" (APA, 467). The aftermath of the Vietnam War is credited as the beginning of the modern conception of PTSD, although psychological impairment after war has long been noted. This period was also the one in which feminists began to document the effect of trauma, particularly early childhood sexual abuse, on women.

More than half the population reports at least one traumatic event in their lifetime. However, only a small percentage of those experiencing trauma will develop PTSD; the American Psychiatric Association estimates that about 8 percent of adults in the United States will experience PTSD at some point in their lives. Women are about twice as likely to develop the disorder as men. Some traumatic experiences are more likely to lead to PTSD, with studies finding over 30 percent of men with combat exposure developing the disorder. For both men and women, rape is highly likely to lead to PTSD, as are **torture**, internment as a political prisoner, and childhood abuse.

PTSD usually appears within three months of the trauma but can appear later, even years after the event. In about half the cases, symptoms will disappear in another three months, but for the remaining cases, symptoms can persist, sometimes for years, often waxing and waning with other life stressors or reminders of the event.

The symptoms of PTSD fall into three categories: intrusion, avoidance, and hyperarousal. Intrusion can take the form of recurrent and intrusive memories, nightmares, or what are termed "flashbacks," dissociative states lasting a few seconds to days in which the person reexperiences the event. Avoidance includes trying to avoid thoughts, feelings, or conversations that remind them of the trauma. Persons with PTSD may feel numb; have less interest in events around them; have less ability to feel emotions, especially those related to intimate involvement with others, and may end up detached from other people and with a sense that they have no future. Hyprearousal means persons with PTSD experience symptoms of anxiety or arousal that were not present before the trauma. These can include difficulty sleeping, hypervigilance, exaggerated startle responses, outbursts of anger, or difficulty concentrating.

Other psychological disorders often accompany PTSD. Depression is a common consequence of the losses experienced in the trauma and the individual's inability to confront the painful feelings. Some individuals may also experience survivor guilt, because they survived the trauma, while others did not. Many people also attempt to blunt the symptoms of PTSD by abusing **alcohol** or other drugs.

Learning theory is usually used to explain the presence of the avoidance behaviors and the hyperarousal in PTSD, but the intrusive symptoms are harder to explain. It has been theorized that cognitive processing involves a "completion tendency" that keeps trauma information in active memory. It has been shown that a shift in perceptions follows trauma, resulting in a loss of belief in the meaningfulness of life and in one's own invulnerability and worth. The task of recovering meaning involves reexamining and reinterpreting the event.

Attempts have been made to identify factors that increase the likelihood that trauma will result in PTSD. More extreme traumas, that is, those that have larger and more intense stressors over a longer period of time and those that are more unpredictable and uncontrollable, are more likely to result in PTSD. There are some indications that neurohormonal changes observed following PTSD may have a genetic factor. Childhood abuse increases the likelihood of PTSD following trauma. Factors such as active coping styles, the use of humor and **religion**, and social support can reduce the risk of PTSD. *See also*: **Dissociative Identity Disorder (DID)**; **Rape Trauma Syndrome**.

Suggested Reading: American Psychiatric Association, *Diagnostic and Statistical Manual of Mental Disorders, Fourth Edition, Text Revision (DM-IV-TR)* (Washington, DC: Author, 2000); Mardi J. Horowitz, *Stress Response Syndromes*, 2nd ed. (New York: Aronson, 1986); Ronnie Janoff-Bulman, *Shattered Assumptions: Toward a New Psychology of Trauma* (New York: Free Press, 1992); F.H. Norris, "Epidemiology of Trauma: Frequency and Impact of Different Potentially Traumatic Events on Different Demographic Groups," *Journal of Consulting and Clinical Psychology* 60 (1992): 409–418; C.S. Widom, "Posttraumatic Stress Disorder in Abused and Neglected Children Grown Up," *American Journal of Psychiatry* 156.8 (1999): 1223–1239; R. Yehuda, "Psychoneuroendocrinology of Post-traumatic Stress Disorder," *Psychiatric Clinics of North America* 21.2 (1998): 359–379.

MARGARET GIBBS

PREDATORS. *See* Sexual Predators.

PREGNANCY. The **survivor** of a rape who finds she is pregnant faces many difficult choices, which in turn increase the psychological trauma of the rape. She must choose whether to terminate the pregnancy. If she opts for an **abortion**, the stress of this could compound the already complex effects of the assault itself. In some areas, where abortions are difficult to obtain, **infanticide** may result. If abortion is illegal, the medical and social risks involved increase. Following Germany's defeat in World War II, the number of rapes committed by occupying soldiers, mainly of the Red Army, was so large that hospitals were authorized to provide abortions, though normally illegal.

If a raped woman opts to have the baby, she faces the decision of whether to raise the child. It may be problematic at times for the mother to disassociate the child from the attacker, particularly if there is a physical resemblance. If the child is the result of **incest**, further complications arise. People may ostracize the child of rape, especially if the assailant was a member of an enemy group. Some medieval European penitentials taught that women should not be condemned if they left to die by exposure an infant conceived during a rape, but they did have to perform penance.

In some places, any sexual encounter by a woman outside of marriage is likely to be the cause of her death in order to redeem her **family**'s honor. Therefore, a rape resulting in pregnancy may prove to be a woman's death sentence. Unwed mothers were frequently shunned in earlier eras and continue to be so in some areas of the world today. If the woman is already in a sexually active relationship, the paternity of the child may be unclear unless a DNA test is done. Without confirmation of paternity, her partner will often have difficulty accepting the child.

On the other hand, if the rapist becomes aware of the child's existence, he may assert his parental rights, including the right to **consent** (or not) to adoption. The mother is then faced with a lifelong relationship with her assailant and additional worries for the child's well-being. Many states have therefore established laws that deny parental rights to the father if the child was conceived as a result of rape.

Late medieval and early modern English law courts employed the Galenic model of reproduction, which denied the possibility of pregnancy resulting from rape. Galen, an ancient Greek physician, believed that both men and women produced "seed." A woman only released her "seed" upon orgasm, which in turn only happened if the experience had been enjoyable and hence consensual. The belief that women could not conceive if raped was carried to the British American colonies.

In the 1990s, a study found that women who are raped are more likely to become pregnant than women who engage in consensual intercourse, thereby asserting that there may be a biological imperative for rape (Gottschall and Gottschall). This report, based on insufficiently small sample groups (about 400 in each group), is dangerous, as some men may try to employ it to condone rape. Since few men rape for reproductive reasons—rape is an issue of power, not sex—the results and purpose of the study are even more questionable.

One instance where pregnancy was a desired outcome of an assault is the systematic rapes of women in the civil wars in Croatia and **Bosnia-Herzegovina**. Here, women and girls were repeatedly raped, often with the aim of impregnating them. Both the rapes and the resultant pregnancies worked to tear families apart, to undermine a **religion**, to blur ethnic identities, as well as to humiliate and psychologically (and not infrequently physically) destroy the opposition. *See also*: **Morning-After Pill; Paternity Testing; Stigma.**

Suggested Reading: John Boswell, *The Kindness of Strangers: The Abandonment of Children in Western Europe from Late Antiquity to the Renaissance* (New York: Random House, 1990); Jonathan A. Gottschall and Tiffany A. Gottschall, "Are Per-Incident Rape-Pregnancy Rates Higher Than Per-Incident Consensual Pregnancy Rates?" *Human Nature: An Interdisciplinary Biosocial Perspective* 14.1 (2003): 1–20; Atina Grossmann, "A Question of Silence: The Rape of German Women by Occupation Soldiers," in *West Germany under Construction: Politics, Society, and Culture in the Adenauer Era*, ed. Robert G. Moeller (Ann Arbor: University of Michigan Press, 1997), 33–52; Dorothy Q. Thomas and Regan E. Ralph, "Rape in War: The Case of Bosnia," in *Gender Politics in the Western Balkans: Women and Society in Yugoslavia and the Yugoslav Successor States*, ed. Sabrina P. Ramet and Branka Magas (University Park: Pennsylvania State University Press, 1999), 203–218.

TONYA MARIE LAMBERT

PREVENTION. *See* Rape Prevention.

PRISON RAPE. While incarcerated in detention facilities, men, women, and youths can be subjected to **sexual harassment**, sexual brutality, and rape. Rape within a prison setting can happen through multiple combinations of circumstances and perpetrators (individuals who carry out the rape of another). Prison rapes can be perpetrated as prisoner upon prisoner in which either a single individual or a gang of individuals is responsible for the rape of another inmate. In addition, prison staff might rape their own prisoner(s).

Prisoner rape is denounced as a violation of human rights by the United States and by many in the international community. Several organizations, such as Amnesty International, and a growing number of international governing bodies have even recognized **sexual assault** upon prisoners as a classification and method of **torture**. In the United States, prison rape is recognized as a violation of the prisoner's Eighth Amendment U.S. constitutional rights, which expressly prohibit cruel and unusual punishment.

Statistical studies of the U.S. prison population provide only an overview and a glimpse of the frequency and vulnerability of prisoners to being raped while in an American prison. At present such sexual crimes occurring within prison facilities are not reflected in the U.S. Bureau of Justice's annual crime statistics, which provides reporting on sexual and other crimes. Information about the extent of prison rape in the American prison system is therefore largely dependent, then, on other studies and sources of investigation. Typically, these existing and available studies have limited information about the national occurrence and scope of prison rape in the United States—because generally information about prison sexual assaults is often available from only a few prisons within select regions of the United States.

But from such studies as these, specifically one regarding male prison inmates, appears the ratio that 1 in 10 men report being anally raped while in prison. Rates for women being sexually assaulted in prison vary greatly and appear dependent on the facility in which they are incarcerated. Although women do experience forced sexual assaults and **sexual coercion** in prison, according to a report in 1996 by Cindy Struckman-Johnson, women prisoners are more likely to be sexually harassed. Youths, of both genders, are particularly vulnerable to sexual assault when placed in detaining circumstances with an adult prison population. With the problems of overcrowding and understaffing in the current prison system, perpetrators can more easily exploit the vulnerabilities of both the prison system itself and ultimately the vulnerabilities of their future victims.

Although anyone certainly can become a victim of sexual assault, prisoners with mental disabilities or of diminutive size or male prisoners with otherwise perceived feminine traits are significant targets for sexual violence in prison. Among male and female prisoners, often the newest inmates who may have yet to form the protection of gangs, who are younger or who are lacking other resources for defense, become those prisoners facing the most potential risk for perpetual sexual victimization.

In prison environments, sexual assaults happen to both men and women, across all age groups and sexual orientations, with some similar yet distinct characteristics and effects. The common misuse of the expression for prison sexual assault as being **"homosexual rape"** can lead both male and female victims to feel that their sense, definition, and experience of what is masculine or feminine, as well as what is meant by sexuality, is at risk. **Gay and lesbian survivors** of prison rape can equally blame themselves for their sexual orientation for increasing their perceived vulnerability for their sexual assault.

In addition to the direct injury of sexual violence to their bodies, men and women who are sexually assaulted during their prison incarceration also are subjected to the very real dangers of sexually transmitted diseases (STDs). In prison settings STD prophylaxis (prevention) and treatment is not often, if at all, available. HIV transmission rates alone, according to one study, are 10 times higher in the prison population as compared with a general population of nonprisoners. For women prisoners, **pregnancy** intervention methods are also too frequently nonexistent. Prisoners can be reluctant to report their sexual assault to the prison authorities for fear of retaliation, stigmatization, or additional violence threatened by their perpetrators. For these assaulted prisoners, their victimization then extends further by reducing their opportunities to receive prompt medical intervention. Immediate and early medical care can have clear and powerful effects on the disease outcomes of STDs and HIV, as well as pregnancy.

Because of the very nature of their confinement and restricted freedoms, it is important to consider that for many prisoners experiencing sexual violence in prison, they can continue to be sexually victimized throughout the duration of their incarceration sentence—which could be years or a lifetime. As a potential survival strategy, then, prisoners may make multiple concessions, including sexual victimization itself, in order to avoid or assert some control over the outcome of further acts of violence.

More nationwide and thorough studies are needed to better assess the extent and consequences of prison rape. Such studies would, in addition to raising awareness of prison rape, provide information about preventing those circumstances unique to sexual assault in prison environments and identify the specific needs for treating these rape victims as well as their perpetrators. *See also*: **HIV/AIDS**.

Suggested Reading: Amnesty International, http://www.amnestyusa.org/; Human Rights Watch, htp://www.hrw.org/; Daniel Lockwood, *Prison Sexual Violence* (New York: Elsevier Science, 1980); Stop Prisoner Rape, http://www.spr.org/; Wayne Wooden and Jay Parker, *Men behind Bars: Sexual Exploitation in Prison* (New York: Plenum, 1982).

JENNIFER H. PROFITT

PROFILING. Profiling is the analysis of an unsolved violent crime to determine identifiable characteristics of the unknown offender. The profile consists of subjective opinions created by forensic behavioral specialists and is intended for use by criminal investigators and others in the criminal justice system. Clinical psychologists or psychiatrists lacking experience in the investigation of violent crime created most profiles until the late twentieth century. Since then, the Federal Bureau of Investigation's (FBI) National Center for the Analysis of Violent Crime (NCAVC), retired FBI agents, and selected **law enforcement** officers who have studied with the NCAVC prepare criminal profiles. Profiling forms one part of a criminal investigative analysis. Other services that can be included in an analysis are recommendations for investigative techniques, interrogation methods useful for particular types of suspects, and trial strategies, as well as opinions regarding manner of death.

In 1972, the FBI Behavioral Science Unit at the FBI Academy informally initiated law enforcement's involvement in profiling. The FBI's involvement in criminal profiling grew out of the realization that similar offenders committed similar crimes for similar reasons because the underlying motivation is basically the same. The FBI then formalized the program in 1978 after unanticipated demand and began assigning cases to individual investigators. In 1984, the National Center for the Analysis of Violent Crime supplanted the Behavior Science Unit. NCAVC coordinators in various geographic regions check submitted cases for the necessary materials and for suitability to profiling.

The NCAVC prepares profiles for those cases that meet their requirements, keeping case materials for future reference. These materials, the details of each violent crime and its distinguishing features, are stored in their computer database. Database searches allow the agency to determine whether particular crimes are possibly linked to earlier crimes, meaning that there is likely a serial criminal involved. Services are provided free to legitimate governmental criminal justice agencies, while nongovernmental agencies pay a fee. The criminal profiler needs no particular educational degree or attributes, although a background in the behavioral sciences is helpful. Characteristics of good profilers include investigative and research experience, common sense, intuitiveness, the ability to isolate emotions, the ability to analyze a situation and arrive at logical conclusions, and the ability to reconstruct the crime using the criminal's reasoning process.

Profiling's primary purpose is to save investigative hours by narrowing the focus of a criminal investigation. Profiling is an art rather than a science, and experts advise that it should never be the first or only investigative method that an investigator utilizes. Investigators are advised to conduct all conventional methods first and use profiling if the case remains unsolved, as profiling will rarely lead to the direct solution of a case. Profiling will not identify a specific person as a suspect in the crime. Instead, it will identify a personality type that investigators can use to help determine or eliminate potential suspects. To be eligible for profiling, a case must involve a crime or series of crimes of violence or potential violence with an unknown offender, and all other major investigational leads must have been exhausted. **Serial rapes** are among those crimes that are particularly appropriate for profiling. The investigating law enforcement agency must include a case materials map, a victim statement, and a victimology, or summary of known facts about the victim. The interview of the rape victim and its documentation are the most important factors in rape profiling. There should be no information that identifies particular suspects in order to avoid damaging the profiler's objectivity. If there is not sufficient behavior to analyze, the NCAVC will be unable to profile the case.

The profiling process in rape cases follows three basic steps: determining from the victim the rapist's behavior, analyzing that behavior to determine the rapist's motivation, and stating the characteristics and traits of the person who would commit rape in the manner indicated by his/her behavior. The forms of offender behavior that profilers analyze include verbal statements, the type and sequence of sexual acts, and the amount of physical force used by the offender. The motivation for the crime is exhibited through the rapist's behavior and can include hostility, anger, need for affection, concern, degradation, and punishment. A profile's format may vary from preparer to preparer, but the information remains essentially the same. The most common formats are outlining, which allows quick identification of specific characteristics, and narrative style, which provides more detail.

Profiles can include both the general characteristics of the stranger rapist and the specific characteristics of different categories of rapists. *Power reassurance (compensatory) rapists* are the least violent and aggressive, using only enough force to control their **victims** and often expressing concern for the victim's welfare. They suffer from low self-image, and their basic purpose is to elevate their self-status. *Anger retaliation rapists* see themselves as masculine and socially competent but harbor deep hatred for women. Their basic purpose is to get even with all women through hurting a specific victim. *Power assertive rapists* exhibit selfish behavior with no regard for the victim's welfare, attempting to express their virility and dominance through rape. *Sadistic rapists* are the most dangerous because they exhibit compulsive personalities and rape with the clear intent to harm the victim. Many sadistic rapists often escalate to **murder**, although the act of killing is secondary to the act of rape. They express no remorse for their actions. Most profiles include the rapist's approximate age, sex, race, marital status, occupation type, hobbies, approximate year and style of vehicle, arrest history, appearance and grooming habits, residential information, and victim-offender relationship. Profiles also include an offender's personality characteristics, such as temperament, intelligence, emotional adjustment, pathological behavioral characteristics, and ability to interact socially and sexually. *See also*: **Prosecution; Serial Rape and Serial Rapists; Sex Offenders.**

Suggested Reading: A.N. Groth, *Men Who Rape* (New York: Plenum Press, 1988); Robert R. Hazelwood and Ann Wolbert Burgess, *Practical Aspects of Rape Investigation: A Multidisciplinary Approach* (Boca Raton, FL: CRC Press, 1995); Ronald M. Holmes and Stephen T. Holmes, *Profiling Violent Crimes: An Investigative Tool* (Thousand Oaks, CA: Sage, 2002); Brent Turvey, *Criminal Profiling: An Introduction to Behavioral Evidence Analysis* (San Diego: Academic Press, 2002).

MARCELLA TREVIÑO

PROSECUTION. Statistics show that 9 out of every 10 women who are raped will choose not to report the rape to authorities. Rape **victims** often feel guilty and embarrassed after a rape, and insensitive police officers and/or hospital personnel can accentuate these feelings of responsibility for being the victim of a sexual crime. Many rape victims choose silence over prosecution because they know that a trial would force them to face the rapist and relive the horrors of the rape in front of a crowded courtroom, where they might not be believed and might be accused of lying or even encouraging or consenting to the rape. High-profile rape cases like the 1991 cases of William Kennedy Smith in Florida and Mike Tyson in Indiana have given rape victims an illuminating view of how victims may be treated during rape trials. Even if a rape victim is willing to report the crime, she/he knows that the rapist is unlikely to be arrested and even less likely to be prosecuted and imprisoned for the crime. If the rapist is imprisoned, he is likely to serve only a few years, and the rape victim may have been threatened with revenge.

Before the women's movement of the 1970s, rape victims were often interviewed by insensitive police officers who questioned a woman about what *she* did to provoke the rape. In response to the feminist call-to-arms on the subject of rape and the creation of **rape crisis centers**, the attitude of police officers has changed for the most part. Rape crisis advocates who support rape victims throughout the process of dealing with the aftermath of rape have called attention to improper actions in dealing with rape victims, and it has become standard practice to develop training for all those who regularly come into contact with rape victims.

Successful prosecution of a rape case depends to a significant degree on the quality of evidence accumulated by those who gather physical evidence from the victim and the crime scene. Technical experts can often analyze evidence to form a complete picture of the rapist and of his habits. Criminologists have identified four major categories of evidence that help prosecutors build a case against a rapist: forensic, circumstantial, eyewitness, and direct evidence. Forensic evidence, such as fingerprints, footprints, body fluids, hairs, and fiber, can scientifically connect a rapist to a crime scene. Circumstantial evidence may point to a particular individual as a rapist. Eyewitnesses can place an individual or a vehicle at the scene of the crime. Direct evidence like drivers' licenses and photographs of the victim may highlight a direct link between the rapist and the victim. Collateral evidence, such as reading, viewing, and collecting habits, that may seem minor on the surface may indicate a particular interest, pattern, or behavior that leads to the arrest and conviction of a rapist.

One reason that it has become easier for prosecutors to convict accused rapists is that both federal and state laws have become more responsive to the realities of law. For example, in 1975, the Michigan legislature passed rape reforms that became the model for other states. The Michigan law set up four categories of **sexual assault** based on the seriousness of the crime in gender-neutral language that included offenses against males, as well as against females. The categories were based on the seriousness of the offense, the amount of force or coercion used, the degree of injuries inflicted, and the age and incapacitation of the victim. This new definition of rape also expanded the traditional definition to include penetration by an object and placed the burden of proof on the defendant. States also passed **rape shield laws** so that a victim is not put on trial for her/his sexual history and repealed laws that required prompt reporting and proof of **resistance**. Prosecutors at both the state and federal level have been assisted by improved technology, which may provide solid evidence that the accused rapist committed the crime in question. It may also clear the accused rapist of the crime. DNA evidence has been particularly useful in solving rape crimes, and its use has become more widespread. For example, in August 2003, the New York Police Department announced that it would review sexual crimes of the past 10 years using DNA profiles. In light of new technology, Nevada has no statute of limitations on rape cases, and other states are extending the statute of limitations.

The behavior of the investigating officer who may be the first person to interview a rape victim is extremely important to the emotional well-being of the victim and to the prosecutor who depends on investigating officers to conduct initial interviews and to gather evidence at the crime scene. Before specific rape training was instituted, officers might refuse to believe a woman was raped if she had not actively resisted, if the rape had not been witnessed, or if the victim was not physically injured or noticeably traumatized. Most police officers are now trained to understand that initial reactions of rape victims vary greatly. While one victim may be in shock, another may try to pretend the crime never happened. Another victim may have hysterics, and still another may appear calm and in control on the surface. Experts have suggested a number of things the police can do to help rape victims. The police should make rape cases a high priority because rape is a crime with grave consequences. Officers should ensure the safety of the victim and get immediate medical attention when it is needed. The initial interview should be as painless as possible in comfortable and nonthreatening surroundings. No more than two police officers should be present at the interview. When questioning the victim, police officers should ask open-ended questions as well as those that require specific answers. Specific information might include whether or not the victim knew her attacker, what kinds of smells or sounds were evident, what the weather was like, whether the victim had noticed a stranger hanging around or had received obscene phone calls, and whether the victim observed particular physical attributes of the attacker. The officer should also discuss legal procedures with the victim so that she/he will know what to expect. It is important that investigating officers be supportive, patient, and gentle with the victim and tactful with the victim's **family**.

Before the prevalence of **rape education** and training, many rapes were never prosecuted because prosecutors did not believe victims were raped. Estimates of false rape charges vary from as low as the 2 percent suggested by rape crisis counselors to the 25 percent claimed by antifeminists. Prosecutors do have clues that point to a false rape claim. If a victim recants her testimony after giving inconsistent testimony or if a victim's testimony is not borne out by the evidence, the prosecutor may ask for a lie detector test. If the victim fails, the prosecutor may drop the case. A number of false rape claims picked up by the **media** have led some members of the public to think the incidence of false allegations of rape is higher than the evidence shows.

A charge of rape does not have to be false for the prosecutor to refuse to prosecute or to agree to a lesser charge (plea bargain). A prosecutor looks at how strong the case is, whether the victim is a child or is mentally incapacitated, whether the attacker was a current or previous sexual partner, and whether **alcohol** or drugs were present. Other factors in the decision may include the background of the defendant, the victim's attitude and ability to withstand the trial, and the perceived level of threat to society from the accused. In some cases, state and federal prosecutors are never involved in rape cases. For example, when rapes occur on college campuses involving the alleged rape of one student by another, the school may engage in damage control by responding to the rape through campus policies. The highly publicized sex scandals within the Catholic Church have generally been dealt with (or ignored) by Church officials. When rape occurs in the military, military procedures take precedence over civil remedies.

All professionals who work with rape victims are responsible for keeping the victim informed of legalities at all levels. It may be up to the prosecutor to explain the legal process to the victim, and this process may vary from state to state. The first step in a rape charge is usually to file a complaint against the attacker, who will then be arraigned in court, generally within a day or two. After the arraignment, a probable cause or preliminary hearing takes place at which all principals are required to be present. The prosecutor attempts to connect the accused with the crime, while the defense lawyer tries to prove there is no connection. If the accused does not make an appearance in court, the police will make an effort to locate him. If the preliminary hearing reveals sufficient evidence to bind the accused over for trial, a trial date is set. The trial is usually held in front of a jury that will determine guilt or innocence. If the accused is found guilty, a sentence will be handed down, and the accused will be imprisoned.

For a trial, the prosecutor's case files will include the following if well prepared: transcripts of the original call to the police; the first interview conducted at the crime scene; interviews with the nurse and doctors who examined the patient at the hospital; a list of physical evidence linking the suspect to the crime scene; a follow-up interview with the investigating officer(s); personal notes taken during the preliminary hearing; statements of eyewitnesses; and statements given to a private investigator if one was used.

The rape victim's testimony may be the most important variable in determining the guilt of the accused, and the prosecutor needs to carefully question and prepare the victim for the trial. Interviews with all witnesses should be conducted personally so that no surprises emerge in the course of the trial. Ideally, the prosecutor's notes for the actual trial should be so detailed that they include 90 percent of the closing statement. Successful prosecutions are the most important factor in a rape victim's recovery. *See also*: **Campus Rape; Clergy, Sexual Abuse by; Law Enforcement; Rape Kit; Secondary Rape.**

Suggested Reading: Joy Satterwhite Eyman, *How to Convict a Rapist* (New York: Stein and Day, 1980); Rob Hall, *Rape in America: A Reference Handbook* (Santa Barbara, CA:

ABC-CLIO, 1995); Susan Halpern, *Rape: Helping the Victim* (Oradell, NJ: Medical Economics Company, 1978); Robert R. Hazelwood and Kenneth V. Lanning, "Collected Materials in Sexual Crimes," in *Practical Aspects of Rape Investigation*, ed. Robert R. Hazelwood and Ann Wolbert Burgess (Boca Raton, FL: CRC Press, 2001), 221–232; William Heiman, rev. and updated by Ann Ponterio and Gail Fairman, "Prosecuting Rape Cases: Trial Tactic Issues," in *Practical Aspects of Rape Investigation*, ed. Robert R. Hazelwood and Ann Wolbert Burgess (Boca Raton, FL: CRC Press, 2001), 347–364; Judith May-Parker and Lucia Kiwala, *Guidelines for Police Training on Violence against Women and Child Abuse* (London: Commonwealth Secretariat Team, 2000); Barbara J. Rodabaugh and Melanie Austin, *Sexual Assault: A Guide for Community Action* (New York: Garland STPM Press, 1981); Cassia Spohn and Julie Horney, *Rape Law Reform: A Grassroots Revolution and Its Impact* (New York: Plenum Press, 1992).

ELIZABETH R. PURDY

PROSTITUTION. Within the last century, views on the relationship between prostitution and rape have remained divided. Some have seen prostitution, or the commercial sale of sex, as an intrinsic if unfortunate aspect of human civilization. Others perceive prostitution *as* rape, while still others regard the cultural stigmatization and criminalization of prostitution as the crucial problems and advocate decriminalization and redefining prostitutes as "sex workers." Providing them with the same legal protections afforded other citizens would reduce their vulnerability to coercion, violence, and in particular, rape. To date, however, positions on this controversial topic have been limited by scarce research on pimps, victimizers, and clients and inadequate attention to male prostitutes.

Historically, human cultures have regarded prostitutes as deviant and outcast women, but early in the twentieth century, suffragists redefined them as "white slaves" compelled into commercial sex by "third parties," or by organized cartels that ran an "international traffic in women." For these antiprostitution activists, no woman could give genuine **consent** to prostitution but rather was coerced into an inherently degrading form of sexual **slavery**. Commercial sex denied women the rights of ownership over their bodies and moral characters, and it occurred because men demanded sexual access to women and denied them equal economic, familial, social, educational, and legal rights and opportunities.

None of the parties to the current debate deny that all classes of prostitutes, including streetwalkers, independent call girls, and brothel workers, are victimized at alarming rates by assailants confident that the women will not report rape because they live outside the law. Moreover, legal scholars wonder whether or not prostitutes can *claim* rape or only the theft of their services, even in contexts in which they are not engaged in commercial sexual activities. For instance, a man who knows a woman (or man) is a prostitute could rape her or him, then claim he had had a monetary dispute with the sex worker. Statistics attest to the difficulties prostitutes face when they do report rape. Under most circumstances, they are denied protection of law. In the United States, police often call such reports "unfounded," meaning that no crime ever occurred, and in many other countries prostitutes never file reports.

Legal scholars concur that current laws against prostitution are hard to enforce, create an underworld culture that jeopardizes prostitutes, confuse victims with victimizers, and foster conditions in which "bosses" force prostitutes to service clients or perform particular sex acts against their will. For these reasons, some feminists see rape as inherent in prostitution and thus want to see sex work eliminated by giving prostitutes other economic choices. They also battle against **pornography**, which they perceive as perpetuating a culture of rape and sexual commodification of women. These thinkers stress the high correlation between childhood sexual abuse and later involvement in prostitution and therefore view commercial sex as a lifelong continuum of sexual exploitation and violence countenanced by male-dominated cultures. However, incidents of sexual abuse of male children remain underreported, and almost half of American women experience some form of **sexual assault**, sexual abuse, or **sexual harassment** during their lives but still do not become prostitutes. Hence, statistics should not be dismissed but regarded with some caution.

Others draw different conclusions from the high vulnerability of prostitutes to rape and exploitation. For them, prostitutes should not be characterized as social or psychological "types" but rather as sex workers whose chief problems emanate from exploitative labor relations, social stigmatization, and lack of legal protections. According to this view, prostitution does not mean rape, but it often entails rape because current social policies reflect fear and hatred of prostitutes and perpetuate the crimes committed against them. Dominant cultural attitudes condemn ascribing monetary value to sexual activities and treat sexual pleasure as something inherently different from other pleasures, such as food and drink, which do have monetary value. According to such thinkers, the issue of degradation is irrelevant because it involves beliefs about the place that sex "should" have in human relations. In addition, they distinguish between consensual commercial sex acts between adult prostitutes and clients and the crime of rape. Calls for more discipline and legal punishment of prostitutes, and more recently, their abusive employers, have never worked. Insisting on dealing with the "here and now," such thinkers believe that providing sex workers with legal and labor protections makes distinct the now blurred boundaries between prostitution and rape. Writings by women and, to a lesser extent, men in the sex industry on the whole confirm the above view, while attesting to the impossibility about drawing single theoretical conclusions about this complex issue.

Some see prostitution as rape, a violation of human rights, and a means of maintaining male dominance over women. Others contend that treating sex work as a legitimate form of decriminalized labor would considerably lessen the rape and exploitation of such workers. However, in order to gain fuller understanding of prostitution and rape, far more research into the pimps, victimizers, and above all, *clients* who create the demand for commercial sex is required, for as long as men remain excluded, changes in attitudes toward sex and power cannot occur. *See also*: **Trafficking in Women and Children.**

Suggested Reading: Melissa Farley, ed., *Prostitution, Trafficking, and Traumatic Stress* (Binghamton, NY: Haworth Maltreatment and Trauma Press, 2004); Kelly D. Weisberg, ed., *Applications of Feminist Legal Theory to Women's Lives: Sex, Violence, Work, and Reproduction* (Philadelphia: Temple University Press, 1996).

CORINNE E. BLACKMER

R

RACE AND RACISM. Based on scientific notions of heredity, race is a modern concept that has been employed by human and natural sciences to describe and distinguish groups of living beings, both animal and human. As a cultural category, race is interwoven with concepts of nationality, the understanding of a people as nation, and notions of citizenship. In the United States the dual legacy of **slavery** and immigration has had a particular impact on how citizenry relates to race, despite the fact that citizenship in the United States is based on *ius soli*, or place of birth, as opposed to *ius sanguinis* (law of blood). As a biological category, race differentiates organisms within a certain species. In more general use, the term *race* has been applied to discriminate between persons of different phenotype, that is, skin color and texture of hair, ethnic descent, and cultural tradition. For cultural studies, race has become the ultimate trope of difference.

The highly loaded but vague term *racism* refers to all forms of political, economic, and social discrimination based on supposedly hereditary racial and ethnic differences. Racist ideologies are considered to have had a long history that can be traced back to ancient history and myths as well as to the **Bible**. They found their scientific grounding during the Enlightenment and the Victorian age, especially with the emergence of theories of evolution, such as Charles Darwin's monumental work *On the Origin of the Species by Means of Natural Selection* (1859), and with a practice of ethnography that tended to biologize so-called primitive people. During the rise of nation–states in the eighteenth and nineteenth century, colonialism and imperialism were legitimized in part by Eurocentric notions of cultural and racial superiority. Discriminating human races on genetically based phenotypes, scientific theories of race also held that differences in phenotype correspond to certain character traits. Nineteenth-century criminology defined social deviancy as a hereditary trait. The most significant and lasting effect of these notions of race is that racial and ethnic differences were increasingly perceived as "natural."

Resisting scientific racism and discrimination on the basis of race, class, and gender, cultural criticism has argued for decades that race cannot be reduced to biological essences but instead needs to be seen as a cultural construct that separates social groups and represents relations of power. Findings of molecular biology and most recently the Human Genome Project have reinforced the notion that race appeals to nothing that science can register as "real." Instead, novel insights of genetic research have affirmed claims of critical anthropology that there is more genetic variation within one race than there is between one race and another.

In the United States race emerged as a representation of the relation between **Native Americans** and European colonizers, yet even more prominently of the master/slave relation, and therefore as superimposed upon class and economic relations. In the nineteenth-century United States, culture race theories managed to retain the hierarchical difference between white Americans and **African Americans** even after the Civil War (1861–1865) and the period of Reconstruction (1865–1877), while at the same time transforming that difference from an economic into a biological divide. Laws that discriminated persons on the basis of their race—the so-called Jim Crow legislation in the United States—served to perpetuate social and cultural segregation and were oftentimes violently enforced, especially in cases of so-called miscegenation. During the 1920s, fears that "darker" races could outnumber the white "Nordic" races dominated a growing interest in " 'other' cultures," including African American cultural expression. In the United States such xenophobic sentiments led to adjustments of immigration laws in 1921 and 1924.

Racist ideologies and the science of race took devastating turns with the eugenics movement of the early twentieth century. Preoccupied with hereditary hygiene and the health of the "national body," eugenics was appropriated by fascism and its appeal to a superior "Aryan" race and paved the way to the near extinction of European Jews during the reign of German national socialism. At the same time European eugenics had a strong impact on medical sciences in the United States, which engaged in experiments involving African Americans as well as mentally and physically challenged persons.

The construction of race has involved high degrees of systemic and systematic violence. Throughout the twentieth century, wars have involved crimes against humanity such as racial **genocide** and so-called **ethnic cleansing**. Moreover, the construction of race has been closely conjoined with constructions of class, gender, and sexuality. More specifically, theories of race and racist ideologies have informed notions of racialized sexualities, which project the sexual preferences and practices of racial or ethnic "others" as deviant and prone to violence. Nineteenth-century U.S. culture thus brought forth a hierarchy of ethnicities with African Americans positioned at the bottom, below the Irish. Capitalizing on constructions of racialized femininity, antebellum American culture projected the image of a black female nymphomaniac, which was used to legitimate the institutionalized rape of African American women during slavery. Resting on the theory of racial retrogression, which assumed blacks to relapse further into primitivism after the controlling force of slavery was abolished, Southern postbellum culture tended to scapegoat African Americans for all political and economic tensions of the time. Racist fictions, such as the novels of Thomas Dixon, not only projected African Americans as corrupt and uncivilized; the criminal nature of the black male supposedly culminated in an irrepressible lust for white women. Like Irish men and males of the lower classes, African Americans were projected to be prone to sexual violence. Such claims in turn legitimized the use of violence against all blacks as a disciplinary practice for racial control.

The so-called myth of the black rapist—the image of the oversexed and bestial African American man—is by no means a postbellum phenomenon, however. In the 1840s, proponents of slavery insisted, for instance, that the descendants of Ham had overdeveloped sexual organs and were the original Sodomites of the Old Testament, thereby also acknowledging the homophobic and homoerotic dynamic that inform projections of racialized sexuality. However, the image of the black rapist rose to nationwide prominence only after emancipation. It marked a significant change in the American rhetoric on body and sexuality and a moment in American cultural history that generated notions of difference still current today. While the—mostly merely alleged—rape of white women by black men was read as the rape of the South after Reconstruction, as an attack on white civilization and moral purity, the sexual violation of black women has rarely registered in American culture. Black womanhood epitomized European perceptions of Africans as primitive, animallike, savage, and seemingly immune to such violation. As black women's injuries appeared negligible, their rape remained without retribution. Black femaleness has therefore been engendered as a condition of unredressed injury.

The discourse on rape, whether employed in the **media,** in historiography, or in fiction, has been overdetermined by distinct and nationally specific histories of racial and ethnic conflict, by a discourse on race and ethnicity that itself has tended to overdetermine issues of class. This underlines that representations of race, class, gender, sexuality, and sexual violence constitute dense transfer points for relations of power. Narratives of sexual violence therefore do not ponder an alien and uncontrollable part of human nature but the power dynamics of a particular culture.

While race has for a long time been employed primarily as a concept that separates the "other" from the norm or self and thus politically and socially marginalizes ethnic groups, in the final decades of the twentieth century, race has been reclaimed by these groups as a parameter of an appreciated difference and employed for a distinct identity practice and politics. In the United States such race pride had already gained visibility during the Harlem Renaissance, the rise of African American cultural expression during the late nineteenth century up to the 1930s, and was expressed both more emphatically and more aggressively by the Black Aesthetic and Black Power Movements in the 1960s and 1970s. Since African American culture has historically associated matters of race, ethnicity, and nation, the link between race, racialism, and nationalism becomes particularly evident in this context. Black nationalism and other expressions of racial solidarity need to be understood as a reaction and counterforce to systematic racial discrimination, which involved legal segregation as well as extreme forms of physical violence such as lynch justice and continued racial discrimination. To this day racist ideologies and politics remain a means to establish and perpetuate power relations. *See also*: **Interracial Rape; Nazis; Rape-Lynch Scenario.**

Suggested Reading: Angela Davis, *Women, Race and Class* (New York: Random House, 1983); Paula Giddings, *When and Where I Enter: The Impact of Black Women on Race and Sex in America* (New York: Morrow, 1984); Evelyn Brooks Higginbotham, "African-American Women's History and the Metalanguage of Race," in *Revising the Word and the World,* ed. VéVé A. Clark, Ruth-Ellen B. Joeres, and Madelon Sprengnether (Chicago: University of Chicago Press, 1993), 91–114; Walter Benn Michaels, "Race into Culture: A Critical Genealogy of Cultural Identity," *Critical Inquiry* 18.4 (June 1992): 655–685; Robyn

Wiegman, *American Anatomies: Theorizing Race and Gender* (Durham, NC: Duke University Press, 1995).

SABINE SIELKE

RAPE, CAUSES OF. Because rape has many meanings and social contexts, its precipitating factors depend on the social and cultural context in which it occurs, and any theory advanced to explain rape may explain only particular forms of it. Also, many theories explain acts of violence more generally, with rape being only one of many ways in which men (usually) attack other men, women, and children. Further, which types of rape get theorized depends upon which forms of it are understood to exist and be social problems. Rape in marriage, for instance, was legal for many decades in the United States, as sex was considered a husband's entitlement and a wife's duty. Similarly, the rape of black women by white male "owners" was institutionalized under **slavery**. In such cases, rape is best explained as enabled and motivated by a legalized sexual entitlement to specific women by specific men. In other cases, after slavery, for example, white men used rape as much to signal their **resistance** to the freedom sought by black men as for sexual exploitation.

Rape takes place most often when there is social hierarchy—among men in prison, by men in marriage, by soldiers at war, by those who have enslaved another group, by adults who control children, and by those preying upon people with physical or mental disabilities. Rape is often an expression of possession, sexual entitlement, dominance, and intimidation. Hence some causal accounts suggest that it is the desire for this dominance that precipitates rape. However, this cannot explain rape committed by someone who does not necessarily think of the action as intimidation, dominance, or rape.

It is the **victims** who describe rape as *not sexual* and as rendering them powerless or subordinate to the perpetrator. Conflating the perspective of perpetrator and victim has led some to assert that rape is caused by a desire to find unwilling people to force into sex. This view presumes that rapists realize they are raping, which they often do not. It also presumes that the goal is not sexual, though others have emphasized the cultural conflation of sexual arousal and aggression.

The conflation of sexual pleasure and women's subordination to men is perpetuated in much mainstream **pornography**, leading some feminists to suggest that images celebrating and sexualizing violence against women cause rape by encouraging a dangerous misunderstanding of real women's desires. This causal account is captured in Robin Morgan's second-wave political slogan, "Pornography is the theory for which rape is the practice" (Lederer, 140). This view cannot explain rape committed before pornography was prevalent, neither does it explain male-on-**male rape**. That rape occurs from male to male and not necessarily by gay-identified perpetrators confirms, for some, that rape is about violating another rather than gaining sexual pleasure and, for others, suggests that the cause of rape is the socialization to a masculinity that stresses aggression and goal-oriented sexuality over intimacy. Such socialization leads men to interpret the behaviors of others to suit their own desires and may cause rape by blinding them to someone's disinterest or unwillingness to have sex. Some scholars suggest that some men are frustrated by their lack of access to women, with whom they feel entitled to have sexual access.

In this sense the cause of rape has to do with men's anxieties around women's shifting position in society, in which women's complicity is no longer institutionally enforced. As such, rape is caused by frustrated entitlement or by anger at a woman's unavailability or unwillingness to accept men sexually.

Some suggest rape signals a failure of communication, while others have shown how rape is a means of communication. Some, particularly in college **rape prevention** programs, suggest that miscommunication is a cause of rape and that women, in particular, must communicate more carefully, lest men take a "maybe" or silence for a "yes" to have sex. This view presumes that men are in fact trying to get **consent** and would not rape if women only communicated more clearly. However, it has been argued that men *are* communicating with women, but with a disproportionate authority to define situations and an arrogant sense of confidence about women's desires, which they carry out with intimidation and force. When rape occurs by a gang of men on a woman, it has been suggested that the cause is men's desire to bond socially and sexually with one another but at the expense of an unwilling woman, who serves as a heterosexual alibi for homophobic men. Fraternity **gang rape**, then, may communicate men's erotic attraction to one another. In organized conflict, the rape of women might signal from one male group to another, "We have won this war." Given that men are primarily those sacrificed in war, some have theorized that men rape because they have learned that their own bodies are expendable and constantly under threat of violence by other men. Men thus do not have the respect for the sovereignty of women's (or other men's) bodies because they do not have body sovereignty themselves.

Evolutionary psychologists, noting that the majority of rapes are committed by men whose victims are young women of reproductive age, suggest that rape is caused by an evolved sexual psychology adapted for an earlier human environment in which the men who sought sexual encounters with many fertile women would have had greater reproductive success, thus establishing sexually aggressive behavior as human male nature. Men who were cooperative with and respectful of women would not have been such successful breeders and therefore would not have survived to reproduce men like themselves. This view presumes that human male sexually aggressive behavior was once adaptive and has a biological component that was/is heritable.

Other causal accounts emphasize the symbolic meaning of male and female bodies, arguing that a heterosexist culture conceives of a man's body as strong and impenetrable, while deeming a woman's body naturally violable. Such a way of imagining the gendered body, often fueled by authoritative scientific accounts, can lead men to feel that they are capable of, and even prone to, rape, while leading people to act as though women's bodies are rapeable and incapable of stopping a man. Rape may be caused by various combinations of factors. For example, aggravated, **serial rape** is likely caused by a combination of factors different from those causing **marital rape**. *See also*: **Advertising; Blame the Victim Syndrome; Campus Rape; Wartime Rape.**

Suggested Reading: Tim Beneke, *Men on Rape* (New York: St. Martin's Press, 1982); Jacquelyn Dowd Hall, "The Mind That Burns in Each Body: Women, Rape, and Racial Violence," *Powers of Desire: The Politics of Sexuality* (New York: Monthly Review Press, 1983); Neal King, "Knowing Women: Straight Men and Sexual Certainty," *Gender & Society* 17.6 (December 2003): 861–877; Laura Lederer, *Take Back the Night: Women on Pornography* (New York: William Morrow, 1980); Nancy Matthews, *Confronting Rape: The Feminist*

Anti-Rape Movement and the State (New York: Routledge, 1994); Martha McCaughey, *Real Knockouts: The Physical Feminism of Women's Self-Defense* (New York: New York University Press, 1997); Stephen Montagna, "Men-Only Spaces as Effective Sites for Education and Transformation in the Battle to End Sexual Assault," in *Just Sex: Students Rewrite the Rules on Sex, Violence, and Campus Activism*, ed. Jodi Gold and Susan Villari (Lanham, MD: Rowman & Littlefield, 2000), 181–188; Peggy Reeves Sanday, *Fraternity Gang Rape: Sex, Brotherhood and Privilege on Campus* (New York: New York University Press, 1990; Michael Scarce, *Male on Male Rape: The Hidden Toll of Stigma and Shame* (New York: Perseus, 1997); Diana Scully, *Understanding Sexual Violence: A Study of Convicted Rapists* (Boston: Unwin Hyman, 1990); Randy Thornhill and Craig T. Palmer, *A Natural History of Rape: Biological Bases of Sexual Coercion* (Cambridge, MA: MIT Press, 2000).

MARTHA MCCAUGHEY

RAPE, DEFINITIONS OF. The definition of rape varies by time period, place, and gender. A common perception of rape is that it involves the nonconsensual penile penetration of the vagina—*per vim stuprum*, or "intercourse by force," as the ancient Romans termed it. Many countries define rape as such. For example, in the Czech Republic, only vaginal penetration is considered to be rape, while oral or anal penetration must be prosecuted under blackmail laws. In Namibia, vaginal penetration is also central to the definition of rape, though penetration may be only partial. It also must have been the intention of the accused to penetrate the victim's vagina, though it is difficult to understand how such an action could occur accidentally. In Fiji, only vaginal penetration by the penis is considered rape. However, if a husband forces his wife to have intercourse with him, this is not considered to be rape or a crime. This has been the case throughout much of history and is the case in many nations today. Bahamian law specifically exempts spouses from being charged with rape. By 2000, only 26 countries worldwide had laws recognizing **marital rape**, among them Australia, Austria, Barbados, Bulgaria, Canada, Denmark, Ecuador, France, Germany, Honduras, Iceland, Ireland, Mexico, Namibia, New Zealand, Norway, the Philippines, Poland, South Africa, Spain, Sweden, Trinidad/Tobago, and the United Kingdom. Marital rape became a crime in Zimbabwe in 2001. In the United States, marital rape is also illegal, though 33 states have qualifications concerning the amount of force necessary for a nonconsensual sexual act in marriage to be considered rape. Some countries like Colombia provide lighter penalties for marital rape because lack of **consent** is difficult to prove within a conjugal situation. It is also difficult to prove in the case of prostitutes. Medieval canon law declared it impossible to rape a prostitute, and many contemporary secular courts concurred.

Toward the end of the twentieth century, some countries adopted broader definitions of rape. In 1996, the Italian government ruled that proof of premeditation was no longer necessary to prove rape. In 1997, Germany passed new rape laws that recognized acts of sexual violence not involving penetration as rape. Germany also expanded the definition of force to include psychological as well as physical coercion. These laws are written in gender-neutral language, thereby acknowledging that men as well as women may be the target of sexual violence and that women as well as men may be the assailant. Many countries still define a **sexual assault** where both the victim and the assailant are men as **sodomy** and not rape. Danish law recognizes as rape acts of sexual violation it calls "equivalent" to penile penetration of the vagina. These can include anal, oral, or vaginal penetration by the penis or any other body part or foreign object. The broadest definition of rape is that employed by the International Criminal Tribunal for Rwanda (working for the United Nations) in 1998. The Tribunal considered rape to be a **war crime** and an act of **genocide** and further defined it as "a physical invasion of a sexual nature, committed on a person under circumstances which are coercive." This definition does not limit the type of sexual act, the gender of the victim, or the sets of circumstances that can be deemed coercive.

Another factor involved in defining rape is identifying the **victim** of the crime. While it is the woman who is attacked and suffers the physical and emotional trauma, according to the laws of many states, past and present, it is not the woman against whom the crime is legally committed. Among the medieval English and Ndebele of Africa, compensation was paid to the father or husband of the woman. In modern Zimbabwe and Canada, rape is a crime against the state, not an individual.

The rape laws of most countries also make distinctions based on the age of the victim. Unlike the situation of marital rape, the age of the victim has long been considered a factor in determining whether an act of sexual intercourse is defined as rape (that is, consensual or nonconsensual). Generally, if the victim is a legal minor, consent is supposed to be irrelevant. Minors are not thought to be capable of making informed decisions about whether to engage in sexual intercourse. In English rape laws, this special distinction regarding the rape of a minor has been in effect since 1576 when a separate law was established to deal with the rape of girls 10 years of age and under. Three centuries earlier, Statute of Westminster I (1275) had deemed consent a nonissue when the victim was under the age of 12. However, Statute of Westminster II (1285) only confused matters, and it was not until 1576 that any further attempt was made to deal with the rape of a minor. The age of consent varies from country to country: In Paraguay, it is 12; Canada, 14; Swaziland, 18. In Namibia, a girl cannot consent to sexual intercourse until she is 12, but a boy may by the age of 7.

Opinion has varied according to time and place as to what sort of crime rape is. Should it be considered primarily a crime of violence? Perhaps its sexual nature should be emphasized? Kim Philips's study of legal treatises, statutes, and trial records reveals that in England rape changed from being considered a crime of violence (twelfth–early thirteenth century) to a crime of sex (early thirteenth–late fourteenth century) to a property crime (late fourteenth–late fifteenth century). *See also*: **Rape History in the United States; Rape Law; Statutory Rape.**

Suggested Reading: Sophie Day, "What Counts as Rape? Physical Assault and Broken Contracts: Contrasting Views of Rape among London Sex Workers," in *Sex and Violence: Issues in Representation and Experience*, ed. Penelope Harvey and Peter Gow (New York: Routledge, 1994), 172–189; Kim M. Philips, "Written on the Body: Reading Rape from the Twelfth to Fifteenth Centuries," in *Medieval Women and the Law*, ed. Noel James Menuge (Woodbridge, Suffolk: Boydell Press, 2000), 125–144.

TONYA MARIE LAMBERT

RAPE, ABUSE & INCEST NATIONAL NETWORK (RAINN). Founded in 1994 by Scott Berkowitz with support from Atlantic Records, Warner Music Group, and singer/songwriter Tori Amos, the Rape, Abuse & Incest National Network (RAINN) maintains a national rape and sexual abuse hotline that connects callers to local **rape counseling centers**, as well as a Web site (http://www.rainn.org) that provides information about the problem of **sexual assault**. In this way, RAINN works to bring national attention to the issue of rape and sexual abuse while at the same time linking its **victims** to the resources of their communities. The National Sexual Assault Hotline, (800) 656-HOPE, automatically forwards callers to their nearest local rape counseling center. In 2003, RAINN maintained affiliations with over 1,000 counseling organizations, providing connections to all of the rape crisis centers in 24 states, with less coverage in other states. By March 2003 the National Sexual Assault Hotline had received 600,000 calls, and its call volume had increased nearly 25 percent compared to the previous year. RAINN attributed this to an expansion of its outreach efforts, including promotions appearing in the national **media**. For instance, a public service announcement following a Lifetime Network special on sexual assault led to a 75 percent increase in calls to the hotline. In 1997 Congress honored RAINN both for its work with crime victims and for its efficient operation as a not-for-profit, non-government-funded organization. RAINN relies completely on donations from individuals and corporations and has been lauded as an example of the private sector's ability to provide a valuable public service. RAINN maintains its national offices in Washington, D.C. *See also*: **Rape Education; Rape Prevention.**

SHARON A. KOWALSKY

RAPE COUNSELING. In *One Night: Realities of Rape*, a 2002 book by rape survivor Cathy Winkler contends that rape victims are raped three times. First, they are raped by the perpetrator of the crime, then they are raped by the social system that frequently blames the **victim** of the rape. Finally, Winkler believes that rape victims are raped by the legal system that fails to provide justice. In 1986, the film *The Ladies Club* depicted a group of women who were traumatized not only by the man who had raped them but also by the legal system that refused to enact justice. In retaliation, the group of women, which included a surgeon, castrated the rapist. The film illustrated the rage and frustration experienced by most rape victims. Rape victims tend to divide their lives into two periods: before and after the rape. In "Rape Poem," poet Marge Piercy compares being raped to "being pushed down a flight of cement steps . . . being run over by a truck . . . being bitten on the ankle by a rattlesnake . . . and going headfirst through a windshield."

The support system that surrounds the rape victim is significant in the recovery process. Victims who are able to talk about the rape experience and their feelings heal more quickly than those who remain silent. Some victims find it easier to talk to an objective listener, such as a rape crisis counselor, than to talk with **family** and friends. The traumas that accompany the crime of rape may also call for professional counseling. This professional may be a psychiatrist, a psychologist, or a psychiatric social worker. Various studies have shown that rape victims who seek counseling suffer less long-lasting trauma than those who do not.

The aftermath of rape may stay with a rape victim for the rest of her/his life, but counseling may reduce the severity of the trauma. **Survivors** of rape experience what has been identified as **rape trauma syndrome** (RTS), a form of **posttraumatic stress disorder (PTSD).** Rape survivors usually go through four stages of trauma on their way to recovery: shock and disbelief; confusion, fear, depression, and anger; resolution and coping; and adjustment. They may also experience feelings of helplessness, guilt, degradation, dependency, vulnerability, hysteria, and embarrassment. Studies have revealed that up to 94 percent of rape survivors exhibit signs of RTS within one week of the rape, and up to 50 percent continue to display trauma symptoms over the next 12 months. Those who are close to the rape victim may also experience the effects of trauma, particularly a sexual partner or a parent. Studies have revealed that 60 to 80 percent of intimate sexual relationships do not survive after a partner is raped. Parents often feel they have failed as parents because they could not protect their child.

Rape victims may also experience a number of physical symptoms associated with rape trauma. These may include disturbances in sleep patterns, nightmares, changes in appetite, feelings of numbness, nausea, vomiting, gastric disturbances, and physical pain or discomfort. Evidence suggests that rape victims, particularly those who are victims of sustained abuse, may be more likely to develop serious disease, such as diabetes, gynecological conditions, and Parkinson's disease. In extreme cases, the rape victim may lose the ability to function normally. For example, a rape victim may choose to stay in bed rather than face the emotional and/or physical problems that seem insurmountable. Some rape victims find it impossible to deal with the trauma, and evidence shows that between 17 and 20 percent of rape victims attempt suicide. **Alcohol**, drug abuse, and clinical depression are frequent consequences of rape. Rape counselors may work with medical doctors or other professionals to provide comprehensive care for survivors of rape.

All rape victims do not handle trauma in the same way. A child who knows and loves her/his attacker may experience the aftermath of rape differently from a child who is raped by a stranger. A victim of sustained sexual abuse may experience deeper trauma than the victim of a single attack. An adolescent rape victim may have trouble engaging in normal dating activity. A woman who is raped by an intimate sexual partner or a date may experience a deep-rooted distrust in other relationships. A woman who is raped by a stranger may feel guilt and wonder whether she encouraged it by her attire or by being in a particular location. A black woman may experience rape trauma differently than a white woman or a victim of an Eastern culture. An elderly rape victim or a mentally challenged individual may be unable to fully comprehend rape trauma. A heterosexual male may begin to doubt his own sexual orientation. A homosexual male may decide not to report a rape because of a perceived bias against gay men in general. A prisoner who is raped may not be in a position to stay away from his/her attackers and may not have access to needed support and counseling. Because rape is experienced in unique ways and because recovery involves a number of distinct variables, a professionally trained rape counselor may be needed to meet individual counseling needs.

When a rape victim seeks the help of a professional counselor, the counselor may use the American Psychiatric Association's *Diagnostic and Statistical Manual* to identify the presence and extent of posttraumatic stress disorder. The counselor will question the rape victim about the rape to determine the level of threat involved and specific features of the attack. Counselors will question the rape victim about memories and dreams of the rape and the presence of particular stimuli that are connected to the experience. The counselor will be interested in how the rape victim deals with daily activities and with interrelationships. The rape survivor may experience all or some of the following symptoms: feelings of detachment and constriction, a lack of interest in her/his surroundings, sleep disturbance, irritability, difficulty concentrating, hypervigilance, exaggerated startle response, increased perspiration or heart rate, change in appetite, increased nervousness, body image disturbance, sexual problems, self-blame, low self-esteem, and fear of being alone. All of these symptoms are normal reactions to severe trauma and should respond to professional counseling. *See also*: **Rape Crisis Centers**.

Suggested Reading: Ann Wolbert Burgess and Lynda Lytle Holmstrom, "Rape Trauma Syndrome," *American Journal of Psychiatry* 131 (1974): 981–986; Robert Hazelwood and Ann Wolbert Burgess, *Practical Aspects of Rape Investigation: A Multidisciplinary Approach* (Boca Raton, FL: CRC Press, 2001); Linda Ledray, *Recovering from Rape* (New York: Henry Holt, 1994); Marge Piercy, "Rape Poem," in *Circles on the Water* (New York: Alfred A. Knopf, 1982), 164–165; Cathy Winkler, *One Night: Realities of Rape* (Walnut Creed, CA: Altamira, 2002).

ELIZABETH R. PURDY

RAPE CRISIS CENTERS. As a result of the women's movement of the 1960s and 1970s, women began to develop a clearer understanding of rape and its aftermath. In 1971, New York Feminists held a Rape Speak Out to inform women about the prevalence of rape in the United States and to motivate feminists to form rape crisis groups. The first rape crisis center was established in Washington, DC in 1972 and was followed by centers in Los Angeles, California, and Seattle, Washington. It was a point of pride in most early centers not to accept funding from what was considered the patriarchal power structure. In 1974, Pittsburgh Action against Rape became the first rape crisis center to receive federal funding, and by the 1990s rape crisis centers had become mainstream, with the majority of centers accepting public funding, frequently from United Way or from **law enforcement** agencies. In 1994, the **Violence against Women Act** of 1994 funded grants for rape crisis centers through the Department of Justice. Early rape crisis centers tended to be run by untrained volunteers. With the shift to government funding, rape crisis centers moved toward formal organizational structures, the use of professionals as counselors, and extensive training of volunteers. Rape crisis centers were formed on college campuses, where students were particularly vulnerable to **date rape** or acquaintance rape because of the prevalence of **alcohol**, drugs, and a party atmosphere. By 2001, over 1,200 rape crisis centers had been established around the country, an average of 24 per state.

Typical functions of rape crisis centers include providing 24/7 hotlines; individual or group counseling; escort service to police stations, hospitals, and courts; advice on testing for **pregnancy, HIV/AIDS**, and sexually transmitted diseases; and educating the public about rape, **rape prevention**, and **rape counseling**. Antirape **education** also includes teaching police officers, who are often the first on the scene of a rape, not to blame the victim by asking insensitive questions. Many law enforcement agencies have formed their own task forces to educate personnel on the unique problems of rape investigations, and hospitals sometimes provide nurses trained in rape crisis. Former Representative Constance Morella (R–MD) addressed the frequent complaint that rape victims do not always receive adequate emergency care by sponsoring the Compassionate Care for Female Sexual Assault Survivors Act to mandate access to contraception in emergency rooms. The bill remained in committee in 2003 but was expected to be reintroduced in 2004.

In 1974 the concept of **rape trauma syndrome** (RTS), a form of **posttraumatic stress disorder**, was promulgated. Understanding what a victim is experiencing helps counselors to devise the proper treatment. One study revealed that 94 percent of rape victims experience RTS within a week of the attack, and 50 percent continued to suffer from RTS up to a year after the attack. Normally, one would expect a rape victim to call a rape crisis center immediately; but, in practice, centers have received calls as long as 20 years after the rape occurred. The **Rape, Abuse & Incest National Network (RAINN)** offers a 24/7 hotline at 800-656-HOPE or instant Web access at http://www.rainn.org/ to link women to state rape crisis centers in their areas.

The aftermath of rape is extensive and has a tendency to spiral out toward everyone it touches. In addition to the **victim** and her family and friends, the trauma affects rape crisis counselors, police officers, victims' advocates, and lawyers. Not only do those who work with rape victims share the emotional burden, but they become highly frustrated over the low rate of prosecutions and the knowledge that 98 percent of accused rapists never serve time in prison. Modern definitions of rape include rape of children and men as well as rape of adult women and encompass various sexual acts in addition to the traditional definition of penetration of the vagina by the penis. Even though the expanded definition indicates increased awareness of rape, it is somewhat frustrating because rape crisis workers realize that the overall goal of eradicating rape has never been, and may never be, met. *See also*: **Rape Kit.**

Suggested Reading: Ann Wolbert Burgess and Lynda Lytle Holmstrom, "Rape Trauma Syndrome," *American Journal of Psychiatry* 131 (1974): 981–986; Linda Ledray, *Recovering from Rape* (New York: Henry Holt, 1994); Mary E. Odem and Judy Clay-Warner, eds., *Confronting Rape and Sexual Assault* (Wilmington, DE: Scholarly Resources, 1998); "National Sexual Assault Hotline," Rape, Abuse & Incest National Network (RAINN), http://www.rainn.org/; Claire M. Renzetti et al., eds., *Sourcebook on Violence against Women* (Thousand Oaks, CA: Sage, 2001).

ELIZABETH R. PURDY

RAPE CULTURE. A rape culture is one in which rape and other sexual violence against women and children are both prevalent and considered the norm. In a rape culture, rape and sexual violence are accepted as inevitable and are not challenged. The term *rape culture* originated in the 1970s during the second-wave **feminist movement** and is often used to describe contemporary American culture as a whole.

A rape culture, according to the editors of *Transforming a Rape Culture*, "is a complex set of beliefs that encourages male sexual aggression and supports violence against women." A rape culture believes that sexual aggression in men is biologically determined, rather than learned behavior. In turn, it considers women to be sexually passive and meant to be dominated by men. Consequentially, a normal sexual encounter is represented as a heterosexual man forcing himself upon a woman. Thus in a rape culture, rape is the model for most sexual activity.

A rape culture supports rape and violence by tolerating such abuse. In regard to criminal justice, the number of sexual assaults is high, while the rate of arrests, prosecutions, and convictions of assailants is low. Excuses are often found to explain why men commit rape, or why the violence against the **victim** is justified. Many times the rapist's actions are implied to be out of his control: He simply could not help himself. This viewpoint positions rape as an expression of sexual desire, rather than the enactment of power, control, and anger. Women are socialized into believing that men are naturally sexual aggressors and that it is a woman's responsibility to take precautions against being attacked. A rape culture blames the assault on the actions of the victim (such as her walking alone, drinking **alcohol**, or being in a date's apartment), rather than questioning the behavior of the rapist.

A rape culture reinforces its beliefs by promoting **rape myths**, false or biased information about rape, rape victims, and rapists. Rape myths work to deny that instances of forced or coerced sex are actually rape. Rape myths make excuses for the rapist or minimize the effects of the rape on the victim. As a whole, rape myths elide the phenomenon of rape, refusing to acknowledge that any problem exists. Examples of rape myths include the following: Women secretly want to be raped; it is rape only if a weapon is used; and women are aroused by sexual violence. In a rape culture, rape myths are learned and perpetuated by the general culture, but especially the **media**: in advertisements, television shows, **films**, and music videos.

Images of sex and violence are intertwined in a rape culture. The media often portrays normal sex as sadomasochistic, "a dirty, low, and violent act involving the domination of a male over a female" (Herman, 39). Rape, when portrayed as such, is often eroticized and depicted as "rough, unwanted sex, that is nevertheless sexy" (Pearson, 12). At times the rape victim is even portrayed as being aroused by the assault, having subconsciously wanted to have sex with her attacker. This portrayal of rape in the media trains men to become aroused by violent sex. In a rape culture, rarely is sex portrayed as shared, loving intimacy; instead, violent imagery abounds that fosters the mentality that there is little difference between regular sex and rape.

Feminist critics believe that rape culture will flourish as long as women do not realize the same legal, economic, and social privileges as men. In turn, the rape culture will continue to legitimatize rape and sexual violence as normal expressions of male sexuality, and more women and children will be victimized as a result. In order to eliminate rape, many see that the mechanisms of the rape culture first need to be confronted. *See also*: **Advertising**; **"Blaming the Victim" Syndrome**.

Suggested Reading: Emilie Buchwald, Pamela Fletcher, and Martha Roth, *Transforming a Rape Culture* (Minneapolis: Milkweed Editions, 1993); Dianne F. Herman, "The Rape Culture," in *Women: A Feminist Perspective*, ed. Jo Freeman (Mountain View, CA: Mayfield, 1989), 20–44; Alyn Pearson, "Rape Culture: It's All Around Us," *off our backs* 30.8 (August 2000): 12.

ROBIN E. FIELD

RAPE EDUCATION. Rape education, an integral part of **rape prevention**, seeks to educate women, men, and children about rape. Educational programs can vary in purpose, presentation topics, duration, and target audience. They may be offered at a community center, a **rape crisis center**, a religious institution, at summer camp, in a classroom, or in the workplace. Some educational programs are tailored according to age, sex, race/ethnicity, physical ability, and personal need. Some use an exclusive curriculum and audience in order to address group-specific needs, while others will more broadly address rape for a general audience.

A rape education curriculum may include a discussion of the facts and myths of rape, the legal definition and aspects of **prosecution**, a distinction between rape and sex, ways to effectively communicate about sex, rape avoidance and **self-defense** options, what to do if you or someone you know is raped, and resources for learning more and getting help. One successful program, "Safe, Sane, and Sexy," was developed by the Rape Education and Prevention Program at Ohio State University in 1983. Part of a series of workshops for incoming first-year students, it teaches women and men how to communicate about sex, how to understand the difference between rape and consensual sex, the relationship of **alcohol** and drugs to consensual sex, birth control and infection prevention options, and how to recognize warning signs of an unsafe situation.

One of the challenges for effective rape education is the inclusion of resources and information that represents and reaches a diverse population while also adequately addressing specific cultural concerns. For instance, programs may be for women only, Asian women, male survivors, or visually impaired individuals. A women-only rape education program can address gender-specific concerns related to violence against women and women's self-defense. This may meet the needs of many women, yet it inadequately addresses important and specific issues such as experienced by an immigrant woman dependent on her abuser, or the conflict an **African American** woman may experience reporting her rape by a black man due to racism and societal alienation of black men. In other words, personal experiences and educational needs vary according to individual and cultural factors. Thus, experts recommend that programs include both broad-based comprehensive programs and narrow-focused group or need-specific programs.

Rape education programs are often included in rape prevention programs and therefore may offer services other than educational presentations. They may provide counseling and support group services, victim advocacy, crisis intervention, distribution of printed educational materials, and community or college activism. For example, "**Take Back the Night**," an annual antiviolence against women march and speak-out that started in the 1970s, combines rape education and prevention efforts. Participants learn about rape through guest speakers, printed material, skits, poetry readings, personal stories, and self-defense and martial arts demonstrations, while also taking part in raising community awareness and actively reclaiming the right to be free of violence. This is part of a broader prevention agenda whereby community members are informed about antiviolence resources and services, volunteer opportunities, and antirape and social justice organizations.

While women have been at the forefront of rape education and prevention efforts, it is important to note that men are increasingly active in this movement. Since the 1990s, men have worked in alliance with women to form groups to educate themselves and other men in an effort to stop rape. One such program, Men Can Stop Rape, is a nationally recognized group of men and women based in Washington, D.C. Their mission is to teach men and boys to be actively involved in ending men's violence through awareness, activism, and education.

The benefits of rape education are numerous. They facilitate shared experiences, build solidarity, dispel myths, bring awareness to various groups, share resources, decrease victim blame, teach self-defense and assertiveness skills, raise awareness about consensual and safer sex, and promote violence prevention.

Suggested Reading: Kimberly Lonsway and Chevon Kothari, "Acquaintance Rape Education: Evaluating the Impact of a Mandatory Intervention," *Psychology of Women Quarterly* 24.3 (September 2000): 220–232; "A Rape Prevention Program in an Urban Area: Community Action Strategies to Stop Rape," *Signs* 5.3 (1980): 238–241; Jonathan C. Stillerman, "Preventing Rape: .A Male and Female Approach," 1999, *World College Health*, http://

www.worldcollegehealth.org/020399b.htm; Robin Warshaw, *I Never Called It Rape* (New York: Harper & Row, 1988).

HEATHER SCHMIDT

RAPE HISTORY IN THE UNITED STATES: SEVENTEENTH CENTURY. The physical act of rape has a long history across time and space. How the act of rape will be interpreted by society and punished by the courts is constructed by the social and cultural context in which it occurs. The east coast of North America in the seventeenth century presented some particularly distinguishing features. These settlements, huddled along the Atlantic Ocean, formed the nucleus of the future United States. In the seventeenth century, however, they were still a series of separate colonies with legal institutions shaped by both their relationship to England and their own particular environments. In addition to the indigenous inhabitants, the population consisted of new arrivals of both European and African descent, some who were free and some who were slaves or indentured servants. Together these factors make discussion of rape in seventeenth-century America a complicated one.

In the oldest southern colonies, Virginia and Maryland, English law was adopted with regard to rape. The crime of rape was a capital offense and first had to be heard by a grand jury. If the grand jury brought in a true bill, the case was tried by a petit jury in the Virginia General Court. This court had jurisdiction over criminal offenses affecting the life or well-being of individuals, and the juries were required to come in with unanimous verdicts. Rape was rarely brought to the attention of courts; in fact, the extant General Court records reveal no such cases prior to 1670, and only one has been found at the county level. These statistical findings do not mean that rape was nonexistent in the southern colonies; rather, it can be assumed that those few women who did make charges were women who defied legal, social, and cultural barriers and wide-ranging fears for their survival. Legally, women did not serve as judges or jurors, though they could be called to testify. It was other more visceral and personal matters that caused women to fear charging men with rape or to win unanimous verdicts from male juries if they did. There is evidence that southern magistrates simply did not believe women's accusations, unless they were against black men. The powerful landowning men of the southern colonies were often related by marriage and not inclined to turn against each other in questionable behavior related to women or slaves. In addition, numerous factors abridged women's abilities to charge and testify against men in court. Isolation on far-flung landholdings, fear of physical force, the fact that indentured servants could be sold or have their terms extended as punishment, and the fact that wives could not legally be raped all contributed to women's fears to legally challenge men's violent sexual behavior. Taken together, such factors and fears provided a chilly climate for women who wanted to charge men with rape or attempted rape.

For slaves, the matter of rape was one fraught with both sexual and economic politics. Female slaves did not legally own their bodies; their masters did. As a result, the **sexual assault** of slave women by their masters, male members of his **family,** and by extension, friends and white men in general, was simply not regarded as a crime. The South stereotyped black men as oversexed, brutal, and especially dangerous to white women. Statutory laws in the southern colonies reflect that anxiety. The rape of a white woman by a slave was a capital crime, and slaves convicted of attempted rape could be castrated. The facts reveal a different reality, however. Because slave men were expensive and highly necessary property, white judges and juries made exceptions for both crimes. This was especially true if any shadow could be cast on the behavior or reputation of the woman. This was more likely the case if the woman was poor and perceived as not acting according to the rules of conduct for a Southern "lady." In the instance of sexual assault, then, sex and class could and did trump race when it came to meting out punishments for rape in the early slave South.

In colonies to the north, the attitudes toward rape were not shaped by the culture and economics of slavery but by the religious attitudes of Puritanism. Puritan culture predisposed men to believe that women existed to serve men's needs and had no right to reject demands of any kind made by men. Puritan men might be powerless before God and nature, but they could dominate women and demand their submissiveness. Together these attitudes encouraged some men who were frustrated by their life circumstances, including being unmarried, to force themselves on women.

Proof of such observations rests in statistics that show 91 percent of the men accused of rape or attempted rape were single and used physical strength to commit their crimes, not weapons of violence. In other words, men forced women to submit to them, as they had been taught they should. Attackers often stopped the assault when women proved particularly assertive in their **resistance**. This undoubtedly reinforced the stereotype that women who did not sufficiently resist an attack really wanted to be raped. Servants constituted one-third of **victims** in New England but only 10 percent of the female population. Because at least the risk of severe punishment was present if a man was convicted of a sexual assault, the perpetrator was more likely to choose a young domestic servant working in his home and dependent on him for her livelihood, perhaps even money she earned for her family. Taken together, this offers an explanation for men's propensity to choose the most vulnerable and easily available targets.

Rape was a capital offense in the colonies. Continuing a tradition from the Middle Ages, though, the punishment could differ depending on the age and marital status of the woman. The rape of married and espoused women, and girls under 10, was considered all the more dreadful because it injured the marital bonds, called the legitimacy of children into question, and compromised men's legal relationship to wives and minor daughters established through coverture. Cotton Mather, a leading Puritan clergyman for three-plus decades in the seventeenth century, prescribed fines, whipping, or marriage (if the victim consented) in the instance of single women being raped. The fines were partially allocated to the father. Girls under 10 were protected because, as in a **statutory rape** today, it was believed that they could not properly **consent** to intercourse. Moreover, because the **Bible** saw intercourse as an act of procreation, not possible with a 10-year-old girl, it was seen as an even more heinous crime, similar to **sodomy** and **bestiality**.

Just as it is today, accusing a man of rape was a difficult proposition. New England Puritans believed the testimony of female accusers because they thought such women would be so terrorized by the attack that they surely would resist, and if overpowered, they would not be able to lie about the incident. However, women who accused men of rape also found themselves challenged about whether they resisted enough or cried out when the attack occurred. A few women, in fact, were punished for complicity because the authorities did not believe they had resisted enough. Puritans also believed that a woman had to have an orgasm in order to conceive, so if she accused someone of rape and then turned out to be pregnant, they assumed she must have given her consent to the act and lied about the accused. If it was determined at a later date that the woman had lied about the incident, she could be charged with either adultery or fornication. Given the difficulties of being believed, the threat of losing your reputation, or even the possibility of being convicted of a crime, it is not surprising that, as in the southern colonies, few rapes were actually reported.

Of the men accused of rape in seventeenth-century New England, six were hanged and one was branded, but the great majority were whipped or fined. About one-third were acquitted or the disposition was unknown. In half the cases, words other than rape were used to describe the incident, indicating that some rape was seen to be more odious than other rapes, and perhaps making sure that the perpetrator could avoid the death penalty. Discrimination took form in New England in attitudes toward **Native American men**, as it did in the South toward **African American** men. An Indian man who raped a nine-year-old Indian girl was sold into servitude, but a white man who raped an Indian woman only received a fine. *See also*: **Indentured Servitude; Rape Law; Slavery.**

Suggested Reading: Richard Godbeer, *Sexual Revolution in Early America* (Baltimore: Johns Hopkins University Press, 2002); Lyle Koehler, *A Search for Power: The Weaker Sex in Seventeenth-Century New England* (Urbana: University of Illinois Press, 1980); Mary Beth Norton, *Founding Mothers & Fathers: Gendered Power and the Forming of American Society* (New York: Alfred A. Knopf, 1996); Merril D. Smith, ed., *Sex without Consent: Rape and Sexual Coercion in America* (New York: New York University Press, 2001); Diane Miller Somerville, "Rape, Race, and Castration in Slave Law in the Colonial and Early South," in *The Devil's Lane: Sex and Race in the Early South*, ed. Catherine Clinton and Michele Gillespie (New York: Oxford University Press, 1997).

DONNA COOPER GRAVES

RAPE HISTORY IN THE UNITED STATES: EIGHTEENTH CENTURY. Eighteenth-century Americans understood rape as penis-vagina sexual intercourse committed with physical force and against a woman's will. They had no concept of sexual battery nor of any prosecutable **sexual assault** that did not include an attempt at sexual intercourse. Only women were understood to be **victims** of rape. (Male-male **sodomy** was a crime whether forced or consensual.) Sexual intercourse with girls under 10 years old was considered rape regardless of their degree of **consent. Marital rape** was an impossibility—women gave their perpetual consent to their husband's sexual overtures by saying, "I do" at marriage. For most of the eighteenth century, rape was a capital crime, punishable by death. (After the American Revolution, some states began to eliminate the death penalty, but a rape conviction could still lead to decades of incarceration.)

However, early American courts applied such severe penalties neither equally nor frequently: Courts were especially hesitant to execute upstanding white men for rape. Indeed, all rape prosecutions were implicitly structured along racial lines. Cases involving raped white women were much more likely to be prosecuted than those involving women of color. Conversely, nonwhite (especially **African American**) defendants were far more common targets of rape prosecutions than were white men. These distorted prosecutions contributed to the myth—still powerful today—that black men were likely to rape white women.

All women in eighteenth-century America might fall victim to a sexual assault, but some women had far more protection against sexual attackers than did others. Enslaved and African American women had the least legal and social protection from rape. Legally, a white man could be prosecuted for raping an enslaved African American woman. However, many colonies passed laws that prevented slaves from testifying against whites in court. Since a victim's testimony was usually crucial to a successful **prosecution**, few slaves could win a rape prosecution against any white man. Even free African American women could rarely bring a rape prosecution against white men, because early Americans believed that black women were naturally promiscuous and thus unlikely to resist a rape. Accordingly, there is no known conviction of a white man for raping a slave or free African American woman in the eighteenth century, even though we know that many white men forced slaves to have sexual relations with them. The eighteenth-century judicial system purposefully ignored the many rapes of nonwhite women: more than 95 percent of the victims of prosecuted rapes were white.

Although white women had more legal protection after a rape, reporting and prosecuting a sexual assault was never easy. A victim had to convince her husband or father to take her to court to complain about the attack, then had to tell a magistrate what had happened, and then had to repeat her story to courtroom lawyers, jury members, and judges. Many legal officials believed that women often lied about rape, so would try to disprove women's stories whenever possible. Because respectable women were supposed to resist sexual relations, legal officials believed that women would charge men with rape to preserve their reputation when they regretted having illicit, though consensual, sexual relations. However, there is little evidence of such false rape charges in early American court records. Conversely, there is much evidence that legal officials carefully cross-examined rape victims, trying to prove that they had not truly resisted a sexual attack. Victims could prove their **resistance** by showing that they had physical injuries, that they had cried for help, that they immediately filed charges, and that they were sexually chaste. These standards ignored the ways that sexual assaults often occurred and the many layers of mediation by **family** and friends that usually preceded a legal complaint. In many ways, eighteenth-century rape victims were considered guilty of consenting to the sexual interaction unless they could prove their innocence. Such unrealistic expectations and unfair treatment meant that many victims chose to avoid legal involvement after a sexual attack.

Courts were most likely to believe a white woman's claim of rape against a black man. All colonies convicted black men of rape more often than white men. Black men were often tried at separate courts without many legal protections. Most notably, they could be convicted by a majority decision, rather than the unanimous jury decision required for whites. Many colonies also passed special laws mandating exceptionally harsh punishments for slaves who raped or tried to rape white women. Southern colonies that abolished the death penalty for white rapists continued sentencing black rapists to death well into the nineteenth century. Overall, about three-quarters of the men executed for rape in the eighteenth-century were of African descent. Black men could also be executed for attempted rape, while white men would usually be punished with a fine, whipping, or imprisonment. At every stage of prosecution, black defendants were treated much more harshly than white defendants.

While colonial Americans originally feared that **Native American** men would rape

Anglo-American women during wartime, by the eighteenth century, they believed that Native American men were unlikely to rape white female captives. Many Native Americans believed that sexual relations would weaken a warrior's powers, so would refrain from all intercourse (including rape) during war. Some Native American leaders repeatedly complained, however, that Anglo-American traders and travelers had sexually assaulted Native American women, but few of these cases were prosecuted in American courts.

In many ways, eighteenth-century colonists used rape as a tool of colonialism. By harshly punishing nonwhite men for rape of white women, early Americans enacted a sexual system that supported their increasingly racially divided society. Sexual access to white women would be reserved as a privilege of white men, and protection from sexual attacks would be reserved to white women. Together, this treatment of rape turned a sexual attack on a woman into a means to institutionalize the racial power inequities and racial discrimination that have continued for centuries. *See also*: **Interracial Rape; Slavery.**

Suggested Reading: Sharon Block, "Lines of Color, Sex, and Service: Comparative Sexual Coercion in Early America," in *Sex, Love, Race: Crossing Boundaries in North American History*, ed. Martha Hodes (New York: New York University Press, 1999), 141–163; Cornelia Hughes Dayton, *Women before the Bar: Gender, Law, and Society in Connecticut, 1699–1789* (Chapel Hill: University of North Carolina Press, 1995), 231–284; Alice Nash, " 'None of the Women Were Abused': Indigenous Contexts for the Treatment of Women Captives in the Northeast," in *Sex without Consent: Rape and Sexual Coercion in America*, ed. Merril D. Smith (New York: New York University Press, 2001), 10–26.

SHARON BLOCK

RAPE HISTORY IN THE UNITED STATES: NINETEENTH CENTURY. Rape was seen as a crime throughout the nineteenth century. The statutes of virtually every state and territory that made up the United States in the nineteenth century defined the crime of rape generally as the unlawful carnal knowledge of a woman by a man forcibly and against her will. From a reading of the statutes, it would seem that one could easily discern when a man had raped a woman and that all a prosecuting attorney had to prove to earn a conviction was that the defendant had forced his accuser to have sexual relations with him. Such was not the case, however, because American law in general and rape law in particular are far more complicated when put into practice.

Men were highly suspicious of women who brought a rape charge. Nineteenth-century legal and medical writers frequently invoked the admonition of Lord **Matthew Hale**, Chief Justice of the King's Bench in England from 1671 to 1676, who warned that while rape was a serious offense worthy of severe punishment, it was also a charge that women tended to bring out of spite or embarrassment. Some legal authorities insisted that women accused men of rape to blackmail them into marriage or get money or exact revenge. They also worried that a woman might claim she had been raped when she had merely been seduced. These were points of concern because many legal officials believed that if jurors—and only men served on juries in the nineteenth century—allowed their emotions to govern their intellects, they would convict innocent men of rape. For this reason, judges created exceptional rules of law intended to protect defendants in rape cases, and they modified or altered generally accepted legal doctrines to make it difficult for a woman to prove that she had been raped. Authorities who insisted that defendants in rape trials needed specially crafted rules to protect them from false accusations offered no proof that women who brought rape complaints did so out of spite or for purposes of blackmail.

Rape convictions were difficult, though not impossible, to achieve in the nineteenth century. Two key elements of the crime of rape were force and **resistance**. For an act of sexual intercourse to constitute a rape, most courts required proof that the defendant had used actual force to accomplish his end, and all courts mandated proof of penile penetration. Merely threatening a woman with a knife or a gun did not suffice as the kind of force the law demanded for a rape conviction. Rather, to be actual force, the man had to stab or shoot or in some way physically maim the woman. Fraud was not an element of rape, unless the statute expressly stated that it was. A woman could not claim rape if she had been tricked into giving her consent. To constitute resistance, a woman had to fend off her attacker successfully, unless she could show that an extenuating circumstance had prevented her from so doing. To judges and jurors, consummation indicated **consent**, or at least strongly suggested it. Judges devised the "half consent" and the "ultimate consent" doctrines for cases where women claimed they had resisted to the utmost of their abilities, yet the man still managed to consummate the act. Under the half consent doctrine, defendants argued that if the woman's resistance was equivocal, it amounted to a partial consent, which was as good as a whole consent. Defendants used the ultimate consent rule to assert that even though their accusers initially resisted their efforts at **seduction**, they eventually gave in and ultimately consented to the intercourse.

Some women found it more difficult to achieve rape convictions in nineteenth-century courts than others. Social factors such as the race, ethnicity, socioeconomic status, or religion of the accused and his accuser influenced rape case outcomes. Slave women occupied a very precarious position because slave codes made them the chattel property of their masters, who were immune from rape prosecution if they forced their slave women to have sexual relations with them. Some historical evidence indicates, however, that if a man who had no property rights in a slave woman had intercourse with her without her master's permission, he may have been subject to criminal prosecution. Recently, historians have demonstrated that the assertion that black males were prone to rape white females did not prevail in slave times but came about after emancipation. They have also shown that it is a **rape myth**. Urban working-class women had a difficult time convincing jurors to convict their assailants of rape, as did Hispanic and Asian women living in the West, because class-biased and racist ideologies portrayed such women as immodest and unchaste.

In the nineteenth century, only a man could commit a rape, and he could commit it only against a woman. A woman could be convicted of a rape as an accomplice if she aided and abetted in the commission of the crime, but she could not be charged as the actual perpetrator. Nineteenth-century **rape law** did not recognize what today is **homosexual rape**, though a man who compelled another male to engage in sexual relations could be charged with forcible **sodomy**. Rape law defined sex with female children under a specified age of consent, usually 10 or 12, as rape even in the absence of force or resistance. While today such an act is referred to as **statutory rape**, in nineteenth-century law, the crime was known as the carnal knowledge and abuse of an infant female. *See also*: Hispanics/Latinos; Native Americans; Rape History in the United States; Slavery; Southern Rape Complex.

Suggested Reading: For important appellate court cases, see *People v. Abbot*, 19 Wend (NY) 192 (1838); *Camp v. State*, 3 Ga 417 (1847); *Brown v. State*, 11 SW 412 (1889). For important treatises, see Joel Prentice Bishop, *Commentaries on the Criminal Law*, 2nd ed., 2 vols. (Boston: Little, Brown, 1858); Emlin McLain, *A Treatise on the Criminal Law* (Chicago: Callaghan and Co., 1897).

MARY BLOCK

RAPE HISTORY IN THE UNITED STATES: TWENTIETH CENTURY. Definitions of rape and **sexual assault** have varied from one historical period to another and one culture to another. The United States in the twentieth century saw tremendous shifts in private and public understandings of this phenomenon. Contemporary attitudes toward rape, which continue to evolve, are based in large part on the developments of the twentieth century.

In the first half of the century, discussions of rape generally were taboo, but when the issue did arise, it typically treated rape as an expression of sex and passion and not as violence. The issue involved at least three interlocking themes. The first of these was Freudian psychoanalysis and sexology, which had a tremendous popular impact in the United States, reaching beyond academic and clinical contexts and into the popular realm. Freudians interpreted rape as perverse sexual behavior and rapists as mentally ill individuals. Freudian psychology viewed rapists as having surplus, uncontrollable sex drive. In this view, rapist behavior was an illness to be treated, not a widespread social problem to be prevented. Thus, rape was viewed from the perspective of the perpetrator, not the **victim**.

The second theme that marked most discussions of rape from 1900 to the 1960s was **race and racism**. The history of rape in the United States is inseparable from this theme. In earlier periods, "rape" of enslaved women by their white male owners was legally impossible. Black women were stereotyped as promiscuous and indiscriminate in their sexual choices, and black men were portrayed as sexually ravenous, particularly toward white women. Following **slavery**, and halfway into the 1900s, black men were subjected to extralegal murders called lynching, allegedly for the rape of white women but often without formal rape charges and always without a court conviction. White lynch mobs intimidated the entire **African American** community with threats of violence. Writers such as **Ida B. Wells** alluded to the sexual abuse of black women by white men, which received little attention in the legal realm or in the press. Together, lynching of black men and rape of black women served to reinforce white supremacy once slavery was over. Lynching finally stopped in the 1950s, largely due to the activism of the Association of Southern Women for the Prevention of Lynching.

The third theme is that of victim behavior. Legally, rape has always been considered a crime. The law of rape in the United States was inherited from English common law, which stated that a man committed rape when he had "carnal knowledge" of (sexual intercourse with) a woman, not his wife, by force or threat of force, without her **consent** and against her will. Until law reforms of the 1970s, rape cases were marked by evidentiary distrust of women's charges. Most states had laws that required corroboration, or independent evidence, of rape claims before a case could be tried. Many state laws required judges to instruct juries that rape charges were easy to make and hard to prove, no matter how innocent the accused. All states exempted husbands from rape charges by their wives, and in practice, this exemption was extended to their "voluntary social companions." Women who brought rape complaints found their own sex lives scrutinized for signs that they had been sexually active prior to the rape; those who had could not expect prosecutors to move forward with rape charges or juries to convict. Even if such cases went to trial, victims could expect defense attorneys to present evidence of their previous sexual experiences, creating the impression that a woman who has said yes to sex would not say no again. Thus, **rape trials** often focused greater attention on the victim than on the perpetrator.

The antirape movement of the 1970s challenged all that was "known" about rape. The movement grew out of the feminist mobilization of the 1960s that challenged sexism and discrimination against women in all aspects of society. Antirape campaigners challenged the myths of rapists and rape victims and redefined the crime from the victim's point of view.

The feminist antirape movement developed its analysis of rape not out of psychological research or racist stereotypes but out of the testimonies of victims themselves. In rape speakouts and **Take Back the Night** marches, victims dispelled many of the dominant **rape myths**, some of which still have force. For example, most rape victims told of rapes by friends, husbands, doctors, employers, and other acquaintances—demonstrating that rape was not the act of a few psychotic individuals but by men who otherwise fit a "normal" psychological profile and who were previously known to the victim. They also testified that most rapes were intraracial, dispelling the myth of the black rape of white women. The antirape movement found that women's **clothing**, behavior, and actions rarely had anything to do with their rapes; this prompted a focus on the perpetrator's behavior rather than the victim's.

The antirape campaign sought to redefine rape not as a crime of sexuality and passion but of violence and control. This was revealed in movement efforts to reform rape laws. One well-known reform was rape shield, which limited the evidence of a victim's sexual past that could be admitted at trial. The movement also sought to remove the marital exemption for rape, to develop a degree structure for rape, and to remove evidentiary roadblocks to **prosecution** such as corroboration requirements. All of these initiatives were an attempt to create victim-friendly rape laws that would force the legal system to take sexual assault seriously. Thanks to the antirape movement, many of the misconceptions of rape have been dispelled, all of the states have undergone law reform, and **rape crisis centers** now provide victims with 24-hour care and advocacy. In spite of these changes, challenges still persist: For example, in most jurisdictions, **date rape/acquaintance rape** is not taken as seriously as rape by a stranger, and overall, myths of black men's propensity to rape white women are strong. In addition, some writers have asserted that feminists have "gone too far" in redefining unwanted sex as rape.

The issue of rape underwent radical transformation in the course of the twentieth century. An issue once shrouded in secrecy, racism, and victim blaming is now likely to be treated quite differently in public policy and popular opinion, and the availability of crisis centers has addressed the needs of victims. It remains to be seen whether these changes in attitudes and public policy will produce an end to the problem of rape in our society. *See also*: **Marital Rape; Rape Law; Rape Shield Laws.**

Suggested Reading: Maria Bevacqua, *Rape on the Public Agenda: Feminism and the Politics of Sexual Assault* (Boston: Northeastern University Press, 2000); Susan Brownmiller, *Against Our Will: Men, Women and Rape* (New York: Simon and Schuster, 1975); Patricia L.N. Donat and John D'Emilio, "A Feminist Redefinition of Rape and Sexual Assault: Historical Foundations and Change," *Journal of Social Issues* 48.1 (1992): 9–22; Susan Estrich, *Real Rape* (Cambridge: Harvard University Press, 1987).

MARIA BEVACQUA

RAPE KIT. A rape kit, also known as a **sexual assault** evidence kit (SAEK), is a collection of evidence from a rape or sexual abuse **victim** after an assault. The exam varies by state and situation but can involve the following: a vaginal exam; swabbing of vagina, anus, and gums; blood and urine samples; combing of pubic hair; pulling of hairs from pubic area and head; photographing of bruises, cuts, or abrasions; scraping underneath or clipping of fingernails; taking of victim's underwear; and hearing the victim's account of the assault. This extensive examination may provide blood, semen, hair, saliva, skin, or fibers—all of which could aid in arresting and convicting a suspect. Exams are completed by emergency room doctors, nurse practitioners, or a sexual assault nurse examiner (SANE), a specially trained forensic nurse examiner. The examination, handling, collecting, and assembling of samples for the rape kit can take up to four hours, after which the contents of the kit becomes evidence and is handed over to police.

Victims seeking help within 48 to 72 hours after an assault are typically encouraged to have a rape kit collected so that the physical evidence will be on file if the victim or state chooses to prosecute. When evidence is collected properly, the kit can be used by police and courts to convict rapists by matching DNA found in or on the victim with the suspect's DNA. Historically, many states did not have the money to process every rape kit that was turned into evidence—a cost of about $500 per kit in private labs—especially when the rapist was a stranger to the victim. Consequently, the kits were not processed for matches with known criminals in the Federal Bureau of Investigation (FBI) DNA database that has been in operation since 1990.

In recent years, state and federal governments have worked to pass laws to provide funding for standardized rape kits, to process backlogged and future rape kits even when there is an unknown suspect, and for the training of more SANE nurses. The Debbie Smith Bill was introduced by U.S. Representative Carolyn Maloney and Senator Maria Cantwell in 2001, followed by the Rape Kit DNA Analysis Backlog Elimination Act of 2002, introduced by Representative Jerrold Nadler and Senator Hillary Clinton, and the DNA Sexual Assault Justice Act of 2002, introduced by Senator Joseph Biden and Representative Anthony Weiner. In addition, several states have changed their statute of limitations for rape prosecution, allowing for longer statutes when DNA evidence is uncovered. The passing of these laws will help victims use standard scientific evidence in rape trials and can help exonerate falsely imprisoned suspects. *See also*: **DNA Collection and Evidence.**

Suggested Reading: National Rape Evidence Project, http://www.rapeevidence.org; Deborah Parnis and Janice Du Mont, "Examining the Standardized Application of Rape Kits: An Exploratory Study of Post-Sexual Assault Professional Practices," *Health Care for Women International* 23 (2002): 846–853; U.S. Congress, Senate Committee on the Judiciary, *The DNA Sexual Assault Justice Act of 2002* (Washington, DC: GPO, 2002).

JACKIE GRUTSCH MCKINNEY

RAPE LAW. In 1680, **Matthew Hale,** the British jurist whose description of the English common law became the foundation for many American laws, stated: "It is true, rape is a most detestable crime, and therefore ought severely and impartially to be punished with death; but it must be remembered that it is an accusation easily to be made and hard to be proved; and harder to be defended by the party accused, though ever so innocent" (Bohmer, 317). Over 300 years later, the ambivalence reflected in Hale's statement on the law of rape remains a fixture of American jurisprudence. A more modern articulation of the two competing goals of rape law is given by law professor Angela Harris: (1) to protect individuals from nonconsensual sexual acts and (2) to ensure that accused individuals are not convicted of crimes of which they are innocent or crimes that they could not reasonably have known they were committing (52).

Susan Brownmiller became one of the first scholars to shatter the silence surrounding the history, sociology, and criminal law of rape with the publication of *Against Our Will: Men, Women and Rape.* Brownmiller was the first person to argue that rape was a crime of violence, not passion, when she argued that rape is "nothing more or less than a conscious process of intimidation by which all men keep all women in a state of fear" (15). She also gave a detailed history of rape law, discussing the crime's origins in property rights, such that rape initially involved a claim by one man against another man for damage to his property. Indeed, the word *rape* comes from the Latin *rapere,* which means to steal. In common law (i.e., under traditional law), rape was defined as an act of sexual intercourse undertaken by a man with a woman, not his wife, against her will and by force. Since the publication of *Against Our Will,* rape law has undergone a series of reforms that have resulted in the repeal or modification of earlier statutes in all 50 states.

The first wave of reforms began in the early to mid-1970s. Reformers attacked all aspects of this traditional definition, including the exemption of spouses; the gender-specific nature of the language, which did not allow for male **victims**; the exclusion of all sexual acts other than penile-vaginal intercourse; and the condition that victims be forcefully compelled, known as the **"resistance** requirement." In addition, activists and scholars sought to remove the various legal obstacles to proving that the rape had occurred—motivated by concerns that the victim, rather than the defendant, ended up being put on trial. Requirements of victim corroboration, admission of testimony on the victim's prior sexual history at trial, **rules of evidence** that required the victim to physically resist her/his attacker, and the notion of "fresh complaints" (i.e., the notion that charges of rape made to the police several days or weeks after the incident were false on their face) were all attacked.

The political climate was generally favorable to reform proposals, though there was resistance from defense attorneys concerned with changes infringing upon the rights of the accused. The result was a series of compromises in many states resulting in the deletion of specific provisions within the reform package or the substitution of a weaker version of a particular change. One example of a provision frequently deleted from early reform bills was the elimination of the **marital rape** exemption, a change that would not come until the second wave of reform. While some states adopted all the proposed changes through comprehensive reform bills, others made only minor revisions through a series of individual changes over time.

Four of the most common reforms enacted by legislatures have been identified. First, states redefined the crime of rape by adopting a series of graded offenses, rather than one sole crime, which were distinguished by the presence or absence of various "aggravating conditions." Reformers believed that these changes would remedy the aforementioned deficiencies of the traditional common-law definition as well as improving its precision by clearly stating a series of criminal behaviors. Each one of the graded offenses was described in gender-neutral terms and defined in terms of the circumstances surrounding the crime, including: the seriousness of the crime (penetration versus other sexual contact); how much force was used by the perpetrator; whether and to what extent the victim was injured; the age and incapacitation of the **survivor**; and whether or not a felony in addition to the **sexual assault** had been committed. In addition, most states eliminated the terms *rape* and **sodomy** and instead used terms like *sexual assault, sexual battery*, or *criminal sexual conduct*. Finally, many statutes redefined the term *penetration* to encompass a broader spectrum of actions committed by perpetrators. The Michigan statute, which is regarded as a model rape reform law by many scholars and activists, defined sexual penetration as "sexual intercourse, cunnilingus [**oral sex** performed upon a female], fellatio [oral sex performed upon a male], anal intercourse, or any other intrusion, however slight, of any part of a person's body or of any object into the genital or anal opening of another person's body, but emission of semen not required" (Spohn and Horney, 22).

Second, states addressed criticisms of the common-law statutory phrase "by force and against her will," which made an individual's nonconsent a critical component of the crime. This statutory element led to the development of what has been termed the "resistance requirement" whereby an individual was required to "resist to the utmost" or at least to demonstrate "such earnest resistance as might be reasonably expected under the circumstances" (23). In fact, many resistance requirements were further strengthened by state courts that overturned cases in which they believed insufficient resistance had been mounted. In a case in which the victim had struggled and screamed, the Wisconsin Supreme Court reversed the defendant's conviction, stating that "there must be the most vehement exercise of every physical means or faculty within the woman's power to resist the penetration of her person, and this must be shown to persist until the offense is consummated" (23).

Both activists and police officers insisted that these requirements actually increased the chances that an individual would be severely injured during a sexual assault. Their criticisms were augmented by feminists and legal scholars who stated that such resistance was not required from victims of any other violent crimes such as robbery, and furthermore, such inquiries shifted the focus of the trial toward the victim's behavior and character rather than the defendant's criminal actions. Many states chose to address these criticisms by eliminating resistance by the victim as one of the elements prosecutors had to prove at **rape trials**. Other states chose to more specifically define circumstances that satisfied the force requirement such as the use or display of a weapon or the injuring of a victim. A third approach taken by reformers of the **consent** standard sought to define the concept of consent itself more clearly. In Illinois, the legislators of 1985 chose to define consent as "a freely given agreement to the act of sexual penetration or sexual conduct in question" (24).

The third area of reform concerns the corroboration requirement. The corroboration requirement harkens back to the concerns expressed by Lord Hale about the easiness of levying a false rape accusation out of vengefulness, regret, or due to "mental imbalance," as well as the difficulty in disproving any such allegation. Despite a lack of empirical evidence concerning the frequency of false accusations and/or convictions, many states enacted a corroboration requirement that required that prosecutors present evidence other than the victim's testimony concerning the essential elements of the case (i.e., the attacker's identity, penetration, nonconsent). In addition to corroboration or as an alternative, some states required that judges issue a "cautionary instruction" to juries that was modeled after Hale's (in)famous statement. In attacking the corroboration requirement, reformers charged that the laws were sexually discriminatory (because the word of a woman was viewed as not being sufficient) and unnecessary (because judges and juries were, "if anything," biased against rape victims rather than defendants). In addition, critics pointed to the particular difficulty of obtaining evidence of a crime that usually takes place in private and therefore without any other witnesses, stating that reforms would lead to both an increased pool of prosecutable rape cases and an increased conviction rate. The majority of jurisdictions subsequently abolished both the cautionary jury instructions and the corroboration requirement through either legislation or court rulings.

Finally, through the enactment of **rape shield laws**, reformers were able to exclude a significant amount of evidence regarding the victim's prior sexual conduct. Previously, under common law, such evidence had been allowed into court in order to question the victim's **credibility** and therefore prove that she had in fact consented to sexual intercourse.

> The notion that the victim's prior sexual conduct was pertinent to whether or not she consented was based on the assumptions that chastity was a character trait and that, therefore, an unchaste woman would be more likely to agree to intercourse than a woman without premarital or extramarital experience. Simply stated, the assumption was "if she did it once she'd do it again." (25)

Critics argued that these assumptions were based on outdated stereotypes that provided courts and juries with little or no guidance on the issue of credibility or in determining what happened on this specific occasion. Such criticisms were well received, and by 1985 almost all of the states and the federal government had adopted rape shield laws that encompass a range of restrictiveness concerning admissibility.

The 1986 Texas statute offers an example of a less restrictive approach whereby no evidence of sexual conduct was categorically excluded, but rather each individual judge is instructed to hold a private hearing to determine whether or not the evidence's inflammatory nature is outweighed by its relevance or helpfulness. Michigan, on the other hand, completely prohibited the admission of evidence concerning a victim's prior sexual history as of 1985 with only two narrow exceptions, though even the exceptions must first be deemed valuable and relevant by the judge before they are admitted. Other jurisdictions attempt to offer more of a balance between the rights of the complainant and the accused; some, like California, distinguish between evidence of past sexual history to prove consent, which is inadmissible, and evidence relating to credibility, which is allowed. Reformers hoped that rape shield laws would ensure that survivors would no longer be subjected to "a second brutalization in court" (27).

In a second wave of reform, activists moved beyond the legal hurdles both before and during trial, in order to further question the definition of rape itself. In addition, spousal rape statutes that reformers had been forced to abandon during the first wave of reform were enacted in most jurisdictions, making the assault of one's spouse a crime.

Many of the broad effects reformers in the 1970s and 1980s anticipated to arise out of these changes did not ultimately occur. Rape is still a significantly underreported crime, particularly **date rape/acquaintance rape,** which is taken less seriously than stranger rape. Consent standards and force/resistance requirements are still being debated, if not in legislatures, then in courtrooms, prosecutors' offices, and police stations, as well as the public at large. Current legal scholarship has focused on the evolving definition of consent, attempting to take into account and explain the different perceptions of the same encounter reported by survivors and defendants through nuanced interpretations of the language.

These are some of the most significant changes in American rape law, with an emphasis on the first wave of reforms enacted during the 1970s and 1980s. The law of rape is constantly evolving—yet increasingly activists and scholars are turning to other mediums in order to effect change such as community outreach and education with specialized training for those working within the criminal justice system. While the statutory construction of the law remains a site of struggle, how those statutes are interpreted, enforced, and perceived has increasingly become the focus of both scholarly and activist inquiry. *See also*: **Prosecution; Rape, Definitions of.**

Suggested Reading: Carol Bohmer, "Acquaintance Rape and the Law," in *Acquaintance Rape: The Hidden Crime*, ed. Andrea Parrot and Laurie Bechofer (New York: John Wiley and Sons, 1991), 317; Susan Brownmiller, *Against Our Will: Men, Women and Rape* (New York: Simon and Schuster, 1975), 15; Susan Estrich, *Real Rape: How the Legal System Victimizes Women Who Say No* (Cambridge, MA: Harvard University Press, 1987); Leslie Francis, "Introduction," in *Date Rape: Feminism, Philosophy, and the Law*, ed. Leslie Francis (University Park: Pennsylvania State University Press, 1996), viii; Angela P. Harris, "Forcible Rape, Date Rape, and Communicative Sexuality: A Legal Perspective," in *Date Rape: Feminism, Philosophy, and the Law*, ed. Leslie Francis (University Park: Pennsylvania State University Press, 1996); Cassia Spohn and Julie Horney, *Rape Law Reform: A Grassroots Revolution and Its Impact* (New York: Plenum Press, 1992).

STEPHANIE L. SCHMID

RAPE-LYNCH SCENARIO. Nearly 3,000 Americans were lynched from the late nineteenth through the early twentieth centuries. The vast majority of these were **African American** males who died at the hands of white mobs. The purported "crime" of many of these victims was the rape of or inappropriate sexual conduct with or in the presence of white women. This scenario—an accusation of sexual impropriety or criminality against a black man, followed by mob violence that often ended in the brutal murder of the accused rapist—was an all-too-common occurrence in the late nineteenth-century South, a period often considered the nadir in American race relations.

Accusations of black rape or **sexual assault** carried great weight in the South because much of the region at this time had become convulsed with fears or anxiety about black-on-white rape, although there is little evidence to substantiate such concerns. Regardless, a perceived misstep or sexual advance by a black man toward a white woman was often offered up as an excuse for mob violence. Many white communities, believing that blacks only responded to such displays of extralegal "justice," simply refused to allow such alleged sexual infractions to proceed through the criminal justice system, despite the high rates of execution for black men convicted of the rape or attempted rape of white women.

Lynching has been variously defined over the years, but the term generally applies to a variety of extralegal actions by groups of varying sizes in response to a perceived violation of law or a breach of custom. Rituals that were sometimes observed in lynching include allowing a **victim** or the victim's **family** member to take the lead in the attack; the mutilation of the alleged attacker; the cooperation of law officials working actively, though perhaps covertly, with the mob; welcoming large audiences to witness the spectacle of lynching; and finally, the grisly commercialization of lynching that produced picture postcards commemorating lynching or the selling of body parts as grisly mementos, a development that coincided with the rise of consumer culture in America.

While the ostensible reasons for lynching varied wildly over region and time, according to most white southern contemporaries, the primary motivation for mob action against a black man was sexual misconduct, broadly defined as rape. Many types of behaviors when committed by black men in the presence of white women had connotations of sexual aggression that most likely would not have been the case had the male been white or the female black. Knocking on the door of a white woman home alone, for example, might very well be interpreted as a sexually menacing act. Scaring a white woman or making direct eye contact with a white woman could precipitate a lynch mob. And, of course, word about consensual sex across the color line would frequently energize the white community into taking action against the suspected black offender. Much of the white South believed no "sane" or proper white woman would ever consent to sex with a black man, virtually rendering all forms of sex between black men and white women coerced, or rape.

Although statistically sexual assault was not the most frequent reason given for most racially motivated lynchings, lynching apologists, nonetheless, fixated on black rape as the chief cause of most lynchings, in large measure to justify a heinous and savage practice to those outside the South. Radical racists invoked the sanctity of white womanhood, falling back on the gendered mores of the Victorian culture, to sanction the racial violence that pervaded much of the South at the turn of the century, fully cognizant that economic and political competition, which in reality undergirded much of the fatal white-on-black violence, would carry little currency outside the South. Pervasive repulsion at black rape thus transcended regional borders and shored up support outside the South for "extreme" measures like lynching, or at least helped to mute the criticism of lynching.

Southern politicians were especially adept at harnessing rape fears to garner support for lynching. Rebecca Latimer Felton of Georgia, suffragist, Prohibitionist, and the first woman to serve in the U.S. Senate, unabashedly called for the lynching of black rapists, crying that "if it takes lynching to protect woman's dearest possession . . . then I say lynch a thousand times a week if it becomes necessary."

Despite claims that the rape of white women was the primary cause of lynching, sexual offenses constituted only one of many reasons for lynching. Critics of lynching, mostly black activists, denounced such claims as constructed merely to mask indiscretions by white women who flouted racial taboos by becoming intimately involved with black men. Once exposed, such women, rather than risk community opprobrium or rejection, "cried rape," prompting antilynching activist **Ida B. Wells** to label the charge of black rape "the old thread-bare lie." She suspected as well that other motivations, like political agency and the economic viability of the black community, which proved threatening to whites, lay at the heart of lynching. Wells was joined by other African Americans, like Frederick Douglass, John Mitchell, and Mary Church Terrell, and by organizations like the National Association for the Advancement of Colored People (NAACP) and the Committee on Interracial Co-operation, in the fight against lynching. One grassroots organization, the Association of Southern Women for the Prevention of Lynching, headed by white woman Jesse Daniel Ames, worked tirelessly for federal legislation to outlaw lynching.

Antilynching activists faced an uphill battle combating popular renderings of rape and race in the South. The themes in Thomas Dixon's popular novel, *The Clansman* (1905), which glorified the birth of the Ku Klux Klan largely by showcasing the sexual threat black men posed to white women of the South after the Civil War, played to a much wider national audience in its celluloid offspring, *Birth of a Nation* (1916). Huge crowds attending the cinematic spectacle expressed revulsion at the rape scenes and became receptive to lynching as a "natural" way to combat "the usual crime" of black-on-white rape. Ironically, in the twentieth century, race liberals of the South, both black and white, employed **literature** as a vehicle to protest the savagery of lynching and in particular to expose as sham the ruse of black rape. Mississippi novelist William Faulkner, most notably, turned the table on white male lynchers whom he suspected of harboring feelings of sexual repression. In *Light in August* (1932), Joe Christmas is brutally mutilated and lynched for the alleged murder of a white woman. The leader of that white mob, Percy Grimm, thus exorcises his own sexual frustrations by lynching Christmas, a man of mixed race, who was demonized for his freer views about sex. Lillian Smith, James Baldwin, and W.E.B. Du Bois, to name just a few authors critical of the rape-lynch scenario, followed suit. *See also*: **Race and Racism; Southern Rape Complex.**

Suggested Reading: W. Fitzhugh Brundage, *Lynching in the New South: Georgia and Virginia, 1880–1930* (Urbana: University of Illinois Press, 1993); W. Fitzhugh Brundage, ed., *Under Sentence of Death: Lynching in the South* (Chapel Hill: University of North Carolina Press, 1997); James E. Cutler, *Lynch Law: An Investigation into the History of Lynching in the United States* (New York: Longmans, Green, 1905); Philip Dray, *At the Hands of Persons Unknown* (New York: Random House, 2002); Stewart E. Tolnay and E.M. Beck, *A Festival of Violence: An Analysis of Southern Lynchings, 1882–1930* (Urbana: University of Illinois Press, 1992).

DIANE MILLER SOMMERVILLE

RAPE MYTHS. Rape myths are widely held inaccurate beliefs about how and why rape happens. Myths are either untrue and unfounded ideas misconstrued as facts (**victims** want to be raped) or partially true yet atypical experiences that get applied uncritically to all **sexual assault** cases (strangers rape women in dark alleys). These myths are learned through cultural socialization by our **family**, peers, religious instruction, **schools, media,** and community. Rape myths usually include the following ideas: victims deserve, cause, invite, ask for, or want to be raped; victims who get raped could have avoided it and therefore are at fault; and victims are sexually promiscuous, or they are sexually active with the offender, and thus she/he was a willing partner in a sex act.

Racist, classist, and sexist stereotypes about victims, perpetrators, and violence play a key role in the development and maintenance of rape myths. For example, one stereotype is that of the black male rapist who attacks white women. This has little basis in reality. About 80 percent of **sex offenders** violate victims within their same racial group. The exception to this is **Native American** women who are almost always raped by non-Native men, according to the Bureau of Justice Statistics. Because of racist stereotypes that have continued since colonialism and American **slavery**, white women have been socialized to be cautious of black male strangers, and nonwhite women have been largely overlooked as victims of assault.

Sexist stereotypes have made women's sexuality the focus when it comes to understanding rape. The mythical belief that women who are raped bring it on themselves makes scrutiny of their sexual activity, as well as their dress and behavior, culturally acceptable. Stereotypical views that women should be sexually available and pleasing to husbands or lovers perpetuate myths that women cannot be raped in marriage, in a relationship, or on a date. In this situation, common cultural responses might be: She knew what she was getting into, she just regretted sex and called it rape, and it cannot be rape because it is her duty as a wife to please her husband.

Furthermore, racist and classist stereotypes interconnect with sexism. Women who are viewed as virtuous and moral—usually white, not impoverished, married, heterosexual, and law-abiding—may be accepted as true victims and solicit more sympathy and more justice-seeking than women perceived as promiscuous or immoral—nonwhite, working-class or poor, rural, unmarried, homeless, sex worker, sexually active, and queer. While these stereotypes fuel rape myths about women, they also shape myths about men by completely invalidating them as victims of sexual assault.

Rape myths not only produce and maintain ideas about victims and offenders; they shape and consequently narrow our understanding of violence and the way rape is defined. For example, one commonly held belief is that a rape crime can only be defined as such if it happens to a "moral and believable" woman who is attacked by a deviant male stranger. This scenario does happen, but using it as a standard obscures the majority of sexual assault experiences and facts of rape. Furthermore, it relies on stereotypical ideas about violence, which often measures the level of crime, appropriate legal response, and assessment of victim harm by the visual signs of physical injury. In reality, most **child rape** and adult rape do not reflect "obvious" bodily injury. Thus, this myth minimizes the trauma of rape and contributes to misguided and ineffective legal and societal responses to rape.

Rape myths, and the stereotypes that fuel them, profoundly affect society's understanding of and response to rape. They increase a survivor's feelings of blame and shame, discourage them from seeking help and reporting, and can harm their recovery; relieve offenders of responsibility and make arrest and **prosecution** more difficult; influence the way society, media, and the legal system treat **survivors** and respond to rape; allow society to minimize or excuse the prevalence of rape and the effect it has on us all; and teach all women and men the wrong ideas about rape, which in turn falsely informs them about effective **rape prevention** methods and assistance services.

Dispelling rape myths and working toward ending rape require reevaluation in light of the facts of rape. Sexual intercourse without **consent** is always rape regardless of the circumstances and characteristics of the victim or offender. It is rape whether or not a weapon was used, excessive force was used, there are visible signs of violence, or a victim fought back. No one owes sex because they are dating, married, "sexually teasing," prostituting, or previously or currently engaging in other consensual sexual activity. No one deserves or does something to invite rape. Rape is always the responsibility of the offender.

While sexual assault occurrences vary, there are common characteristics obscured by rape myths. Most adult and child rape survivors know or are acquainted with their offender. The majority of rape victims are women and children, but adult men are also sexually assaulted. According to the Bureau of Justice Statistics, most rapes in the United States occur in or near a victim's home or an acquaintance's home, and a rape is just as likely to occur during the day as it is in the evening. Moreover, almost all sexual violence is perpetrated by men within their racial group, and research on rapists reveals that most are clinically sane, have sex regularly, hold jobs, and appear as "normal" members of society.

In conclusion, rape myths are prevalent, and many people believe they are true and factual. They affect individual, cultural, and institutional understanding of and responses to rape. Thus, dispelling rape myths and exposing the racism and sexism that fuel them are imperative to ending rape. *See also*: **"Blaming the Victim" Syndrome; Male Rape; Prostitution; Southern Rape Complex.**

Suggested Reading: Bureau of Justice Statistics, http://www.ajp.usdaj.gov/bjs/pub; Angela Davis, "Rape, Racism and the Myth of the Black Rapist," in *Women, Race & Class* (New York: Random House, 1981), 172–201; Mary P. Koss, "Hidden Rape," in *Rape and Sexual Assault*, vol. 2, ed. A.W. Burgess (New York: Garland, 1998); Anthony J. Urquiza and Beth L. Goodlin-Jones, "Child Sexual Abuse and Adult Victimization with Women of Color," *Violence and Victims* 9.3 (1994): 223–232; Robin Warshaw, *I Never Called It Rape* (New York: Harper & Row, 1988).

HEATHER SCHMIDT

RAPE OF LUCRETIA. The Rape of Lucretia is the legendary event that led to the expulsion of the kings of Rome in 509–510 B.C.E. Many important turning points in Rome's history were marked by either the rape or attempted rape of a woman. For the Romans, rape apparently brought together the two divine origins of the nation—the god of war, Mars, and the goddess of love, Venus—and hence was critical in furthering the development of the state. Early sources for the story of the Rape of Lucretia are the historian Livy, and the poet Ovid, who wrote between the end the the first century B.C.E. and the beginning of the first century C.E. The Rape of Lucretia has also been the subject of a Shakespeare play and numerous paintings.

The story begins when the Romans attack Ardea, a neighboring city. Tarquinius Superbus, the Roman king, had launched the assault in order to distract the people, who were unhappy with the king's program of forced labor. The assault on Ardea rapidly turned into a siege. One evening a group of young princes gathers to drink and pass the time. Collantinus Tarquinius bragged that his wife was more virtuous than anyone else's. In order to prove it, the men agree to travel to each other's houses that very night to see how their wives are spending their time. As they visit each house, the princes discover the royal wives are engaged in drinking parties just like their husbands. When they reach the home of Collatinus, however, they find his wife, Lucretia, and her maids are busy spinning wool, a sign of female virtue. Collatinus wins the contest. But the favorite son of the king, Sextus Tarquinius, becomes inflamed with passion, either because of Lucretia's beauty, or because he wants to destroy her virtuous reputation. He returns to Collatinus's house, and

Lucretia welcomes him as a guest. When the household is asleep, he creeps into Lucretia's room. At first Tarquinius promises marriage and the crown; then he threatens Lucretia with his knife. She is willing to die to preserve her chastity, so Tarquinius tells her that he will kill her and a slave, arranging the bodies so that he can claim he caught her in the act of adultery and killed her on behalf of the **family**. Unable to stand this idea, Lucretia allows him to rape her. The next day she calls her husband and her father home, instructing them to bring along trustworthy friends. They arrive, she tells them what Tarquinius has done, and asks them to swear that they will avenge her. The men try to convince Lucretia that she has done nothing wrong. She surprises them by crying out that no woman shall have the opportunity to use Lucretia as an excuse for immoral acts and then stabs herself. As her husband and father look on in horror, Brutus (another member of the royal family) pulls the knife from Lucretia's body and swears that he will avenge her by deposing the king. Lucretia's body is carried to the Forum, where the people rally around Brutus and expel the king. Brutus and Collatinus become the first two Roman Consuls, and the republic is born.

Scholarly treatments of the rape of Lucretia often focus on the political consequences of the act: a political revolution and the founding of the Roman republic. Others focus on the religious and dramatic qualities of the story. When the political outcome is emphasized, the characters of Brutus and Sextus Tarquinius are often the main focus of the analysis, rather than Lucretia. Scholars of ancient **religion** have pointed out the ritual nature of the rape and its aftermath, essentially reading Lucretia as a sacrificial victim who is killed to purify the state and society. Others have focused on the dramatic nature of the story. In Livy's telling, the action is so close to **theater** that subsequent dramatists have found it easy to adapt. In another interpretation, the rape is seen as further evidence that the Romans drew on both the violent and creative aspects of their collective identity, making rape a quintessentially Roman way of marking important turning points in the development of the polity. Finally, feminist scholars have pointed out the ways in which this story dramatizes the position of Roman women who are treated as symbols and pawns to be exchanged and violated by men as part of their competition for political power. Although these interpretations vary widely, it is clear that the Romans felt that rape was central to their own political and cultural origins. *See also*: **Art; Mythology; Rape of the Sabine Women.**

Suggested Reading: I. Donaldson, *Rapes of Lucretia* (Oxford: Clarendon Press, 1982).

APRIL BULLOCK

RAPE OF NANKING. On December 13, 1937, after six months of intense fighting in the Yangtze Valley, Nanking, the capital of Nationalist China, fell to the Japanese. This was a major victory in Japan's quest to dominate Asia. It was followed by seven weeks of carnage known as the Rape of Nanking. Mass executions slaughtered the Chinese Army, 260,000 to 350,000 civilians were killed, and up to 80,000 women and men were raped. These atrocities were designed to terrorize the Chinese people, demean them, break their will, and allow Japan to easily subjugate the population. The few missionaries in Nanking tried unsuccessfully to protect women from being raped. Though the Rape of Nanking made headlines around the world, the international community did not investigate the rapes until after the war.

Rape has always been a technique of warfare, but according to rape expert **Susan**

Brownmiller, only the Pakistani treatment of Bengali women in 1971 compares to the violence, pain, and humiliation bestowed by Japanese soldiers on the people of Nanking. Under the command of General Iwana Matsui and Prince Asaka Yasu-hiko, soldiers and officers systematically went through the city, raping all women, regardless of their ages. Chinese men were also sodomized or forced to commit necrophilia or **incest** in front of laughing troops. The women, raised to prize chastity, fiercely resisted the Japanese. Women went into hiding, tried to pass as men, refused to bathe, and threw up or voided on their attackers, but the violence continued. When bored, soldiers gang raped Buddhist nuns, sliced open the vaginas of young girls to assault them more efficiently, impaled women's vaginas, took pornographic pictures of their victims, and ripped fetuses out of pregnant women for amusement. Many of these women were then sent to the front lines in other areas of Asia and the Pacific to serve as unpaid sexual slaves for the Japanese military.

A soldier explained the rapists' attitudes toward Chinese women: "We just thought of her as something like a pig." When the military police made token efforts to stop the rapes, the soldiers began to kill women to cover the abuse. Victims were disemboweled, had their breasts cut off, and were nailed to walls. There was no limit to the capacity for human degradation and sexual perversity.

Many of the women who survived were faced with unwanted pregnancies. Because the Japanese had used rape as a tactic to terrorize and humiliate the Chinese people, pregnant women faced the unthinkable consequence of bearing and raising an enemy's child. To date, not a single Chinese woman has admitted that her child was the result of these rapes. Yet Western observers reported mass suicides of pregnant Chinese women in 1938, and numerous half-Japanese babies were killed at birth by their scarred mothers.

Historians blame Japanese military culture for the extent of the **torture.** Young boys in Japan were trained from an early age for military service. Teachers also instilled an intense hatred of the Chinese and preached of Japan's racial superiority. Thus, boys were ready to join the army and conquer China. However, they found the military life to be arbitrary, cruel, and based on rank. Thus, the soldiers who came to China were filled with rage and looking for someone "lower" than themselves on which to take out their frustrations. Chinese women, because of their "inferior" racial and gender status, were ideal targets for the soldiers' aggression. Military superstition also promoted the sexual abuse of women. Many Japanese soldiers believed that raping **virgins** made them more powerful in battle. Other soldiers wore amulets made from their victims' pubic hair to protect them from injury.

As Westerners alerted their home governments of the atrocities taking place in Nanking, the Japanese high command stepped in. Rather than punish the soldiers, they created a system of military **prostitution** based on the sexual slavery of Asian women. Those from Nanking were among the first exploited as "**comfort women.**" Under the puppet rule of Chinese collaborators, the situation in Nanking quieted. The survivors often turned to opium as an escape. Even after the Japanese surrender in 1945, the people of Nanking continued to suffer lives of silent poverty, shame, and chronic physical and mental pain. Anxious to make alliance with Japan in the Cold War era, neither Westerners nor the Chinese government held the Japanese government accountable for the Rape of Nanking. *See also*: **Bosnia-Hergezovina; Nazis; War Crimes; Wartime Rape.**

Suggested Reading: Timothy Brooks, ed., *Documents on the Rape of Nanking* (Ann Arbor: University of Michigan Press, 2000); Iris Chang, *The Rape of Nanking* (New York: Penguin, 1997).

MARY LINEHAN

RAPE OF THE SABINE WOMEN. The Rape of the Sabine Women is part of the legendary story of the founding of Rome. It is the second in a series of rapes or attempted rapes that mark important turning points in the early history of Rome. The first of these, the rape of Rhea Silvia by the god Mars, produced the legendary founder of Rome, Romulus. The ancient sources for the story include Livy's *Early History of Rome* and Ovid's *The Art of Love*, both produced at the end of the first century B.C.E.

Shortly after Romulus established the city of Rome (c. 750 B.C.E.), he was faced with the problem of creating a stable population base. Rome's citizens consisted of the rabble of other towns that had either joined up with Romulus's army or had responded to his call for people for the new town (he granted asylum to all who responded). There was a severe shortage of women. Romulus sent envoys to neighboring cities asking for the right of intermarriage and hence alliance. They were sent packing by their neighbors who felt that Rome's power was already too great or that the Roman rabble were simply unfit for intermarriage. When the envoys returned disappointed, Romulus formulated a plan to abduct women from neighboring communities. The Romans invited their neighbors, including the Sabines, to celebrate a new religious festival in Rome. While the theatricals were under way, the Romans set upon the young women from neighboring cities and abducted and raped them. The women's relatives fled in confusion. While the other cities attacked Rome and were quickly defeated, the Sabines bided their time and waited for some months to wage war against Rome to avenge this wrong. In the meantime, Romulus and the Romans apparently won the women to their cause; various sources report that they promised legal marriage and a glorious future for their offspring and whispered words of love. When the war finally comes, the Sabine women stand between their families of birth and marriage, pleading with both to spare themselves and their children further exposure to the horrors of war between relatives.

Scholarly interpretations of the Rape of the Sabine Women stress different aspects of the story. The Rape of the Sabines has been used to explain the origins of the Roman marriage ceremony. Many of the specific customs associated with Roman marriage can be found in the story of the Sabines. Carrying the bride across the threshold, for example, may commemorate these first, forced marriages. But for most scholars, the central meaning of the rape is political. Those who rely on the Roman historian Livy tend to view the rape as simply the easiest and most practical solution to the problem of building a stable population for the newly founded city. These interpretations focus primarily on the latter intervention of the Sabine women on the battlefield and its happy consequences for the Romans. Other interpretations focus on the Roman poet Ovid's account of the rape, which gives more narrative attention to the terror and suffering of the women and the lustfulness of the Romans. In some interpretations, Ovid's narration of the fear and pain of the **victims** of the rape is viewed as evidence of a protofeminist interest in the consequences of rape for its victims and in the role of rape in perpetuating **patriarchy**. For other scholars, however, Ovid's attention to the sufferings of the victims is a result of an inability to separate the violence and sexuality that are both part of rape. In this interpretation, political and sexual violence are inescapably linked; indeed, there is no clear demarcation between them. Whichever of these interpretations is favored, it is clear that the Rape of the Sabines was one of the most important stories the Romans told about themselves and their community, which was founded on love and war, passion and violence. *See also*: **Abduction (Kidnapping)**; **Art**; **Mythology**; **Rape of Lucretia**; **Theater**.

Suggested Reading: Mary Beard, "The Erotics of Rape: Livy, Ovid, and the Sabine Women," in *Female Networks and the Public Sphere in Roman Society*, ed. P. Setala and L. Savunen (Rome: Acta Instituti Romani Finlandiae XXII, 1999); Susan Deacy and Karen F. Pierce, eds., *Rape in Antiquity: Sexual Violence in the Greek and Roman Worlds* (London: Duckworth, 1997).

APRIL BULLOCK

RAPE PREVENTION. Traditionally, rape prevention knowledge has largely been a set of well-intentioned but misled ideas passed word of mouth by our peers, families, **schools**, religious institutions, and communities. The focus has historically been on female **victims** of rape and the ways in which women should avoid being assaulted. The methods were based on what is now considered victim control, controlling women's behavior to prevent a potential assault. New ideas about rape revealed that this restricted the freedom of women, not the freedom of rapists. Furthermore, it was argued that the traditional avoidance techniques—do not go out at night, dress conservatively, walk in groups—were not effective, especially in light of facts that show most victims are assaulted by someone they know in their own home or the home of an acquaintance. Thus, traditional rape prevention information was based on **rape myths** and focused avoidance methods on women's behavior in stereotypical stranger rape scenarios.

Rape prevention, as a philosophy as well as a set of responses to rape, emerged from the women's movement and antiviolence movement beginning in the 1960s. The analysis came out of women's personal and collective experiences of violence and sexism. In informal discussions and consciousness-raising groups, women became aware of shared experiences. This shifted the understanding of rape from being an individual problem to a societal and cultural one. It further challenged the idea that rape was an isolated event that happened at random with infrequence, exposing the fact that rape was, and is, frequent, usually planned, and a culturally embedded behavior. Furthermore, violence, including **sexual assault**, came to be viewed as connected to all forms of oppression and the consequential injustices.

This analysis of rape and violence has changed and influenced our fundamental cultural understanding of all violence. One of the most important contributions to this changed perception was the development of a feminist redefinition of rape. Feminists argued that rape was motivated by the desire for power and control, not sex. Additionally, feminists pointed out that the prevalence of rape in our society was fueled and maintained by the subordination of women. Challenging the idea that rape is an act motivated by the attainment of sex has enabled the antiviolence movement to embrace men who have been victims of rape and other types of violence. It has also opened up space for understanding hate-motivated crimes related to race, **religion**, sexuality, and physical ability. Further, understanding rape as a desire for power and control has shifted responsibility from victims to offenders.

A change in the way rape and other forms of violence were analyzed called for a new understanding and response to rape. Therefore, rape prevention strategies were developed to address the range of cultural issues contributing to sexual assault. For example, a systemic strategy for ending rape may require ending power imbalances resulting from oppression and inequality. This may include addressing poverty, improving institutional education, and ending oppression related to race, gender/sex, ethnicity, heterosexuality, physical ability, and appearance. Rape prevention strategies also include direct education and empowerment of individuals. This may incorporate rape education programs that inform women and men about the realities and myths of sexual assault. It may include information on effective strategies for risk reduction and rape avoidance such as assertiveness, confrontational skills, and **self-defense** options.

Rape prevention programs often work on a broad scale, educating individuals and communities, as well as working with **law enforcement, hospitals**, and **rape crisis centers**. Programs may provide or offer referrals for **rape counseling**, victim advocacy, and crisis intervention. Education and prevention programs also strive to make **survivors** and offenders aware of the services available. Thus, rape prevention programs can educate about and prevent rape, as well as provide services for survivors and their friends and family.

Although there are rape prevention services established in many communities and universities, there are still communities, especially nonmetropolitan or rural areas, without rape crisis centers or specially trained hospital staff. Most universities and law enforcement agencies remain ill prepared to handle **date rape/acquaintance rape** complaints because of the prevalence and complexity of the cases. Further, some universities lack specific penalties for sexual assault, prosecute under the student conduct code, and do not ensure confidentiality for the victim.

Even with these challenges, rape prevention information and services have become successfully widespread. People have a better awareness and understanding of sexual assault. Popular magazines and television shows have featured various aspects of rape and recovery to a diverse audience. **Rape education** programs are being offered in classrooms, churches, and at community awareness events. Seeking out crisis intervention and counseling is becoming more acceptable. Several men's groups have been established to work toward stopping rape. More information is available to rape survivors previously not served well—men, disabled and mentally impaired individuals, people of color, and queer and transgendered individuals. Self-defense is making headway as an effective tool to avoid assault. Since the 1980s, programs for women and children have increased, and multiple training options have become available. Lastly, with the 1994 creation of the **Rape, Abuse & Incest National Network (RAINN)**, the National Sexual Assault Hotline, access to information is quicker and better disseminated across diverse groups. The national 24-hour rape hotline for men and women allows them to get referral information for their local rape crisis centers and counselors. These efforts have made significant strides in the goals of rape prevention—improving rape education, awareness, knowledge of self-defense options, and services—combining to make stopping rape a greater possibility. *See also*: **Campus Rape.**

Suggested Reading: Pauline Bart and Patricia O'Brien, *Stopping Rape: Successful Survival Strategies* (New York: Pergamon Press, 1985); Martha McCaughey, *Real Knockouts: The Physical Feminism of Women's Self-Defense* (New York: New York University Press, 1997);

Andrea Parrot, *Acquaintance Rape and Sexual Assault: A Prevention Manual* (Holmes Beach, FL: Learning Publication, 1991); Nadia Telsey, *Self-defense from the Inside Out: A Women's Workbook for Developing Self-esteem and Assertiveness Skills for Safety* (Eugene, OR: Published by the author, n.d.).

HEATHER SCHMIDT

RAPE SHIELD LAWS. Beginning in the 1970s, several states within the United States began passing "rape shield laws." These laws protect rape **victims** from public scrutiny by prohibiting the media from broadcasting or publishing their names and protect them in court by preventing their previous sexual histories from being revealed. Before the laws were enacted, the sexual history of a victim could be brought before the court and used to defend the rapist. If the defense showed that the woman had sexual relations with the man prior to the rape, many judges and juries took that to mean that the woman was "asking to be raped." Rape shield laws allow rape victims to be treated fairly in the court system instead of putting them on trial.

Rape shield laws have been open to intense scrutiny, and some are being challenged. Critics point out that the language of many of the laws is extreme. For example, the Massachusetts law states, "Evidence of the reputation of a victim's sexual conduct shall not be admissible in any investigation or proceeding before a grand jury or any court of the commonwealth." Numerous constitutional lawyers have pointed out that the rape shield laws may, in some cases, violate the constitutional rights of the accused. The Sixth Amendment clearly states the rights of the accused in a trial. If the accused has evidence in his defense, it may not be admissible to the court if the rape shield laws forbid it. It is almost universally agreed that rape shield laws have done more good than harm, but their validity is still being tested in the legal system. *See also*: *Cox Broadcasting Corporation v. Cohn*; *Michigan v. Lucas*; Rape Law; Rules of Evidence; Secondary Rape.

Suggested Reading: General Laws of Massachusetts, http://www.state.ma.us/legis/laws/mgl/233-21B.htm. "J. Tanford & A. Bocchino, Rape Victim Shield Laws and the Sixth Amendment," http://www.law.harvard.edu/publications/evidenceiii/articles/tanford.htm; Cathy Young, "Excluded Evidence: The Dark Side of Rape Shield Laws," *Reason.com* (February 2002), http://reason.com/0202/co.cy.excluded.shtml.

ARTHUR HOLST

RAPE STATISTICS. Rape statistics are gathered to understand, respond to, and prevent rape. Statistics provide information about rape **victims,** offenders, circumstances of the crime, reporting, victims' experiences and feelings, recovery, effectiveness of **self-defense** and preventative measures, **prosecution,** and conviction. They have been used to dispel **rape myths** as well as sexist and racist stereotypes by confirming what we know about rape and how victims and **survivors** experience rape. Statistics are an important tool for **rape prevention** education because they raise awareness about rape and about the need for changes in societal responses to rape.

Some of the main and important rape statistics include the following: An estimated 12.1 million women have been raped at least once in their lifetime, and 39 percent of them experienced more than one rape; over 80 percent of victims are assaulted by someone they know or are newly acquainted with; the Women's Safety

Project, based on in-depth face-to-face interviews with 420 women, indicated that 97.6 percent of women reported they had experienced some form of sexual violation, and extrapolating from their findings, they reported that more than 1 in 3 women are raped in adulthood, the 1999 Bureau of Justice Statistics reports that 9 percent of all rape happens to men; the Center for Disease Control reported that of those participants in their national telephone survey, 84 percent of rape victims did not report their offense to the police; with the exception of **Native American** rape victims, the 1994 Bureau of Justice Statistics reports 80 to 90 percent of all rape cases involve people of the same race, and they also report that most **sexual assault** occurs in or near the victim's home or the home of someone they know; and 98 percent of all rape victims will never see their attacker caught, tried, and imprisoned. Almost half of all convicted rapists are sentenced to less than one year behind bars.

There are both institutional and individual barriers contributing to underreporting and inaccurate rape statistics. Institutionally, there is deliberate underreporting by **law enforcement**, universities, and other institutions like religious entities to protect their reputation or to avoid the extra work and time required to deal with cases; the classifying of sexual assault is sometimes done inaccurately because a belief in rape myths dismisses the assault as a crime or because the crime categories in the classification system do not allow for accurate or detailed reporting; the Federal Bureau of Investigation cannot adequately monitor reporting accuracy; and most rape victims do not report to law enforcement agencies.

The reasons for not reporting sexual assault are numerous and complicated. Misled beliefs about rape and violence influence a rape victim's understanding of their experience and his/her choice to report and/or seek medical attention and crisis services. For example, what an individual believes constitutes rape, which is often minimized if she/he knew the offender and if there are not visible signs of injury, and whether she/he believes that what happened is a crime worth reporting are central to deciding whether to report the crime. This is tied to issues of being a rape victim: the fear of being blamed, the fear of not being believed, and the **stigma** attached to being raped. Add to this the fears and anxieties related to characteristics of and/or the relationship of the victim or offender—being gay, being a male survivor, being raped by a husband or lover, being raped by someone who shares the same racial or cultural community, especially oppressed groups, being raped by a prominent person, and being victimized in a small or close-knit town with little privacy or lack of resources (especially if the victim is not out as gay, is a male survivor, or belonging to an oppressed group).

Even with underreporting and inaccuracies, both of which the U.S. Bureau of Justice Statistics acknowledges as problems, statistics continue to be gathered through the national crime incident reporting system established in the 1970s. Alongside this local and state crime reporting system, researchers have been conducting surveys and gathering data to document rape. One of the keys to their success has been anonymous self-reporting whereby individuals have the opportunity to report sexual violence without the same level of inhibitions previously mentioned.

When considering the accuracy of rape statistics, it is important to consider that most rape cases are not reported or reflected in reports. Look for consistency among research statistics. Multiyear trends are usually more reliable than single year. Consider the methodology, the size of the sample, the characteristics of the sample (race, age, sex, sexuality, and socioeconomic class, for example), and any political bias influencing a statistical gathering organization. *See also*: **Rape Law**.

Suggested Reading: Bureau of Justice Statistics, http://www.ojp.usdoj.gov/bjs/pub; Bureau of Justice Statistics, *Violence against Women* (Washington, DC: U.S. Department of Justice, 1994); Centers for Disease Control and Prevention, http://www.cdc.gov/ncipc/factsheets/rape.htm; Mark Fazlollah, "Experts Question Accuracy of New Rape Statistics," *Women's Enews*, http://www.womensenews.org/article.cfm/dyn/aid/587; Lawrence A. Greenfield, *Sex Offenses and Offenders: An Analysis of Data on Rape and Sexual Assault* (Washington, DC: Bureau of Justice Statistics, U.S. Department of Justice, 1997); The National Women's Study, *Rape in America: A Report to the Nation* (Arlington, VA: National Center for Victims of Crime, 1992); Melanie Randall and Lori Haskell, "Sexual Violence in Women's Lives: Findings from the Women's Safety Project, a Community Based Survey," *Violence against Women* 1.1 (1995): 6–31; Senate Judiciary Committee, "The Response to Rape," 1993; Robin Warshaw, *I Never Called It Rape* (New York: Harper & Row, 1988).

HEATHER SCHMIDT

RAPE TRAUMA SYNDROME. "Rape trauma syndrome" (RTS)—first delineated by Ann Wolbert Burgess and Lynda Lytle Holmstrom in their now-classic 1974 article of the same name and elaborated in numerous publications thereafter—is a term used to describe the stress response pattern commonly exhibited by **victims** in the aftermath of rape or attempted rape. Before the advent of second-wave feminism, psychological investigations of sexual violence were overwhelmingly preoccupied with the character of the perpetrator, the victim's experience being largely ignored. Redirecting scholarly attention to the problem of female victimization, Burgess and Holmstrom were instrumental in facilitating the remediation of that neglect.

Rape trauma syndrome, as originally conceived, involved two distinct stages—acute and long term—both composed of diverse psychological, somatic, cognitive, and behavioral elements. Beginning immediately after the assault and persisting for days to weeks thereafter, the acute phase encompasses both the initial impact of the rape, which may be communicated through an expressive or guarded emotional style, along with a series of related symptoms (i.e., feelings of fear, anger, guilt, and humiliation; sleep and appetite disturbances; intrusive imagery; and diverse somatic complaints) reflective of the extreme disruption that rape engenders. Victims next enter a period of reorganization that may extend from weeks to years during which they struggle to come to terms with the assault and make whatever practical adjustments are required to enhance their daily functioning, such as changing their telephone number or residence and seeking sustained support from **family** and friends. This phase is distinguished by persistent dreams and nightmares, traumatogenic fears and phobias, and difficulties in personal relationships, all grounded in the circumstances of the rape. There is significant variation in the precise nature, intensity, and duration of symptoms, depending in part on such factors as education, culture, personality, and the violence of the attack; in whatever combination they are manifest, however, these effects provide persuasive evidence of the profound impact of rape upon its many victims.

Researchers have since modified a number of the ideas and assumptions embedded in Burgess and Holmstrom's typology. For example, some have reconceptualized RTS as a three- rather than a two-stage process. On a more substantive level, subsequent studies have sought to address the deficiencies of the original sample, for instance, broadening its parameters to take account of **date rape/acquaintance rape**, which is today recognized as the most prevalent form of **sexual assault** in the United States. In addition, whereas early work in the field dealt exclusively with female victims, for whom sexual assault was then, as it is now, a notoriously commonplace ordeal, it has since been applied to raped males, who have been found to evidence strikingly similar symptomatologies. As a result of these changes, RTS is today a more nuanced and sophisticated diagnostic instrument, cognizant of distinctions in types of rape, the experience of victimization, and the range of potential therapeutic approaches available for improving a victim's postassault functioning. Yet it is by no means immune to criticism. Especially compelling is the claim that RTS effectively pathologizes what are in fact entirely normal responses to rape, in the process removing the crime from the broader social and political context in which it continues to thrive. Questions have also been raised concerning the syndrome's general applicability, developed as it was from a sample of victims who reported their rapes, when the vast majority does not. Likewise, the exclusion of institutionalized women from sampling designs remains problematic, given the extraordinarily high rates of past sexual abuse observed within that population.

Professional perceptions of the utility of the rape trauma syndrome paradigm have also shifted over time. It continues to be widely utilized within the fields of nursing and **law enforcement**, while its stature among **physicians** and psychologists has diminished. Indicatively, RTS does not appear as an independent diagnostic category in the current edition of the American Psychiatric Association's *Diagnostic and Statistical Manual of Mental Disorders* (popularly known as "DSM-IV"), which instead considers rape one of numerous factors that may incite **posttraumatic stress disorder (PTSD)**. Although there is some disagreement as to whether RTS should be construed as an independent entity or a form of PTSD, the latter view now predominates. Indeed, rape victims constitute the single largest group to whom that diagnosis is applied. A parallel process of debate and refinement has occurred within law. While there is no national consensus regarding the admissibility of expert and lay testimony on RTS, most states that have decided the question agree that the likelihood of prejudice against the defendant (or, less often, the alleged victim) is so great that it may not be employed to show whether or not a rape has occurred. However, such testimony is widely permitted for other purposes, most notably to rebut a defense of **consent** or fabrication and to elucidate aspects of a victim's postassault behavior that may appear counterintuitive to jurors. **Rape law** reform notwithstanding, the behavior of the complainant continues to be subjected to intense scrutiny, routinely exceeding that applied to the defendant, to whom comparable diagnostic labels are seldom applied.

The identification of rape trauma syndrome is generally seen as marking an important advance in the recognition of rape's manifold harms. Since the 1970s, a vast body of literature—much of it undertaken from a feminist standpoint—has been generated on the nature of victimization, the process of recovery, and individual treatment modalities. Although RTS has been largely superseded by the PTSD diagnosis, many of its central findings have endured. The proliferation of studies of rape victimology and the crucial insights they have generated have made a vital contribution to ongoing efforts to combat sexual violence, raising professional and public awareness of the prevalence of rape and its often devastating consequences. *See also*: **Dissociative Identity Disorder (DID)**; **Male Rape**.

Suggested Reading: Ann Wolbert Burgess and Lynda Lytle Holmstrom, "Rape Trauma Syndrome," *American Journal of Psychiatry* 131 (1974): 981–986; Deryck Calderwood, "The Male Rape Victim," *Medical Aspects of Human Sexuality* 21 (1987): 53–55; Patricia A. Frazier and Eugene Borgida, "Rape Trauma Syndrome: A Review of Case Law and Psychological Research," *Law and Human Behavior* 16 (1992): 293–311; Susan Stefan, "The Protection Racket: Rape Trauma Syndrome, Psychiatric Labeling, and Law," *Northwestern University Law Review* (1994): 1271–1345.

LISA CARDYN

RAPE TRIALS. During the 1990s a number of highly publicized rape trials and sex scandals catapulted the social problem of rape into public consciousness. The William Kennedy Smith, Mike Tyson, and Marv Albert rape trials, the Clarence Thomas–Anita Hill **sexual harassment** case, and the President Bill Clinton–Monica Lewinsky affair drew attention to the complexity of sexual issues and the deepseated ambiguity of interpreting **sexual assault**. Although rape trials represent only one component in the study of violence against women, the public drama of the trial and the highly political and emotionally charged issues implicated in it provide a novel empirical forum for exploring our cultural practices and the role of the legal institution in society.

The rape trial has been seen to be the centerpiece of feminist theoretical and applied policy interest. Theoretically, rape trials represent a context for understanding male domination and oppression not only in the legal system but also in society more generally. In terms of criminal justice policy, such trials stimulated a massive legal reform movement to (1) increase reporting, **prosecution**, and conviction of rape; (2) improve the harrowing degradation ceremony of the victim during trial; and (3) expand public awareness of sexual assault and alter prejudicial stereotypes of rape, rapists, and **victims**.

In the late 1960s and 1970s feminist researchers demonstrated that the law was not neutral, objective, or rational but ideologically grounded in gender-specific practices. The rape trial was the most public and symbolic manifestation of male domination in law and society. According to feminist theorists like **Catharine MacKinnon** (1987), law as practiced in the rape trial was interpreted in male terms, so that if a woman knew the man, was out on a date with him, dressed provocatively, failed to resist to the utmost, was promiscuous and so on, then she could not have been *legally* assaulted. And legal scholar Susan Estrich noted in her 1987 book *Real Rape* that in contrast to real rape, in which a stranger jumps out of the bushes, the law failed to protect victims of *simple* rape (e.g., dates, acquaintances). If the victim's complaint reached the courtroom, then her sexual history and other highly prejudicial and irrelevant extralegal facts could enter the trial. At trial, the victim would be *raped* a second time, as the defense attorney attempted to transform the victim's experience into routine consensual sex. Thus rape was a discriminatory and criminal practice, keeping women in their place, restricting their freedom of movement and sexual autonomy, instilling a chronic and unsettling fear, and depriving them of their rights; and if physical coercion was not enough, the rape trial functioned as the default option: the legal machinery for legitimating sexual assault and reproducing male domination. Empirical studies of the rape trial illustrate in concrete and moment-by-moment detail precisely *how* domination operates, how interpretations of sexual violence are constituted, and how we perform our sexually gendered identities. That is, such trials have been seen to constitute a vivid and normative representation of how our gender roles should function in society.

This theoretical interest worked in concert with the applied agenda of transforming how the legal system handled rape cases. Responding to the systemic bias in the legal system, proponents of rape reform targeted the rape trial as both the vehicle and object of massive policy change because of its role in legitimating sexual violence. Beginning in the early 1970s feminist scholars, activists, and lawyers (often in conjunction with more conservative law-and-order politicians) successfully lobbied for statutory reforms in the adjudication of rape cases, so that by the 1990s most of the 50 states in the United States as well as the federal government had implemented sweeping trial reforms. New statutes included the following: a gender-neutral degree structure to reflect the seriousness of the assault (first-degree or aggravated sexual assault included the use of a weapon and violence, whereas second-degree occurred without the use of a weapon, etc.); removal of the corroboration requirement, which placed an undue burden of proof on the prosecution; less focus on the victim's resistance than on the amount of force or threat of force employed by the assailant; and most important, rape shield evidentiary rules that prohibited introduction of the victim's sexual history during trial, unsavory and irrelevant details that not only humiliated the victim on the stand but also had a chilling effect on instrumental outcomes of reporting, prosecution, and conviction. In addition to instrumental changes, rape reformers anticipated significant changes in cultural stereotypes about rape—for example, the rapist as primarily a stranger myth.

Although reformers were optimistic about the instrumental outcome of reform, recent criminal justice evaluation questioned whether reform achieved the intended results. The most comprehensive study to date (Spohn and Horney) found that anticipated outcomes post reform failed to materialize, though perhaps some symbolic change occurred in the public's attitude toward rape crimes. Susan Estrich also noted that proposed reforms were of little help to victims of simple rapes, the majority of cases, which involve men the victim knows, dates, meets at a bar, and so on, because these cases still revolve around issues of **consent** and moral-sexual character. Reformers and evaluators provided a number of reasons for lack of success: the courtroom work group, which may decide to admit sexual history evidence; traditional attitudes of jurors; and the prosecuting attorney's office, which operates with a "downstream" orientation to convictability and may thus decline to prosecute a case with only slim prospects of gaining a conviction trial.

A major problem with legal, criminological, and feminist research on the implementation and evaluation of reform was a neglect of what the adversary process looked like. Instead of looking at the nitty-gritty details of trial processes or the law in action, lawyers and rape reformers felt they could understand rape trials and base reforms on abstract legal theorizing or the law on the books. For example, Vivian Berger's highly influential 1977 article on the rape trial noted that rape victims were treated differently than victims of other crimes, but rather than prove this empirically, she used a hypothetical illustration of a male robbery victim being blamed on cross-examination for his complicity in the robbery, a fictitious example designed to highlight the absurdity of blaming rape victims for their assault at trial.

Recent research has gone beyond philosophical theorizing to study the details of actual rape trials. If we think about how a woman's experience of violation is disqualified and made to look like consensual sex, one aspect of the trial becomes transparently relevant. Rape trials are not about truth or falsity but winning and losing, and that, in turn, depends on which side can best wield language as a persuasive tool of power. It has been noted that "our law is a law of words" (Tiersma, 1); and this is especially so in the he-said-she-said type of rape trial. Evidence, inconsistency, **credibility**, moral character, sexual history, force, consent, and coercion are produced and interpreted through courtroom language. And courtroom language in the rape trial, like other contexts, is a difficult object to harness or control. Rather than being a neutral tool for representing reality, language shapes, constitutes, and mediates legal reality at every turn in the trial. Facts are always constructed through this creative, inferential, and moral medium of culture. For example, in the William Kennedy Smith rape trial, defense attorney Roy Black referred to the victim's former boyfriend as "Your daughter's father." Through such a simple depiction of kinship relations, Black legally circumvented rape shield statutes to offer an allusive reference about the victim's sexual history: that she had a child out-of-wedlock. In the rape trial, sexual history and damaging character inferences are routinely produced through ordinary characterizations like the above. Defense attorneys and defendants employ the same ordinary use of language to make the victim's experience look like consensual sex in the courtroom.

Recognizing this crucial role of language in the rape trial, a number of sociolinguists and legal scholars have begun to study how language constructs our sexual identities, molds evidence and our interpretation of facts, and circulates ideas about sexual violence. Researchers have also considered the role of language in the implementation and evaluation of legal change in the trial, grounding their proposals in the empirical details of language and ideology—the law in action. A number of specific—yet quite controversial—proposals have been put forth for modifying the use of language in the rape trial, such as the use of an intermediary who would translate the defense attorney's questions to the victim into less abusive forms. In the William Kennedy Smith rape trial, it was found that rape shield constrains the defense attorney from introducing explicit sexual history information but not the more typical subtle forms. It was noted that reforms may have little impact due to a combination of the adversary culture of winning at all costs and the microlinguistic power of language in constituting legal reality.

Future research needs to calibrate (if any and to what extent) the linguistic and ideological differences among rape trials, other criminal cases, and even civil litigation, perhaps starting from the assumption of similarity and then moving on to document differences empirically and systematically rather than anecdotally or hypothetically (or basing them on advocacy claims). Such an approach would allow researchers to suspend presuppositions about the gender specificity of the rape trial and include other variables, including the systemic features of the adversary system and its role in the revictimization process. This would also permit comparison with other types of offender-victim categories, such as female-female or male-male. The challenge is to consider what linguistic legal reforms, if any, are possible to make the rape trial fair for both victims and defendants. *See also*: **Celebrity Rapists; Rape Shield Laws.**

Suggested Reading: Vivian Berger, "Man's Trial, Woman's Tribulation: Rape Cases in the Courtroom," *Columbia Law Review* 77 (1977): 1–103; Maria Bevacqua, *Rape on the Public Agenda: Feminism and the Politics of Sexual Assault* (Boston: Northeastern University Press, 2000); David Brereton, "How Different Are Rape Trials?" *British Journal of Criminology*

37 (1977): 242–261; Susan Ehrlich, *Representing Rape: Language and Sexual Consent* (New York: Routledge, 2001); Susan Estrich, "Palm Beach Stories," *Law and Philosophy* 11 (1992): 5–33; Susan Estrich, *Real Rape* (Cambridge: Harvard University Press, 1987); Lisa Frohmann, "Discrediting Victim's Allegations of Sexual Assault," *Social Problems* 38 (1991): 213–226; Catharine MacKinnon, *Feminism Unmodified* (Cambridge: Harvard University Press, 1987); Gregory Matoesian, *Law and the Language of Identity: Discourse in the William Kennedy Smith Rape Trial* (New York: Oxford University Press, 2001); Gregory Matoesian, *Reproducing Rape: Domination through Talk in the Courtroom* (Chicago: University of Chicago Press, 1993); Cassia Spohn and Julie Horney, *Rape Law Reform: A Grassroots Revolution and Its Impact* (New York: Plenum Press, 1992); Andrew Taslitz, *Rape and the Culture of the Courtroom* (New York: New York University Press, 1999); Peter Tiersma, *Legal Language* (Chicago: University of Chicago Press, 1999).

GREGORY M. MATOESIAN

RAPISTS. *See* Celebrity Rapists; Serial Rape and Serial Rapists; Sex Offenders; Sexual Predators.

REAL RAPE. *Real Rape* is the title of a widely debated and highly influential book, authored by legal scholar Susan Estrich, subtitled "How the Legal System Victimizes Women Who Say No," and published by Harvard University Press in 1987. Triggered in part by Estrich's own experience of having been raped by a stranger in 1974, the study calls for a new understanding of rape. For too long, the author insists, rape has been recognized only when the perpetrator was unknown to the victim and extrinsic violence or multiple assailants were involved. Both legal institutions and rape **victims** therefore need to acknowledge that so-called simple (acquaintance) rape is as real a rape as is aggravated or stranger rape. In more than 90 percent of all rapes, perpetrator and victim are acquainted with each other prior to the assault. However, due to misconceived racialized notions of male and female sexuality, legal institutions have tended to distrust certain victims in such cases, forcing them to prove that their own behavior did not provoke the assault.

Estrich not only shows that cases of simple rape equal conquests of **credibility** in both common and modern law approaches; she also foregrounds that despite major reforms of American and Canadian **rape law** in the 1970s the so-called force doctrine remains an efficient means to screen out simple rapes and to blame victims for their own violation. Aiming at redefinitions of "**consent**," "force," and "coercion," Estrich's argument insists on reading rape cases in new ways. Employing the term *real rape* in "an argument for change" (7), her study contributed considerably to victims' sense of their own violation, to the rise of the term **date rape**, to the comprehensive feminist conception of rape, and to a broad awareness of the continuum of sexual violence against women and men. *See also*: **Date/Acquaintance Rape.**

Suggested Reading: Susan Estrich, *Real Rape: How the Legal System Victimizes Women Who Say No* (Cambridge: Harvard University Press, 1987); Andrea Parrot and Laurie Bechhofer, eds., *Acquaintance Rape: The Hidden Crime* (New York: Wiley, 1991).

SABINE SIELKE

RELIGION. Major world religions, including Judaism, Christianity, Islam, Buddhism, and Hinduism, have functioned as societal forces that contribute to rape-prone discourse and behavior. They have neither clearly nor persistently condemned rape practices and theories. One reason for this age-old problem relates to androcentric views on women and sexuality. Androcentrism has made religious authorities and laypeople question a victim-survivor's rather than a rapist's sexual and religious integrity. Sacred texts, religious doctrines, rituals, and laws have silenced raped women, children, and even men and made it possible to discard charges of rape.

Yet with the emergence of the global **feminist movement** in the twentieth century feminist scholars began exposing the rape tolerance of many religious traditions. Often personally committed to the religion under consideration, they critique rape-prone religious discourse and offer alternative religious theories and practices. To date, feminist theologians and scholars have primarily focused on Christian and Jewish traditions; research on other religions is in the early stages. Some of the positions on rape surfacing from Judaism, Christianity, Islam, Buddhism, and Hinduism are discussed here.

Jewish **literature** has included discussions on rape, perhaps because the Hebrew **Bible** contains many rape texts. Among the most horrific stories is the **gang rape** of a woman called "a concubine" who dies after the nightlong raping and is subsequently cut into twelve pieces by her cowardly husband (Judges 19). Another prominent story describes the rape of Princess Tamar, who is sexually assaulted by her half brother Amnon (2 Samuel 13). Rape laws appear in Deuteronomy 22:22–29. Postbiblical literature also refers to rape. For instance, in Ketubot 39a–b and 51b of the Babylonian Talmud, the rabbis acknowledged the pain of a raped woman and prohibited **marital rape**. Also the medieval rabbi Maimonides recognized the innocence of a woman forced into sexual intercourse (Biale, 239–255). Still, rabbinical discourse did not abandon the idea of rape as a marital rather than a criminal matter, and so they did not prescribe criminal punishment for the rapist. Instead rabbinical texts focused on the raped woman who, however, was given substantial decision-making power (Hauptman, 77–97).

Christian theologians did not make rape an explicit topic in most of their treatises. Hardly ever were biblical rape texts included in the lectionary, the prescribed selection of biblical texts read during Christian worship services. Consequently, even today many Christians remain unaware of biblical rape prose and poetry. Still, some theologians articulated their views. One of the earliest is the patristic writer Jerome (347–420 C.E.). Although Jerome was generally opposed to suicide, he advised women to commit suicide after rape because "[he] [Christ] has no power to crown one who has been corrupted" (Jerome, 138). Another patristic theologian, Augustine (354–430 C.E.), contested Jerome's position dominant in the Roman Empire. In his work *The City of God*, Augustine prohibited suicide after rape because in his view rape was ultimately for a woman's own good. It helped her to deepen her faith and to purify her soul.

In later centuries, some Christian mystics relied on rape metaphors to describe their union with God. The fourteenth-century mystic St. Teresa of Avila felt overwhelmed by divine shafts of love. The seventeenth-century poet-mystic John Donne pictured himself as being overshadowed by the divine presence. He wrote: "Batter my heart, three-person'd God . . . you ravish [i.e., rape] me" (Cooper-White, 89). Mostly, however, Christian theologians did not concern themselves with rape. Encountering the issue, for instance, in biblical texts, it has been noted that they usually redefined rape as **"seduction"** or "love."

Islam dealt with rape mostly in legal practice. In Pakistan the so-called *Hudud* Ordinance has regulated rape since 1979. Accordingly, rape is included as an "offense of *Zina*" (by force), which criminalizes extramarital sexual relations. One of the stipulations is that four Muslim adult men must have witnessed the sexual transgression. Predictably, raped Muslim women rarely come forward with charges of rape. Not only do they face death threats from male **family** members who want to restore the family honor, raped women might also receive the death penalty by the state if they cannot prove their innocence. So-called honor killings are a considerable problem in Muslim countries, even in those not ruled by Islamic law. Muslim feminists criticize the discriminatory legal practice. They maintain that the Qur'an, the Islamic holy book, does not support the current interpretation of Islamic jurisprudence or the male honor system. To them, *zina* does not include nonconsensual sex or rape. Moreover, the Qur'an charges not to doubt the character of a woman.

Another religious tradition, Buddhism, tells stories of nuns who struggle with male sexual force. One of them is the beautiful Subhā. Attacked, Subhā tries to instruct the man about the delusions of physical pleasure and beauty. When he does not let her go, she mutilates herself in front of him by pulling out one of her eyes. Immediately the rapist's "passion disappeared," and he exclaims: "I wish you well, chaste lady; this sort of thing won't happen again" (Wilson, 168). Perhaps the story reinforces the stereotype that beautiful women are more endangered by rape than other women. Some interpreters maintain that in this story the woman turns from an object to a subject. Subhā succeeds in being treated as a "woman of insight—a seer and not just a sight to be seen" because she was willing to eschew "the female gaze" (169).

In the Nyingma lore is a story about Lady Yeshe Tsogyel (sometimes Tsogyal), an eighth-century Tibetan princess, who greets her rapists enthusiastically and transforms the event into the occasion for their enlightenment. According to the text, Lady Yeshe Tsogyel defines the rape as a "lustful disposition" and "creative vision of the deity." She seems neither victimized nor vengeful. Some scholars therefore consider her as the most powerful female Buddhist archetype and a tantric adept.

Hindu literature also contains references to rape that scholars mention in the context of marriage customs. For instance, the foundational text of the Hindu religion, the Mahābhārata, includes narratives that praise "marriage by capture." Even Lord Krishna, one of the major divine figures in Hinduism, is sometimes characterized as "a bold woman-snatcher" (Meyer, 68–69). Stories tell of men like Bhāshma, the son of Cāntanu, and Duryodhana who abduct women. In these tales the **abductions** involve forced sexual intercourse, but eventually the women come to love their abductors and **consent** to marriage. One story tells of Arjuna who sees Krishna's sister, Subhadrā. Krishna encourages Arjuna to "carry her off by force," which he does. In time, Arjuna marries the willing Subhadrā. Moreover, myths and rituals about goddesses, particularly the goddess Kāli, know of sexual violence. Some interpreters view these texts as religious sublimation for the manifold rapes of women and girls. Women who are violated in society become mythical men-killers. As a result of this religious dynamic, men and women have been seen to ignore the actual violence against women and girls.

Furthermore, the Upanishads, sacred Hindu texts, contain a passage that excuses the rape of a woman who is unwilling to consent to sexual intercourse: "If she should not grant him his desire, he should bribe her. If she still does not grant him his desire, he should hit her with a stick or with his hand, and overcome her, saying: 'With power, with glory I take away your glory!' Thus she becomes inglorious" (Pinkham, 68). Dalit ("Untouchables") opponents to the Hindu caste system quote these and other passages to demonstrate the prejudicial nature of Hinduism. They also describe the system of the Devadasi as an illustration for the prejudicial thought patterns of this religion. The system of Devadasi coerced young pubescent girls, often from the Dalit cast, to be offered to the deities in Brahmanic temples. After "the first night," traditionally spent with a priest or a wealthy man, the girls were forced into lifelong **prostitution**.

In conclusion, prejudices and stereotypes about rape permeate much of religious discourse and practice. Consequently, religious leaders and thinkers have rarely sided with raped victim-survivors. Only with the emergence of feminist critique are rape-prone religious literature, ritual, myth, and beliefs recognized for their harm of women. It remains to be seen whether the feminist critique will substantially change religious traditions so that they foster a rape-free world. *See also:* **Mythology; Tribal Customs and Laws.**

Suggested Reading: Rachel Biale, *Women and Jewish Law: An Exploration of Women's Issues in Halakhic Sources* (New York: Schocken Books, 1984); Sarah Caldwell, *Oh Terrifying Mother: Sexuality, Violence and Worship of the Goddess Kāli* (New Delhi: Oxford University Press, 1999); Pamela Cooper-White, "Rape," in *The Cry of Tamar: Violence against Women and the Church's Response* (Minneapolis, MN: Fortress Press, 1995, 77–99); Judith Hauptman, *Rereading the Rabbis: A Woman's Voice* (Boulder, CO: Westview Press, 1998); Human Rights Watch, "Broken People: IX. Attacks on Dalit Women: A Pattern of Impunity," http://hrw.org/reports/1999/india/India994-11.htm; Jerome, *The Letters of St. Jerome: Ancient Christian Writers*, vol. 1 (Westminster, MD: Newmann Press, 1963); Johann Jakob Meyer, *Sexual Life in Ancient India: A Study in the Comparative History of Indian Culture* (Delhi: Motilal Banarsidass, 1971); Mary Pellauer, "Augustine on Rape: One Chapter in the Theological Tradition," in *Violence against Women and Children: A Christian Theological Sourcebook*, ed. Carol J. Adams and Marie M. Fortune (New York: Continuum, 1998), 206–241; Mildreth Worth Pinkham, *Woman in the Sacred Scriptures of Hinduism* (New York: Columbia University Press, 1941); Asifa Quraishi, "Her Honor: An Islamic Critique of the Rape Laws of Pakistan from a Woman-Sensitive Perspective," in *Windows of Faith: Muslim Scholar-Activists in North America*, ed. Gisela Webb (Syracuse, NY: Syracuse University Press, 2000), 102–135; Susanne Scholz, "Was It Really Rape in Genesis 34? Biblical Scholarship as a Reflection of Cultural Assumptions," in *Escaping Eden: New Feminist Perspectives on the Bible*, ed. Harold C. Washington et al. (Sheffield: Sheffield Academic Press, 1998), 182–198; "What Is the Devadasi System," http://www.dalitstan.org/books/decline/decline11.html; Liz Wilson, *Charming Cadavers: Horrific Figurations of the Feminine in Indian Buddhist Hagiographic Literature* (Chicago: University of Chicago Press, 1996); Lady Yeshe Tsogyel, http://www.dabase.net/padskydan.htm.

SUSANNE SCHOLZ

REPORTING. *See* **Media; Rape Shield Laws.**

RESISTANCE. Resistance is opposing another's will. When the desires of human beings conflict, resistance defines the boundary between their wills. Passive or active, expressed or unexpressed, subtle or violent, brief or sustained, premeditated or spontaneous, resistance is always an opposing force against the advancing will of another. And given that desires often conflict, resistance pervades human relations.

Nowhere in human relations do desires more frequently conflict than when pursuing sexual pleasure. The pursuit of shared sexual pleasure is rife with advances and resistance. Moreover, differing personal experiences and beliefs about sexuality easily make another's desires unclear. For many, the interplay and ambiguity of desires contribute to sexual pleasure. Indeed for some, dramatic staging of roles provides an opportunity when one's own resistance to another's will can be safely and pleasurably overpowered. Rape occurs when one person's resistance to another's sexual intentions is overpowered without **consent**. Rape is when one's boundary of resistance against a conflicting will is trespassed. Regardless of ambiguities, overpowering someone's resistance to sexual activity can cause irreparable trauma and is legally inexcusable.

Evidence of resistance has an important role in the legal determination of a rape **victim**'s lack of consent. In many cases, a victim's resistance is unambiguous, making determination and **prosecution** of rape relatively straightforward. If the perpetrator had to forcibly overcome significant physical resistance by the victim, indications like bruises and cuts will likely be left on the victim's body. Historically, evidence of a high level of physical resistance was required for prosecution: "[T]he female must resist to the utmost of her ability, and such resistance must continue till the offense is complete" (*Reidhead v. State*, 31 Ariz 70, 71, 250 P. 366, 377 (1926)). This is often called the force-resistance requirement. **Rape law** reformers have since argued that a standard of "utmost resistance" is not sensitive to interpersonal dynamics present during rape. They argue that dynamics like severe imbalances of social power, a victim's fear of bodily harm, or misinterpretation of intentions must be considered when determining the level and type of resistance required for demonstrating nonconsent. Legally, "reasonable resistance" has come to replace "utmost resistance." Consequently, other forms, like verbal resistance, would be sufficient indication of nonconsent.

While a broader consideration of resistance is more useful for describing the violation of a victim's will, it forces legislation to navigate problematic ambiguity in human relations. Interpreting another person's sexual behavior can be difficult. Even more difficult is determining people's desires and resistance from the third-party vantage point of the court. Nonphysical resistance rarely leaves clear evidence. For instance, a person may have rebuffed another's advances by clearly saying "no," and then, for fear of bodily harm, have submitted to the other's persistence. In this case, determination of the victim's consent may be limited to judging between their conflicting stories. Such judgment is further obscured when the individuals have had a prior relationship.

More complex problems arise from disagreement over the forms and extent of resistance necessary to constitute rape. Should a verbal "no" be enough resistance? Is one always responsible for asking about another's desires or communicating one's own? Who is responsible for a misunderstanding? What if one resists after initially submitting? Disagreement in society about the nature of sexuality, sexual ethics, and gender relationships contributes to both the difficulty and the importance of achieving consensus on clear standards. Beliefs about appropriate sexual behavior and responsibility differ widely. For example, some believe that for a woman to be "respectable," she must initially offer "token resistance," even though she actually wishes to engage a man sexually. As such, her "no" is interpreted as "yes." Such beliefs are often called **"rape myths"** by rape law reformers. Rape myths like this one can influence a man's response to a woman's actual resistance. They can also influence court members who are deliberating over a case of accused rape. Reformers often focus on dismantling rape myths through wide social education movements, arguing that misinterpretation of resistance must be addressed by changing fundamental beliefs about sexuality prevalent throughout society.

The boundary between wills that resistance creates, whatever form it takes, is the site where shared sexual pleasure can become rape. Having one's resistance to another's will for sexual pleasure overpowered can cause serious physical harm, traumatically alter one's sense of self, and forever affect one's relation to other people. Considering the amount and forms of a victim's resistance is crucial for the legal prosecution of rape cases. But given the inherent ambiguity of human relations, the difficulty in determining forms of resistance by a third party, and conflicting social beliefs about sexuality, the nature of resistance to rape will remain a site of constant public dispute. *See also*: **Rape Prevention**.

Suggested Reading: Susan Ehrlich, *Representing Rape: Language and Sexual Consent* (New York: Routledge, 2001); Alan Soble, ed., *The Philosophy of Sex: Contemporary Readings*, 4th ed. (Lanham, MD: Rowman and Littlefield, 2002).

JUDSON ODELL

ROHYPNOL. Rohypnol, known in clubs and on the street as "Roofies," "Roche," and the "Forget-me pill," is primarily purchased for its use in situations of "**drug-facilitated sexual assault.**" Rohypnol is particularly dangerous since it is tasteless, odorless, and dissolves easily in carbonated beverages. As with many other club drugs, its sedative and toxic effects are increased with the use of **alcohol**. However, even without the use of alcohol, a dose as small as one milligram can impair a victim for as long as 8 to 12 hours. While Rohypnol is generally administered orally by dissolving it in a drink, it can also be ground up and snorted. Chemically, Rohypnol is categorized in the class of drugs known as benzodiazepines (e.g., Valium, Xanax, and Versed). Although it has not been approved by the federal Food and Drug Administration for medical use in the United States, it is manufactured and distributed by Hoffman-LaRoche in 64 countries as a treatment for insomnia, as a sedative, and as a presurgical anesthetic.

The symptoms of Rohypnol include muscle relaxation, sleepiness, nausea, difficulties in speaking or even moving, visual problems, hypotension (low blood pressure), hallucinations, and blackouts that last from 8 to 24 hours. Chronic use can lead to physical and psychological dependence. Withdrawal is also dangerous in that it can lead to headaches, confusion, numbness, convulsions, and shock. Rohypnol can produce profound anterograde amnesia (i.e., people cannot remember the events that they experienced while under the effects of the drug). Even under hypnosis, these events cannot be recalled because they were not actually processed. Consequently, **survivors** of **sexual assault** who were given Rohypnol cannot identify their attackers. *See also*: **Ecstasy; Gammahydroxybutyrate (GHB); Ketamine**.

Suggested Reading: National Women's Health Information Center, "The 'Date Rape' Drug," http://www.4woman.gov/faq/rohypnol.htm.

JUDITH A. WATERS AND SHARON A. DROZDOWSKI

ROIPHE, KATIE (1968–). Author of *The Morning After: Sex, Feminism and Fear on Campus* (1993), Katie (Katherine) Roiphe criticized feminists for enlarging the definition of rape to include sexual contact brought about by verbal coercion on the grounds that this expanded definition of rape reinforced the stereotype of women as weak and passive. Roiphe claimed that the emphasis on "verbal coercion" was a mask for claims that "women need to be protected from men who don't share their social background." Roiphe also alleged that many female college students who are motivated by guilt or regret over consensual sexual encounters make false claims of **date rape**. Her characterization of the political climate on college campuses as dominated by overly vigilant feminists resonated with many conservative critics. Because Roiphe was in her twenties when her ideas first garnered national attention, her work is often cited as that of a "Generation X" feminist, in contrast to older feminists whose theories about rape centered on the importance of believing a woman's accounts of her own experience. Critics of Roiphe believe that she trivializes the reality of rape. Her critics also point to Roiphe's sheltered Manhattan upbringing and Ivy League education when describing the limits of Roiphe's perspective. Roiphe is also the author of *Last Night in Paradise: Sex and Morals and the Century's End* (1997), a discussion of sexual behavior in the HIV-fearing, post–sexual revolution era. Her first novel *She Still Haunts Me: A Novel* (2002) is a fictionalized account between Charles Dodgson (who wrote under the pen name Lewis Carroll) and Alice Liddell, the inspiration for *Alice in Wonderland*. *See also*: **Dworkin, Andrea; Feminist Movement; Freidan, Betty; MacKinnon, Catharine A.; Pornography; Steinem, Gloria.**

Suggested Reading: Katherine T. Bartlett, Angela Harris, and Deborah Rhode, eds., *Gender and the Law: Theory, Doctrine and Commentary* (New York: Aspen Publishers, 2002).

BRIDGET J. CRAWFORD

RULES OF EVIDENCE. Guidelines for what can and cannot be used as evidence in a **rape trial** are found in the rules of evidence of the jurisdiction in which the defendant is tried. The purpose of these rules is to clarify all forms of acceptable evidence that are relevant to the scope of a trial so that defendants can mount the most complete defense possible. In both state and federal rules, there exists a rape shield provision that limits the evidence that a defendant can introduce about the **victim**'s prior sexual history.

The Federal Rules of Evidence offer an example of such a provision. Under the original Rule 404(a)(2) (regarding the introduction of character evidence for crime victims, including victims of rape), rape defendants could present evidence of the victim's past sexual behavior in mounting a defense that the sexual act in question was consensual. However, the broad scope of the rule permitted wide-ranging inquiries into the sex lives of rape victims, thus distracting juries from the defendants' conduct, embarrassing and harassing the victims, and discouraging victims from pressing charges or cooperating with prosecutors.

For this reason, a new Federal Rule of Evidence (Rule 412) was included in the Privacy Protection for Rape Victims Act of 1978, which was signed into law by President Jimmy Carter on October 30 of that year. The rule's intent was "to protect rape victims from the degrading and embarrassing disclosure of intimate details about their private lives" during the course of rape trials, which would presumably encourage more victims to report instances of **sexual assault** and to cooperate with prosecuting attorneys.

Rule 412 prohibits the introduction at trial of reputation or opinion evidence of a rape victim's sexual history. The justification for that rule is that prior consensual sexual acts are irrelevant to the issue of whether a victim consented to have sex with a particular person at a particular time. Three important exceptions to Rule 412 were included to protect the defendant's interest in presenting a full defense. The first concerns evidence that a rape defendant has a constitutional right to introduce; the second is for evidence of sexual behavior between the victim and persons other than the defendant, which the defendant offers as proof that he was not the source of semen or injury; and the third is for past sexual behavior between the victim and defendant, which the defendant is allowed to offer in order to show consent. In the second and third instances, such evidence can be introduced only when the trial judge finds that it is both relevant and more probative than prejudicial. *See also*: **Cox Broadcasting Corporation v. Cohn**; **Michigan v. Lucas**; **Rape Shield Laws.**

Suggested Reading: Barbara E. Bergman and Nancy Hollander, *Wharton's Criminal Evidence*, 15th ed. (Eegan, MN: West, 2001), 4: 41.

GREGORY M. DUHL

S

SCHOOLS. A wide range of sex-related crimes are perpetrated against children ranging in ages from approximately 4 to 18 years old. For younger children, the studies and stories confirm that a wide incidence of molestation and rape with an object are most common. At the other end of the age spectrum, forcible rape and **drug-facilitated sexual assault** are typical, as well as daily **sexual harassment.** Gay/lesbian/bisexual/transsexual–identified youth suffer harassment relentlessly. Students identified as "disabled" by others have a much greater chance of being sexually assaulted.

Interact, the **rape crisis center** of Wake County, North Carolina, provides recent national statistics in their report "N.C. 2001 Rape Statistics: Children at Highest Risk." The following **rape statistics** are cited in this report:

- Boys and girls ages 19 and under are the most frequent **victims** of rape.
- Approximately 1.8 million adolescents in the United States have been the victims of **sexual assault.**
- Thirty-three percent of sexual assaults occur when the victim is between the ages of 12 and 17.
- Females comprised 82 percent of all juvenile victims.
- Teens 16 to 19 years of age were 3.5 times more likely than the general population to be victims of rape, attempted rape, or sexual assault.
- Twenty-three percent of all **sexual offenders** were under the age of 18.
- An offender was arrested in 32 percent of the cases involving victims ages 12 to 17.
- Forty-two percent of girls younger than 15 years reported that their first sexual intercourse experience was nonconsensual.

Due to the pandemic of sexual violence in schools in the United States, the government stepped in to monitor and implement solutions for the situation. One resolution was the Safe and Drug-Free Schools and Communities Act of 1994. This act provided funding for school-based violence prevention programs. The National

Center for Education Statistics was funded to research violence in the schools, and the result was a report titled *Violence and Discipline Problems in U.S. Public Schools: 1996–97*. The center found that 10 percent of crimes reported to school officials were violent in nature ("murder, suicide, rape or sexual battery, physical attack or fight with a weapon, or robbery"). Four thousand rapes, defined as "rape, fondling, indecent liberties, child molestation or sodomy," were reported in schools that year. For every 1,000 students in schools around the country, according to this report, 0.1 reported rape to a teacher, counselor, or principal. In contrast, the **National Crime Victimization Survey** of 1995 surveyed persons in their homes and showed a much larger percentage of minors as the victims of sexual crime: For every 1,000 12- to 14-year-olds, 3.5 reported rape, and out of every 1,000 15- to 17-year-olds, 6 reported.

While there is a marked increase of reporting outside the school, this is not entirely due to the incredible safety of the public institutions of learning in the United States. In many schools, abstinence is the only sex education taught. The prevalence of **rape myths** among students *and* teachers is widespread. If there is no understanding adult to turn to, or the child/adolescent/young adult is not believed because of his or her past behavior, the crime may go "unreported." Therefore, surveys such as the education study cited can make public schools seem like safe havens. However, the reality of the students' situations can become so unbearable that the circumstances may warrant involvement with the courts for resolution. That was the case in an instance of sexual harassment that has changed national school policy.

In May 24, 1999, Title IX, a 1972 amendment to the Constitution, was challenged in a lawsuit filed in *Davis v. Monroe County Board of Education* by parents of a fifth-grade girl who had been repeatedly sexually harassed. The crux of the case was the charge that the school had purposely ignored the case and that the harassment impeded the student's education. The school board lost the case, and the plaintiff was awarded damages. The result of that case is that a student can now sue any school for one-on-one sexual harassment charges when the proper criteria are met. *See also*: **Campus Rape; Campus Security Act (Clery Act)**.

Suggested Reading: Interact, "N.C. 2001 Rape Statistics: Children at Highest Risk," http://www.interactofwake.org/home.htm; Julie Lewis, "Supreme Court Updated: *Davis v. Monroe County Board of Education*," American Association of School Administrators, http://www.aasa.org; Ryan Morgan, "Colorado University Faces Title IX Suit in Rape Case," *The Denver Post*, October 21, 2002; "Statement by Pascal D. Forgione, Jr., Ph.D., U.S. Commissioner of Education Statistics," *Violence and Discipline Problems in U.S. Public Schools: 1996–97*, National Center for Education Statistics," http://nces.ed.gov/.

EMILY RIVENDELL

SCOTTSBORO BOYS CASE. On March 31, 1931, two white women, Victoria Price (age 21) and Ruby Bates (age 17), claimed that they had been beaten and raped by a gang of nine **African American** youths while traveling illegally on board a train through northeastern Alabama. The women's allegations sparked a national furor over the case of the "Scottsboro Boys." Advocates for the defense claimed that the women's "low moral character" cast doubt on their charges of rape. The **prosecution** argued that the women deserved equal protection under the law and that evidence of semen found on the women indicated that they had been sexually assaulted. Set against the backdrop of the Great Depression, the case highlighted many of the racial, gender, and class tensions evident in the New South.

Price and Bates claimed that they had hopped freight trains to travel to Chattanooga in search of work and were attacked on board the train as they returned to Alabama. The women claimed that the defendants were armed with knives and guns and that they traveled together in a gang. The women's descriptions were at odds with the physical characteristics and origins of the defendants. Charlie Weems, Clarence Norris, Ozie Powell, Olin Montgomery, and Willie Roberson were from Georgia, whereas Haywood Patterson, Andy and Roy Wright, and Eugene Williams were from Tennessee. The defendants' ages ranged from 12 to 20 years, with Roy Wright being the youngest. Olin Montgomery was nearly blind, and Willie Roberson suffered from syphilis and gonorrhea and had to walk with a cane; physicians concluded that sexual intercourse would have been extremely painful for Roberson.

The first trial took place from April 6 to 9, in Scottsboro, Alabama; a series of four trials and numerous retrials would take place over the next six years in Scottsboro and in Decatur. **Physicians** who examined the women testified that they found little evidence of **sexual assault**; they did acknowledge that both Price and Bates had had recent sexual intercourse, citing the presence of "nonmotile" (inactive) semen present in the victim's bodies two hours after the alleged rape. All of the defendants claimed to be innocent; however, several of the men offered conflicting accounts of the train, and Norris and Patterson accused several of the others of committing the crime. The initial trials resulted in a guilty verdict for eight of the defendants; twelve-year-old Roy Wright was awarded a mistrial due to his age. Judge Alfred Hawkins sentenced the eight others to death by electrocution. The case became a cause célèbre as northern papers decried the "legal lynching" of eight men on flimsy evidence. Both the International Labor Defense (ILD) wing of the Communist Party of the United States and the National Association for the Advancement of Colored People (NAACP) worked on behalf of the defendants; however, these organizations remained at loggerheads throughout the proceedings. The ILD considered the NAACP too moderate; members of the NAACP thought the Communists were jeopardizing the defendants' lives to provide propaganda for spread of communism. Eventually the ILD, the NAACP, and the American Civil Liberties Union (ACLU) would form a joint partnership to establish the Scottsboro Defense Committee in 1935.

Subsequent trials would castigate the female accusers; defense attorneys claimed that both women had engaged in interracial relationships and had worked as prostitutes in Alabama. Defense attorneys suggested that the women leveled rape charges to distract public attention from their own vagrancy and criminal background. In *Powell v. Alabama* (1932) and *Norris v. Alabama* (1932), the U.S. Supreme Court overturned convictions, citing inadequate counsel and procedural errors.

In 1933, Bates recanted her testimony, claiming that she and Price had fabricated the rape charges in an effort to escape arrest for vagrancy. She claimed that both Price and herself had had voluntary sexual intercourse with male acquaintances the night before the alleged rape. By this point, however, Bates appeared to have received financial assistance from the ILD, and her testimony was considered suspect; after the trial she briefly toured the country as a guest speaker for the ILD. She also wrote to the defendants in prison, appeared with their parents at rallies on their behalf, and met with four of the men who were released in 1937.

Subsequent proceedings (1935–1937) resulted in renewed convictions for four defendants, but in 1937, Alabama prosecutors dropped charges against Montgomery, Roy Wright, Roberson, and Williams. Charles Weems was released from prison in 1943; the following year Andy Wright and Clarence Norris were also released; however, both men broke parole by moving north and were sent back to prison. Ozie Powell remained in prison on unrelated charges. Haywood Patterson escaped from prison in 1948 and moved to Detroit, where he was eventually convicted of manslaughter in another case and returned to prison. In 1976 Alabama Governor George Wallace pardoned Clarence Norris, the sole living defendant in the Scottsboro case. Bates died that same year; Price remarried and moved to Tennessee. Price maintained her story of rape until she died in 1982.

The Scottsboro trials remain an infamous example of the racial prejudice and suspicion black men faced in the South. The economic circumstances that led Price and Bates to ride the rails in search of work, legal or otherwise, received little attention at the time. Most contemporary historians and legal scholars concede that Price's and Bates's claims of rape were specious, yet allegations of rape made by white female accusers carried more weight in a society dominated by white supremacy. *See also*: **Gang Rape**; **Interracial Rape**; **Rape-Lynch Scenario**.

Suggested Reading: Dan Carter, *Scottsboro: A Tragedy of the American South*, rev. ed. (Baton Rouge: Louisiana State University Press, 1979); James Goodman, *Stories of Scottsboro* (New York: Pantheon Books, 1994); Kwando Mbiassi Kinshasa, *The Man from Scottsboro: Clarence Norris in His Own Words* (Jefferson, NC: McFarland, 1997); Haywood Patterson, *Scottsboro Boy* (Garden City, NY: Doubleday, 1950).

REGAN SHELTON

SECONDARY RAPE. *Secondary rape* is the term commonly given to describe the process of investigation that agencies, institutions, or individuals perform when questioning a rape **victim**. It is considered "secondary" rape because the event has the same characteristics as the primary or original rape: It exerts power, it is invasive, it is destructive of privacy, and it denies the victim control over his or her body and person. For these reasons, some women also use the term *secondary rape* to describe being forced to give birth after conceiving from a rape.

An example of secondary rape is when police question the victim in a way that treats her or him as a perpetrator rather than a person who was injured. Officers might use language that casts doubt on the victim's complaint, is accusatory, or insinuates that the victim did something to instigate and cause the rape. Even within the last decade police have regarded some rape complaints with suspicion. Black women, poor women, or women considered to be promiscuous are often not believed. Before U.S. states began enacting laws against **marital rape** in the 1970s, married women of any social class or background could not charge their spouses with rape. By extension, police also would not accept complaints of rape from a live-in partner of either sex.

During the processing of the crime, the victim goes through many stages of secondary rape. She or he is questioned and subjected to inspection and photography of the body parts that were penetrated, touched, injured, or covered with semen or other body fluids. The bright lights and awkward positions put the victim in the same or more vulnerable circumstances from a psychological point of view than the original rape. Once again the privacy and integrity of the individual is compromised and invaded. Getting evidence in a rape case results in a secondary rape for many individuals because it contains many of the elements of the primary rape.

After **law enforcement** and medical personnel question and obtain evidence from the victim, a period of time elapses while the legal system arranges for identification of the perpetrator and for a court hearing. During this time, the victim is urged to seek professional help in dealing with the trauma. As the event fades from the present, healing begins to take place. However, since the law requires the victim to testify against the perpetrator or perpetrators if they are found, the shock of going to court and facing his or her attacker, as well as having to answer the attorneys' questions, may awaken the profound psychological distress and the victim is forced to relive the rape once again, this time in public. *See also*: **Rape Kit**; **Rape Trauma Syndrome**.

Suggested Reading: Susan Brownmiller, *Against Our Will: Men, Women and Rape* (New York: Fawcett Columbine, 1975); Lee Madigan and Nancy Gamble, *The Second Rape: Society's Continued Betrayal of the Victim* (New York: Lexington Books, 1989).

LANA THOMPSON

SEDUCTION. Seduction is generally understood as an act or phenomenon aimed at misleading a person or a group of people. Enticed by a seducer, for instance, the seduced is supposedly led astray and persuaded to engage in acts that are considered to be morally wrong or unlawful. In a more figural sense of the term, groups of people are said to be seduced by political ideologies and economic systems, for example, by the mechanisms of global consumer culture. Holding strong sexual overtones, the concept seduction tends to suggest that, oftentimes in addition to an imbalance in age or mental maturity, the relationship of seducer and seduced is characterized by a social, economic, gender, or racial hierarchy. Due to its multiple moral and ethic implications, the term *seduction* thus involves a fluid dynamics of power and guilt, which engages both the seducer, who acts with an intention to mislead, and the seduced, who seemingly allows herself or himself to be led astray.

As a highly contested term, *seduction* is frequently employed to distinguish consensual sexual acts from sexual acts that involve physical coercion. While the concept seduction entails the overriding of the conscious will of the seduced by the seducer, oftentimes by rhetorical or verbal coercion or the powerful physical presence of seducer or seductress, historically it has also implied a certain degree of **consent** on the part of the seduced. Seduction therefore seems to operate somewhere between courtship and rape. By convention, since any equivocation and acquiescent gesture on the victim's, traditionally the woman's, part signal seduction, merely their absence and unequivocal **resistance** mark rape. The term *seduction* therefore tends to displace the guilt from the perpetrator to the victim. Feminist criticism holds that legal institutions have tended to reduce cases of rape to seduction narratives, which in turn redefined rape as constituted not by the violator's coercion but by the victim's nonconsent.

The tendency to view seduction and rape as binary opposition is partly due to the significance of the seduction motif, in both its comic and tragic mode, for literary history. Projecting fictions of premarital sexuality leading to loss and the downfall of both seducer and seduced, early British and American novels, such as Samuel Richardson's *Clarissa* (1747–1748) and Susanna Rowson's *Charlotte Temple* (1791), established the seduction motif as the dominant figure of (hetero-)

sexual encounter/seduction The cultural effect of seduction fictions on the construction of sexuality, as well as gender, class, and race relations, has been manifold. Even though Victorian seduction narratives upheld a single standard of chastity for men and women and channeled both female sexuality and patterns of manhood, seduction narratives have tended to establish gender differences as difference in sexuality and to project female sexuality as victimization. As a counterforce to enlightened ideas, seduction narratives insisted that new liberties and the decline of parental control of marriage made women increasingly vulnerable and thereby triggered the fetishization of **virginity** as capital. Identifying premarital sexuality with economic danger and social death, seduction narratives were geared to limit female desire to matrimony where sexual intercourse, consensual or not, is a legitimate act and "duty." At the same time seduction narratives have lastingly equivocated the violence that sexual acts possibly entail, overriding the difference between consensual and nonconsensual sexuality.

The term *seduction* also gained prominence in psychoanalysis. In the 1890s, **Sigmund Freud** proposed a theory of the aetiology of neuroses called the seduction theory, which argued that neuroses resulted from the aftereffects of sexual abuse in childhood. Unable to discern whether his patients' traumatic memories were triggered by imagined or real scenes of abuse, Freud discarded this theory, however, and turned toward the exploration of infantile sexuality and the Oedipal complex instead. Feminist critics retrospectively take this abandonment as a turning away from the widespread sexual abuse on children. They also objected to Freud's conception of female sexuality as by nature masochistic, which has contributed to a general tendency to blur the distinction between seduction and rape and to write sexual violence out of the social text. *See also*: **Literature, World and American; Rape, Definitions of.**

Suggested Reading: John Forrester, "Rape, Seduction, and Psychoanalysis," in *Rape*, ed. Sylvana Tomaselli and Roy Porter (Oxford: Basil Blackwell, 1986), 57–83; Christine Froula, "The Daughter's Seduction: Sexual Violence and Literary History," *Signs* 11.4 (1986): 621–644; Saidiya Hartman, "Seduction and the Ruses of Power," *Callaloo* 19.2 (1996): 537–560; Jenny Newman, ed., *The Faber Book of Seductions* (London: Faber, 1988); Sabine Sielke, "Seduced and Enslaved: Sexual Violence in Antebellum American Literature and Contemporary Feminist Discourse," in *The Historical and Political Turn in Literary Studies*, ed. Winfried Fluck, *REAL—Yearbook of Research in English and American Literature* 11 (1995): 299–324.

SABINE SIELKE

SELF-DEFENSE/SELF-DEFENSE COURSES. Anyone confronted by an attacker has the legal right to resist actual or threatened violence. Self-defense is the act of resisting with whatever force or means reasonably necessary. Since rapists utilize violence, weapons, and threats, individuals should be prepared to resist attacks with physical, verbal, and psychological strategies. Any amount of physical **resistance** increases the likelihood of stopping a conflict and avoiding rape, without increasing chance of injury. Self-defense classes, based mostly on martial arts from Asia and military hand-to-hand combat techniques, prepare individuals to react with precise maneuvers in order to terminate any attack with a single technique.

Classes offer hands-on training in avoidance skills, threat assessment, crisis de-escalating techniques, and physical defense techniques from standing and fallen positions. Classes prepare individuals against grabs, punches, kicks, armed attacks, and multiple attackers. Instructors teach maneuvers to escape from various positions during attempted rape, no matter how large or strong the attacker. Students learn legalities, such as what constitutes unnecessary force. Courses are taught incrementally, gradually increasing levels of contact and simulation. Instructors address fears and concerns. Upon completion, students should know a variety of options when facing attack.

Other maneuvers taught include jabbing the bridge of the nose, kicking the groin or shins, grabbing and jerking the testicles, breaking out of single- or double-wrist grabs, escaping from front- and back-body grabs (bear hugs), escaping choke holds, removing a weapon from an attacker's possession, releasing oneself from hair grabs, and breaking ribs.

Particularly devastating maneuvers include kicking an attacker's kidneys, punching the solar plexus nerve center using a single-knuckle fist, jamming thumbs deep into eye sockets, and grabbing the throat to squeeze the trachea shut. These disabling techniques can leave an attacker in severe pain, in sudden shock, unconscious, even dead.

Physical resistance should only be used when physical attack is imminent. Legally, individuals must not use more force than is reasonably necessary to escape or terminate the attack. For success, individuals must react in the first few seconds of an attack. They must immediately analyze the situation, location, appropriateness of force, and chances of escape. Each attack is different. Through training, techniques become second nature and move from concepts to instinctive reactions based on muscle memory.

Verbal strategies are another component of self-defense. Screaming "fire" is psychologically more agitating than "rape." It should cause public response. **Victims** can also begin to immediately yell about recognizing the attacker, the police branding the attacker as a rapist, or resurfacing after years to inform the attacker's partner, children, and coworkers of the incident. If these statements are made during or after rape, attackers may **murder** to avoid later detection.

Remaining calm, victims might convince rapists there is no physical or psychological threat. Statements about having a venereal disease or **HIV/AIDS** or suggesting that sex would be pleasant without a weapon present can be deterrents. After distracting or calming attackers, a surprise physical technique can be exercised.

Other nonphysical resistance strategies include keeping several feet of distance between oneself and others and keeping one hand free when carrying objects. When neither hand is free, there is a greater risk of being targeted.

Psychological deterrent strategies include urinating, defecating, or vomiting on oneself, pretending to be insane, or pretending to faint. Rapists may panic, may no longer feel sexually aroused, or may feel that the dominance and control set out for has been accomplished.

Some methods, such as begging or crying, have not been shown to be effective and may also increase risk of injury. While compliance may reduce the chance of injury, it does not help avoid attack. Chemical sprays can be effective, but they are only useful if accessible in a matter of seconds.

Self-defense classes are usually taught by martial arts and **law enforcement** communities. They may be offered specifically to women or may specifically address

rape prevention. Classes are usually free or low cost at martial arts clubs, college campuses, and women's or community centers.

Self-defense knowledge is critical to surviving rape. A counterattack must be swift and brutal to stop an attacker whose mind is made up to harm. In the end, victims act, react, or take no action based on instinct, intuition, location, and personal choice. Rape is a crime whether victims resist or not. *See also*: **Rape Education; Rape Myths.**

Suggested Reading: Paul Henry Danylewich, *Fearless: The Complete Personal Safety Guide for Women* (Toronto: University of Toronto Press, 2001); Michael Vassolo, *The Manual of Unarmed Self-defense* (Fort Lee, NJ: Barricade Books, 1999).

ELIZABETH JENNER

SERIAL RAPE AND SERIAL RAPISTS. Serial rape is a type of criminal offense that only became recognized by the general public in the 1970s. According to the Federal Bureau of Investigation (FBI) definition, serial rape involves sexual attacks upon 10 or more stranger **victims**; however, local police forces and the general public frequently use the term after more than two similar rapes have occurred. The reluctance of victims to report rapes and the absence of effective police procedures may mean that this type of rape is an old phenomenon only recently identified. Stylized verbal scripts demanded from the stranger victim, sadistic or violent behavior, the rapist's inability to penetrate his victim or to climax, and the collection of souvenirs mark serial attacks.

The few studies conducted upon serial rapists show that these men, particularly the most violent ones, are usually white males of European ancestry who target white females. Black rapists, by contrast, are known to cross color lines. Most offenders enjoy stable employment, live with someone, and have been married at least once. Significant numbers of these men experienced troubled childhoods, with many reporting juvenile **alcohol** abuse, cruelty to animals, fire setting, stealing, and assaults against adults. A majority of rapists, 68 percent, began their sexual predation as voyeurs.

The FBI has used interviews with serial rapists to group this type of offender into four camps: power-reassurance, power-assertive, anger-retaliatory, and anger-excitation. All of the men in the categories share a psychosexual trait that drives them to repeatedly attack. Unable to match reality to their sexual **fantasies**, the men feel the need to try again, thereby creating a process that results in serial sex crime. The pattern of behavior of serial rapists is similar to that of serial killers since many murderers begin their criminal careers as rapists and often intersperse murders with nonlethal sexual assaults.

The power-reassurance attacker is the most common type of serial rapist. Often referred to as the "gentleman rapist," he bolsters his masculinity through the exercise of power over women. Victims are preselected through surveillance or peeping activities, surprised, and usually attacked in the evening or early morning. The rapist may have several potential victims, all in the same vicinity, lined up. If one potential assault is foiled, the rapist will often seek another victim nearby on the same night. He will take souvenirs from his victims and keep a record of his crimes.

The power-assertive rapist, the second most common type of serial rapist, uses his attacks to express his "natural" dominance over women. Unlike the power-reassurance rapist, this rapist is regarded as a selfish offender who is unconcerned over the welfare of his victim. He will often use a con approach and then force the victim to engage in repeated **sexual assault**s. The victim is often left in a state of partial nudity at the assault location, which will be a place of convenience and safety for the offender.

The anger-retaliatory rapist is motivated by feelings of rage and retaliation: He wants to "get even" with women. The victims are symbols of someone else, often exhibiting certain appearance, dress, or occupational similarities. Sex is used to punish and degrade, and the attacks are typically frenzied with excessive levels of force. Since the attacks occur as the result of an emotional outburst, they lack premeditation. There is little planning or advance victim selection. The attacks are sporadic and can occur at any time of the day or night.

The anger-excitation rapist, the least common type, achieves sexual excitement from observing the victim's reaction to physical or psychological pain. The rapes, characterized by fear and brutality, may involve **torture**. The offender uses a con approach, attacks and binds the victim, and then takes her to a preselected location that offers privacy. He will usually keep her for a period of time and may make a visual or audio record of his activities.

Contrary to public perception, most serial rapists attack in the homes of the victims. According to FBI researchers, only 6 percent of rapes occurred in streets or alleys, with another 6 percent of victims attacked in parking lots or on highways. Serial rapists are more likely to attack in the summer in neighborhoods characterized by ethnic diversity, high population turnover, and multiple unit dwellings.

The study of serial rape is still in its infancy. Difficulty in recognizing the presence of a serial rapist and difficulty in capturing such an attacker have resulted in a lack of knowledge about such **predators**. *See also*: **Murder; Sex Offenders; Voyeurism**.

Suggested Reading: Philip Jenkins, *Intimate Enemies: Moral Panics in Contemporary Great Britain* (New York: Aldine de Gruyter, 1992); D. Kim Rossmo, *Geographic Profiling* (Boca Raton, FL: CRC Press, 2000).

CARYN E. NEUMANN

SEX OFFENDERS. The scope of sex offenses changes over time, mirroring shifts in cultural attitudes about acceptable sexual practices. Cultural attitudes also influence whether sex offenders are perceived as criminals, mentally ill, or a dangerous combination of both. The first edition of the American Psychiatric Association's *Diagnostic and Statistical Manual* (DSM) included the term "sociopathic personality disturbance," with "sexual deviation" listed as a subtype. DSM-IV (1994) lists exhibitionism, fetishism, frotteurism, **pedophilia**, sexual masochism, sexual sadism, transvestic fetishism, and **voyeurism** as psychosexual disorders. These disorders are not, however, synonymous with sex crimes. Not everyone diagnosed with a psychosexual disorder commits a criminal act. State and federal laws define sexual offenses, further complicating categorizing sex offenders by geographic jurisdiction. A sex offender, therefore, is someone who has committed or attempted to commit any type of illegal or nonconsensual sexual act and/or any sexual behavior involving children under the legal age of **consent**, based upon the laws governing the location where the sexual behavior occurred.

In 1835, James Cowles Prichard (1786–1848), an English physician, blamed criminal behavior on "moral insanity," a defect causing perversions of natural impulses and inclinations. Francis Galton (1822–1911), an English scientist, founded the study of eugenics and advocated limiting reproduction to "suitable" people. Richard von Krafft-Ebing (1840–1902), a German psychiatrist, believed heredity was a factor in "moral degeneracy," which could lead to rape. His *Psychopathia Sexualis* (1886) included one of the earliest scientific studies of sexual murderers. He was instrumental in popularizing the idea that homosexuality was a form of mental illness. The widespread influence of these two men led to laws in the United States imposing sterilization on sexual deviants.

Early in the twentieth century, "sex psychopath" laws allowed indefinite confinement of sex offenders to protect the public. However, mental hospitals did not have effective treatments for sexual deviants. In 1949, Egas Moniz (1874–1955), a Portuguese neurologist, won the Nobel Prize for his pioneering work with prefrontal lobe brain operations. Lobotomies were performed on sexual deviants until the early 1970s, when new psychoactive drugs became available. After World War II, there was growing concern for the civil rights of accused sex offenders and recognition that there was a racial imbalance in the population of sex offenders who were prosecuted and punished within the legal system. In 1977, the U.S. Supreme Court ruled that the death penalty for rapists was unconstitutional. The second-wave **feminist movement** resulted in new theories about sex offenders. **Susan Brownmiller**'s landmark publication ***Against Our Will*** (1975) contended that rapists are not sexual deviants at all but extreme examples of "normal" maleness within a patriarchal society that is hostile toward women. The term *sexual aggressive* was first used in 1977 to classify offenders who rape or carry out other forceful sexual acts. Gaps in valid statistical data were acknowledged, and it became obvious that there was still only limited understanding of the motivations of sexual offenders.

During the last two decades of the twentieth century, criminal theories about sex offenders gained dominance over sociopsychiatric theories. Politicians allocated less funding for therapeutic programs for sex offenders and community mental health services. Controversial **sexual predator** commitment laws, registration and community notification laws, and chemical **castration** laws were enacted during the 1990s. New DNA identification databases allow various jurisdictions to track and monitor known sex offenders. The Jacob Wetterling Crimes against Children and Sexually Violent Offender Registration Act of 1994 brought about state sex offender registration systems. In 1997, the U.S. Supreme Court's ruling in *Kansas v. Hendricks* legalized indefinite postsentence detention of sexually violent predators as a form of "civil commitment" to protect the general public. In contrast, the International Association for the Treatment of Sexual Offenders (IATSO), founded in 1998, believes that effective treatment, rather than punishment, will result in the reduction of repeat assaults by sex offenders.

The latest example of shifting cultural values defining the scope of sexual offenses occurred in June 2003, when the U.S. Supreme Court ruling in *Lawrence v. Texas* decriminalized private, same-gender sexual activity between consenting adults in all 50 states. This landmark decision typifies the ongoing controversies involved with human sexuality, civil rights, and legal definitions of sex offenders. *See also*: **Megan's Law; Serial Rape and Serial Rapists.**

Suggested Reading: American Psychiatric Association, *Dangerous Sex Offenders: A Task Force Report of the APA* (Washington, DC: Author, 1999); Helen Cothran, ed., *Sexual Violence: Opposing Viewpoints* (Detroit: Gale, 2003); George B. Palermo and Mary Ann

Farkas, *The Dilemma of the Sexual Offender* (Springfield, IL: Charles C. Thomas, 2001); Louis B. Schlesinger, *Sexual Murder: Catathymic and Compulsive Homicides* (New York: CRC Press, 2004); Bruce J. Winick and John Q. La Fond, eds., *Protecting Society from Sexually Dangerous Offenders: Law, Justice, and Therapy* (Washington, DC: American Psychological Association, 2003).

BETTY J. GLASS

SEXUAL ABUSE ACT OF 1986. In 1986 Congress passed the Sexual Abuse Act in an attempt to deal with the problem of proliferating **sexual assaults**. The bill, applied to all federal jurisdictions, provided for fines, imprisonment, or both for individuals who forced other persons to engage in sexual acts against their will or with those who were unable to give **consent**. It also expanded the definition of sexual assault to include acts of a sexual nature beyond the limited identification of vaginal penetration of a female by a male and recognized that males could also be **victims** of sexual abuse. A separate section of the bill expanded protection for children of both sexes.

On November 7, 1986, the Sexual Abuse Act of 1986 became Public Law 99-654. The new law punished individuals who used force in sexual acts and who threatened their victims with threats of death, serious bodily harm, or kidnapping. It specifically banned sexual acts with individuals who were unconscious and made it a crime to render a person unconscious through drugs or other intoxicants. The section of the law pertaining to children attempted to stem the tide of child **pornography** and expanded the Mann Act to protect male children from being taken across state lines for the purpose of sexual acts.

According to the Federal Bureau of Investigation's Uniform Crime Reports for 1986, 90,434 forcible rapes were reported to authorities, and some estimates suggest that only one in five sexual assaults are reported. Since the new law applied only to federal jurisdictions—prisons, post offices, military bases, and Indian reservations—the majority of sexual assault cases were unaffected. Congress passed a more inclusive bill with the **Violence against Women Act** in 1994. *See also*: **Statutory Rape.**

Suggested Reading: Maria Bevacqua, *Rape on the Public Agenda: Feminism and the Politics of Sexual Assault* (Boston: Northeastern Press, 2000).

ELIZABETH R. PURDY

SEXUAL ASSAULT. The topic of sexual assault generates much interest, in both popular and academic discourse. Many terms are used to refer to abusive sexual behavior, and *sexual assault* falls between the more specific crimes like rape and the more general categories like **sexual harassment**. For example, sexual assault may include rape, but some harassing behaviors will not be seen officially as sexual assault. As a legal term, definitions of sexual assault may differ depending on which country you happen to be in, or even which part of which country (for example, both Australia and the United States have rape/sexual assault laws that vary by state). The differences between such laws appear to have limited impact in terms of practical outcome, that is, convictions. But the differences in terminology tell something about the broader political trends in understandings of sexual assault.

So why does it matter whether we call a sexual violation a rape or a sexual assault? This debate is important for two reasons. First, some suggest that the official definitions of crimes like rape do not reflect the experience of all **survivors,** just those assaults that fit with our stereotypes. Second, rape cases are notoriously difficult to deal with in the criminal justice system, resulting in failure to secure conviction for many attackers. Some argue that these problems could be improved by using the term *sexual assault* instead.

One problem with the term *rape* is that it is often gender specific. The crime of rape originates from an era when men "owned" women, and therefore rape was almost a crime against a man's property rather than against women as individuals. Many countries have retained a definition of rape that refers only to the penile penetration of female **victims** by male perpetrators. This means that "rapelike" crimes such as nonconsensual **sodomy** are therefore seen as different from (and even less serious than) the more stereotypical penile rape of women by men. Including all "rapes" within one gender-neutral category of sexual assault could promote equality between survivors (and between perpetrators' sentences). However, others feel that as most victims of rape are women and most perpetrators are men, the gender specificity of "rape" is important, and therefore sexual assault should only refer to other sexual violations.

The second problem with the category of *rape* is that it tends to focus on sexual intercourse, which can lead to victim blaming. In contrast, the term *sexual assault* focuses attention on the problem of sexual violence, drawing parallels with other kinds of violent crime such as robbery. It is common for crimes of sexual assault to be graded in terms of seriousness, with reference to the level of violence of the crime. Some argue that this is a good thing because it allows a variety of kinds of assault within one simple category to be recognized. Others feel this is a problem, because it suggests that some forms of sexual violation, such as **date rape** or **sexual coercion,** are somehow less serious because they less commonly involve overt physical force. The increasing popularity of the term *sexual assault* reflects an international trend toward seeing rape as a crime of violence, as gender neutral, and as the perpetrator's responsibility. However, in both practical and symbolic terms, the value of using *sexual assault* rather than *rape* remains contested, and the debate looks set to continue for some time. *See also*: **Prosecution; Rape Law; Rape Trials.**

Suggested Reading: P.L.N. Donat and J. D'Emilio, "A Feminist Redefinition of Rape and Sexual Assault: Historical Foundations and Change," *Journal of Social Issues* 48.1 (1992): 9–22; J. Gregory and S. Lees, *Policing Sexual Assault* (London: Sage, 1999).

RUTH GRAHAM

SEXUAL ASSAULT, DRUG-FACILITATED. The definition of "rape" specifies sexual activity that takes place when a person (female or male) is physically forced, verbally threatened, or under the influence of drugs that render him or her incapable of making a free decision or resisting a **sexual assault.** Acquaintance rape (**date rape** is a subcategory) involves someone being forced to have sexual contact against his or her will with a person previously known to the survivor. It is now a felony to give an unsuspecting person one of the date rape drugs with the intent of committing a violent act, including rape, upon that person. The law-imposed penalties include fines and prison terms for importing or distributing more than one gram of these drugs. Despite the efforts of the criminal justice system at developing deterrents, the use of date rape drugs appears to be increasing. While **gammahydroxybutyrate (GBH), Rohypnol,** and **ketamine** are considered the primary date rape drugs, **Ecstasy** and **alcohol** (either alone or in combination with one of the other drugs) have been and continue to be used in cases of sexual assault by impairing the judgment of the target. For example, women who use Ecstasy actually want to be touched and held by partners who may have been complete strangers only 10 minutes before the sexual contact.

The scenarios associated with drug-facilitated sexual assault have distinct patterns with respect to the players, the circumstances, and the scripts:

1. The targets include women alone (the most frequent situation), women with companions (who may also be drugged to prevent their intervention), and men alone or with companions. In each case, the predator or predators assess the vulnerability of the target.
2. Most of the predators are men, alone or in groups.
3. The settings include bars, clubs, fraternity houses, private homes, cars, or any place where the act will not be easily discovered or interrupted.

The scenario generally follows a typical sequence with the perpetrator first making overtures of friendship or efforts at **seduction**. Eventually, an open drink will be adulterated with one of the easily dissolvable, odorless, and tasteless date rape drugs. The target will eventually develop symptoms of weakness and dizziness; the timing depends on the specific drug and the dosage. The predator will then offer to drive the potential victim home or even to the hospital. The victim will experience an 8- to 24-hour "blackout." The only evidence of a crime may be bruises and disarranged or missing **clothing**. The **survivor** may have a strong suspicion that a sexual attack had occurred, but she (in most, but not all cases, the target of sexual assault is a woman) will have absolutely no memory of the event. The question arises as to whether her memory could be restored through the use of hypnosis. The answer is a deafening "no." If the survivor seeks medical attention, there will be no evidence of the use of drugs. If she reports her suspicions to the school authorities or the police, in all probability, nothing will happen because the survivor has no evidence and may not know who was involved.

In data supplied by the Women's Health and Counseling Center and by the Bureau of Justice Statistics, we find that 25 percent of college-aged women have either been raped or have survived an attempted rape. Eighty-four percent of the women who were raped knew their assailants. Although women from the ages of 16 to 24 years are at the greatest risk of being raped, no one is completely safe. In a survey, 1 in 12 male students had committed acts that meet the legal definition of rape. Eighty-four percent of the men, who had committed rape, stated that what they had done was definitely not rape. Only 27 percent of the women who were sexually assaulted perceived themselves rape **victims**. Seventy-five percent of the male students who committed rape and 55 percent of the female students involved in a rape situation had been drinking alcohol, using drugs, or both. One third of the male sample stated that they would commit rape if they could get away without detection. Twenty-five percent of the male respondents believed that rape was acceptable under the following conditions: (1) if the woman asked the man to go out, (2) if the man paid for the date, and (3) if the woman agreed to go to the man's room after the date. In addition, a predator may feel entitled to sex if he is invited to the woman's room, or if he thinks his status as an **athlete** or celebrity gives him special rights. While it is not possible to eliminate all risk factors, there are behaviors that will reduce the danger. These include not putting oneself in high-risk situations and watching for warning signs. However, experienced predators know how to behave so that the defenses of intended victims and others are not activated. At parties, stay with people who can be trusted. In addition, never drink from an open container.

There are several signs that drugs are being used in college dorms. For example, Visine bottles are used to store GHB. An "X" marked on the door of a dorm room indicates that Ecstasy is available. Sometimes an extreme focus on weight control by women students can indicate that club drugs that suppress appetite and cocaine are being used on the campus. Students may not see the use of club drugs as a problem because many students believe that club drugs are not as dangerous as cocaine. *See also*: **Campus Rape; Fraternities; Rape Statistics.**

Suggested Reading: Robert J. Ascolese, *Pathways to Recovery: The Psychology and Spirituality of Substance Abuse Prevention and Treatment* (New York: Recovery Assistance Foundation, 1995); Club Drugs.org, http://www.clubdrugs.org; Jaime Diaz, *How Drugs Influence Behavior: Neurobehavioral Approach* (Upper Saddle River, NJ: Prentice Hall, 1997); Harold E. Doweiko, *Concepts of Chemical Dependency*, 5th ed. (Pacific Grove, CA: Brooks/Cole, 2002); John P. Morgan, "Designer Drugs," in *Substance Abuse: A Comprehensive Textbook*, ed. Joyce H. Lowinson, Pedro Ruiz, Robert B. Millman, and John Langrod (New York: Lippincott, Williams, and Wilkins, 1997); Partnership for a Drug-Free America, http://www.drugfreeamerica.org; Substance Abuse and Mental Health Association's National Clearinghouse for Alcohol and Drug Information, http://www.health.org.

JUDITH A. WATERS AND SHARON A. DROZDOWSKI

SEXUAL COERCION. Sexual coercion is incorporated within the broader spectrum of *sexually abusive behaviors*, from rape and **sexual assault** to **sexual harassment** and emotional blackmail. The concept of coercion does not rely on notions of overt physical violence to define what counts as nonconsensual sexual contact. Instead, the focus is on freely given **consent**. Sexual coercion is therefore about more subtle processes of gaining sexual access and includes more "everyday" behaviors. And so because sexual coercion is a more everyday occurrence, it is harder to draw the line between behavior that is criminal and behavior that is simply undesirable or unethical. At the root of the issue is how violence has been relied upon to define consent.

From the 1970s onward, the feminist perspective has dominated many of the debates around rape and sexual assault, because mainstream research has shown so little interest in the topic by comparison. The feminist perspective has been useful because it showed that most **victims** are women and most perpetrators are men and located rape as one aspect of men's violence toward women. Understanding sexual assault as part of a broader pattern was a powerful shift in political and critical awareness. But it reinforced a problematic association between the seriousness of sexual assault and the existence of physical violence.

The problem with focusing on violence is that while the traditional stereotype of rape as physically violent reflects adequately some people's experiences, it does not account for all nonconsensual sexual contact. The vast majority of rapes and other unwanted sexual attentions are committed by someone the victim knows, where the use of physical violence is much less likely. For example, there are debates about the extent to which rape takes place in society, because many rapes, such as **date rape**, do not fit the stereotype. Mary Koss, a key academic commentator on the prevalence of rape, argues that official **rape statistics** have consistently underestimated the number of rapes. This is because those collecting official data have used a narrow definition of *rape*, which may not include victims who were not physically forced because they were incapacitated. Discussion of the relationship between violence and coercion is important because these terms define what counts as consent to sexual activities and therefore what counts as nonconsent.

In response to the focus on violence, there is a growing interest in sexual coercion, particularly in the United States. Research on sexual coercion typically focuses on understanding people's everyday experiences of sexual consent that is not freely given. Many of these studies are associated with the study of U.S. college campus populations. A leading academic in the field is Charlene Muehlenhard, whose work goes beyond consensus definitions of unacceptable sexual behavior to look at relatively "everyday" incidence of "normal" sexual behavior and the role of coercion in that context.

The move away from a focus on sexual violence toward sexual coercion represents a more inclusive definition of unacceptable behaviors that are not necessarily gender specific. For example, using emotional blackmail to get someone to agree to sexual intercourse is an option open to both men and women. Men as victims are the minority, and female perpetrators are rare, but there is a need to account for the events where men are coerced and women are sexually coercive—where consent is not just an issue about threat of physical violence but a question of meaningful and honest communication about free choice. Some argue that this shift toward a broader definition of sexually abusive behavior is problematic because it criminalizes too much "normal" social behavior. Others may find it problematic that the explicitly gendered nature of serious sexual assaults is less pronounced in the more everyday sexual coercions like emotional blackmail. But it is increasingly hard to justify talking about sexual assault and rape without also discussing the relevance of coercion to the concept of consent. *See also*: **Campus Rape; Legislation, Sexual Harassment.**

Suggested Reading: J.A. Allison and L.S. Wrightsman, *Rape: The Misunderstood Crime* (Newbury Park, CA: Sage, 1993); P.Y. Martin and R.A. Hummer, "Fraternities and Rape on Campus," in *Violence against Women: The Bloody Footprints*, ed. P.B. Bart and E.G. Moran (Newbury Park, CA: Sage, 1993), 114–131; C.L. Muehlenhard and J.L. Schrag, "Nonviolent Sexual Coercion," in *Acquaintance Rape: The Hidden Crime*, ed. A. Parrott and L. Bechhofer (New York: Wiley, 1991), 115–128; C.L. Muehlenhard, S.C. Sympson, J.L. Phelps, and B.J. Highby, "Are Rape Statistics Exaggerated? A Response to Criticism of Contemporary Rape Research," *Journal of Sex Research* 31.2 (1994): 144–146.

RUTH GRAHAM

SEXUAL DOUBLE STANDARD. Understanding the history of rape and sexual exploitation in the United States includes examining the role of the sexual double standard in our social and legal culture. From colonial times to the present, American laws governing sexual crimes and **family** law have been shaped by gender prescriptions, and the sexual double standard is firmly imbedded in the larger criminal justice system.

The term *sexual double standard* suggests that women are held to a different standard than men and that their words and actions are questioned based on their virtue or lack of virtue. The notion of distrusting women's words is particularly evident in rape cases across time. In colonial Connecticut, the magistrates focused on the character of both parties, but as time went by, the focus of character shifted entirely to the female, and the validity of women's words became suspect. In short, if a woman failed to live up to the standards of female purity, many courts viewed her as a willing participant in illicit sex and not a **victim** of rape. Courts across the United States followed the same pattern by applying different standards of sexual behavior to men and women. While men were allowed great latitude in acting out sexually, women who failed to protect their own virtue outside of marriage received little sympathy from the court system.

During the early twentieth century, courts continued to apply unequal standards of morality based on gender. The rise of the juvenile courts system is a good example. As urbanization, industrialization, and economic growth transformed American society, young people had more freedom to engage in illicit sex as community and family controls changed. Moral and legal reformers sought to control juvenile sexual delinquency through state legal intervention and introduced reformatories and eventually a large juvenile court and correctional system. The court system identified female sex delinquents as a serious social problem and routinely investigated young girls' sexual histories. In many cases judges ordered further actions including the use of required compulsory physical examinations, treatment for venereal disease, placement in correction facilities, or in extreme cases, forced sterilization. Furthermore, these same courts labeled girls who found themselves pregnant, whether by choice or as rape victims, as sexual delinquents. In contrast, these very same courts did not require boys to describe their sexual histories or face institutionalization for their sexual misconduct. Rape prosecutions were even less likely, depending on the character of the female party.

The sexual double standard can be seen in a number of examples across time and speaks volumes to the role that social constructions of gender continue to have in measuring the guilt or innocence of female rape victims. *See also*: **Gender Roles**.

Suggested Reading: Cornelia Dayton Hughes, *Women before the Bar: Gender, Law & Society in Connecticut, 1639–1789* (Chapel Hill: University of North Carolina Press, 1995); Mary E. Odem, *Delinquent Daughters: Protecting and Policing Adolescent Female Sexuality in the United States, 1855–1920* (Chapel Hill: University of North Carolina Press, 1995).

DANELLE MOON

SEXUAL HARASSMENT. The federal government of the United States defines *sexual harassment* as "any repeated or unwanted verbal or physical sexual advances; sexually explicit derogatory statements; or sexually discriminating remarks made by someone in the workplace which are offensive or objectionable to the recipient, give discomfort or humiliation, or interfere with the recipient's job performance." Sexual harassment is one of the serious causes of workplace violence. Behavior that begins as seemingly innocuous comments can eventually escalate to rape and other forms of physical assault. The term *workplace* has been extended beyond corporate offices, factories, fieldwork outside the office, and public facilities to **schools** and universities, including military academies and other institutions of learning. When the law was first formulated in 1964, sexual harassment was seen as an extension of sex discrimination with a male in a position of power and a woman in the more vulnerable role. Now the law has been redefined to cover same-sex relationships or a woman in the supervising role with a male subordinate. Both employees may be on similar levels of responsibility. In any case, the clear implication is that the organization tolerates such behavior. Consequently, an employee may believe that he or she is entitled to engage in harassing behavior since management has a history of ignoring complaints.

Essentially, there are two categories of sexual harassment that can lead to charges and perhaps even litigation: "quid pro quo" and "hostile environment." In the case of quid pro quo, the predator may begin by trying to seduce the target. If that strategy is unsuccessful, the predator's behavior may become more threatening, or he or she may use managerial power to promise a raise, a promotion, or special training opportunities. In academic institutions, grades may become contingent on sexual favors. In the corporate world, there is always the threat of loss of employment or other job actions. While the demands are frequently coupled with the enticement of job-related advantages, the message is implicitly one that involves negative consequences. Many targets are afraid to report incidents of sexual harassment because they think that no one will believe them or that people will assume that they contributed to the situation by their own behavior.

Behaviors defined as sexual harassment include indirect remarks, offensive touching, active aggression without physical contact, such as phone calls and letters, and actual sexual abuse, including sexual propositions, unwelcome hugging, sexual touching, and kissing. The aggressive nature of these acts is tantamount to assault. In many cases, the harasser begins to behave with such impunity that the target fears to be alone or unprotected in places where the harasser might find him or her. A hostile environment where many employees find themselves in an atmosphere of loutish behavior including continuous salacious remarks, pornographic materials in shared areas, and generally unpleasant physical behavior that remains unchallenged by management can lead to a class-action litigation by everyone in the workplace. The Civil Rights Act of 1991 states that job-related bias based on sex, disability, **religion**, or national origin will be punished in the same manner as cases based on the race of the claimant. Punitive damages that are now covered by law can be very costly to individuals and employers accused of sexual harassment. Moreover, employers can no longer plead ignorance if they should have been aware of the situation. Organizations, including universities, must develop and post sexual harassment policies with stated consequences to the harasser. Expeditious investigation is part of the process. Employers are motivated to eliminate sexual harassment in the workplace since Supreme Court decisions have placed the responsibility for a hazard-free environment squarely on the shoulders of management.

In order to come to a fair decision with respect to a complaint, it is thought that claims of sexual harassment must be investigated to determine validity, the level of seriousness of the event(s), and the appropriate consequences for those involved. Both human resources and the legal departments should be concerned. Everything must be carefully recorded. If the organization does not appear to be acting in an unbiased manner, any future litigation will result in a higher judgment against management. Possible consequences include the following disciplinary actions against a known harasser: oral and written warnings, reprimands, suspension, probation, lateral transfer, demotions, and discharge for cause. Redress of the claimant's situation is expected (e.g., a promotion once withheld should be given and unfair grades should be changed).

Many **survivors** of sexual harassment are afraid to report the event(s) since they fear retaliation and being blamed for the situation by their peers or families. If these incidents are not reported, however, the administration cannot take formal action. The targets of sexual harassment frequently make anonymous calls to counseling offices and human resources departments asking for advice on how to handle an incident without making a formal report. It is extremely difficult to convince a predator to stop his or her behavior without the weight of the organization and its remedies to deter further acts. In some areas of the world, sexual harassment may not be recognized as a crime. In the United States, **victims** of sexual harassment are encouraged to tell someone in a position of authority immediately and keep a "paper trail" (record) of the events. If nothing comes of the report, experts advise consulting an attorney. *See also*: **Legislation, Sexual Harassment.**

Suggested Reading: Patricia Brownell and Albert R. Roberts, "Domestic Violence in the Workplace," in *Handbook of Violence*, ed. Lisa Rapp-Paglicci, Albert R. Roberts, and John Woldarski (New York: John Wiley and Sons, 2002); "Facts about Sexual Harassment," http://www.eeoc.gov/facts/fs-sex.html "Revised Sexual Harassment Guidance: Harassment of Students by School Employees, Other Students, or Third Parties," Office for Civil Rights, http://www.ed.gov/offices/OCR/shguide/; Judith A. Waters, Robert I. Lynn, and Keith Morgan, "Workplace Violence: Prevention, Intervention Theory and Practice," in *Handbook of Violence*, ed. Lisa Rapp-Paglicci, Albert R. Roberts, and John Woldarski (New York: John Wiley and Sons, 2002).

JUDITH A. WATERS AND DANIEL GROSS

SEXUAL MUTILATION. Sexual mutilation is the alteration or modification of the victim's body before, during, or after a rape, which is different from "female genital mutilation." In the former, the act is a deliberate demonstration of sexual sadism that is specific to each perpetrator and is culturally unacceptable; in the latter, it refers to a cultural practice of alteration of the labia and clitoris and is accepted by those cultures that practice it.

Examples of sexual mutilation abound. They date from antiquity and myth. For example, in ancient Greek **mythology**, Tereus raped Philomela, cut off her tongue, and imprisoned her so that she could not speak of the crime. Perhaps the best-known historic cases are those victims of Jack the Ripper. More recent perpetrators were Theodore Bundy whose rape and killing sprees went from Florida to Utah (early 1970s), Christopher Wilder, who chose dark-haired beauty queens for his victims (1980s), Danny Rolling, "The Gainesville Murderer" (1990), and the **sexual predators** who worked as a team, Lawrence Bittaker and Roy Norris (late 1970s).

The methods used in mutilation are limited only by the imagination of the offender. Hammers, pliers, and electric cattle prods, wires, pins and needles, biting, whipping, burning, insertion of foreign objects into the rectum or vagina, pouring caustic substances on the skin, bondage, amputation, asphyxiation to the point of unconsciousness, application of electric shocks, and insertion of glass rods in the male urethra are some examples.

When sexual mutilation accompanies a rape, the victim is frequently killed. However, mutilation after death occurs as well. When the victim is mutilated while alive, domination, infliction of pain, and suffering are important to the rapist. Sexual sadism has been seen as a persistent pattern of becoming sexually excited in response to another's suffering. Perpetrators find the suffering of the victim sexually arousing.

Postmortem evidence sends a different message. Often the mutilation is symbolic or sends a message to investigators. In the case of Edward Gein, he mutilated the bodies of his victims and kept trophies. One woman was hung and eviscerated like large game. Jack the Ripper cut away nipples, vaginas, uteruses and abdominal organs from his victims. Danny Rolling decapitated the head of one of his victims and left it facing the door, anticipating the horror of the first observer of the crime scene.

Mutilation is not always of the genitals. Lawrence Bittaker and Roy Norris stabbed ice picks into the auditory meatus of young girls. They planned and rehearsed each aspect of their rapes from modifying the inside of a van to practicing the routes they would take after abducting their victims. Their choice was teenagers, one from each age group from 13 to 19. Theodore Bundy squeezed superglue in girls' eyes to render them sightless. During the rapes, he bit them on the buttocks and breasts.

In 1978, Lawrence Singleton raped, then hacked off the arms of a teenage runaway. Singleton was imprisoned but later released only to kill a woman. Disposition of these offenders is fraught with controversy because so many of them repeat their behaviors once freed. *See also*: **Foreign Object Rape; Serial Rape and Serial Rapists**.

Suggested Reading: Patricia Cornwell, *Portrait of a Killer* (New York: G.P. Putnam's Sons, 2002); Robert Hazelwood, V.A. Park, Elliott Dietz, and Janet Warren, "The Criminal Sexual Sadist," *FBI Law Enforcement Bulletin* (February 1992), http://www.fbi.gov/publications/leb/leb/htm.

LANA THOMPSON

SEXUAL PREDATORS. A sexual predator, legally, is one who has previously committed a violent sex crime and been found by a judge and jury to suffer a "mental abnormality" or "personality disorder" that makes him "likely to engage in predatory acts of sexual violence" (Revised Code of Washington). Florida Statutes defines sexual predators as "repeat **sexual offenders**, sexual offenders who use physical violence, and sexual offenders who prey on children." Because of his inherent propensity to repeat the harmful acts, the predator remains a menace to society even after released from incarceration. Frequently, despite outrage and protest from previous **victims** and their families, he is released and reenters society only to commit a similar or more violent offense.

One of the most heinous examples of a sexual predator who escalated his modus operandi was Earl Shriner, who, in 1990, after being released from prison, attacked, raped, and sexually mutilated a 7-year-old boy. Shriner, a 40-year-old white male, had a lengthy record that began at age 16, when he killed a 15-year-old girl, his schoolmate. In his midtwenties, he kidnapped and assaulted two teenage girls. Although he was incarcerated for 10 years, authorities thought that he should not be released but instead committed to a state hospital. However, two factors precluded his continued detention. Since he was not diagnosed mentally ill, a psychiatric hospital would not accept him, and since he did not commit any sexual offenses while detained, the institution could not extend his sentence. Obviously, while under lock and key, he did not have the opportunity to stalk and rape young victims.

The first attempt at legislation to deal with sexual predators was made in 1930 with two considerations: the protection of society and rehabilitation for the offender by either removal from society and punishment or treatment (or both). In Minnesota, if one was diagnosed as having a psychopathic personality, then that person could be confined in a mental institution or "an asylum for the dangerously insane." By 1940, both the U.S. Supreme Court and the Minnesota court found that definition to be too vague because voyeurs, exhibitionists, and other nonpredatory behaviors were being included in the sexual psychopath laws. The next 20 years witnessed a series of changes, and by the 1960s, 28 states had sex offender commitment laws. In some states, parole and probation were required after release as a way to keep track of the predators. Then, with the rise in civil rights in the late 1960s, predators, too, were given protections. A reversal began with the right to counsel, the right to be heard, to be confronted with witnesses against him, to cross-examine, and the right to offer his own evidence. The existing laws that required sentences of indeterminate hospitalization were challenged. Treatment became voluntary rather than mandatory. By 1990, only 13 states had "sexual psychopath" laws.

One reason that the psychiatric profession supported the repeal of these laws was that the term *sexual psychopath* was neither medical nor legal but an "amalgam . . . that allowed treatment in a manner consistent with a guarantee of community safety" (Group for the Advancement of Psychiatry). In other words, the intervention neither changed the perpetrator nor prevented further offenses. Psychiatry had no disease entity for such a person but could only classify the phenomena as a behavior.

The new legal term was the *sexually violent predator*, a person charged or convicted of a sex crime and who has "a mental abnormality or disorder which makes the person likely to engage in predatory acts of sexual violence" (Lieb, 2). This allowed the state to detain an individual involuntarily after the sentence for the offense expired until such time as the predator was deemed safe to be at large. But this act was challenged and in 1995 it was revised.

On May 17, 1996, President Bill Clinton signed **Megan's Law**, named after a seven-year-old New Jersey girl who was raped and murdered by a sexual predator who lived across the street. Soon after, Louisiana and other states enacted sexual predator and sex offender registration and notification laws. While some jurists feel this law causes humiliation and invasion of privacy for a person who has "served his time," others feel this is a reasonable compromise between indeterminate incarceration and release of a dangerous person.

On March 5, 2003, the Supreme Court ruled that notifying communities of sex offenders information and specifically that of placing photos of sex offenders on the Internet is not infringing on sex offenders' rights, outlined in the Constitution. *See also*: **Pedophilia; Serial Rape and Rapists.**

Suggested Reading: Andee Beck, "The Little Boy: What Do We Need to Know," *Tacoma News Tribune*, February 7, 1990, S9; Committee on Psychiatry and the Law, *Psychiatry and Sex Psychopath Legislation: The 30s to the 80s*, report No. 98 (New York: Group for the Advancement of Psychiatry, 1977), 861; Kristin Gordon, "Sex Offender Info Still Online," *Lancaster Eagle Gazette*, March 6, 2003, http://www.lancastereaglegazette.com/news/stories/20030306/topstories/1120684.html; Roxanne Lieb, "Washington's Sexually Violent Predator Law: Legislative History and Comparisons with Other States," Washington State Institute for Public Policy, December 1996, http://www.wa.gov/wsipp.wagov/rptfiles/Wasexlaw.pdf; Donna D. Schram and Cheryl Darling Milloy, "Community Notification: A

Study of Offender Characteristics and Recidivism," Washington State Institute for Public Policy, October 1995, http://www.wa.gov/wsipp/crime/pdf/chrrec.pdf.

LANA THOMPSON

SEXUALLY TRANSMITTED DISEASES (STDs). *See* HIV/AIDS.

SLAVERY. The system of slavery has been a central feature of world history and is directly tied to the physical and cultural rape of different peoples across time. In the fifteenth century, European nations competed for new world markets and launched a new era of bondage by turning African slavery into a transatlantic business. The resulting greed and competition tore African men, women, and children from their native communities and forced the diaspora of slaves throughout the Western world. The early slave traders largely focused on male slaves to fulfill the labor demands of sugar, rice, and tobacco production. Once plantation owners firmly rooted slavery in the American colonies, the sex ratio between male and female slaves leveled out. This shift led to the formation of slave communities where slave families suffered under a barbaric system of physical and sexual abuse.

Historians disagree over the political and economic rationale for the system of American slavery, yet there is little disagreement over the dehumanizing and oppressive features of slavery and the formation of power relations that reinforced unnatural bonds between whites and blacks that rested on the economic and reproductive labor of slaves. To fully appreciate the social conditions that fostered this sexual and reproductive exploitation, one must understand how gender and race shaped Southern society as a whole. Both merged into Southern codes and cultural attitudes that grew dependent upon gender prescriptions, the dominance of **patriarchy,** and the laws that governed domestic relations between husband and wife, parent and child, and slave and master. Gender prescriptions reveal a complex set of social relations in the Southern society grounded on patriarchal rule. Both Southerners and Northerners promoted unequal relationships between men and women through the theory of the "Cult of True Womanhood." This theory maintained that white women were pure, pious, submissive, and dependent. Southern men used this theory to justify their manhood and reinforced paternalism grounded on a violent code of honor. This same code of honor placed white women on a pedestal, while consigning black women to a life of bondage and sexual exploitation. The sexual misconduct of white women was not treated lightly, particularly if they engaged in illicit sex with black men. White female sexual misconduct dishonored the reputation of the **family,** and therefore all male kin had an interest in preserving female purity. Ironically, maintaining race purity became a central feature of Southern law and served as a means to enforce sexual purity among white women, while men's sexual misconduct went unpunished as shown by the increase in the mulatto population.

In contrast to white women's virtue, the female slave stereotype of "Jezebel" and the history of forced reproduction tell the story of male sexual misconduct, **sexual coercion,** and sexual violence. Many Southern whites believed that black women, like the biblical Jezebel, lacked self-control of their libidos and were the antithesis of the true white woman. This imagery of Jezebel exposes European and American perceptions formulated during and after contact with African culture. The nature of a female slave's work in the rice, tobacco, and cotton fields often meant that they were semiclad to complete the work. Exposure to women's bodies during slave auctions and slave beatings reinforced the perceptions of promiscuity and imprinted this stereotype in the minds of white society. As with all stereotypes, there is some element of truth, but in the case of the female slave, she was coerced to give her body for slave breeding and reproduction and in some cases became the mistress of her slave owner or entered the "Fancy Trade" of **prostitution** and concubinage.

Southern antebellum slaveholders shaped by a unique social system reinforced the **sexual double standards** for both white and black women. In reality, these standards, brought on by the exploitation and illicit sex of white men, created mixed-race families, revealing the inherent flaws of Southern honor and laws governing rape. At the same time, Southern **rape laws** reveal a systematic discrimination based on gender, class, and race. These same laws provide a historical framework for understanding the pervasiveness of the sexual double standards in rape cases today.

Rape and property laws defined different levels of behavior, and the punishments meted out varied in degree based on color. Southern courts punished blacks more harshly than whites, thus exposing a dual system of justice and the contradictions of a slave society. The enforcement of rape laws and definitions of property blended together in a legal system reinforced by gender, class, and race stratifications.

Southern white men believed that black men were obsessed with white women. During the colonial period, black men convicted of rape could expect **castration**, and by the antebellum period the punishment increased to the death penalty. The harshness of punishments against black rapists in part reflected white society's obsession with female sexuality and the view that it owned white women's bodies and would protect them as property. These same beliefs tied white men's masculinity to family honor and white female purity. Rape not only dishonored the woman and entire household, it also challenged the racial and social order of Southern slave society.

Slavery created a dual and contradictory system at all levels. Southern law reinforced the protection of white women as property, while justifying the sexual exploitation of black women. White slaveholders held absolute power over their slave population and could rape their slaves at will without fear of punishment. The systematic sexual exploitation of black female slaves and their mulatto offspring reveals a society weighted down by public and private violence. Rape laws did not apply or protect black female slaves from the abuses of their masters. Instead, these women shouldered the double burden of their gender and race.

In contrast to white men's experience, black men accused of raping black women faced punishment for assault and battery laws. In the case *George v. State of Mississippi* (1859), the court overturned a death sentence of a convicted black male slave on the basis that the law did not recognize rape between African slaves. Masters, not the state, regulated sexual intercourse between slaves. In this case, the court ruled that the black male slave could be tried for assault and battery, regardless of gender, and slaves lacked legal standing under common law. The Civil War sharpened Southern views on **sexual assault** of black women, and for the first time legal scholars promoted laws that protected slave women from rape. New rape codes offered some protection to black women, but courts dispersed punishments unequally based on race. White men convicted of raping white women faced imprisonment, whereas black men convicted of raping white women faced certain death. In contrast, men convicted of raping black women, whether free or slave, faced fines and punishments according to the courts' discretion. Southern jurisprudence punished rape offenders unevenly based on two separate legal standards centered on race and gender. Black men and women were the double **victims** of a society grounded on racism and sexual exploitation, while the court's assessment of white women's virtue depended on their sexual purity. Judges could label women who had engaged in illicit sex as willing participants rather than victims and in turn, offer little protection from the court. In reflection, Southern antebellum laws governing illicit sex and rape reveal an obsession with female sexuality and a general distrust of female rape victims; whether black or white, the sexual double standard prevailed.

The history of slavery and its concomitant sexual exploitation serves as a reminder that past and present rape laws focus on female purity, limiting the effectiveness of laws designed to protect women from continued sexual exploitation. *See also*: **Race and Racism; Rape Law; Southern Rape Complex.**

Suggested Reading: Peter W. Bardaglio, *Reconstructing the Household: Families, Sex, & the Law in the Nineteenth-Century South* (Chapel Hill: University of North Carolina Press, 1995); Catherine Clinton, *Tara Revisited: Women, War, & the Plantation Legend* (New York: Abbeville Press, 1995); Deborah Gray White, *Ar'n't I a Woman? Female Slaves in the Plantation South* (New York: W.W. Norton, 1985).

DANELLE MOON

SODOMY. On June 26, 2003, the U.S. Supreme Court ruled that it was illegal to criminalize the act of sodomy between consenting adults. The Court's decision, *Lawrence et al. v. Texas*, overturned the centuries-old traditional basis of the laws, which criminalized nonprocreative sex. It also set a precedent to halt the use of sodomy statutes to stigmatize same-sex relations—a trend that had gained momentum over the past quarter-century in the United States. The Supreme Court decision, however, clearly supported the ongoing **prosecution** of nonconsensual acts of sodomy, including rape and **sexual assault**.

The definition of sodomy, which formed the basis of the American laws, can be traced to the time of the reign of England's King Henry VIII. Originally, it was defined as anal intercourse between a man and a woman, between two men, or between humans and beasts. The sixteenth-century frameworks of both the ecclesiastical and civil laws designated these acts as sex for nonprocreative purposes and thereby synonymous with both a sin against God and a crime. The term *sodomy* itself derives from the story of the kingdoms of Sodom and Gomorrah. According to the Old Testament **Bible** (Genesis 18–19), both kingdoms were completely destroyed because of the wickedness of all the male inhabitants, who were all deemed as sinners against God.

Over the centuries, the definition evolved to include all sexual acts outside of procreative sex—namely, both **anal** and **oral sex**. Therein, the precedents from the early Judeo-Christian religious, ethnic, and moral beliefs became the basis of the sodomy laws in early colonial America. Many of these continued to the present day, with the notions of sin and immorality being implicated in the laws. The state of Rhode Island, for instance, aptly reflected these sentiments in entitling their legislation as an "Abominable and Detestable Crime against Nature." From the founding of America until the latter decades of the twentieth century, the sodomy legislation was only sporadically enforced and most commonly ignored if the participants were consenting adults having sexual relations in private. However, the *Lawrence* decision, and the position of many activist groups, cites that the laws have been used in recent decades to stigmatize and criminalize same-sex couples and sexual relations. The Supreme Court decision is thereby important as it strikes down the use of the legislation to criminalize sodomy for moral reasons or to stigmatize same-sex couples. Right-to-privacy, gay rights, and international human rights lobbyists applauded the ruling of the Court.

Lawrence stressed the importance of using the laws to address the continuing scenarios where sodomy is a criminal act. This includes nonconsensual sodomy, sexual assault, coerced sodomy, and other forms of rape. Sodomy with minors, whose youth legally renders them as incapable of providing **consent**, is also outside of the law. Some prosecutors suggest that the charge of sodomy is levied when there is insufficient evidence to garner a conviction on the more comprehensive charges of sexual assault or rape.

The Supreme Court ruling clearly delineated the current interpretation of the boundaries between legal and criminal sodomy. However, the religious association with immorality and sin still continues in the popular belief system of many Americans. Influential religious organizations and structures, such as the Vatican, continue to uphold their opposition to all nonprocreative sexual acts. Therefore, criminal charges for bona fide sodomy, such as in a rape or in sex with minors, continues to elicit strong sentiments and public opinion, beyond the physical tragedy of the assault, from those who view the act as sinful, immoral, and criminal. *See also*: **Legislation, Illegal Sex Acts.**

Suggested Reading: Richard Godbeer, " 'The Cry of Sodom': Discourse, Intercourse, and Desire in Colonial New England," *William and Mary Quarterly* 52.2 (1995): 259–286; David C. Nice, "State Deregulation of Intimate Behavior," *Social Science Quarterly* 69.1 (1988): 203–211; Bert F. Oaks, " 'Things Fearful to Name': Sodomy and Buggery in Seventeenth-Century New England," *Journal of Social History* 12.2 (1978): 268–281.

LAURIE JACKLIN

SOUTHERN RAPE COMPLEX. The American South's near-hysterical fear of black men as rapists of white women, often referred to as the "rape complex" or "rape myth," has been one of the most salient aspects of race relations in that region since the late nineteenth century. Such fears, imagined and irrational, had little basis in reality. Regardless, a virtual obsession among southern whites about the sexual danger black men posed to white women proved to be a powerful tool of racial control and dominance, effectively helping to deny black men access to political, economic, and social equality, while increasing white women's dependence on their men folk for protection.

The rape complex has long intrigued scholars of the American South. For much of the twentieth century, sociologists, psychologists, physicians, and historians have analyzed the white South's preoccupation with black male sexuality. Once viewed as a universal and timeless aspect of southern society, white fears of black rape were believed to have been a direct legacy of **slavery**. Early analysts of this phenomenon, heavily influenced by the psychoanalytic teachings of **Sigmund Freud**, claimed that slaveholding white men constructed an imaginary black rape threat to assuage their own guilt about sexually exploiting slave women. Native southerner and social critic Wilbur J. Cash in a seminal work, *Mind of the South* (1941), who is largely credited with coining the term "rape complex," also cited the region's infatuation with the notion of pure white womanhood as contributing to ideas about a black rape threat. The symbol of virtue, honor, and purity, white women thus were "desexed" in the minds of many whites. The exaggerated purity and ostensible passionlessness of white womanhood stood in contrast to the hypersexual and savage black man.

Historians found these Freudian explanations of the southern rape complex persuasive and borrowed heavily from them in historical treatments of the topic. Foremost, Winthrop Jordan offered the first in-depth historical insight into the complex relationship between sexual ideology and race in his pathbreaking study of early race relations, *White Over Black* (1968). White American perceptions about black sexuality, he argued, stemmed from early English contact with Africans in Africa. Partial nudity, gossip about black male genitalia, and the practice of polygamy fueled racist notions about **bestiality** and licentiousness in Africans, which carried over to **African American** slaves.

White stereotypes about black sexuality thus played an important role in the development of the rape complex. Whites believed blacks were innately immoral and uncivilized, therefore more susceptible to "natural" impulses, including sex. Recent historical works, however, have suggested that while colonial and antebellum whites tended to view blacks as more passionate and even promiscuous, white fears of black rape did not emerge until well after slaves had been emancipated, thus shifting the origins of the rape complex to the late nineteenth century. Not until the late 1880s did the white South seem to become gripped by fears of black rape. White southerner Philip Alexander Bruce is believed to have been the first to present the "problem" of the "black rapist" to a large readership in 1889. What followed in print and speeches was a veritable flood of rabid diatribes about black men's propensity to rape white women, accompanied by ominous predictions for the white South if the black man's urges were not held in check. Racial segregation and disfranchisement of black men were thus served up as necessary to protect the region's white females. Turn-of-the-century southern politicians quickly gauged the political hay they could reap by employing the rhetoric of the "black-beast-rapist." On the floor of the U.S. Senate in 1907, for example, Senator Benjamin Tillman of South Carolina provocatively described the state of siege under which southern women lived, fearful of lurking black men whose breasts pulsated "with the desire to sate their passions upon white maidens and wives." The father of three daughters, Tillman explained he would rather find any one of them "killed by a tiger or a bear" and retain her **virginity** rather than suffer the fate of being "robbed of the jewel of her womanhood by a black fiend."

Political rants about the "black-beast-rapist" were shored up by published "scientific" studies in various fields that set out to examine and quantify the "Negro rape problem." In 1896, Frederick L. Hoffman, a statistician employed by the Prudential Insurance Company, published a demographic study that purported to show incidence of rape by blacks wildly out of proportion to their numbers in society. Hoffman blamed innate sexual immorality, a propensity for crime, and a tendency for blacks to "misconstrue personal freedom into personal license." **Physicians** also weighed in on the debate about the "new Negro crime." One medical study traced the proneness of black men to rape white women to the "hereditary influence" of African ancestors, the Ashantee warrior who had been accustomed to knocking his prospective bride with a club and then dragging her into the woods.

Images of black **sexual predators** were especially bountiful on the pages of fiction composed by turn-of-the-century native white southerners caught up in the "Lost Cause" mentality, the defensive posturing taken by many after the Civil War that hailed the Confederate cause as honorable and glorious. Using the Reconstruction-era South as the stage, southern novelists used the pen to attack federal Reconstruction policies, notably those granting blacks political equality. Empowered with new-found political rights, these authors wrote, black men now set their sights on "social equality," the right to take white women as wives and lovers. The most successful of these novels was Thomas Dixon's *The Clansman* (1905), which director D.W. Griffith transformed into *Birth of a Nation*, the nation's first major motion picture epic. The dénouement of the novel is a scene in which an innocent, young white girl is sexually assaulted by a bestial ex-slave. The stereotype of the black rapist that inhabited the pages of southern fiction, and was later more widely consumed by **theater** and movie audiences, became indelibly etched on the minds of Americans and appeared to validate the claims of twentieth-century southerners who sought (invented) historical justification for their own social attitudes and behavior, including racial segregation, disfranchisement, and lynching.

While endemic throughout the South by the turn of the twentieth century, images of black rapists did not go unchallenged. African American activists understood the connection between the white perception about the black sexual threat and the spasms of lynching that punctuated parts of the South well into the 1920s. Frederick Douglass, for one, publicly implied what most blacks instinctively knew: that the allegation of black rape was a ruse offered up to rationalize mob **murder**. Others suggested that consensual relations between black men and white women precipitated allegations of rape. Alex Manly, editor of the Wilmington (NC) *Sentinel*, claimed charges of black rape grew out of attempts by white women to cover up clandestine affairs across the race lines. No one was more outspoken about the "racket" of black rape than antilynching advocate **Ida B. Wells**. Like Manly, Wells attributed many accusations of black-on-white rape to black men betrayed by their white lovers who, fearing the scorn of neighbors and **family**, cried rape.

While historians are divided on the causes of the southern rape complex, most agree that something unique to the 1890s is responsible. The 1890s was, of course, the nadir of race relations in America, when the most vitriolic forms of racism emerged and when the most devastating manifestations of racism became institutionalized. Black political power was certainly center stage as fusionist politics threatened to craft interracial political coalitions. The threat of interracial, intraclass alliances, some say, was the impetus for southern Democrats to appeal to the protection of white womanhood as a ploy to unify whites of all classes. Women's historians interject that the "rape complex" had a devastating impact on white women as well as black men. The encroachment of industrialization into the rural South disrupted traditional gender and family roles in the South and gave rise to a new class of working women who increasingly flouted patriarchal domination. The creation of a black "bogeyman" encouraged white women to depend on their white men. Thus, the rape myth not only served the political ends of white supremacists but reined in wayward white women as well.

Ample evidence testifies to the continuing staying power of the rape complex and to its resilience as a political issue well into the twentieth century and beyond the borders of the South. Studies of the American criminal justice system reveal, for example, that black men convicted of raping white women receive more severe sentences than for raping black women and more severe sentences than white rapists whose victims are black or white. Fears of black rape also infused the 1988 presidential election when a George Bush campaign ad attempted to portray Democratic nominee Michael Dukakis as soft on crime. The ad criticized a prison furlough program in Massachusetts supported by Governor Dukakis, citing the case of Willie Horton, an African American who committed an assault and a rape in Maryland after failing to return to prison on his weekend pass. A mug shot of Horton, some say, was designed to play on white fears of the savage black man as rapist of white women. The following year, racial and political tensions were stretched taut in New York City when a group of racist white teens in the Bensonhurst section attacked and killed a 16-year-old black youth, Yusef Hawkins, in part because some mistakenly believed he was in the Italian American neighborhood to visit a white girl. The rape complex, while it has clearly diminished in potency and pervasiveness in the early twenty-first century, nonetheless continues to shape the contours of American race relations. *See also*: **Interracial Rape; Rape-Lynch Scenario.**

Suggested Reading: Wilbur J. Cash, *Mind of the South* (1941; reprint, New York: Vintage Books, 1991); George M. Fredrickson, *The Black Image in the White Mind: The Debate on Afro-American Character and Destiny, 1817–1914* (Middletown, CT: Wesleyan University Press, 1971); Jacquelyn Dowd Hall, " 'The Mind That Burns in Each Body': Women, Rape, and Racial Violence," in *Powers of Desire: The Politics of Sexuality*, ed. Ann Snitnow, Christine Stansell, and Sharon Thompson (New York: Monthly Review Press, 1983); Winthrop D. Jordan, *White over Black: American Attitudes toward the Negro, 1550–1812* (1968; reprint, New York: W.W. Norton, 1977); Ida B. Wells, *On Lynchings* (reprint, Salem, NH: Ayer, 1991); Joel Williamson, *The Crucible of Race: Black-White Relations in the American South since Emancipation* (New York: Oxford University Press, 1984).

DIANE MILLER SOMMERVILLE

STATUTORY RAPE. Statutory rape is sexual intercourse with an unmarried person who is under the "age of **consent.**" That age ranges from 14 to 18 across the United States, although in most states it is 16. As the crime rests solely on the age of the **victim,** force is not required. The laws are supposed to protect young people from engaging in potentially coercive sex, which may not be recognized as meeting a legal definition or popular perception of forcible rape, before they are physically or emotionally ready. As such, they are often used to prosecute the abuse of young children and teens. But their wording also allows the **prosecution** of consensual sexual relationships between any underage person and any other person if they are not married to each other.

During the colonial period, the age of consent was usually 10 or 12. But in the late nineteenth century, an alliance of organizations such as the Women's Christian Temperance Union, suffragists, and some conservative religious groups and workingmen's organizations lobbied to have the age raised to 16 or 18. Male legislators complied but at the same time made prosecutions more difficult. Some states required the female victim to be able to prove she was a **virgin** at the time of the crime. Others allowed perpetrators to claim that they had made a "mistake of age" and thought the female older than she was.

In the 1970s, as part of a nationwide effort to change **forcible rape** laws, feminists were successful in most states in having these two stipulations repealed. They also lobbied for differential penalties for the crime, depending on the ages of the victim and the perpetrator; generally, the younger the victim, the more severe the penalty.

Two other types of changes did not go uncontested. First, the laws were made "gender neutral." While originally they prosecuted a male who had sex with an underage female, as amended the laws can prosecute any person who has sex with any underage person. Second, while originally the laws stated only that the victim be under a certain age, feminists lobbied for "age spans" that required that the perpetrator be a certain number of years older than the victim. These spans vary from two to six years across the states that adopted them but are generally set at three or four years so that teens close in age are not prosecuted.

Radical feminists believed that gender-neutral language and age spans would detract from their concern that males were always the more powerful party in heterosexual relationships, even if they were the younger party. Religious conservatives, with a more traditional view of gender roles, felt that only males should be punished and also wanted a perpetrator who fell within an age span to still be punished so as to send the message that nonmarital sex was always wrong. Sex radical feminists, as well as **gay and lesbian** groups, feared that gender-neutral laws might be used disproportionately against homosexuals and also felt that age spans did little to counter the laws' invasion of sexual privacy.

In the 1990s, renewed attention was given to statutory rape laws as the U.S. welfare system was revamped. Congress exhorted the states to prosecute the crime more effectively, so as to deter teen **pregnancy** and thereby lower the number of people dependent on welfare. While many states increased prosecutions, it is debatable whether such action would lower the welfare caseload; only about 1 percent of public assistance recipients are underage teens with children.

Given all of the debates over the laws' purposes and over who should be prosecuted, their implementation sometimes undercuts their stated purpose of protecting the young and vulnerable. First, if someone underage is married, his or her sexual activity is not illegal regardless of the character of his or her relationship. Second, some states still retain the "mistake of age" defense, so that young people who appear older or try to act older are outside the law's protection. Third, some states still allow the prosecution of a perpetrator the same age as or younger than the victim. Fourth, an underage person cannot stop a prosecution by claiming that he or she felt that the activity was consensual. Fifth, males in committed relationships with underage females may have to register as **sex offenders** and thus be barred from seeing their partners, as well as from approaching day care centers or school playgrounds at which some of them have children.

The question remains as to how one can effectively protect children and teens from sexual abuse while at the same time allowing consensual sexual activity to go unprosecuted. *See also*: **Child Rape; Rape Law.**

Suggested Reading: Leigh Bienen, "Rape III: National Developments in Rape Reform Legislation," *Women's Rights Law Reporter* 6.3 (Spring–Summer 1980): 170–213; Carolyn Cocca, *Jailbait: The Politics of Statutory Rape Laws in the United States* (Albany: State University of New York Press, 2004); Michelle Oberman, "Turning Girls into Women: Reevaluating Modern Statutory Rape Law," *Journal of Criminal Law and Criminology* 85 (1994): 15–78; Mary Odem, *Delinquent Daughters: Protecting and Policing Adolescent Female Sexuality in the United States, 1885–1920* (Chapel Hill: University of North Carolina

Press, 1995); Frances Olsen, "Statutory Rape: A Feminist Critique of Rights Analysis," *Texas Law Review* 63 (1984): 387–432.

CAROLYN E. COCCA

STEINEM, GLORIA (1934–   ). Feminist organizer and writer, Gloria Steinem was born in Toledo, Ohio, to Leo Steinem and Ruth Nuneviller Steinem. After her 1956 graduation from Smith College, Steinem received a fellowship to study in India, where she absorbed grassroots organizing skills from followers of Gandhi. In 1960 she moved to New York City where she worked for *Help!* magazine and freelanced for *Life, Esquire, Glamour,* and other publications. Steinem cofounded *New York* magazine in 1968, serving as its political columnist until 1972. She came to the women's movement in 1969 after attending a meeting of the Redstockings, a radical feminist group, during which women described their experiences with **abortion.** Her consciousness raised, Steinem embraced feminist activism. In 1971–1972, she and others founded *Ms.* magazine, a groundbreaking publishing venture that drew attention to women's issues.

Steinem became extraordinarily influential; in addition to *Ms.,* her regular appearances on national television as well as constant lecture tours on college campuses and elsewhere brought the women's movement to wide popular audiences. An adept organizer, Steinem was also instrumental in founding the National Women's Political Caucus, Voters for Choice, the Women's Action Alliance, the Ms. Foundation for Women, and the Coalition of Labor Union Women.

Since the 1970s she has dedicated her career to writing, editing, fund-raising, public speaking, and organizing on behalf of feminist issues, receiving numerous awards for her writing and public service. Over the course of her career, Steinem has written and spoken widely on violence against women, including childhood sexual abuse; **date rape/acquaintance rape** and **marital rape;** the relationship between rape and **pornography;** and rape as a **war crime.** From its inception, *Ms.* magazine has published regularly on these topics. Two publications were particularly pathbreaking and controversial. When porn actress Linda Marchiano (Linda Lovelace) asserted that the film *Deep Throat* depicted her own rape, Steinem was among the first to publicize the story, writing "The Ordeal of Linda Lovelace," the May 1980 cover story, which drew attention to relationships between rape and pornography. In the 1980s, the magazine initiated what became a highly contentious discussion of rape on college campuses. Building on Karen Barrett's September 1982 article "Date Rape: A Campus Epidemic?" *Ms.* invited Kent State University psychologist Mary P. Koss to collaborate with the magazine to study the project, part of the magazine's effort during these years to bring feminist scholarship to popular audiences. With support from the National Institute for Mental Health as well as the National Center for the Prevention and Control of Rape, and carried out under Koss's direction, the project was the most far-reaching study on patterns of **sexual assault** at institutions for higher learning at that time. The results, reported in the landmark 1988 study *I Never Called It Rape: The Ms Report on Recognizing, Fighting and Surviving Date and Acquaintance Rape,* became the source for the often quoted and contested figure that one in four women have been victims of some form of sexual assault. Steinem's papers as well as the records of the Women's Action Alliance are housed at the Sophia Smith Collection at Smith College; *Ms.* magazine records are held by both the Sophia Smith Collection and the Schlesinger

Library. *See also*: Feminist Movement; Rape History in the United States: Twentieth Century.

MARLA MILLER

STIGMA. Rape stigma is the negative perception of a rape **survivor**'s reputation, manifested in insinuations or openly expressed misconceptions that the assault was somehow "invited" by the **victim**'s behavior.

Stigma normally takes three common forms: self-stigma, **family** stigma, and social stigma. Self-stigma is the tendency of many victims to blame themselves for the assault. It is a deep emotional condition with tragic effects on the person's quality of life, self-esteem, and readiness to have a regular sexual relationship. Not infrequent is family stigma, an often hostile attitude of family members who blame or force the victim to keep silent. An early example of family stigma is described in the **Bible**, in the story of Tamar, raped by her half brother and later told by her brother to hide the truth. Social stigma is the reproach on the victim's reputation conveyed in the general feeling that the victim's behavior contributed to the incident. Rape stigma is a pervasive and persistent phenomenon whose peculiarity becomes evident when one realizes the difference between the attitude toward rape survivors and that reserved for victims of nonsexual assaults. Whereas the society in general is strongly compassionate toward persons crippled by drunk drivers, for example, the sexual element of rape automatically raises doubts as to the victim's role in a rape.

An especially unfortunate consequence of stigma is that victims are further traumatized and have few ways to break the cycle of injustice. According to various estimates, due to the fear of social stigma, rape is a dramatically underreported crime. When reported, many rapists go unpunished, as their defense attorneys capitalize on the victim's self-stigma and manage to convince the grand jury that the sexual encounter was consensual. Victims often avoid being named in **media** coverage. Often advised against speaking out, rape survivors let themselves be shamed into silence, which according to some experts only adds insult to injury. Silence does little to resolve the emotional distress a raped person has been subjected to. Speaking out is not easy either, as those who choose this option are more or less openly accused of using the incident with a view to fame. But as advocates of speaking out argue, because rapists often threaten to kill their victims, going public is a way to break the rapists' power over their victims. *See also*: **"Blaming the Victim" Syndrome; Rape Counseling; Rape Crisis Centers; Tribal Customs and Laws.**

Suggested Reading: K.K. Baker, "Sex, Rape, and Shame," *Boston University Law Review* 79 (1999): 663–716; T.R. Miller et al., *Victim Costs and Consequences: A New Look* (Washington, DC: U.S. Department of Justice, 1996).

KONRAD SZCZESNIAK

SURVIVORS. Throughout history and around the world, people have been raped by strangers, dates, **family** members, multiple attackers, and gangs. They have been trafficked and forced into **prostitution** or sexual **slavery**. Women have been forced to become wives and concubines. Rape survivors are female and male, adults and children, homosexuals and heterosexuals. They endure physical and psychological consequences of their ordeal for months or years, if not a lifetime.

Sexual crime is an affront to the person. Some can get over the sex act, but the sense of dehumanization remains. Survivors are devastated by the sense of losing their personal power and ability to make choices. Psychological consequences can be severe. They can include **posttraumatic stress disorder**, depression, anxiety, panic attacks, constant fear, sleep disorders, nightmares, flashbacks, denial, problems forming relationships, intimacy difficulties, constant anger, emotional shutdown, debilitating self-blame or shame, overeating or loss of appetite, substance abuse, and more. Survivors may lose all sense of being safe. Collectively, these reactions are called **rape trauma syndrome**. Symptom intensity may increase if survivors revisit the rape scene or a similar situation.

Some individuals are more susceptible to certain psychological responses than others. Today, almost half of **date rape** survivors tell no one of their ordeal, thereby increasing the potency of any physical and psychological problems. But support is critical. For instance, posttraumatic stress disorder can be minimized, even prevented, if **victims** receive clinical help soon after rape.

Physically, survivors may suffer mild to severe injuries, usually from being choked or beaten. Injuries most often include bruising of skin, vaginal walls, or cervix, severe bleeding, tearing of the anus, and swelling of the labia. There may also be **pregnancy**, venereal disease, or **HIV/AIDS**.

Sociologically, there is lasting **stigma**, often not of the victim's own making. Society often places a stigma on rape victims that is hard to escape. Rape becomes a component of a person's identity for life.

Survivor recovery depends heavily upon the amount and quality of support from **law enforcement**, medical and rape crisis communities, family, and friends. Psychiatric help may be needed beyond ongoing counseling. Friends and family should take the rape seriously, listen, and verbally praise victims for surviving.

Survivors may be comforted by having a friend at their side during police reporting. Counselors from **rape crisis centers** are familiar with police procedures and can attend interviews to support survivors. Survivors may request to speak to an officer of the same sex, but one may or may not be available.

If survivors injure or kill an attacker, feelings of guilt may occur. Some individuals feel guilty for not having fought harder. Often, survivors question whether or not they are responsible for the rape. They may ask, "Do I look like I want to be raped?" They attribute elements of fault to themselves. It is important to remember that guilt lies with the rapist. Anything individuals do to remain alive during attack should be respected.

With an under 50 percent arrest rate for reported rapes, it is little wonder that constant fear, which plagues the majority of survivors, continues long term. Symptoms of posttraumatic stress can surface years after the incident.

Rape prevention or other **self-defense** classes are one method for survivors to tackle fears, build confidence, and regain a sense of control. Some survivors turn to community or political action as another method to find empowerment and help prevent rapists from consuming the lives of others. Whatever the methods, finding outlets, support, empowerment, and relief from psychological trauma is imperative to the recovery and well-being of survivors. *See also*: **Rape Counseling**.

Suggested Reading: Dianna Daniels Booher, *Rape: What Would You Do If . . . ?* (New York: Julian Messner, 1981); Robin Warshaw, *I Never Called It Rape: The Ms. Report on Recognizing, Fighting and Surviving Date and Acquaintance Rape* (New York: Harper & Row, 1988).

ELIZABETH JENNER

T

TAILHOOK CONVENTION OF 1991. An event synonymous with **sexual ha-rassment** within the **U.S. military**, the Tailhook affair was a sex scandal named after the 1991 convention of the Tailhook Association at the Las Vegas Hilton Hotel. The Tailhook Association is a private organization devoted to supporting U.S. Naval Carrier Aviation and ensuring a continued strong national defense. The association comprises aviators on active duty, as well as reserve and retired navy and marine corps pilots, defense contractors, and others.

During the association's 1991 convention, naval aviators were reported to have molested, to varying degrees, women officers and nonmilitary personnel. Details of the incidents were revealed following lawsuits filed by Lieutenant Paula Coughlin and other women who claimed to have been sexually assaulted by intoxicated pi-lots. Among the most notorious activities associated with the scandal was "the gauntlet." In each of the three nights of the 1991 convention, in a particular hallway of the hotel, drunken male officers encircled women and grabbed at their breasts, crotches, and buttocks, attempting to strip off their clothes. In total, at least 26 women were forced to run the gauntlets, and it was revealed that a significant number of women did so freely and knowingly, some even baring their breasts. According to various witnesses questioned in the course of the investigation, poke-and-grab gauntlets had been a Tailhook tradition for at least 15 years. It was com-mon for intoxicated males to run nude past onlookers, an activity described by witnesses as "streaking," and to publicly expose their genitals, which is commonly referred to as "ballwalking."

The Tailhook case is significant for its role in exposing the U.S. military's fre-quently sexist attitude toward women, which became evident in the navy's reluc-tance to conduct a viable investigation into cases of sexual harassment. According to an independent report by Deputy Inspector General Derek J. Vander Schaaf, investigators purposely blocked the investigation and were said to make untoward remarks about women's role in the military.

The inadequacies of the investigation through regular navy channels and an earlier dismissal of her complaints prompted Lt. Paula Coughlin to bring the case to the court. She sued the Tailhook Association, the Las Vegas Hilton Hotel, and the Hilton Hotels Corporation for failing to provide adequate security for guests. On October 24, 1994, U.S. District Judge Philip M. Pro read the verdict, finding the defendants guilty of negligence.

The shock that accompanied the scandal prompted the navy to confront the problem of sex abuse. It was recognized that the Tailhook incident resulted from both a failure in leadership and a navy culture indulgent toward **sexual coercion**. To rectify the situation, sensitivity training was proposed, along with a zero-tolerance plan that stipulated, among other things, that sexual offenders and "senior officers who question the role of women in the military" be summarily dismissed from duty. Additionally, an initiative was proposed to enhance professional opportunities for women.

These reforms were introduced amid protests from military members who claimed the affair had been blown out of proportion and that the measures taken may have been motivated by opportunism rather than commitment to the military. This point was based on evidence that a large number of female personnel appeared to have freely participated in the Tailhook events and, indeed, denied feeling victimized. Furthermore, it was pointed out that there existed the possibility that careers could be destroyed unfairly, based on mere suspicion of sexual impropriety. Such was the case of one commander who was denied promotion in 1995 on the grounds that he was in Las Vegas at the time of the 1991 Tailhook Convention, even though he proved he had not been in any way implicated in the scandal. Finally, the suicide of Admiral Jeremy Michael Boorda, who felt hounded by the accusers, had perhaps the most sobering effect on the Tailhook whistleblowers.

The Tailhook affair had consequences for the Tailhook Association as well. After the navy withdrew its official support of the organization and many of its members left its ranks, the Tailhook Association had no option left but to introduce measures prohibiting sexual harassment. When the organization was once again accused of similar cases of misconduct at its 2000 convention, a navy investigation found no evidence to support the allegations and cleared the Tailhook Association of any wrongdoing. *See also*: **Alcohol**.

Suggested Reading: Jack Kammer, "Recovering from a Tailspin," *Reason Magazine* (January 1994); Derek J. Vander Schaff, *Tailhook 91—Review of the Navy Investigations*, report released by the Department of Defense, September 1992; Tailhook Association, http://www.tailhook.org/.

KONRAD SZCZESNIAK

TAKE BACK THE NIGHT MOVEMENT. Take Back the Night is an event designed to promote awareness of sexual violence against women and to assert that sexual violence, or violence of any sort, will not be tolerated in our communities. Take Back the Night protests rape, **domestic violence**, **sexual harassment**, and any acts of physical brutality. These events are meant to empower women to take a stand against violence and refuse to be victimized.

The first Take Back the Night took place in Europe in the early 1970s, and the first large-scale Take Back the Night in the United States took place in San Francisco in 1978. As its focus was primarily to rally against **pornography** and demand street safety, more than 5,000 marchers demonstrated at night in San Francisco's pornography strip, blocking traffic and chanting slogans such as, "No more profits off women's bodies."

Today's Take Back the Night events are primarily local events organized by colleges and universities or women's organizations. Composed of rallies and/or marches, many Take Back the Nights occur in April, which is **Sexual Assault** Awareness Month. The precise format of each Take Back the Night varies. Many begin in the early evening with a march through a highly populated area, with participants carrying signs and chanting slogans such as, "Survivors Unite / To Take Back the Night" and "Join Together / Free Our Lives / We Will Not Be Victimized." A **survivor** of sexual violence or councilor from a **rape crisis center** may give a speech on **date rape**, childhood sexual abuse, or other relevant topics. A speak-out, where women read poems, tell of their own assaults, or request a moment of silence, allows participants to share their experiences with sexual violence. Many Take Back the Night events end with a candlelight vigil and an exhortation to confront the issue of sexual violence every day in one's actions, speech, and thoughts.

Some Take Back the Night events limit participation to women only, asking men to offer support by giving a donation or providing child care. Organizers of these events argue that Take Back the Night is a time for women to stand in solidarity to reclaim their bodies and the streets without the help or "protection" of men. Their critics argue that restricting the event to women excludes the group it should be addressing—men—and alienates those men who do want to lend their support. Regardless, Take Back the Night provides an important means of discussing rape and other sexual violence and decrying its prevalence in our communities. *See also:* **New York Radical Feminists (NYRF)**.

Suggested Reading: "Take Back the Night," Campus Outreach Services, 2002, http://www.campusoutreachservices.com/resources/tbtnhistory.htm.

ROBIN E. FIELD

THEATER. Since the times of the ancient Greeks, plays have been written about **victims** of rape. Many societies that produced such plays understood rape and its consequences in very different ways, and punishments for rape in these plays take many different forms. In consequence, the plays provide valuable insights into the values of these societies. Many plays begin after the rape has occurred and present the **victims'** lives, the lives of their children, and the lives of the men who raped them. Plays in which a rape is attempted are relatively common. Plays in which a rape actually occurs are quite rare.

For the Greeks and Romans, calling an act of sexual violence rape depended on whether the victim was male or female, a citizen, or a slave. Rape was usually defined as a crime against a male citizen's property, not as an act of violence against another human being. Early Greek dramas of the classical period often treat the subject of rape in the context of war. The victims are generally women and children enslaved by the victorious enemy. The best known examples deal with the Trojan War and its aftermath, such as Euripides's *The Trojan Women* (415 B.C.E.) and Aeschylus's *Agamemnon* (458 B.C.E.). Other Greek dramas make reference to the rape of mortals by gods. In these plays, such as Euripides's (*Ion*), both the victim and the attacker are considered outside the reach of human law, and they are often revered for producing children with superhuman qualities.

In the later Greek New Comedy, rape is presented in contexts that are entirely human. Menander's *The Arbitration* (310 B.C.E.) is about a wealthy citizen who rapes but then marries his victim, the daughter of another citizen. The Roman comedies of Plautus and Terence are largely modeled after those of Menander and deal with similar situations, including the fates of the children born to the victims. These plays are more concerned with human law than divine intervention and with plots that generate marriages across economic divides.

In plays of the Renaissance, rape is portrayed not just as a physical assault but as a loss of honor, which means a profound loss of social status. Spanish Renaissance dramas, including those by Lope de Vega, Tirso de Molina, and Calderón de la Barca, portray female characters who have "lost their honor" and must find a way to regain it. In Calderón's *Life Is a Dream*, the protagonist, Rosaura, restores her honor by marrying her rapist. In Renaissance terms, this is considered an acceptable way to restore Rosaura's lost honor, as well as a suitable punishment for her rapist, since he is forced to renounce a more advantageous marriage. English Renaissance writers place great emphasis on rape or attempted rape as a crime against the husband and/or father, as well as against the victim. Shakespeare's revenge tragedy *Titus Andronicus* and his later romance *The Tempest* are both examples. Ben Jonson's satire *Volpone* is a particularly bleak look at the ways in which men covet their neighbors' property, including their wives.

Rape was also regarded as a crime against honor and property in the Age of Reason, but with a difference in emphasis. Western dramatists at this time begin to discuss the subject of legal and economic independence as a way for women to protect themselves from predatory males and abusive husbands. This arises directly from a profound shift of ideas, first articulated by Thomas Hobbes and John Locke, implying that since men and women are born equal, they also have the right to own their own bodies, their own sexual pleasure, and their own economic independence. The Restoration comedies of Aphra Behn, John Vanbrugh, and William Wycherley contain witty and explicit discussions of these new insights. In France, Molière explores similar themes in his plays. Many plays of this period portray situations of attempted rape where a woman cannot rely on a male relative to intervene and so has only her own wits to save her. In consequence, rape begins to be seen as a crime against the individual and as a violation of rights to self-determination.

This understanding extends from the eighteenth century to the present. The majority of plays are still written by men, but some begin to show an increasing sensitivity to the vulnerability of the politically and economically disenfranchised, and rape is depicted as an oppressor's weapon. Tennessee Williams's *A Streetcar Named Desire* (1948) portrays a complex woman caught in tragic circumstances, where rape is used as a weapon to destroy her sense of self. William Mastrosimone's play *Extremities* (1982) depicts a similar situation, but the victim, in a stunning reversal, takes revenge upon the man who attempts to rape her by subjecting him to analogous acts of violence that break him down.

Rape becomes an important theme in several late-twentieth-century dramas documenting the experience of minority women. Robbie McCauley's performance piece *Sally's Rape* and Eve Ensler's *The Vagina Monologues* show examples of the violence perpetrated by dominant white, heterosexual males upon disenfranchised minorities. Other playwrights begin to portray rapes enacted in front of the audience, where the rape is presented not only as a physical violation of the victim but as a metaphor for the colonization of the culture that the victim represents. These plays include Howard Brenton's *Romans in Britain* and Alice Tuan's *Some Asians*.

Drama is no longer just a medium for writing about rape, however. Dramatic techniques are now becoming part of highly specialized therapeutic treatments for rape victims. Drama is also being used by student-run theater groups as a means to educate students about rape, especially **date rape** and its devastating consequences. *See also*: **Art; Films, Foreign; Films, U.S.; Literature, World and American.**

Suggested Reading: Ann E. Nyman, "Sally's Rape: Robbie McCauley's Survival Art," *African American Review* 33.4 (Winter 1999): 577–587; Anita K. Stoll and Dawn L. Smith, eds., *The Perception of Women in Spanish Theater of the Golden Age* (Lewisburg, PA: Bucknell University Press; Cranbury, NJ: Associated University Presses, 1991).

DOMINICA BORG

TORTURE. The World Health Association, in its 1975 Declaration of Tokyo, presents the following definition of torture: "the deliberate, systematic, or wanton infliction of physical or mental suffering by one or more persons, acting alone or on the orders of any authority, to force another person to yield information, to make a confession, or for any other reason." Torture can include both physical and psychological methods. Physical torture can include beatings, electric shock, stretching, burning, asphyxiation, rape, and other traumas. Psychological methods include threats, isolation, sleep and sensory deprivation, mock executions, excessive stimulus, and forced witnessing of other traumas. Such physical and mental abuse is often inseparable as **victims** are subjected to combinations of violence against them. The use of all such methods of torture has specific intents, most often for political effects, to overpower and coerce into submission as well as dehumanize its victims.

Some risk factors for being tortured may include the following:

- Refugees or individuals with political asylum status
- Immigrants from a country with totalitarian history
- Members of a minority group in their country of origin
- Members of a minority political party in their country of origin
- Individuals in countries torn by civil war
- Individuals in countries where the military has governmental control
- Prisoners of war
- Individuals with a history of arrest or prison detention
- Individuals participating in antigovernment organization(s)

Human rights organizations estimate that approximately 123 countries condone and use torture on their citizens. Other figures place the number of individuals who have been tortured between 1.1 and 8 million people worldwide. According to J.M. Jaranson, in *Caring for Victims of Torture*, there are an estimated 400,000 **survivors** of torture living in the United States. However, because torture is often perpetuated in secrecy and attempts are made to suppress its extent from both the regional and international public, the numbers of victims can only be estimated.

Sexual torture with implements and animals, and acts of forced sex committed by the torturers or others, is often a central and common method in the torture process of men, women, and children. Yet many judicial agencies and governing institutions still separate, in legal language, rape from the torture experiences. Importantly, author Lucinda Finley writes, "Legal language does more than express thoughts, it reinforces certain world views and understanding of events." The move to include rape as a classification of torture has political and treatment implications. Such a change in language could provide additional legal protections that victims of other methods of torture receive. The psychological aftermath experienced by a rape victim and a torture victim is comparable diagnostically. Many survivors will meet the same criteria for **posttraumatic stress disorder**, yet by continuing to classify rape as a separate "bad act" that is not judged as heinous or as despicable as torture, victims are denied equal access to human rights law. In short, current policies or beliefs perpetuate **rape myths**, such as rape is just sex.

A practical illustration of this cognitive splitting off of rape as somehow a different form of torture occurs in the way services are delivered to survivors. For instance, a refugee may receive services for every type of torture he or she endured except rape. The rape would be treated as requiring a separate and completely different set of services. This fractured treatment approach continues to marginalize rape victims and adds to the likelihood that treatment for the torture experience that includes rape will be incomplete. The centrality of rape embedded in a torture experience has lasting implications for victims in ways that are qualitatively different, indeed worse, than other forms of torture. The distortion that is often experienced by rape survivors serves to isolate them in their intimate relationships and in their communities. For example, if a person has been intentionally electrically shocked or burned, they would not expect to encounter those forms of punishment when they returned to their home or community, yet that same person is very likely to encounter—indeed, be expected to engage in—sexual relations with an intimate partner not just once but repeatedly over time.

With so many traumas superimposed simultaneously it is difficult to develop one clear "torture syndrome." As with any extraordinarily difficult experience, recovery is an arduous and ongoing process. The survivor of torture will face many factors that mediate his or her recovery. The factors of the traumatic experience of torture are a composite of biological predisposition, coping mechanisms, and other variables that serve as protective influences over the individual's psychological functioning. Central to the understanding of recovery from rape in particular is the understanding that being raped meets the definition of torture as fully as other forms of torture. *See also*: **Prison Rape**.

Suggested Reading: Metin Basoglu, *Torture and Its Consequences: Current Treatment Approaches* (Cambridge: Cambridge University Press, 1992); Susan Brownmiller, *Against Our Will: Men, Women and Rape* (New York: Fawcett Columbine, 1975); Lucinda M. Finley, "Breaking Women's Silence in Law: The Dilemma of the Gendered Nature of Legal Reasoning," *Notre Dame Law Review* 64 (1989): 886–888; J.M. Jaranson, *Caring for Victims of Torture* (Washington, DC: American Psychiatric Press, 1998); Harvey M. Weinstein, Laura Dansky, and Vincent Iacopino, "Torture and War Trauma Survivors in Primary Care Practice," *Western Journal of Medicine* 165 (1996): 112–118.

JENNIFER H. PROFITT

TRAFFICKING IN WOMEN AND CHILDREN. Human trafficking occurs for many purposes. Most women and children are trafficked for **prostitution**, some for marriage, and many for exploited labor. Women who are trafficked for domestic labor often end up being sexually exploited as well. Some children are trafficked for adoption. Increasingly, especially in African countries, there are reports of children being trafficked for organs.

There are enormous difficulties in producing accurate assessments of trafficking. The International Organization of Migration (IOM) attempted to estimate numbers of trafficked women in Europe for the European Union and concluded that accurate numbers were not possible. However, the United Nations estimates that trafficking is a $5 billion to $7 billion operation annually, with 4 million persons moved from one country to another and within countries. The U.S. government estimates that 50,000 women and children are trafficked each year into the United States, primarily from Latin America, Russia, the New Independent States, and Southeast Asia.

Traffickers are adept at taking advantage of any unstable conditions such as military conflicts, countries in financial crisis, politically destabilized situations, or refugee camps where women and children are often abducted or recruited. Child sexual exploitation has grown exponentially in all countries but especially in Asian and Latin American countries. Travel agencies, hotels, airlines, businesses, and so-called child protectors are often involved in sex tourism. Some child sexual abusers seem to think that they can avoid AIDS if they have sex with children, but more often, they seek out children because children can be made to fulfill the abusers' demands.

Organized crime is certainly involved in trafficking, but in many cases traffickers and pimps are small-scale operators who are husbands or boyfriends of **victims**. Women are trafficked into the United States, for example, often through other transit countries or across neighboring borders. The women are trafficked by car, bus, boat, and plane.

The conditions of trafficking range from force or coercion to deception, abuse of power, or abuse of a victim's vulnerability. Many women are deceived into thinking they will work as domestics, waitresses, dancers, and models. Others are sold outright and moved around from place to place. Some know that they will engage in prostitution but have no idea of the conditions that await them. Many are women whose vulnerabilities are preyed upon. The majority of women in prostitution have been sexually abused as children. Once in the country of destination, women are held in apartments, bars, and makeshift brothels where they service multiple men per day. Many are raped, beaten, and confined under the worst of conditions.

In most countries, various factors make it nearly impossible for trafficked women to seek assistance and to testify against traffickers and other exploiters. These include death threats to themselves and their families, conditions of isolation and confinement, the violence and control within the sex industry, constant movement from place to place within a strange country, fear of deportation, and the lack of shelters. Additionally, the immigration and criminal justice system in many countries is weighted against trafficked women, for the most part treating them as illegal immigrants.

Trafficking affects mostly all countries, although not all equally. There are sending countries, transit countries, and countries of destination, with some countries in all three categories. In general, the flow of trafficked women and children moves from poorer countries or countries in economic, social, and political crisis, to richer and more socially and politically stable countries.

Many nongovernmental organizations (NGOs) and researchers working in the field of trafficking list various factors that facilitate trafficking. Among them are:

Economic policies. Promoted by international lending organizations such as the World Bank and the International Monetary Fund, these policies mandate "structural adjustments" in many developing regions of the world, pushing certain countries to export women for labor (the Philippines)—making them vulnerable to trafficking—or to develop economies based on tourism (Thailand), with a huge dependence on sex tourism.

Globalization of the sex industry. Globalization of the economy means globalization of the sex industry, which becomes an industry without borders. Large- and small-scale trafficking networks operate across borders, actively recruiting girls and women, especially from villages, city streets, and transportation centers. Also influential is global **advertising**, via the Internet, magazines, and tourism brochures.

Male demand. The so-called customer has been the most invisible factor in promoting prostitution and the trafficking of women for prostitution worldwide. Myths about male sexuality, reluctance to problematize the supposed male "need" for commercial sexual exploitation, male sexual expectations, and the way in which sex has been tolerated as a male right in a commodity culture are all part of this demand.

Female supply based on women's inequality. Gender-based social and economic inequality in all areas of the globe assures a supply of women, especially from developing countries and newly independent states in Eastern Europe. The sex industry is also built on expectations and myths about women's sexuality, the cultural sexual objectification and commodification of women, and a history of childhood sexual abuse of women in prostitution.

Racial myths and stereotypes. Trafficked women are eroticized and sexualized on the basis of stereotypical racial and ethnic features. Sexual advertisements on the Internet, such as those found on the World Sex Guide, also cast prostitution as "natural" to certain groups of women.

Military presence. Armed conflict and civil strife have helped generate trafficking in many parts of the world. Sex industries have been set up around military bases, such as in Okinawa, the Philippines, and Korea, for the rest and recreation of U.S. troops. UN peacekeeping forces have trafficked women in various parts of the world where they have been stationed.

Restrictive immigration policies. Countries want cheap labor, and sex industries want a fresh supply of "exotic" women for prostitution. At the same time, legitimate immigration is becoming more restrictive and discriminatory. Traffickers become the major international players who facilitate international migration because the legitimate channels are so restrictive.

State-sponsored prostitution. State-sponsored prostitution refers to any legal regime in which the system of prostitution itself becomes accepted and legitimated by the State, including by regulation, decriminalization, and legalization of the sex industry. There is good evidence that countries such as Holland and Germany, both of which have recognized prostitution as work and as an economic sector, are precisely the countries into which higher rates of women are trafficked. For example, a report done for the Budapest Group found that 80 percent of the women in the brothels in the Netherlands, a country that has fully legalized pimping, brothels, and buying women for sex, have been trafficked to the Netherlands.

The transnational nature of trafficking means that NGOs and countries must work across borders to confront the problem. Thus it is significant that the concluding piece of international legislation in the twentieth century was the Protocol to Prevent, Suppress and Punish Trafficking in Persons, Especially Women and Children, supplementing the UN Convention against Transnational Organized Crime. It complements the older UN Convention for the Suppression of the Traffic in Persons and of the Exploitation of the Prostitution of Others, often referred to as the 1949 Convention. Together, they are key international tools in the struggle to abolish prostitution and trafficking.

The definition of trafficking, contained in the protocol, helps ensure that all victims of trafficking in persons are protected, not just those who can prove force (Article 3a and b); that victims of trafficking will not bear the burden of proof (Article 3b); that the **consent** of a victim of trafficking is irrelevant (Article 3b); that there is a comprehensive coverage of criminal means by which trafficking takes place, including not only force, coercion, **abduction**, deception, or abuse of power but also less explicit means, such as *abuse of a victim's vulnerability* (Article 3a).

Other major provisions of the UN antitrafficking protocol include that trafficked persons are no longer viewed as criminals but as victims of a crime; that global trafficking will be answered with a global response; that there is now an agreed-upon set of **prosecution**, protection, and prevention mechanisms on which to base national antitrafficking legislation against trafficking; that it is not necessary for a victim to cross a border, subject to provisions listed in Article 3 of the main Convention; that the key actionable element in the trafficking process is the exploitation rather than simply the movement across a border (Article 3a); and that this protocol is the first UN instrument to address the demand that results in women and children being trafficked, calling upon countries to take or strengthen legislative or other measures to discourage this demand that fosters all forms of exploitation of women and children (Article 9.5). *See also*: **Child Rape; Comfort Women; Computers and the Internet; Slavery.**

Suggested Reading: Sheila Jeffreys, *The Idea of Prostitution* (Melbourne: Spinifex Press, 1997); Janice G. Raymond, Jean d'Cunha, Siti Ruhaini Dzuhayatin, H. Patricia Hynes, Zoraida Ramirez Rodriguez, and Aida Santos, *A Comparative Study of Women Trafficked in the Migration Process: Patterns, Profiles and Health Consequences of Sexual Exploitation in Five Countries (Indonesia, the Philippines, Thailand, Venezuela and the United States)*, funded by the Ford Foundation (North Amherst, MA: Coalition against Trafficking in Women, 2002), http://www.catwinternational.org; Amy O'Neill Richard, *International Trafficking in Women to the United States: A Contemporary Manifestation of Slavery and Organized Crime* (Washington, DC: Central Intelligence Agency, 1999), http://www.cia.gov/csi/monograph/women/trafficking.pdf.

JANICE G. RAYMOND

TRIBAL CUSTOMS AND LAWS. Tribal communities, particularly in remote areas of the world, often have different understandings of and customs concerning rape. Some of these customs have evolved into customary law, either operating within a larger state structure or being utilized in a clandestine manner in regions where state authorities have limited control and tribal peoples have either little knowledge of state laws or scant respect for them, preferring their own forms of justice. Thus, understanding tribal customs in the instance of rape involves reorienting concepts of crime as offenses that upset a pattern of social relationships within and between communities, and justice as restorative of these relationships. This holds true historically for tribal communities that operated forms of customary law unmodified by contact with laws in the Judeo-Christian tradition, Islamic laws, or Hindu norms and those whose customs and laws have been modified, even if the modification is unacknowledged.

Scholars argue today that gender discrimination was less pronounced in tribal societies, due to the recognition of women's socioeconomic contributions to the community. Moreover, it has been observed that women's status declines when their economic contribution is reduced, for example, by the introduction of new technology or by the adoption of social practices such as seclusion.

In New Zealand, under traditional Maori law, rape was punishable in some cases with death, since in the Maori view, violence toward a woman was an affront to her and her extended kin group (*whanau*), to be punished and compensated accordingly. The colonially introduced English legal system, now in place, accords women less autonomy and legal standing in comparison with their precolonial status and has eroded their capacity to seek effective redress in cases of sexual violence such as rape.

A similar process has occurred among aboriginal peoples in Australia, where an intense debate took place in the late 1980s concerning rape within the aboriginal community. Feminist scholars argued that colonization had a devastating effect upon male-female relations and that women have lost their traditional power base and are no longer able to take preventative or punitive measures against rapists. However, in the context of wider racism in Australian society, this acknowledgment pits aboriginal women against aboriginal men, who thus continue in their silence about rape within their own community.

In many tribal societies, sexual intercourse is considered consensual, and there is no concept of a sexual offense, which offends the wider community. Customary law regulating sexual behavior is principally concerned with adultery, considered an infringement of the exclusive sexual privilege of the husband over the wife, or vice versa in more equalitarian bands. Offenders among the Garo from Meghalaya (India) can be subject either to customary law, under which the offense is nondiscriminatory in gender terms, or the (colonial) Indian Penal Code, which discriminates against women. Customary punishment is a compensatory fine paid to the husband or wife. However, since kidnapping is a commonly practiced form of marriage among several Northeastern tribes in India, the punishment for which is to make the offender pay the bride-price, this practice begs the question of whether custom prevents women from labeling such actions as rape.

Other customs that raise questions as to the consensual nature of sex include the practice of fraternal polyandry, when the marriage of an elder brother gives the younger brothers in a family sanctioned sexual access to the wife. Polyandry is not the general custom but is found among the Gallongs of Arunachal Pradesh (India). Rape is recognized as an offense by the Mishmis of the Lohit Valley (India). Although the punishment for rape is less than that for adultery, the relative statuses of the offenders' and **victims'** clans are crucial to the question of justice. Nowadays monetary compensation is often substituted for compensation in buffalo.

Anthropologists have sometimes been misinformed as to the customs of tribal societies concerning rape. The most important of such instances involved the research of Margaret Mead in Samoa in 1925–1926. She asserted in her book *Coming of Age in Samoa* (1928) that premarital sexual relations were commonplace and unproblematic in easygoing, harmonious Samoa, that rape was absent and adolescence unmarked by the stresses suffered by youth in Western countries. Her conclusions have now been thoroughly refuted, particularly since Samoa has, and had in the 1920s, one of the highest rates of reported rape in the world. Samoa was distinguished by an unusual form of surreptitious rape (*moetotolo*) whereby a man crept in at night and assaulted a virgin digitally (with his finger), in a reenactment of ritualistic public deflowerings that demonstrated a bride's virginity. In customary law the offense of *moetotolo* carried a substantial fine to be paid in kind by the offender's chief. Forced sexual intercourse carried an even stiffer and humiliating sentence of *saisai*, whereby an offender was trussed up in a public place as if he were a pig ready to be baked.

Among tribal communities in Pakistan and Afghanistan professing Islam and described as having a "feudal culture," tribal councils (*jirga/panchayat*) have been known to order rape or **gang rape**, or effectively endorse action taken by private actors. Ordering rape as punishment might be considered lenient, considering that it is more common for a woman to be killed when suspected of an illicit relationship, for expressing a desire for a choice of marriage partner, for seeking divorce, or because she has been raped. In honor killings, known as *karo-kari*, women are hacked to pieces, shot, or burned to death. The loss of a woman's honor is believed to shame her male relatives particularly, since women embody the honor of men whose property they are considered to be. A man must be able to demonstrate his power to safeguard his honor by killing or obtaining compensation from those who damaged it and thereby restore his honor. In July 2002, the Pakistan Supreme Court strongly criticized the local police in a case in the village of Mirwali in Punjab province, where on June 22, 2002, Mukhtar Bibi was gang raped on the orders of the *jirga*. The council made the ruling to rape her in order to punish her **family** after allegations that her brother had been involved with a woman from a higher-status tribe.

In 2000 in Madhya Pradesh in central India where tribal customs have been influenced by upper-caste Hindu norms, the village council decided to punish a young tribal rape victim, Sonata Bai, for having had an "illicit relationship." According to the current interpretation of Gond tribal custom, she was ordered to have sex in public with her "paramour" in order to "purify herself," effectively, a second rape. She was, however, rescued from this fate by the wife of the chief.

In Papua, New Guinea, the effects of colonization and development have resulted in a reported rate of 45 rapes per 100,000 persons in the 1980s, a higher rate than in the United States, together with a high incidence of gang rape. Sexual violence is perpetuated against a background of political and tribal violence over land disputes. Male cults, which celebrated masculinity by sexually abusing widows and other women without male protection, were traditionally important in some New Guinean communities but have died out under Christian influence. Nevertheless, several authors describing different New Guinea tribes have noted the prevalence of punitive rape as a method of punishing women for transgressing tribal customs. The echoes of these practices can be found today in *rascal* gangs and in the gender ideology still imbibed by young men prior to marriage, which stresses male superiority and the dangerousness of women. Sexual violence occurs today in the context of rapid Westernization, new forms of female subservience introduced by Christian missions, as well as male insecurity concerning female independence and the effects of urbanized lifestyles on male-female relations.

Traditionally tribal societies have both condemned and condoned rape, the majority having customary law treating it as an offense. However, amidst rapid change and development, these societies have been subjected to religious change, concomitant influence on legal norms, and the imposition of colonial penal regimes. In the context of pressure exerted by the societal norms and legal sanctions of dominant traditions, some tribal societies have resorted to utilizing rape as a punishment to control women, whereas others demonstrate their inability to enforce traditional sanctions against rape in the face of alien legal codes. Investigating rape thus highlights the plight of tribal communities worldwide in their struggle to come to terms with colonial histories, development, and globalization. *See also*: **Rape Law**; **Virgins/Virginity**.

Suggested Reading: Diane Bell and Topsy Napurrula Nelson, "Speaking About Rape Is Everyone's Business," *Women's Studies International Forum* 12.4 (1989): 403–416; Derek Freeman, *Margaret Mead and Samoa: The Making and Unmaking of an Anthropological Myth* (Cambridge: Harvard University Press, 1983); Stephanie Milroy, "Milroy Maori Women and Domestic Violence: The Methodology of Research and the Maori Perspective," *Waikato Law Review* 4.1 (Special Issue 1996): 58–76; Laura Zimmer-Tamakoshi, " 'Wild Pigs and Dog Men': Rape and Domestic Violence as 'Women's Issues' in Papua New Guinea," in *Gender in Cross-Cultural Perspective*, ed. C. Brettell and C. Sargent (Englewood Cliffs, NJ: Prentice Hall, 1993), 538–553.

EMMA ALEXANDER

U

UNITED STATES v. LANIER. In *United States v. Lanier*, 520 U.S. 259 (1997), the U.S. Supreme Court held that a criminal defendant indicted for **sexual assault** under a federal statute needed "fair warning" at the time of the alleged assaults that his conduct was criminal under the statute. Lanier, a state court judge, had been accused of sexually assaulting women in his judicial chambers. The United States tried and convicted Lanier under 18 U.S.C. § 242 for willfully acting under the color of Tennessee law to deny the **victims** their constitutional right to be protected from sexual assault.

A panel of the U.S. Court of Appeals for the Sixth Circuit affirmed that judgment, but the Sixth Circuit, in an *en banc* decision, set aside the convictions for lack of notice to the public that 18 U.S.C. § 242 covers sexual assault crimes. The court held that notice occurs only when the violated right (i.e., to be free from sexual assault) is identified under § 242 in a U.S. Supreme Court opinion and only when such right has been applied in a U.S. Supreme Court case that is factually similar to the case before the court.

The unanimous Supreme Court held that the Sixth Circuit's test of notice was too strict, stating that before criminal liability is imposed, due process requires "fair warning . . . of what the law intends." At question was whether the statute clearly established that the alleged conduct was unlawful under the U.S. Constitution at the time at which it purportedly occurred. The Court stated that the rights deprived by the defendant need not have been identified in a prior decision of the Court, and it rejected the suggested requirement of a factually similar case. It also ruled that liability may be imposed under § 242 if, in light of preexisting law, the unlawfulness of the defendant's conduct is apparent. Since the Sixth Circuit used the wrong gauge in deciding whether prior judicial decisions gave fair warning that Lanier's actions were in violation of certain constitutional rights, the Supreme Court vacated the judgment of the appellate court and remanded the case for application of the proper standard. *See also*: **Rape Law.**

Suggested Reading: Maria Bevacqua, *Rape on the Public Agenda: Feminism and the Politics of Sexual Assault* (Boston: Northeastern University Press, 2000).

GREGORY M. DUHL

U.S. MILITARY. Women have always served the military in times of war, originally as nurses and later in secretarial or clerical capacities, but it wasn't until the twentieth century that the armed forces slowly began allowing women to enlist, perform the duties of sailors and soldiers, and receive the benefits of a military career. While instances of **sexual harassment** and assault surely existed before, they came to the forefront as women permeated a previously male world, especially with the introduction of integrated basic training. Issues of power and abuse, gender differences and equality, political correctness and feminism swirled and muddied the picture.

The Navy and Tailhook

The first large-scale scandal occurred in 1991 after the 35th Annual **Tailhook** Symposium, a three-day convention of navy and Marine Corps aviators. The Tailhook Association was originally a private organization, a group of former military men who gathered to drink and reminisce. In the late 1960s, the annual symposium was condoned by the navy, and the assistant chief of Naval Operations became responsible for planning certain functions. In addition to professional development, though, the convention was historically a rowdy weekend, one that led the president of the association to warn attendees beforehand about past instances of inappropriate behavior. Men competed to design the most desirable hospitality suites, and the criteria typically involved the amount of liquor, the number of strippers, and the incidents of wild behavior.

When Lieutenant Paula Coughlin, a helicopter pilot, entered a hotel hallway, she claimed that a gauntlet of officers surrounded her, pulled at her clothing, forced her to the ground, and laughed at her cries for help. After Coughlin publicly accused fellow officers of molesting her, more than 80 women and at least 7 men followed suit, also claiming to have been assaulted. The navy severed its connection with the Tailhook Association immediately, and a series of official investigations followed. A 2,000-page report produced in April 1992 by the Inspector General and the Naval Investigative Service described drunken maulings, women being grabbed and disrobed, and outright assault. It increased public furor over the events and led to further inquiries by the Pentagon and the navy. By the following year, more than 100 officers were being investigated for indecent exposure, assault, conduct unbecoming an officer, and lying to Pentagon officials. Most of the accused received fines or career penalties, and no cases ever went to trial.

Some explanations proffered for the officers' actions included traditions established at previous Tailhook conventions and a celebration mentality stemming from victory in the Gulf War. Men argued that they were judged by a double standard: Women were allowed to act wildly, but men were not. Women argued that serious allegations were essentially dismissed when the accused received few or no penalties for less serious charges. One female navy commander suggested a general misogynist attitude was surfacing as women began to compete for men's jobs in an ever-downsizing military. Most women, however, remained silent, choosing the security of their careers over thin hopes for justice or restitution.

The Army and Aberdeen

Two of the navy's long-term reactions to the Tailhook affair included a push to recruit more women and gender-integrated basic training. The idea was to dilute the masculine aura by increasing the feminine presence. The army followed suit in 1993–1994. By the end of 1996, though, the army was wallowing in charges of **sexual assault** and rape of trainees by sergeants at Aberdeen Proving Ground, a training base in Maryland. The initial incidents occurred between July and September of 1996 and went unchecked until Private Jessica Bleckley made them public. A flurry of additional allegations followed. The army quickly announced that it was filing charges against 3 officers and was investigating nearly 20 more. A hotline was set up and received almost 4,000 calls that resulted in 500 cases that warranted further examination.

Disbelief quickly surfaced over how other sergeants could be unaware such abuse was happening, leading many to criticize the macho-male attitude that permeated the military. To compound matters, new controversies soon came to the forefront. At one point, the alleged **victims** claimed that officials forced them to label the incidents rapes so that the army could strike back with a vengeance and restore its public image. Others claimed the charges were racially motivated because most of the accusers were white, while most of the accused were black. The press questioned the army's ability to investigate itself, raising doubts as to the legitimacy of the entire procedure. Nevertheless, a few relatively quick convictions combined with the army's attempt to demonstrate an appropriate response—**rape prevention** classes for new recruits and sexual harassment training for officers—eventually put the scandal to rest.

The Academies

In 1976, the three U.S. Service academies opened their doors to women and to accusations of sexual impropriety and assault. Although West Point and Annapolis have managed to handle the sensitive issue without public scrutiny, the Air Force Academy in Colorado Springs continues to have problems.

In 1996, the Air Force Academy established a hotline for reporting rapes and averaged five cases per year since that time. Over the years, a handful of male cadets faced courts-martial, and slightly more were dismissed or reprimanded. After several years of relative quiet on the scandal front, however, rape in the military reentered the headlines in early 2003 when female cadets claimed that they had been sexually assaulted by superiors in their chain of command. The cadets further charged that not only were their complaints ignored by authorities but that they were disciplined for reporting it and even told they were partially to blame.

The air force ordered a review of the Academy's procedures for handling rape accusations. A military panel convened to investigate the accusations declared there was no evidence of officials having ignored complaints. A civilian panel established by Congress, however, testified that the Visitors Board charged with overseeing morale and discipline failed to adequately handle the situation. Soon afterward, the air force removed the Academy's leadership, virtually ending the careers of General John Dallager, Brigadier General Slvanus Taco Gilbert III, Colonel Robert Eskridge, and Colonel Laurie Slavec. The new Commandant of Cadets, Brigadier General Johnny Weida, decided that at least one accused cadet would face court-martial.

Rationales and Responses

The sticking point on both sides concerns fear and confidentiality. When the person with the authority to help is also the person committing the crime, the fear of retribution increases, and victims understandably feel hopeless. After a 1993 scandal where a cadet alleged that she was gang raped by three fellow cadets, the Air Force Academy instituted a sweeping policy of anonymity for victims. Leaders at the Air Force Academy in 2003 then claimed that the silence stemming from that regulation prevented them from discovering how deeply the problem permeated the school. Consequently, there has been an about-face. All reports of assault or rape are now reported to the alleged victim's commanding officer. Victim advocates decry this change, leading decision makers into a labyrinth of uncertainty about the right course of action.

Granting victims privacy through hot line reporting mechanisms encourages women to come forward—but only to a point. The number of cases reported via the hotline is 5 times greater than the number of cases investigated and nearly 10 times greater than the number of cases that result in judicial hearings. When the likelihood of conviction is small and the likelihood of humiliation or denigration is great, women often choose not to pursue the charges.

When servicemen face judicial hearings for charges of sexual assault, there is controversy over the legal definition of rape. In civilian cases, sex with force and without **consent** defines rape. In the military, though, the theory of constructive force—an abuse of power wherein the victim fears for her safety, whether or not the accused uses physical force—overshadows the prosecutions. This is how Army Staff Sergeant Delmar Simpson was convicted of raping six women at Aberdeen, even though the victims admitted he never forced them to have sex. Instead, their fear of his authority and his ability to end their military careers constituted force in the court's eyes.

Despite these flaws, the armed services are seeking to remedy the problem, having learned from Tailhook and Aberdeen that the issues loom large and threaten key elements of the military's nature: trust, order, and the chain of command. The navy has established a sexual assault victim intervention program, while the army has instituted sexual assault review boards at its major medical facilities. Even the Department of Veteran Affairs now provides treatment for the trauma of past sexual assaults while in the military. Each scandal leads to a better solution, but few are optimistic enough to believe that rape in the military has been conquered. *See also*: **Okinawa Rape Case; Wartime Rape.**

Suggested Reading: Elizabeth Gleick, "Scandal in the Military: Reports of Rape at an Army Training Base Suggest That the Services' Tolerance for Sexual Harassment Is More Than Zero," *Time*, November 25, 1996; Stephanie Gutmann, "The Road from Aberdeen," *The New Republic*, February 24, 1997; Ted Koppel and Michel McQueen, "Investigating the Investigators," *ABC Nightline*, March 13, 1997; PBS Online, "Frontline: Tailhook '91," http://www.pbs.org/; Hanna Rosin, "How the Army Learned to Love Andrea Dworkin," *The New Republic*, June 23, 1997; Diana Schemo (series of Air Force Academy articles), *New York Times*, June 24, 2003, July 11, 2003, July 17, 2003; Robert Weller (series of Air Force Academy articles), *San Diego Union-Tribune*, February 17, 2003, March 30, 2003, June 7, 2003, July 12, 2003, July 16, 2003.

GREGORY M. DUHL

V

VICTIMS. Rape victims extend as far back as antiquity. The biblical Dinah is raped by Shechem who "saw her, took her, lay with her and defiled her" (Genesis 34). Roman men captured the Sabine women (*see* **Rape of the Sabine Women**) spirited them away from their homes on horseback, and kept them from returning to their families and friends. Fine **art** glorifies the victims of rape, and their perpetrators as beautiful or handsome, sexy or powerful, erotic and virile. In real life, however, rape victims are brutalized, ignored, or harassed by the system that is designed to help them. They are traumatized, stigmatized, or shamed for life, if they are not killed during the attack.

In times of political upheaval or war, rape victims are dehumanized both symbolically and physically as the "other." In contrast to urban victims, these women are not known to their perpetrators and are perceived as "the enemy" or less than human. Victims during the Vietnam "conflict" included young Asian girls raped by American soldiers. The 1990s wars in the Balkans and the term "**ethnic cleansing**" exposed to the world groups of women who were deliberately raped for the purpose of impregnation by the aggressors. In this way, they would be forced to bear the children of their enemies. Examples too numerous to list exist in all countries because when war is waged, the concomitant destruction of the sociopolitical infrastructure leads to a climate conducive to rape.

Until the late twentieth century, rape was defined as "the forcible penetration of the body of a woman, not the wife of the perpetrator"(Russell, 32); therefore, by definition, a wife would not be considered a victim. However, in 1993, all 50 states had removed the spousal exemption from their laws on rape and **sexual assault** so that a married woman could be deemed a victim. Modern society is informed enough to acknowledge that victims are married or single, women, men, boys, or girls; a rape victim can be an infant or an elderly nursing home resident. Gay men are victims of nonconsensual sex, their perpetrators sometimes, but not always, other gay men.

The **National Crime Victimization Survey (NCVS)** in 1990 reported that females between 16 and 19 were at greatest risk of being raped, followed by females 20 to 24, then ages 12 to 15. The socioeconomic status varied directly with the frequency of rape, that is, the lower the status, the more likely a woman was to be raped. Although this survey found that there were no differences in rates between white and black women, it should be noted that the data available on black women was a smaller sample.

A slight majority of rapes occur at night. In one study, half of the rapes reported occurred between 8:00 P.M. and 2:00 A.M. (Kaplan and Weisberg). In another, 66.7% of the rapes took place between 6:00 P.M. and 6:00 A.M. (Hall, 91). If the victim did work, she had a job that characteristically involved face-to-face contact, was highly visible, and required close interactions with males and had an outgoing personality. The job put the victim at risk because often it required nontraditional working hours (early morning or late at night). This made the woman more susceptible to ambush because she was likely to be observed walking alone in the dark. Waitresses, barmaids, and nurses were in these categories. Unfortunately many of the qualities that our culture reinforces positively in women make them more likely to be victims. Women have been socialized to be nurturing and altruistic, to care for others, and to be more concerned about others' needs than their own. Sometimes they become rape victims because these qualities work against them. For example, many of serial rapist (*see* **Serial Rape and Serial Rapists**) and murderer Ted Bundy's victims were eager to help him because he feigned a broken limb and needed help with groceries. Women traditionally had been socialized to be weaker than men, although this has changed in the past 20 years with the promotion of fitness centers, girls' athletics in **schools**, and **self-defense** classes.

There are some behaviors that put women more at risk for rape, but because of gender-role stereotypes, these are difficult to extinguish. In one study, it was found that "one-third of rape victims came into contact with their assailants voluntarily, under circumstances other than hitchhiking" (Kaplan and Weisberg). **Date rape** is one example where this occurs frequently. Out of a group of 623 college students, 22 percent of the women and 16 percent of the men responded that they had experienced at least one incident of forced sexual intercourse on a date" (Hyde, 480).

Rape victims tend to be smaller and weaker than perpetrators, and they generally occupy a less dominant social role. This is evidenced in **prison rape**s of males by more dominant male inmates, **incest** victims, employees who are harassed so much that the behavior escalates to rape, and students who are raped by teachers or trusted mentors. A common myth about the rape victim is that he or she was "asking for it," thereby switching culpability and presenting the victim as the criminal rather than the rapist. When a prostitute or "promiscuous woman" is the victim, her **credibility** is more often challenged than that of other victims.

Because not all victims report their rape experience, there is not enough information about them. In a London study at a **rape crisis center**, 75 percent did not report the crime to the police, even after encouraged to do so. Another study documented that 92 percent chose not to report the rape to **law enforcement** (Temkin). In the United States, the National Crime Victimization Survey indicated that in a three-year period from 1985 to 1988, between 35 and 53 percent of **forcible rape**s were not reported to the police. In 1991, that same survey found that 45 percent did not report the crime. In Boston in 1992, less than 19 percent were reported to the police. In general, when the victims were between 12 and 15, they were more likely to be reported than others. The phenomenon of **secondary rape** by the law enforcement and legal system could explain the reason for underreporting. Ironically, the brutality of the legal system shares more with the rapist than with the counselor of the victim. Perhaps when victims can report their trauma without fear of additional invasiveness, the statistics will be more relevant and accurate. *See also*: **Survivors.**

Suggested Reading: Rob Hall, *Rape in America* (Santa Barbara, CA: ABC-CLIO, 1995); Janet Shibley Hyde, *Understanding Human Sexuality* (New York: Macmillan, 1990); John Kaplan and Robert Weisberg, *Criminal Law* (Boston: Little, Brown, 1986), 1052; Diana Russell, *Rape in Marriage* (New York: Macmillan, 1982), 32; Jennifer Temkin, *Women, Rape and Law Reform*, in *Rape*, ed. Sylvia Tomasselli and Roy Porter (New York: Basil Blackwell, 1986), 16–40.

LANA THOMPSON

VIOLENCE AGAINST WOMEN ACT (VAWA). In response to mounting evidence of violence against women, the U.S. Congress enacted the Violence against Women Act (VAWA) of 1994 to give both the federal government and state and local governments new tools with which to fight **domestic violence** and **sexual assault.** Congress cited Centers for Disease Control statistics that at least one out of every six females in the United States will be beaten or sexually abused in her lifetime. VAWA was originally intended to deal with domestic violence only, but lobbying by the National Coalition against Sexual Assault (NCASA), the **National Organization for Women (NOW),** and other women's groups convinced sponsor Senator Joseph Biden (D–DE) to add rape services and prevention to VAWA.

VAWA established federal penalties for interstate stalking and spousal abuse, created the National Domestic Violence Hotline, and increased federal penalties for repeat offenders. Other provisions of the bill set aside grant money to build or improve **battered women** shelters, increase rape crisis intervention, hire additional police officers, and provide training on rape and domestic violence. President Bill Clinton created the Office of Violence against Women within the Department of Justice. The most controversial aspect of VAW dealt with granting victims the right to bring civil rights suits against their attackers. The Supreme Court overturned this provision of VAWA in 2000 in *United States v. Morrison* (529 U.S. 598).

The success of the VAWA has been documented in a number of ways. Reports of domestic violence have declined by 25 percent. More than 250,000 calls have been received on the National Domestic Violence Hotline since 1986. The American Bar Association reports that overall crimes against women have dropped 21 percent, while Congress estimates that more than 300,000 women and children have been provided with shelter under VAWA.

The 1994 version of the VAWA expired on October 1, 2000. Congress reauthorized the bill, known as VAWA II, and increased funding to $3 billion over a five-year period. VAWA II expanded the number of programs, including provisions aimed at making college campuses safer for females. Other elements of the 2000 bill provide increased protection for children, the elderly, the disabled, and immigrant women who are victims of gender-related violence. The addition of legal assistance for victims also strengthens the bill. The most controversial provision of VAWA II is "Aimee's Law," named after Aimee Willard, a college senior from Philadelphia who was kidnapped, raped, and murdered by a convicted murderer who had been given early release from a Nevada prison. The "Aimee's Law" provision withholds federal funds from states that hand down light sentences for criminals who then commit gender-related violence in other states. *See also*: **Marital Rape; Rape Education; Rape History in the United States: Twentieth Century; Rape Statistics.**

Suggested Reading: Maria Bevacqua, *Rape on the Public Agenda: Feminism and the Politics of Sexual Assault* (Boston: Northeastern Press, 2000); Holly Idelson, "A Tougher Domestic Violence Law," *Congressional Quarterly Weekly Report*, June 25, 1994, 1714; Rhonda McMillion, "Stronger Voice for Victims," *ABA Journal* (December 2000): 98; Office of Justice Programs, Department of Justice, "Office of Violence against Women, 30 April 2003, http://www.ojp.usdoj.gov/vawo/; Claire M. Renzetti et al., eds., *Sourcebook on Violence against Women* (Thousand Oaks, CA: Sage, 2001).

ELIZABETH R. PURDY

VIRGINS/VIRGINITY. Across the world and throughout history, the rape of a virgin has often been deemed a more serious crime than that of a sexually experienced woman. In the past, this has mainly been due to the idea that women are men's property. Nonvirgins were not as desirable on the marriage market. In countries where bridewealth was exchanged, the bride's father could no longer demand as much compensation for the loss of her labor. In countries where the bride's family provided a dowry along with their daughter as an incentive for marriage and as a means to start an independent household, the father of a nonvirgin would be required to offer a much larger dowry to compensate for his daughter's status as "damaged goods." This was the case in medieval England, where there were two preferred methods for settling rape cases out of court. The first involved the rapist supplying his **victim** with a larger dowry, which was supposed to enable her to find a husband despite her past. The second was for the rapist to marry his victim. In so doing, the rapist restored honor to his victim and her **family**. British jurist and scholar Henri de Bracton (d. 1268) argued that the rapist of a virgin should lose his member (i.e., be castrated) since he had deprived her of her hymen.

Being a virgin can help a woman prove to the court's satisfaction that a **sexual assault** was indeed nonconsensual. However, while this has generally been the case, it was not always so. For example, in Renaissance Venice, it was more difficult for an unmarried young woman to prove she had been raped because it was assumed that she was naturally more lustful and seeking to attract a husband using any means possible, whereas in sixteenth-century Augsburg, proving a rape was more difficult for a married woman since she was sexually experienced and therefore presumed to desire intercourse frequently.

Some women, such as Roman vestal virgins and Catholic nuns, have had to maintain their virginity for religious reasons. The rape of such virgins is a crime against the state and deity, as well as the woman, and thus of a much more serious nature. A vestal virgin who lost her virginity was buried alive. Anglo-Saxon laws listed higher rates of compensation for the rape of a nun than other virgins. Since the early days of Christianity, theologians had debated about whether a virgin who was raped was corrupted. The argument was that if a woman remained chaste in mind, then the damage done to her body was of little consequence regarding her purity.

Today, almost every country has a minimum age at which a person can legally consent to heterosexual sexual intercourse. This age varies between 7 (boys) and 12 (girls) to 21 (both). Sexual intercourse with a person younger than this, consensual or nonconsensual, automatically constitutes rape. Over the past 150 years, there has been a growing trend in the Western world of viewing children as innocent creatures devoid of sexual feelings. The result of this new attitude has been an increasing success rate in prosecuting **child rape** and harsher penalties for perpetrators.

Many reasons have been advanced to explain why some men prefer sexual intercourse with virgins, one of which is the desire to be the first person to do so. In the past, male preoccupation with female virginity and chastity was a means of ensuring that the offspring of one's wife were one's own blood children. This allowed men to feel secure in the knowledge that their property would remain within the family. Another rationale had to do with popular perceptions of health and hygiene. In eighteenth-century London, men infected with venereal disease sought out virgins as a cure, believing they could transfer the infection to her via intercourse. Court records attest to the increased problem of virgin rape during this century. Similar folk "cures" are common in regions of present-day Africa, particularly in places where the social fabric has been weakened by war, famine, and economic depression and where the rate of **HIV/AIDS** infection is high. *See also*: **African Women and Girls; Rape Myths.**

Suggested Reading: Anthony E. Simpson, "Vulnerability and the Age of Female Consent: Legal Innovation and Its Effect on Prosecution for Rape in Eighteenth-Century London," in *Sexual Underworlds of the Enlightenment*, ed. G.S. Rousseau and Roy Porter (Manchester: Manchester University Press, 1987), 181–205; Georges Vigarello, *A History of Rape: Sexual Violence in France from the 16th to the 20th Century*, trans. Jean Birrell (Cambridge: Polity Press, 2002).

TONYA MARIE LAMBERT

VOYEURISM. Voyeurism refers to obtaining sexual gratification by observing others who are undressing, naked, or participating in sexual activity. More technically, it is defined as a *paraphilia*, a term designed to avoid the term *perversion*, and used to describe unusual sexual behavior that might be considered problematic for the person involved and contrary to *societal norms*. The use of the words societal norms is important, since voyeurism in its broadest sense is almost normative among men in general as witnessed by the popularity of male-targeted magazines such as *Playboy* and *Hustler*, erotic or pornographic movies, tapes, and Internet sites. The term "Peeping Tom" demonstrates that voyeurism has long been recognized as an aspect of male behavior.

Voyeurism only becomes problematical when it goes beyond the norms. Many adolescent or adult males might take advantage of an opportunity to observe women who are undressed or engaged in sexual activity, if they can do so because the woman's bedroom is in plain sight from their own window or street. Others might masturbate by examining the catalogues of *Victoria's Secret*, projecting their search for the unattainable onto underclothes associated with women. However, to furtively seek out the forbidden sights by climbing a fence to peer through a bedroom window, to use a mirror to peer under women's **clothing**, to look through peepholes into dressing rooms or toilets, or to enter people's homes in order to watch them while they sleep, and similar compulsive obsessive behaviors, brings them to the attention of **law enforcement** officials. The voyeur often masturbates while he engages in such behaviors, and part of the excitement and pleasure of such forbidden sexual behaviors is the risk of discovery.

There is a general belief that voyeurs do not engage in rape, but if it becomes part of a group experience, they might well do so. Some experts see group voyeurism as a factor in **gang rape**, whether such voyeuristic activities take place in college **fraternities**, among the military, or among street gangs.

In the past most paraphilias, or those more likely to engage in such behavior, were male, but that is changing, as the popularity of male strip shows, male go-go dancers, and nude photos of men in women's magazines such as *Cosmopolitan* indicates a female interest in this type of activity. Traditionally the difference has been described as due to men's greater sensitivity to visual stimuli, but the changing behavior of women might well indicate it had a lot to do with the cultural constraints imposed on women seeking out sexual stimuli.

Interestingly, however, only a few states prohibit voyeurism as such, and when the voyeur who becomes a nuisance is arrested, he is likely to be prosecuted under antiloitering and disorderly conduct laws and in extreme cases for unlawful breaking and entering. *See also*: **Media**; **Pornography**.

Suggested Reading: G.G. Abel and C.A. Osborn, "The Paraphilias," in *New Oxford Textbook of Psychiatry*, ed. M.G. Gelder, J.J. López-Ibor, and N. Andreason (New York: Oxford University Press, 2000); John Money, *Love Maps* (Buffalo, NY: Prometheus Books, 1986); D. Symonds, *The Evolution of Human Sexuality* (New York: Oxford University Press, 1979).

VERN L. BULLOUGH

WAR CRIMES. War crimes have been recognized as a feature of war for a long time. However, in 1945 the Nuremberg Charter defined them, for the first time at an international level, as the violation or breach of the laws or customs of war. Only the most serious atrocities are covered as examples in this text, as well as in later International Humanitarian Law treaties. According to the Geneva Conventions of 1949, each party to an armed conflict of an international or noninternational character—either States or other armed groups—must respect and apply the general principles of humanitarian law, whose aim is to restrict means and methods of warfare and to protect war **victims**. In this sense, the legal provisions against war crimes contained in these international instruments are widely recognized as customary international law and have an *erga omnes* character, due to the basic values they seek to protect. Since those obligations imply to treat civilians "humanely," it is conceived today that aggressive acts inflicted on women may constitute the war crimes of rape, outrages upon personal dignity, sexual violence, and **torture**.

In the trials held after World War II in Nuremberg, even if sex crimes committed by German soldiers were reported and sustained by evidence, these offenses were excluded from the jurisdiction of the court, and they could not be prosecuted. Although there still was not a list of gender crimes in the Tokyo Charter, the International Military Tribunal for the Far East could walk a step further, since in their activities it considered that rape of civilian women and medical staff could represent ill-treatment, inhumane treatment, or failure to respect **family** honor and rights.

From this precedent onward, it becomes clear that rape can become a war crime—in domestic legislations, customary laws, and conventional documents—whenever it is committed during the course of an armed conflict. Rape and enforced **prostitution** are explicitly forbidden in the Geneva Convention IV, Article 27, and in the 1977 Additional Protocols (Article 76.1, Protocol I, and Article 4.2.e., Protocol II).

In all wars, rape crimes are committed for a multitude of reasons. One single act of sexual penetration may support a cause of action under several different categories. However, since sex crimes receive no widespread international definition, it remains difficult to achieve in International Humanitarian Law a consensus on the notion of rape. Despite these difficulties, rape is generally understood—in the law of armed conflicts and international jurisprudence—as the sexual penetration of the victim (through vagina, mouth, or anus) by any body part or object. As it can be seen, in this broad sense there is no distinction within the concept based on the gender of victims or aggressors, or regarding the means or effects of the penetration. Punishment of rape as war crimes both in the ad hoc Security Council–created tribunals for the former Yugoslavia and for Rwanda show an important gender issue awareness that could become an undeniable precedent for the working of the International Criminal Court as far as the protection of women's rights during armed conflicts is concerned. *See also*: **Bosnia-Herzegovina; Genocide; Rape of Nanking; Wartime Rape.**

Suggested Reading: Judith Gardam, "Women, Human Rights and International Humanitarian Law," *International Review of the Red Cross* 324 (1998): 421–432; Françoise Krill, "The Protection of Women in International Humanitarian Law," *International Review of the Red Cross* 249 (1985): 337–363; Theodor Meron, "Rape as a Crime under International Humanitarian Law," *American Journal of International Law* 87.3 (1993): 424–428; Catherine N. Niarchos, "Women, War and Rape: Challenges Facing the International Tribunal for the Former Yugoslavia," *Human Rights Quarterly* 17.4 (1995): 649–690.

EMILIANO J. BUIS

WARTIME RAPE. Although the practice of soldiers raping the enemy's women during war is seen throughout history, what is new is the role of **media** and its impact on this subject. Beginning in the 1960s and 1970s significant interest in this topic developed, symbolized best by the publication of **Susan Brownmiller's** *Against Our Will* in 1975. Since then almost unimaginable changes have occurred, in large measure because of the instant reporting of repeated and massive atrocities in former Yugoslavia, especially in **Bosnia-Herzegovina**, and in Rwanda.

In earlier eras, wartime rape and other forms of **sexual assault** on women were the subject of legal and religious concerns about their ownership and value. Today wartime rape is recognized by the international community as a war crime. It can also be prosecuted as a crime against humanity, if evidence confirms wartime rapes resulted from systemic government planning, but crimes against humanity are difficult to establish.

Assertions about soldiers raping during war is not the same as documenting the extent to which this ignominious crime occurs. Knowledge about the number of wartime rapes depends largely on the willingness of the **victims** to speak and the availability of interested agencies to record and investigate complaints. Rarely have these conditions occurred together. For different reasons—some personal, others organizational—both victims and the military seem more willing to remain silent and inert. Only in recent years, for instance, has the world learned that during the spring of 1945, as Russian soldiers advanced and eventually occupied Berlin, they raped nearly 1 million German women.

The rapes committed by U.S. soldiers during the same war are only now being investigated. Obstacles to this research have included the myth that our World War

II soldiers are among "the greatest generation," a scarcity of people and organizations willing to be associated with funding for research on this subject, and the fact that military records on their crimes were kept secret for years.

Questions about who is raped are difficult to answer. Some biological and historical explanations, including the **Bible**, indicate that victims are often young and fecund. Rapes committed by German and American soldiers during World War II suggest that while age may have been an influential factor of victimization, opportunity coupled with desire were likely more important. In the European Theater of Operations the rape victims of American soldiers ranged in age between 4 and 75 years, suggesting that these rapes resulted from unrestrained individual motivation and meeting inadequately guarded females. Men, too, have been sexually assaulted during war, but less often than females. Rarely, women with power during war have encouraged and instructed men to rape.

It would be an error to accept such explanations uncritically because individual acts occur in powerful social contexts. There are, after all, extensive historical records that indicate there are rules and objectives involving wartime rape, including the extent to which rape is informally or formally supported by the military. The following is illustrative:

Mass rape as a cultural and/or genocidal weapon. These rapes are well organized, systematic, and often public. The early and mid-1990s rapes in Bosnia were, according to some observers, committed as a matter of deliberate policy. Similar arguments have been made about the rapes committed by Japanese soldiers in Nanking, China, in 1937, during World War II.

Rape to "wound the honor" of the enemy. These rapes are aimed at the male relatives and friends of the victims. The message is clear—they are wounds to the masculinity, honor, and competence of the enemy soldiers who are unable to protect their women.

Rape as part of military culture. Historically, the military has an unusual configuration of norms about masculinity, sexuality, and women. The confluence of these factors may very well be conducive to rape as witnessed by various sexual assault scandals within the U.S. Army, Navy, and Air Force between the 1980s and 2004.

Rape, revenge, and elevated masculinity. Sport and war **literature** abound with accounts of male behavior that confirm and elevate masculinity. The uniform, an essential element in war, symbolizes membership as well as the range of expected and approved behavior. Powerful military group expectations and indoctrination of masculinity may use rape as a gesture of group solidarity. This explanation of wartime rape has often been applied to the behavior of some American soldiers in the Vietnam War.

Rape as part of the "rules" of war—pay and pillage. Before armies were created with regularized pay, soldiers were often recruited with the promise of booty—including sexual booty—as their reward. This form of payment, including rape, was nonetheless regulated because uncontrolled pillage meant, in effect, the control of the army had been lost.

Rape as gratuitous/random behavior. All modern armies have regulations prohibiting rape. Nonetheless, under certain social conditions, individual soldiers violate such rules despite the threat of severe punishment and victimize civilian female colleagues. Official military records from the U.S. Army for the European Theater of Operation (1942–1945) indicate that individuals and gangs of soldiers raped civilian females in England, France, and especially Germany, where the enemy's women were considered to be fair game. Some of the soldiers found guilty of rape were executed, and most of the executed soldiers were black.

Some critics argue that by calling rape of females a crime against humanity, the international community identified women as the weaker gender in need of protection. Others disagree and claim that it formally brought women within the purview of humanity for the purpose of prosecuting crimes against humanity. Still others argue that the actions of the international community on wartime rape as a crime against humanity do not infringe upon the sovereignty of individual states to prosecute this crime. Clearly, the prosecution of rape under international law is justice long overdue. *See also*: **Genocide; My Lai; Rape of Nanking; U.S. Military; War Crimes.**

Suggested Reading: Anthony Beevor, *The Fall of Berlin 1945* (New York: Viking, 2002); J. Robert Lilly, *La Face Cachee des GI's: Les viols commis par des soldats americains en France, en Angleterre et en Allemagne pendant la Seconde Guerre mondiale* (Paris: Payot, 2003); Randy Thornhill and Craig T. Palmer, *Rape: A Natural History of Biological Bases of Sexual Coercion* (Cambridge, MA: MIT Press, 2000); Georges Vigarello, *A History of Rape: Sexual Violence in France from the 16th to the 20th Century* (London: Polity Press, 2001).

J. ROBERT LILLY

WELLS, IDA B. (1862–1931). Ida B[ell] Wells [Barnett] was an **African American** journalist and activist who demonstrated that, despite popular misconception, most African American men who were lynched were not even *accused* of having raped white women. Her investigative reporting and public speaking were crucial in launching the American antilynching crusade. Born a slave in 1862 in Holly Springs, Mississippi, Wells moved to Memphis, Tennessee, and soon became a leading community activist. In 1889 she became co-owner, editor, and publisher of the Memphis weekly newspaper *Free Speech*. Shocked at the March 1892 lynching of three friends, Wells began investigating lynching cases. Stereotypes of the black male rapist were rife in the post-Reconstruction South, and these fueled vicious lynchings, attended by cheering white crowds, that spread across the South in the late nineteenth and early twentieth centuries. Wells revealed the stereotypes as both false and new, concocted by whites when African Americans began gaining political and economic power. Her statistical analysis of hundreds of lynchings revealed that, according to white sources, most lynching **victims** were not accused as rapists. In a May 1892 editorial, she charged: "Nobody . . . believes the old thread-bare lie that Negro men assault white women." She also implied that consensual sex sometimes occurred between white women and black men. Southern whites' outrage forced her into exile in the North, where she continued her antilynching campaign. Wells (who married Ferdinand Barnett in 1895) spent the rest of the 1890s researching, publishing, and touring to publicize the horrors of lynching. Her publications include *Southern Horrors: Lynch Law in All Its Phases* (1892), *A Red Record* (1895), *Mob Rule in New Orleans* (1900), and numerous articles and reprinted speeches. *See also*: **Rape-Lynch Syndrome; Southern Rape Complex.**

Suggested Reading: Linda O. McMurry, *To Keep the Waters Troubled: The Life of Ida B. Wells* (Oxford: Oxford University Press, 1998); Jacqueline Jones Royster, ed., *Southern Hor-*

rors and Other Writings: The Anti-Lynching Campaign of Ida B. Wells, 1892–1900 (Boston: Bedford Books, 1997); Patricia Ann Schechter, *Ida B. Wells-Barnett and American Reform, 1880–1930* (Chapel Hill: University of North Carolina Press, 2001).

DOROTHEA BROWDER

Resource Guide

SUGGESTED READING

This is a brief list of important books on rape. For more selections, see the suggested reading at the end of each encyclopedia entry.

Barstow, Anne Llewellyn, ed. *War's Dirty Secret: Rape, Prostitution, and Other Crimes Against Women.* Cleveland, OH: Pilgrim Press, 2000. This collection of essays by scholars and activists from all over the world discusses sexual slavery, rape as a war crime, and military culture.

Benedict, Helen. *Recovery.* New York: Columbia University Press, 1994. This is a resource book for rape survivors, their families, and friends.

Bevaqua, Maria. *Rape on the Public Agenda: Feminism and the Politics of Sexual Assault.* Boston: Northeastern University Press, 2000. This book thoroughly examines the roots and impact of the feminist antirape movement. It contains a valuable timeline, appendices, and bibliography.

Brownmiller, Susan. *Against Our Will: Men, Women and Rape.* New York: Fawcett Columbine, 1975. This pathbreaking study is the first comprehensive examination of rape from prehistory to the 1970s.

Buchwald, Emilie, Pamela Fletcher, and Martha Roth. *Transforming a Rape Culture.* Minneapolis, MN: Milkweed Editions, 1993. This collection of essays by activists, educators, policymakers, and scholars from a wide variety of backgrounds offers suggestions, opinions, and their visions on transforming a rape culture.

Chang, Iris. *The Rape of Nanking.* New York: Penguin, 1997. This book is a thorough account of the invasion and rape of the people of Nanking, China, by the Japanese in 1937.

Hazelwood, Robert R., and Ann Wolbert Burgess. *Practical Aspects of Rape Investigation: A Multidisciplinary Approach.* Boca Raton, FL: CRC Press, 2001. This is a textbook that provides information on criminal and forensic techniques.

Lefkowitz, Bernard. *Our Guys: The Glen Ridge Rape and the Secret of the Perfect Suburb.* Berkeley: University of California Press, 1997. This is a highly readable account of the Glen Ridge, New Jersey, rape case. It is well researched and analyzes the connection between athletes, sports culture, and rape.

McCaughey, Martha. *Real Knockouts: The Physical Feminism of Self-defense.* New York:

New York University Press, 1997. This is the only study of the self-defense movement in the context of rape culture.

Parrot, Andrea, and Laurie Bechhofer, eds. *Acquaintance Rape: The Hidden Crime*. New York: Wiley, 1991. This is an excellent overview for educators, psychologists, and law enforcement professionals on acquaintance and date rape.

Roiphe, Katie. *The Morning After: Sex, Fear, and Feminism*. Boston: Little, Brown, 1993. This book critiques acquaintance rape discourse. In particular, Roiphe takes issue with the "one in four women will be a victim of rape" statistic as well as the *Ms.* magazine study Robin Warshaw's book is based on.

Smith, Merril D., ed., *Sex and Sexuality in Early America*. New York: New York University Press, 1998. This collection contains original essays on sex and sex-related issues in early America. Several of the essays focus on rape and sexual coercion.

———. *Sex without Consent: Rape and Sexual Coercion in America*. New York: New York University Press, 2001. This volume of original essays covers rape in North America from the time of first contact by Europeans to the present.

Tomaselli, Sylvana, and Roy Porter, eds. *Rape*. Oxford: Basil Blackwell, 1986. This is an impressive collection of essays by historians, anthropologists, and sociologists.

Washaw, Robin. *I Never Called It Rape: The Ms. Report of Recognizing, Fighting, and Surviving Date and Acquaintance Rape*. New York: Harper, 1988. The first major study of date and acquaintance rape, this book draws on both first-person accounts and scholarly reports.

Wolfthal, Diane. *Images of Rape: The "Heroic" Tradition and Its Alternatives*. New York: Cambridge University Press, 1999. This book is the first in-depth exploration of rape in Western art.

WEB SITES

Boston Globe: Spotlight Investigation Abuse in the Catholic Church. http://www.boston.com/globe/spotlight/abuse. This site was started after the *Boston Globe* published a series of articles that uncovered the scandal in the Catholic Church in Boston. It features this story, along with audio and video material, message boards, and links. It is updated regularly.

Club Drugs.org. http://www.clubdrugs.org/. Sponsored by the National Institute on Drug Abuse (NIDA), this site provides information, trends, and statistics on club drugs and club drug use.

The Gender Ads Project: Gender and Advertising Database. http://www.genderads.com/. This site contains ads with reference to gender. Included are graphic ads depicting women who appear to have been raped or sexually assaulted.

History of Rape: Bibliography, compiled by Stefan Blaschke. http://de.geocities.com/history_guide/horb/index.html. This site is a bibliography of books, articles, dissertations, and conference papers on rape and sexual violence. The bibliography includes mostly English and German titles, but also contains some in other languages. The site is updated regularly.

Torture Survivors Network. http://www.pacinfo.com/eugene/tsnet/. This site was started by the nonprofit Rehabilitation Project for Survivors of Torture from Latin America and the Caribbean. It serves as a forum for torture survivors, therapists, and the general public.

ORGANIZATIONS

Amnesty International
322 8th Avenue
New York, NY 10001
Phone: 212-807-8400
http://www.amnestyusa.org/

This is the web site of Amnesty International USA (AIUSA). Amnesty International is an organization dedicated to promoting human rights and in preventing abuse, including rape and sexual violence.

Human Rights Watch
350 Fifth Avenue, 34th Floor
New York, NY 10118-3299
Phone: 212-290-4700
http://www.hrw.org/

Human Rights Watch is an independent nongovernmental organization. It investigates and publishes information on human rights abuses throughout the world.

National Center for Missing and Exploited Children
Charles B. Wang International Children's Building
699 Prince Street
Alexandria, VA 22314-3175
Phone: 703-274-3900
Hotline: 1-800-THE-LOST
http://www.missingkids.com/

The National Center for Missing and Exploited Children is private and nonprofit. The site provides information on missing and exploited children, includes a cyber tipline, and offers links and resources for parents, law enforcement professionals, attorneys, and the media.

Partnership for a Drug-Free America
405 Lexington Avenue, Suite 1601
New York, NY 10174
Phone: 212-922-1560
http://www.drugfreeamerica.org/

The Partnership for a Drug-Free America "is a private, non-profit coalition of professionals from the communications industry." The site contains information on club and party drugs.

Rape, Abuse & Incest National Network (RAINN)
635-B Pennsylvania Avenue, SE
Washington, DC 20003
Phone: 202-544-1034
National Sexual Assault Hotline: 1-800-656-HOPE
http://www.rainn.org/

RAINN runs the National Sexual Assault Hotline and provides education about sexual assault, its prevention, prosecution, and recovery. The site contains news, links, statistics, and information about rape and sexual violence.

Stop Prisoner Rape
6303 Wilshire Boulevard, Suite 204
Los Angeles, CA 90048
Phone: 323-653-STOP or 323-653-7867
http://www.spr.org/

Stop Prisoner Rape is a human rights organization that seeks to end rape and sexual violence against all prisoners—men, women, and children.

FILMS

See also entries on films—foreign and U.S.—in the encyclopedia.

Feature Films

The Accused (Johnathan Kaplan, 1988). Based on the Big Dan's Tavern rape case, the film stars Jodie Foster as a young woman who is gang raped.

Arrat (Atom Egoyan, 2001). This movie focuses on genocide in Armenia.

Birth of a Nation (D.W. Griffith, 1916). Based on Thomas Dixon's novel *The Clansman* (1905), this movie reflects the views of many white Southerners following the Civil War. It depicts black men as beasts lusting after white women.

The Color Purple (Steven Spielberg, 1985). Based on Alice Walker's Pulitzer Prize–winning book of the same title (1982), the story focuses on the struggles of a black woman in the South who is raped by her stepfather and husband.

Deliverance (James Boorman, 1972). Four city men decide to take a canoe trip in the backwoods of Georgia. One of them is sodomized at gunpoint by a deranged mountain man.

Extremeties (Robert A. Young, 1986). A woman fights back after being attacked and raped.

Rosemary's Baby (Roman Polanski, 1968). This film contains a scene in which a young woman is drugged and raped by the devil, as her husband and a band of Satanists look on.

Talk to Her (Pedro Almodoóvar, 2001). A hospital attendant rapes a young woman who is in a coma. In Spanish, with English subtitles.

To Kill a Mockingbird (Robert Mulligan, 1962). Based on Harper Lee's Pulitzer Prize–winning novel of the same title (1960), the movie reflects on race relations in a small southern town. Part of the story line concerns a lawyer, Atticus Finch (Gregory Peck), who defends a black man accused of raping a white woman.

Virgin Spring (Ingmar Bergman, 1960). This is an adaptation of fourteenth-century legend about a spring that emerges after a young girl is raped and killed. In Swedish, with English subtitles.

Documentaries

The Date Rape Backlash: The Media and the Denial of Rape (Media Education Foundation & FAIR, 1994). This documentary presents a critical examination of the media and backlash against the concept of date rape.

Dreamworlds 2 (Media Education Foundation, 1995). This documentary focuses on representations of women in music videos. Viewers should be warned that images of sexual violence are included.

Male Rape (Films for the Humanities & Sciences, 1997). Male survivors of rape speak about their experiences.

Prison Rape: Part of the Punishment? (Films for the Humanities & Sciences, 2001). ABC News anchor Ted Koppel reports on prison rape. Interviews with former prisoners are included.

Rape: A Crime of War (National Film Board of Canada, 1996). This one-hour documentary film focuses on the rape of women in the former Yugoslavia and discusses the issues involved in trying rape as a war crime.

Index

Page numbers in **bold** type refer to main entries in the encyclopedia.

Gay men, rape of, 121
Gays and lesbians, 87–88
  as survivors of prison rape, 156
Gein, Edward, 232
Gender roles, 88–89
  fairy tales and, 69–70
General Counsel Working Group, 13
Genetic fingerprinting, 59
Geneva Conventions (1949), 268
Genghis Khan, 1
Genital warts, 97
Genocide, 1, 67, 89–91, 90, 165
  rape-murder in, 8, 131
Genovese, Kitty, 91
  rape-murder of, xv
Gentleman rapist, 221
Geographic profiling, 91–92
George v. State of Mississippi, 235
Ghanaian Criminal Code, 9–10
Ghana National Commission on Women
  and Development, 10
Gibeah, rape of anonymous concubine in,
  23, 24
Gilbert, Slvanus Taco, III, 260
Gill, Marcus, 142
Gina (film), 75
Girls, African, 7–11
Glen Ridge (NJ) rape case, xvi, 92–93
Gonorrhea, 97
Goya, Francisco de, 16
Grass, Gunther, 75
Greek mythology
  rape in, 117, 132, 145
  sexual mutilation in, 231
Greek New Comedy, 248–249
Green Bombers, 8
Green Man, 30
Greer, Germaine, 12
Griffith, D.W., 76, 239
Grimm, Percy, 191
Grimm Brothers, 70
Grisham, John, 77
Griswold v. Connecticut, 52
Grober, Bryant, 93
Grosbard, Ulu, 79

Hadrian, 35
Hale, Sir Matthew, xiv, 26, 94–95, 122,
  181, 186, 188
Harlem Renaissance, 166
Harp, Rodrico, 142
Harris, Angela, 186

Harris, Paula, 39. *See also* Central Park
  Jogger
Havelock-Ellis, Henry, 146
Hawkins, Alfred, 216
Hawkins, Yusef, 240
Hays, William H., 77
Hays Code, 77
Health Care Financing Administration,
  102
Hebrew Bible, 23, 207
Henry, Joseph, 44–45
Henry II, King of France, 107
Henry VIII, King of England, 236
Heterosexism, 88
Hill, Anita, sexual harassment charges by,
  203
Hinduism, 206–207
Hindu literature, 208–209
Hippocratic Oath, xiii
Hispanics/Latinos, x, 95–97
History of the Pleas of the Crown, The
  (Hale), xiv, 26, 94
Hitler, Adolf, 67
HIV/AIDS, 40, 97–99
  virginity and, 9
Hobbes, Thomas, 249
Hoffman, Frederick L., 238
Holder, Elma, 102
Holmstrom, Lynda Lytle, 201–202
Holocaust. *See* Ethnic cleansing; Genocide;
  Nazis; War crimes
Homoeroticism, 99
Homophobia, 88, 121
Homosexual rape, 30, 99–101, 121, 156,
  182
Homosexuality, 14, 87, 99, 114, 223
Honor killings, ix
Hoover, Herbert, 124
Hopkins, Sarah Winnemucca, 138
Horney, Julie, 55
Horney, Karen, 56, 72
Horton, Willie, 240
Hospitals and nursing homes, sexual as-
  sault in, 101–102
Hostile work environment, 115, 116, 230
Hsu-Li, Magdalen, 18
Hudud Ordinance, 208
Human Genome Project, 165
Human Rights Commission of Pakistan, ix
Human rights organizations, 250
Human Rights Watch, 8, 97, 275
Hyperarousal, 153
Hysteria, 82, 83

About the Editor and Contributors

CAROL J. ADAMS is an independent scholar living in Richardson, Texas. She is the author of *The Sexual Politics of Meat: A Feminist-Vegetarian Critical Theory* (1990, 2000) and *The Pornography of Meat* (2003), among other publications. She has researched extensively on the connections between violence against women and violence against nonhuman animals.

KWABENA O. AKURANG-PARRY, a Ghanaian poet and historian, is an assistant professor of African history and world history at Shippensburg University, Shippensburg, Pennsylvania. He is completing a book manuscript on rape in Ghana from the precolonial period to the present.

EMMA ALEXANDER is a research associate, Centre of South Asian Studies, University of Cambridge, and Nehru Memorial Museum and Library, New Delhi.

OJAN ARYANFARD is a law student at the University of London and is completing a master's degree in Islam and Muslim-Christian relations at Georgetown University.

JOYCE AVRECH BERKMAN is professor of history and adjunct professor of women's studies at the University of Massachusetts, Amherst. She is editing a volume on the life and writings of the recently canonized Edith Stein.

MARIA BEVACQUA is associate professor and chair of the Department of Women's Studies at Minnesota State University, Mankato. She is the author of *Rape on the Public Agenda: Feminism and the Politics of Sexual Assault* (2000).

CORINNE E. BLACKMER is associate professor of English at Southern Connecticut State University, New Haven.

MARY BLOCK is an assistant professor of history at Valdosta State University, Valdosta, Georgia. Her dissertation was a history of rape law in nineteenth-century America.

SHARON BLOCK is an assistant professor in the History Department at the University of California, Irvine. She has written numerous articles on the history of rape in early America and is completing a book on coerced sex in early America.

CHRISTINA BOREL is a graduate student in gender and cultural studies at Simmons College, Boston.

DOMINICA BORG is assistant professor of theater and dramaturgy at the University of Massachusetts, Amherst.

DOROTHEA BROWDER is a doctoral candidate in women's history, University of Wisconsin, Madison.

EMILIANO J. BUIS is a professor at the Universidad de Buenos Aires, Argentina.

APRIL BULLOCK is assistant professor in the Department of Liberal Studies, California State University, Fullerton.

VERN L. BULLOUGH, State University of New York Distinguished Professor Emeritus, is author of numerous books and articles on human sexuality. He also founded the Center for Sex Research at California State University, Northridge.

LISA CARDYN has recently completed her doctorate in American studies at Yale University. She is revising her dissertation, "Sexualized Racism/Gendered Violence: Trauma and the Body Politic in the Reconstruction South," for publication.

ELAINE CAREY is a professor in the History Department at St. John's University, Jamaica, New York.

CAROLYN E. COCCA is assistant professor of politics at the State University of New York, College at Old Westbury. She is the author of several articles about statutory rape, as well as *Jailbait: The Politics of Statutory Rape Laws in the United States* (2004).

CHRISTOPHER CORLEY is an assistant professor of history and affiliated faculty of women's studies at Minnesota State University, Moorhead. His research focuses on family life, childhood, and adolescence in early modern France.

BRIDGET J. CRAWFORD is an assistant professor of law at Pace University in White Plains, New York. She teaches in the areas of feminist legal theory, estate planning, and taxation.

NING DE CONINCK-SMITH is an associate professor in the Department of Educational Sociology at the Danish University of Education, Copenhagen. She is writing a textbook on the history of twentieth-century Danish childhood.

KELLY DONAHUE-WALLACE is an assistant professor of art history at the University of North Texas, Denton.

SHARON A. DROZDOWSKI is a graduate of the Applied Social and Community Psychology Master's Program at Fairleigh Dickinson University.

GREGORY M. DUHL is an Abraham L. Freedman Fellow at the Temple University James E. Beasley School of Law in Philadelphia. Duhl has written on franchise law, copyright law, the Americans with Disabilities Act, and affirmative action.

DINA RIPSMAN EYLON is a scholar, writer, poet, and a former instructor at the University of Toronto. She is the publisher and editor of *Women in Judaism: A Multidisciplinary Journal*.

ROBIN E. FIELD is a doctoral candidate in the English Department at the University of Virginia, Charlottesville. Her dissertation examines representations of rape in American literature since 1970.

MARIE M. FORTUNE is the founder and senior analyst at the FaithTrust Institute in Seattle, Washington, editor of the *Journal of Religion and Abuse*, and author of *Sexual Violence: The Unmentionable Sin* (1993), among other books.

MARGARET GIBBS, a clinical psychologist with research and clinical interests in women's issues, is a professor of psychology at Fairleigh Dickinson University in Teaneck, New Jersey. In addition, she is a clinical consultant at Alternatives to Domestic Violence in Hackensack, New Jersey.

BETTY J. GLASS is associate professor and women's studies subject specialist for the University of Nevada, Reno Libraries.

JILL GORMAN is visiting assistant professor of philosophy and religion at Rollins College in Winter Park, Florida.

RUTH GRAHAM is a research associate in the School of Population and Health Sciences, University of Newcastle upon Tyne, United Kingdom. She is the author of several works on sexual assault.

DONNA COOPER GRAVES is a history professor at the University of Tennessee, Martin.

DANIEL GROSS is a student in the Clinical/Counseling Masters Program at Fairleigh Dickinson University, Teaneck, New Jersey.

ARTHUR HOLST is an adjunct faculty member of Widener University, Chester, Pennsylvania.

LAURIE JACKLIN is a graduate student at the University of Waterloo, Canada, specializing in the history of medicine.

ELIZABETH JENNER is an independent writer living in Rochester, New York.

SHARON A. KOWALSKY is a graduate student at the University of North Carolina at Chapel Hill.

YVES LABERGE is a film historian who holds a Ph.D. in sociology. He has published more than 200 articles and book reviews in many journals, mostly in France and Canada. He is a member of the scientific board for the Encyclopedia of the French Atlantic (2005).

TONYA MARIE LAMBERT is a doctoral candidate in the Department of History and Classics at the University of Alberta, Edmonton, Alberta, Canada. She studies the history of rape in the late medieval and early modern periods, focusing on England.

J. ROBERT LILLY is Regents Professor of Sociology at Northern Kentucky School of Law, Highland Heights, Kentucky. He is the author of *La Face Cachee des GI's: Les viols commis par des soldats americains en France, en Angleterre et en Allemagne pendant la Seconde Guerre mondiale* (2003).

FRED LINDSEY is an assistant professor of cultural studies at John F. Kennedy University, Orinda, California.

MARY LINEHAN has a Ph.D. in U.S. women's history from Notre Dame. She is finishing a book on prostitution and public policy.

ANDREA LOWGREN is a Ph.D. candidate in the history department at the University of California, Santa Cruz.

JENNIFER MANION is a doctoral candidate in history at Rutgers University, New Brunswick, New Jersey. Her dissertation examines the ways gender and compulsory heterosexuality influenced crime and prison reform during the early American republic.

GREGORY M. MATOESIAN is associate professor in the Department of Criminal Justice at the University of Illinois, Chicago. He is author of *Reproducing Rape* (1993) and *Law and the Language of Identity* (2001).

CATHERINE MAYBREY is a doctoral candidate in the History Department at Loyola University, Chicago. Her research focuses on the history of masturbation in America and its relationship to the medical community and the social construction of gender.

MARTHA MCCAUGHEY is associate professor and director of Women's Studies at Appalachian State University, Boone, North Carolina, and author of *Real Knockouts: The Physical Feminism of Women's Self-defense* (1997).

JACKIE GRUTSCH MCKINNEY is a professor in the English Department at the University of North Carolina, Greensboro.

MARLA MILLER is director of Public History at the University of Massachusetts, Amherst.

DANELLE MOON is an archivist/librarian in Manuscripts and Archives, Yale University Library, and teaches U.S. and women's history as an adjunct history professor at Central Connecticut State University, New Britain, Connecticut.

MICHELLE MORAVEC is an assistant professor of history at William Paterson University of New Jersey, Wayne, where she also directs the Women's Center.

SARA MURPHY teaches literature, cultural studies, and gender theory at the Gallatin School of Individualized Studies of New York University. She is the author of a forthcoming study of women's autobiographical practice and shifting conceptions of experience in nineteenth-century culture.

FLAVIA NELSON is a physician who works in the Department of Neurology at the University of Houston.

CARYN E. NEUMANN is a doctoral candidate in U.S. women's history at the Ohio State University, Columbus, and a former managing editor of the *Journal of Women's History*.

JUDSON ODELL is an independent scholar living in Philadelphia, Pennsylvania.

JENNIFER H. PROFITT is a visiting professor at the Union Institute and University of Cincinnati, Ohio.

ELIZABETH R. PURDY is a political scientist and independent scholar who writes in the fields of politics and government, women's studies, and history, among others.

SARAH L. RASMUSSON is an adjunct professor in the Women's and Gender Studies Program at the College of New Jersey, Ewing. As a journalist her work has appeared in a number of print and online publications.

JANICE G. RAYMOND is professor emerita of women's studies and medical ethics at the University of Massachusetts, Amherst. She is also co-executive director of the Coalition against Trafficking in Women, an international nongovernmental organization. Her most recent book is *Women as Wombs: Reproductive Freedom and the Battle over Women's Bodies* (1994).

EMILY RIVENDELL is completing her master's degree in women's studies at Texas Woman's University, Denton. She researches drug rape and sexual assault.

STEPHANIE L. SCHMID is a candidate for a juris doctorate from the University of California, Berkeley, Boalt Hall School of Law.

HEATHER SCHMIDT is an independent scholar and founding member of the Ohio Women's Network of Self-Defense Instructors and has worked extensively in the antiviolence field. She is working on a book that will provide empowering safety information for women travelers.

SUSANNE SCHOLZ is associate professor of religious studies at Merrimack College, North Andover, Massachusetts. Among her recent publications are *Rape Plots: A Feminist Cultural Study of Genesis 34* (2002) and *Biblical Studies Alternatively: An Introductory Reader* (2003).

REGAN SHELTON is a graduate student in American history and women/gender studies at Rutgers University, New Brunswick, New Jersey. She is completing a doctoral dissertation on gender and violence in the South, 1870–1920.

SABINE SIELKE is chair of North American Literature and Culture and director of the North American Studies Program at the Universität Bonn. Her most recent publications include *Reading Rape: The Rhetoric of Rape in American Literature and Culture, 1790–1990* (2002) and *Fashioning the Female Subject* (1997).

ERIC SKINNER is an independent scholar and writer from the Hudson River Valley area, New York.

MERRIL D. SMITH is an independent scholar living in National Park, New Jersey. She has authored and edited several books, including *Sex without Consent: Rape and Sexual Coercion in America* (2001).

DIANE MILLER SOMMERVILLE is assistant professor of history and director of Women's Studies at Fairleigh Dickinson University, Madison, New Jersey. She is the author of *Rape and Race in the Nineteenth-Century South* (2004).

ROSE STREMLAU is a doctoral candidate in American history at the University of North Carolina, Chapel Hill. She specializes in Native American history.

KONRAD SZCZESNIAK is an associate professor who lectures in psycholinguistics, translation, and Portuguese at Silesian University, Sosnowiec, Poland.

ROSSITSA TERZIEVA-ARTEMIS is senior lecturer, Languages Department, Intercollege, Cyprus.

LANA THOMPSON a specialist in medical and forensic anthropology, has authored *The Wandering Womb: A Cultural History of Outrageous Beliefs about Women* (1999).

DAVID TREVIÑO is a history teacher at Donna Klein Jewish Academy, Boca Raton, Florida.

MARCELLA TREVIÑO is a history instructor at Barry University, Boynton Beach Campus, Florida.

SHONNA L. TRINCH is an assistant professor of Spanish and linguistics at Florida State University, Tallahassee. She is the author of *Latinas' Narratives of Domestic Abuse: Discrepant Versions of Violence* (2003).

JUDITH A. WATERS is a professor in the Department of Psychology at Fairleigh Dickinson University, Madison, New Jersey. Her most recent publication is "Moving on from September 11," an overview of the symptoms and professional responses to the traumatic event, which appeared in *Brief Treatment and Crisis Intervention* in 2002.

LINDA D. WAYNE is a doctoral candidate in women's studies and comparative studies in discourse and society at the University of Minnesota. She teaches in the women's studies and humanities programs at the University of New Hampshire, Durham.

TRACI C. WEST is associate professor of ethics and African American studies at Drew University, Madison, New Jersey. She is the author of *Wounds of the Spirit: Black Women, Violence, and Resistance Ethics* (1999).

CHRISTINE CLARK ZEMLA is an instructor in the history department at Rutgers University, New Brunswick, New Jersey.